This lucid, scholarly, accessible, and reverent commentary will be invaluable for preachers, Bible study leaders, and any thoughtful Christian wanting to study the books of Chronicles. It is detailed enough to address the puzzles, for example when putting Chronicles side by side with Samuel and Kings, and yet without being dauntingly dense. The Application sections are pure gold, informed by a robust confidence that the whole Bible finds its fulfilment in Christ. It is likely to be my 'go to' commentary on these books.

Christopher Ash
Writer in Residence, Tyndale House, Cambridge

These two volumes display excellent linguistic knowledge, fine theological discernment, and most useful practical application of passages. This is what makes them so significant, and they will be welcomed as an outstanding contribution to the books of Chronicles. That Philip Eveson has taken years over this work means that we have the mature mind of the author, and so he presents us with an enlightening discussion that will be of assistance to many.

Allan Harman
Research Professor,
Presbyterian Theological College,
Melbourne, Australia

One's head hurts to think of all the labour Philip Eveson poured into this study of Chronicles – he does the indispensable 'dirty work' and beavers us through the details we need to understand the text. And yet all along his applications keep the kingship of Jesus in clear view. Makes me want to go back and study through 1–2 Chronicles all over again.

Dale Ralph Davis
Author, *My Exceeding Joy: Psalms 38-51*

T0270362

1 & 2 CHRONICLES

Volume 1
Adam to David

Philip H. Eveson

Philip Eveson is the author of a number of Old Testament commentaries that have been well received. After ministering for over twenty-five years at Kensit Evangelical Church and serving as Resident Tutor in Biblical Exegesis and Theology at the London Theological Seminary, he became the Seminary's second principal. In retirement, he has continued to teach the Old Testament and to preach in many parts of the world. He and his wife, Jennifer, now attend Borras Park Church, Wrexham, where his family also worships.

Copyright © 2024 Philip H. Eveson

ISBN 978-1-5271-1103-5
Ebook ISBN 978-1-5271-1151-6

10 9 8 7 6 5 4 3 2 1

Printed in 2024
by
Christian Focus Publications Ltd.,
Geanies House, Fearn, Ross-shire,
IV20 1TW, Scotland, U.K.

www.christianfocus.com

Cover design by Daniel van Straaten

Printed and bound by
Bell & Bain, Glasgow

Contents

Abbreviations

AD	Anno Domini (In the year of our Lord)
AV/KJV	Authorised/King James Version
BC	Before Christ
BDB	Brown, Driver and Briggs *A Hebrew and English Lexicon of the Old Testament* (Oxford: Clarendon Press, 1962)
ESV	English Standard Version
LXX	The Septuagint (The Hebrew Old Testament in Greek)
MSS	Manuscripts
MT	Masoretic Text
NIV	New International Version
NKJV	New King James Version

Preface

I count it a privilege to have had some of the best teachers in their fields of scholarship. They have included three Welshmen. The Reverend Dafydd Rhys ap Thomas introduced me to Biblical Hebrew and the Reverend Professor Dr Bleddyn Roberts first aroused my interest in the various Old Testament ancient texts and versions including the Qumran material that had, at that time, only recently been discovered.[1] Both these men belonged to the faculty of Hebrew and Biblical Studies at the University College of North Wales Bangor. The third Welshman to whom I owe much was Dr David Winton Thomas, Regius Professor of Hebrew at Cambridge University. Additional encouragement in Hebrew at Bangor came from the Reverend Brian Mastin, while the Reverend John St John Hart of Queens' College, Cambridge, encouraged a deeper appreciation of biblical Hebrew in his students through his regular Tuesday evening readings from the Hebrew Bible followed by Lapsang Souchong tea and Madeira cake.

More importantly, I thank God for the blessing of being brought up from birth in a home where the Bible was appreciated as God's inerrant and authoritative word and for opening my eyes to its truths and leading me to know God's Son, Jesus Christ, as my own personal Saviour and Lord. It was in the environment of my home church that I grew up from my earliest years to teenage life listening to challenging messages from the Bible through the ministries of the Reverends D. O. Calvin Thomas and J. Glyn Owen in Trinity Presbyterian Church of Wales, Wrexham. I was also

---

1. The Qumran or Dead Sea Scrolls were found on the northwest shores of the Dead Sea between 1947 and 1956.

privileged in those formative years of my life to be gripped by the powerful preaching of Dr D. Martyn Lloyd-Jones when he visited our town from time to time. In addition, it is important to put on record that I owe it to the Lord for keeping me trusting in the veracity of God's Word and enabling me, however imperfectly, to preach that Word and to teach and write on biblical books and themes.

When I first began studying the Bible as an academic discipline, it was at a period when the negativism of liberal Old Testament scholarship had reached its full flowering in British university circles. One of my Old Testament lecturers, Dr Charles Whitley, recommended as a text-book R. H. Pfeiffer's *Introduction to the Old Testament* (London: A & C Black, 1952), a work that Professor G. R. Driver of Oxford considered to be an 'admirable book … beyond all praise'. On Chronicles, this is what I read: 'The Chronicler made no important contributions to theological thought but presented the notions about God found in the Pentateuch and later in the Psalms' (p. 789). Further on I was informed, 'It is an error to consider the Chronicler as a writer of history. It is futile to inquire seriously into the reality of any story or incident not taken bodily from Samuel or Kings. His own contributions would be classed … as historical fiction … the Chronicler is utterly devoid of historical sense and even of a genuine curiosity about the actual events …' (p. 806).

Thankfully, that incredibly pessimistic estimate of Chronicles has long been superseded by a much more positive appreciation of the work, although its infallibility is still denied by many. I had the advantage of engaging in post-graduate studies when this change of thinking in academic circles was in its earliest stages. Dr Peter Ackroyd, the Samuel Davidson Professor of Old Testament at the University of London, was at the forefront of the new outlook and I profited from the personal tuition I received from him in the theological department of King's College London.

The translation of the Masoretic Text of Chronicles is my own and is purposefully as word for word as possible, in order for readers to appreciate the difficulties of translating some sentences and to observe more easily how the compiler used key words throughout his work. Words or phrases placed in *italics* indicate the additions needed in an English translation to help convey the sense of Hebrew sentences. In transliterating the original languages, I have generally followed the Society of Biblical Literature's academic system. When versification between the printed editions of the Hebrew and English Bibles differs, the Hebrew verse number (and chapter if necessary) is placed in square brackets after the English; for example, 1 Chronicles 6:1 [5:27]. As this is a Christian commentary, I continue to use B.C. and A.D. when referring to historical dates.

I have valued the encouragement of Graham Hind and others who have urged me to complete this daunting assignment which was first given me by John Currid. During a sabbatical in 2005, my wife and I spent over a month at the Reformed Theological Seminary in Jackson, Mississippi, and I place on record my immense gratitude to the Seminary board for allowing me free accommodation and access to all their resources. We first met Dr Currid and his wife while at Jackson and very much appreciated their kindness to us.

An important word of appreciation must go to Malcolm Maclean and all at Christian Focus for their helpful support.

It is only in more recent years since my retirement from the principalship of the London Seminary that I have been able to speed up and finish what I began so long ago. I am grateful that a number of former students have also spurred me on to keep going and not give up. The study and writing of this commentary has been a pleasurable project and it has been exciting to appreciate how the whole of Chronicles leads to Jesus Christ.

Finally, I am indebted to my wife, Jenny, for her love, patience and willingness to read through the whole script, checking my references and correcting flaws in my English. It has been a blessing in retirement to have our family close by and I dedicate this commentary to Ruth and Andrew, my daughter and son-in-law, and to Joshua, Nia, Hannah and Joseph, my grandchildren.

PHILIP H. EVESON
Wrexham, North Wales
May, 2023

Introductory matters

Chronicles is 'God-breathed' Scripture and meant to make us wise for salvation through faith which is in Christ Jesus (2 Tim. 3:15-17). Speaking particularly of the Old Testament, our Lord insisted to His Jewish opponents that these Scriptures 'testify about me' (John 5:39). The whole Bible, Chronicles included, was given for teaching gospel truth relating to the triune God, humanity, the person and work of God's Son, as well as informing us about the church of Christ and the end of all things. Again, like the rest of Scripture, Chronicles is also given to rebuke, correct and instruct us in righteousness. In addition, the things that happened to Israel and its kings as revealed in Chronicles are there as examples, and are written as warnings to us 'on whom the ends of the ages have come' (1 Cor. 10:11). As part of God's Word, Chronicles was 'written for our learning that we through the endurance and encouragement of the Scriptures might have hope' (Rom. 15:4).

One book

As with the books of Samuel and Kings, the Masoretes, those Jewish scholars of the sixth to the ninth centuries A.D., considered Chronicles to be one book and placed their final notes (*masorah finalis*) at the end of what we call 2 Chronicles. They reckoned in a marginal note at 1 Chronicles 27:25 that this verse was the halfway point of the whole work. The Septuagint (LXX)[1] divided it into two distinct parts and this

---

1. The Septuagint, from the Latin for seventy, is the earliest known Greek translation of the Old Testament for the Jewish community in Egypt dating from the 3rd to the 2nd centuries B.C. Legend has it that 72 people were involved in the work, hence the Latin name which is abbreviated with the Roman numerals LXX.

was followed by the Latin Vulgate which, in turn, led to all modern versions doing the same. It was only when the first printed Hebrew edition of the Bible was published in A.D. 1448 that the Masoretic Text (MT)[2] was divided into two books. Reading Chronicles as one book is especially important for appreciating that the reigns of David and Solomon form a single entity that revolves around the planning and building of the temple in Jerusalem.

Titles
The various titles given to this work indicate how Chronicles was once understood. Our English name 'Chronicles' is due to Miles Coverdale (A.D. 1535) following Martin Luther's title, which he owed to Jerome who called the book, the 'chronicle of the whole of sacred history'. In the Hebrew Bible, it is known as 'the words of the days' (*dibʾrē-hayyāmîm*) which can be rendered more idiomatically as 'the Annals' or 'the Chronicles' as in 1 Chronicles 27:24. This title suggests that Chronicles is meant to be a record of past events, a book of history that covers the story of God's people in Old Testament times.

In the LXX, a different title is given to the work. Instead of translating the Hebrew literally as it does in 1 Chronicles 27:24, the Greek translators gave the first part of the work the name *Paraleipomenon A* and the second *Paraleipomenon B*. This Greek title, *Pareleipomenon*, from the verb *paraleipō* 'to leave to one side' or 'to neglect', means 'Things Omitted' or 'Things Passed Over', and suggests that the translators thought of Chronicles as a kind of supplement to the books of Samuel and Kings. Such a title as this is regrettable and is one of the reasons why this part of God's Word has often not received the attention it deserves. It encourages readers to pick out those passages unique to Chronicles, so that the flow and intention of the whole book is lost. While the work does contain much that is paralleled in Samuel–Kings, there are some substantial differences of emphasis and often the new material not found elsewhere is introduced to support these significant points. Chronicles deserves to be read not

2. The traditional Hebrew text of the Jewish Bible together with its pointing system. 'Masoretic' is from the Hebrew for 'tradition'.

as a supplement or appendix to Samuel-Kings, but as an important work in its own right.[3]

Location

Chronicles is located in three different places in the canon of Scripture and from this we can gain further insight into how different Jewish traditions understood its purpose.

According to the Jewish Babylonian Talmud,[4] Chronicles appears at the end of the Writings section, that is, as the last book of the third part of the Jewish canon, and the majority of the Hebrew manuscripts as well as the printed editions indicate this. Matthew 23:35 and Luke 11:51 may reflect this tradition, where mention is made of the blood of Abel and the blood of Zechariah, the first Old Testament martyr mentioned in Genesis 4 and the last martyr cited in 2 Chronicles 24:20-21. Placing Chronicles at the end of the Old Testament canon is quite understandable and appropriate, for it summarises the history of redemption that begins with Adam and ends with the prospect of a return to Jerusalem after the Babylonian exile.

The two most important witnesses to the traditional Hebrew text, Codex Leningrad and the Aleppo Codex, which are of Palestinian origin, place Chronicles at the beginning of the Writings section, although most printed editions of the Bible based on these Hebrew texts still position it at the end, for practical reasons. In this location, heading up the third section of the Hebrew canon, it allows Chronicles to stand as a fitting introduction to the Psalter, especially as there is much material in Chronicles relating to the music and worship of the Temple.

A third location, witnessed first in the Septuagint and now in most modern English versions, is alongside the historical books after Samuel–Kings (known as 1–4 Kingdoms in the LXX). This position provides a fresh perspective on the history

---

3. See further Gary N. Knoppers and Paul B. Harvey Jr. 'Omitted and Remaining Matters: On the Names given to the Book of Chronicles in Antiquity,' *Journal of Biblical Literature* 121/2 (2002), pp. 227-243.

4. *Baraitha*: *Baba Bathra* 14b. The Talmud (Hebrew for 'study') is Rabbinic traditional teaching and is made up of the Mishnah (Jewish oral law) and the Gemara (a commentary on the Mishnah).

of God's people in much the same way as each of the Gospel writers present an account of our Lord's earthly ministry but each conveying or stressing their own particular message.

There are in fact no grounds for insisting that any one position is the earliest or best. And certainly, there is no proof that Chronicles was composed to conclude the Old Testament canon of Scripture, although providentially this position does in many ways, like Revelation for the New Testament, bring together so much that is found in the other canonical books. Thus it provides a most fitting conclusion to this first part of the Christian canon of Scripture.[5]

Author

Like many biblical books, Chronicles is an anonymous work and, for this reason, the author or compiler is conventionally called 'the Chronicler'. Jewish tradition is in no doubt that Ezra was responsible,[6] and I have much sympathy for this ancient tradition that was accepted by the Early Church Fathers. Under the guidance of the Holy Spirit, Ezra was in a very good position to accomplish the task. It is clear that the work comes from the post-exilic period for 2 Chronicles 36:22-23 reports the decree of Cyrus for the return of the Jewish exiles from Babylon, a decree that is expanded at the beginning of the book of Ezra 1:1-4. The date for that decree is put at 539/38 b.c. In the genealogical list pertaining to David's royal family, the line continues in 1 Chronicles 3:17-23 down to two generations[7] beyond Zerubbabel, to his grandsons Petatiah and Jesaiah. Zerubbabel was governor in Judea around 520 b.c. when Haggai and Zechariah were prophesying. A start was made on the new Jewish temple in 536 b.c. and it was completed in 515 b.c. Ezra and Nehemiah were in Jerusalem much later from 458 b.c. to about 430 b.c. The reference in 1 Chronicles 29:7 to the daric, a Persian coin named after Darius I (550–486 b.c.), which was minted in 515 b.c., suggests

5. See Gregory Goswell, 'Putting the Book of Chronicles in Its Place,' in *Journal of the Evangelical Theological Society* 60.2 (June 2017), pp. 283-300.

6. Talmud – *Baba Bathra* 15a: 'Ezra wrote the genealogy of Chronicles unto himself,' i.e. the history down to his own time.

7. Not six generations as some scholars have maintained and certainly not eleven with the LXX.

a date for Chronicles well after that, when it had had time
to circulate around the world. All these points encourage
the belief that Ezra might well have been the author and
especially as he is said to be a scribe and a priest. Chronicles'
interest in the temple and the duties of priests and Levites
furthers the case for Ezra.

But if it is maintained that Ezra was the compiler of
Chronicles, the work must be seen as completely separate
from the book that bears his name, as well as the book of
Nehemiah with which the Ezra volume is closely associated.
Academics throughout the nineteenth century and into most
of the twentieth generally believed that Chronicles, together
with Ezra and Nehemiah, formed a single work. Since
the 1970s, that position has dramatically changed so that
few argue for it today. Though there are some stylistic and
linguistic similarities between the three works that contrast
them with the rest of the Old Testament, there are numerous
differences such as obvious distinctions in emphasis that make
it extremely unlikely that they were originally one. While Ezra
and Nehemiah opposed the mixed marriages that were taking
place in the post-exilic period, Chronicles makes a point of
drawing attention to Israelites who married foreigners but
with no hint of disapproval. Even in the case of Solomon, while
Nehemiah refers to his apostasy on account of his marriage
to foreign women (Neh. 13:26), nothing of this is mentioned
in Chronicles. Chronicles has a different aim in writing from
that of the Ezra–Nehemiah material. It portrays the David–
Solomon period in the best possible light, while expecting
readers to be acquainted with the failings of those kings,
and encourages belief in the unity of Israel focused on the
Davidic king and the Jerusalem temple and seeks to broaden
the international outlook of the Jews, while still warning
against corrupting influences and unholy alliances. Ezra and
Nehemiah, on the other hand, were written to deal with the
specific problems relating to local enemies and the need for the
Jews to be kept separate from pagan and syncretistic worship.
Neither the apocryphal book, 1 Esdras, which contains
2 Chronicles 35–36, Ezra 1–10 and Nehemiah 8:13a, nor the
overlap between the end of Chronicles and the beginning of
Ezra, are arguments strong enough for assuming that all three

formed an original unity. On the other hand, the different emphases and apparent contrary attitudes must not be over exaggerated, because both Chronicles and Ezra–Nehemiah were written to the same people who were meant to appreciate what each was stressing. By ending Chronicles in the way it does, repeating almost word for word the opening of Ezra's book (2 Chron. 36:22-23//Ezra 1:1-3a), the compiler encouraged readers not to forget the teaching and warnings presented in Ezra–Nehemiah. The distinct works were not presenting mixed messages but helping to keep a steady course that avoided extreme positions.

Period

For the post-exilic period from 539 B.C. to around 400 B.C., the biblical books of Ezra and Nehemiah, Esther, Haggai, Zechariah and Malachi are of enormous help. During this time, the temple was rebuilt in Jerusalem and the walls of the city restored. But for the people of God the situation was in many respects totally different to pre-exilic times. The nation of Israel had originally been established as a theocracy so that for the whole of the period from the conquest of Canaan under Joshua until the Babylonian exile God ruled first through charismatic leaders and then through kings. God's law was the constitution, setting out the principles for government and religion. The rulers under God came to be those of Davidic descent with the capital in Jerusalem and it was there that the temple was erected. When the breakaway movement took place in the north, it did not change the situation in the south. In modern jargon, church and state were one. But all that changed after the exile when the Jews returned from Babylon to Palestine.

The Persians were now the superpower and their empire was organized into satrapies. Palestine was one huge satrap called 'Beyond the River' and one of the districts within that satrapy was Yehud (Judea). Although the Jews were allowed to build their temple and maintain their own religious worship, church and state were no longer one in the way they had been before. In so far as the Jews were allowed to govern themselves, it was still a theocracy but they were not an independent nation any more. Those who governed the people were appointed by the pagan foreign power. In the providence of God, one of the early governors appointed by Persia over this Yehud district was Zerubbabel, a descendant of King David. The post-exilic prophets, Haggai and Zechariah, use him and Joshua, who was the high priest at the time, to encourage the people to see them as pointers to the coming Messiah, the anointed priest-king. At the same time, these prophets urged the people to finish building the temple in anticipation of the future glory to come. But Zerubbabel's appointment was short-lived. After that, we read of Ezra acting as a kind of governor, but again, it was by the favour of the Persian authorities and likewise Nehemiah's authority in Jerusalem was as a representative of the Persian king. Nevertheless, God's law was read and the people were to order their lives by it and to that extent the life and worship of the people were the same in principle to what had gone on before the exile. The Jews were distinct from other peoples and nations, but they were ruled by the arbitary will of an external pagan power and for that reason they still regarded themselves as in bondage (Ezra 9:9).

The books of Esther, Ezra–Nehemiah and the post-exilic prophets reveal the kind of situations that Chronicles addresses. There was clearly some disenchantment among the people. Prophets like Isaiah, Amos, Hosea, Joel, Micah, Jeremiah and Ezekiel had predicted that the return would bring times of blessing under a new David and a new temple. Instead, the restoration period had only brought hardship and discouragement and this had led to shoddy worship, marriage breakups and the taking of foreign wives. There was no Davidic king on the throne, instead a foreign pagan power was controlling them, antisemitism flourished, there were local enemies that caused them much trouble, and famine had resulted in economic hardships. We read in Malachi of the complaints of the people. Did God really love them?

The Jews generally needed to be confident that they were the true descendants of Israel, that God's covenant with Israel still applied, that His promises had not been annulled, and that, despite there being no Davidic king representing Yahweh's rule on earth, Yahweh was still on the throne. It was also a time when the temple was no longer admired like the old one and when its staff required special reassurances as they ministered in a second-rate building that would have had no claim to becoming a world heritage site. Judging by what we read in Malachi, temple staff and worshippers had become careless in their service for God. Anything would do for God. Now, it is true that their newly-built temple was on Solomon's old temple site and many of the original temple utensils that Nebuchadnezzar had taken to Babylon had been returned. But there was no ark of the covenant in the holy of holies and no glory cloud had descended upon the newly-built temple as had happened when the tabernacle was erected and when Solomon's temple had been completed. So the Jews certainly needed much encouragement. It was vital for them to appreciate the importance of commitment to Yahweh through trust in God's written word, obedience to His law, belief in the power of prayer and enthusiastic communal worship at the Jerusalem temple.

The overall circumstances are not unlike many situations in today's world. No one lives in a theocratic society ordained by the true God. Christian values are often called into question and in the western world generally, the church is side-lined and treated like other charitable bodies with more rules, regulations and restrictions being applied by the powers that be. Again, as I write, churches in the West are not in a time of revival. Even the best of church members as well as pastors can often carry on the round of religious duties with little zeal or enthusiasm. There may be moments of blessing but these are often followed by long periods of discouragement. God's people can get depressed, lose interest in spiritual matters, and lack the keenness they once had for being about the Lord's work. Commitment can be challenging. Lack of unity can be another factor. In addition, there is a sad increase in church members and ministers divorcing or falling into sexual sins and not a few professing young people end up marrying those with no interest in the gospel. As a result, private devotion – as well as communal worship – suffers considerably and the name of Christ and our God is brought into dishonour. Chronicles speaks to such a situation.

Purpose
Chronicles was written in the first place to interpret the past in order to serve the needs of the writer's own post-exilic

community. It is an historical record but it is a history of God's people that seeks to convey theological lessons and to challenge and encourage God's people to look to the Lord with confidence and hope. There is no thought, as some scholars have suggested, that the compiler is seeking to replace earlier accounts, neither is the work an alternative, contradictory account. Chronicles is covering much of the same period as the previous historical biblical books, but like two artists painting the same landscape, the end product is an accurate portrayal but yet quite distinct and different. While Kings was an exilic work, Chronicles tells the story of Israel from a post-exilic perspective and brings out facets of truth and significant lessons not found nor emphasised in the other historical book. On the other hand, like those previous works, Chronicles is not only an historical book in which fresh information is found, but a sermon. Indeed, it is a series of sermons. The whole work presents a message for the people of the Chronicler's day, and because it is of divine origin, it continues to speak down through the Christian centuries.

Sources
The genealogical material found in the early chapters of Chronicles might suggest that the Chronicler used the Pentateuch and the historical books of Joshua to Kings. Certainly, the parallels between the lists in Genesis and Chronicles are close but the Chronicler may have had access to other genealogical lists that survived the destruction of Jerusalem and the exile.

It is almost universally agreed that the books of Samuel–Kings were the main source of the Chronicler's history of Israel, but if that is the case, most scholars admit that it was not a precursor of our MT that was used. While it is certain the Chronicler knew these canonical works and expected his readers to be familiar with their contents, there is reason for believing that both Chronicles and Samuel–Kings used common sources which account for both the very close similarities and the significant differences between them. Take, for instance, 1 Chronicles 10:9-10 and compare it with 1 Samuel 31:9-10.

It is very possible that the sources cited in the canonical books of Kings are the same prophetic annals used by Chronicles. Kings directs readers for further details to 'the book

of the Chronicles of the kings of Judah' (1 Kings 14:29) or 'the
book of the Chronicles of the kings of Israel' (1 Kings 15:31).
Chronicles, however, refers to many more sources for further
information such as 'the book of the kings of Judah and Israel'
(2 Chron. 16:11; 25:26; 28:26; 32:32), 'the book of the kings of Israel
and Judah' (2 Chron. 27:7; 35:27; 36:8), 'the book of the kings of
Israel' (2 Chron. 20:34) and 'the words of the kings of Israel'
(2 Chron. 33:18). It is a characteristic of the Chronicler to use a
range of vocabulary to express the same point, so it is most likely
that all these sources are one and the same and may in fact be
the same sources that are cited in Kings. Judging by what is said
of King Joash in both Kings and Chronicles, it suggests that 'the
midrash' or 'story of the book of the kings' (2 Chron. 24:27) is
yet another expression for this same comprehensive source for
the history of the nation (2 Kings 12:19[20]). Even the references
in Chronicles to letters, genealogies and various military and
tribal lists not found in other biblical material may well have
come from these same annals of the kings of Israel and Judah.

Some material in Chronicles is paralleled in the books of Ezra
and Nehemiah. This may have some bearing on authorship or
mean that both works are drawing on written or oral sources.
The edict of Cyrus in 2 Chronicles 36:22-23 and Ezra 1:1-3 and
the list of Jerusalem's inhabitants in 1 Chronicles 9:2-17 and
Nehemiah 11:3-19 are obvious examples.

The psalm quoted in 1 Chronicles 16 has parallels in the
Psalter in Psalms 96, 105 and 106. Other source material that
is cited include 'The words of Samuel the seer, and the words
of Nathan the prophet and the words of Gad the visionary'
(1 Chron. 29:29) for his treatment of David's reign and 'The
words of Nathan the prophet, the prophecy of Ahijah the
Shilonite and the visions of Iddo the visionary' (2 Chron. 9:29)
for Solomon's reign. One other source mentioned for David's
reign that may well be associated with a similar one for
Solomon's reign is 'the recounting of the Chronicles of king
David' (1 Chron. 27:24; although many consider 'recounting',
'account' or 'number' [*mispār*] to be due to dittography[8]
and instead read 'book' [*sēper*]). This unique source can be

8. Dittography is the unintentional repetition of a letter, word or phrase by a
person copying from a document.

compared to a similar one for Solomon, 'the book of the words of Solomon' (1 Kings 11:41).

Other prophetic sources mentioned include what 'Isaiah the son of Amoz, the prophet' wrote (2 Chron. 26:22), 'the words of Shemaiah the prophet and of Iddo the visionary' (2 Chron. 12:15), 'the midrash of the prophet Iddo' (2 Chron. 13:22) and 'the words of Hozai' (2 Chron. 33:19), although in the latter case many scholars suggest that instead of a prophet's name, we should translate the word 'hozai' as the LXX does to give 'visionaries' or 'seers'. Another source of special interest relates to 'the words of Jehu the son of Hanani' that has the extra information which it adds here: 'are mentioned in the book of the kings of Israel' (2 Chron. 20:34). This unique statement strongly suggests that this prophetic source is part of the same comprehensive collection of prophetic material mentioned above and contained in what the Chronicler has referred to as the 'book' of the kings either of both kingdoms or specifically of the kingdom of Judah. The later reference to 'the vision of Isaiah the prophet, the son of Amoz, in the book of the kings of Judah and Israel' (2 Chron. 32:32) witnesses to this idea. The added phrase indicates that this prophetic material by Isaiah has nothing to do with the canonical book of Isaiah, but belongs to that larger work relating to the kings of Judah and Israel. 2 Chronicles 33:18-19 may also point in the same direction with 'the words of Hozai' or 'the words of the visionaries' (v. 18) being a section within the larger work described as 'the words of the kings of Israel'.

Finally, there is the expression, 'the Laments' (2 Chron. 35:25), which has often been taken as a reference to the book of Lamentations. But this biblical book concerns the events surrounding the Babylonian exile and does not mention the death of Josiah. Chronicles is referring rather to some other record of laments that included Jeremiah's lament over Josiah's death at the hands of the Egyptian Pharaoh. Again, it is more than likely that, as with the other prophetic works cited, it came from that larger source described as the annals or words of the kings of Israel.

What is interesting in reviewing the sources that Chronicles mentions, is the large amount of prophetic material relating to the kings that was available, including some unique messages by prophets, kings and even foreign rulers including Hiram's letter to Solomon (2 Chron. 2:11-16), the Queen of Sheba's speech (2 Chron. 9:5-8), Pharaoh Neco's message to Josiah (2 Chron. 35:21) and Cyrus's Edict (2 Chron. 36:23). All these communications helped to underline the Chronicler's own message.

Historical accuracy

Especially since the beginning of the nineteenth century, the historical value of Chronicles has been questioned and many critics continue to be sceptical of much of its unique material, Manasseh's repentance being a prime example. In this particular case, the Chronicler is not contradicting the account of Manasseh's reign in Kings and it is no argument to believe that because there is no mention of his exile in any Assyrian sources thus far discovered, that it is therefore suspect. His name does, in fact, appear as a vassal who was forced to provide supplies for Assyria's military and building projects.

The criticism relating to the vast numbers that are often given in Chronicles for those going to war is more substantial. It is not, however, a problem unique to this book, for the same concern affects some of the figures in the book of Numbers and other parts of the Old Testament. It must not be forgotten that numbers are sometimes used symbolically in the Scriptures while at other times large totals are meant to convey the idea of a vast army or group of people without intending to be taken literally. Many totals are given in round figures. A thousand thousand, for instance (2 Chron. 14:8), should not be treated as an actual million people but similar to such hyperbolic language in use today where we speak of 'thousands' turning up to an event when the exact figure of those present would be much smaller. It is also possible in the case of military contexts that the terms 'hundred' or 'thousand' are used in a technical sense for fighting units much like the later Roman 'centurion', which did not always mean an officer over precisely one hundred soldiers. Some have suggested that differences in the figures between the texts of Kings and Chronicles when they are dealing with the same event, is due to textual transmission when numbers were written using alphabetical letters and later misunderstood when writing them out in full (see 2 Chron. 3:15; 4:5 with 1 Kings 7:15, 26). In many of these instances, however, the differences may well be due to distinctive methods of measuring or counting, in which case both are correct.

It is important to stress that God's Word is true whatever scholars might say and though there are some references in Chronicles that at present cannot be substantiated by external means or that seem to contradict what is known from elsewhere, we must admit our ignorance and await further light. Fresh archaeological finds have often confirmed the text of Scripture and silenced the sceptics, although this is rarely admitted in print.

Hebrew text

Concerning the accuracy of the transmission of its text, Chronicles has been well preserved. It should be stressed, however, that in no case does a textual doubt involve a matter of doctrine or principle for life. There is particular uncertainty over the spelling of names. Some textual difficulties were known to the Masoretes who have about ninety marginal notes, as witnessed by both the *Kethib* and *Qere* and the *Sebirin* readings.[9] The Qumran scrolls to date are of no value for the textual study of Chronicles. The LXX is also of limited worth; only in a few cases may it represent a better reading, as for instance in 1 Chronicles 2:24; 4:15; 2 Chronicles 14:6, 9; 19:8; 22:2; 25:8; and 26:5. Often, the LXX variants represent interpretive expansions and omissions of a Hebrew text similar to the MT[10] and will frequently seek to give its own interpretation of difficulties with the Hebrew text. Those responsible for the

---

9. The *Kethibh* ('written') is the reading preserved in the Masoretic Hebrew consonantal text. The *Qere* ('read') indicates the preferred or alternate reading. The consonants that make up the preferred/alternate reading are located in the margin while the pointing for pronunciation is placed in the word found in the written text (*Kethibh*). *Sebirin* ('supposed') are marginal notes concerning an unusual word or usage in the consonantal text and its expected form.

10. See P. J. Williams, 'The LXX of 1 Chron. 5:1-2 as an Exposition of Genesis 48-49,' *Tyndale Bulletin* 49 (1998), pp. 369-71; Leslie C. Allen, *The Greek Chronicles: The Relationship of the Septuagint of I and II Chronicles to the Massoretic Text.* Part 1, *The Translator's Craft*; Part 2, *Textual Criticism*, Vetus Testamentum Supplement 25, 27 *(Leiden: Brill, 1974).*

King James or Authorised Version (AV) did accept in one or
two places the LXX readings as in 2 Chronicles 33:18. I prefer
to resort to the LXX only in exceptional cases. As for the Vetus
Latina or Vetus Itala (Old Latin or Old Italian), that is, the
various Latin translations of biblical texts before Jerome's
Vulgate translation, their main use is in correcting the LXX
text. The Vulgate offers little help with regard to the textual
study of Chronicles.

Structure
There is almost universal agreement concerning the book's
outline. It consists of three or four main parts: an introduction
(1 Chron. 1:1–9:34); the united kingdom of the David–Solomon
era (1 Chron. 9:35–2 Chron. 9); and the Judean kingdom from
division to exile (2 Chron. 10–36). The final part could be
separated to form the divided kingdom period (2 Chron. 10–28)
and a re-united period (2 Chron. 29–36).

Introduction (1 Chron. 1:1–9:34)
This part, like the whole of Chronicles, stretches from the
beginning of human history to the return from Babylonian
exile. It introduces the main themes that are developed in
the remainder of the work. Though it is probably the least
read portion of Chronicles, its importance for understanding
the rest of work cannot be overemphasised. It focuses on the
tribes that formed the bulk of the post-exilic community,
namely, Judah, Levi and Benjamin. Attention is also drawn
to King David's family tree and a list of his descendants is
given through to the period in which the Chronicler wrote
(1 Chron. 2-3).

The United Kingdom of the David–Solomon era
(1 Chron. 9:35–2 Chron. 9:31)
This is the central and most significant part. It briefly
mentions the end of Saul's life before covering David's reign
in the remainder of 1 Chronicles and Solomon's reign in
2 Chronicles 1–9. The contents of these chapters are framed
by a Hebrew root *sbb* that is used in the statement that God
'turned over' the kingdom to David on the death of Saul
(1 Chron. 10:14) and in the comment following Solomon's

death that the division of the kingdom was a 'turn' brought about by God (2 Chron. 10:15).[11] Overall, this section presents a model of kingly rule associated with Yahweh's kingdom. The reigns of David and Solomon are treated as one and complement each other.[12] Two main messages stand out: first, in 1 Chronicles 17:3-14, which finds a parallel in Samuel, Yahweh responds to David's desire to build the temple; second, in 2 Chronicles 7:11-22, which is unique to Chronicles, Yahweh responds to Solomon's prayer of dedication.

It is important to appreciate that David and Solomon are not treated the same as in the Samuel–Kings text. In those earlier historical writings, we have more of the personal history of these kings but in Chronicles that is not the interest. Kingdom concerns predominate with a much more idealistic picture given of the reigns of David and Solomon that encourage the expectation of Yahweh's true anointed king predicted by Israel's prophets.

The Judean Kingdom from Division to Exile
(2 Chron. 10:1–36:23)

This part falls into two sections. In section one, 2 Chronicles 10–28, the Judean kingdom from Rehoboam to Ahaz is covered. Only the southern kingdom is considered, where the legitimate kings of David's line ruled and where the legitimate worship took place in the Jerusalem temple. This kingdom of Judah is often judged against the David-Solomon era. The northern kingdom and its rulers are only mentioned when the two kingdoms are directly in touch with one another, the most obvious example being Jehoshaphat's alliance with Ahab and the disastrous results that followed.

2 Chronicles 29–36 can either be seen as the second section of part three of Chronicles or regarded as a separate fourth part. It presents the history of the one kingdom from Hezekiah to the exile of the Davidic kings, the destruction of Jerusalem and the prospect of a return following the Edict

---

11. See Peter R. Ackroyd, 'The Temple Vessels: A Continuity Theme,' *Supplements to Vetus Testamentum* 23 (1972), pp. 166-81 and reprinted in *Studies in the Religious Tradition of the Old Testament* (London: SCM Press, 1987), chapter 4.

12. H. G. M. Williamson, 'Eschatology in Chronicles,' *Tyndale Bulletin* 28 (1977), p. 140.

of Cyrus. Hezekiah is presented as both a second David and second Solomon reigning over a reunified nation.[13]

While Luke in his genealogy begins with Jesus and ends with Adam the son of God (Luke 3:23-38), Chronicles begins with Adam and his offspring and ends with a world ruler who symbolises Jesus, the Son of God, Yahweh's 'shepherd' and 'anointed' ruler (2 Chron. 36:22-23; Isa. 44:28–45:7).

Main themes
God
It is taken for granted in Chronicles that there is only one true and living God, the creator and supreme ruler of the universe (2 Chron. 36:23). David's prayer acknowledges that all things come from Yahweh, the God of Israel, and that He owns everything (1 Chron. 29:10-15). The conviction concerning Yahweh's sovereignty is something the Chronicler stresses throughout his work, particularly in reference to Israel (1 Chron. 28:5; 29:11). In addition, Yahweh, the transcendent king who cannot be contained in any building, chooses to make His earthly dwelling among His people in the Jerusalem temple (2 Chron. 6:18; 7:1-3). But that local presence cannot be taken for granted. The God who is shown to be very present with His people Israel to help and bless them when they are faithful to Him nevertheless warns them of His very real absence if they forsake Him (2 Chron. 15:1-2).

Early in the introduction, Yahweh is seen as active in human affairs. He killed Er, who was evil in God's sight (1 Chron. 2:3). This verse is also the first of many examples in Chronicles, especially from the lives of the Davidic kings, that show the relationship between human sin and divine punishment. Achan provides another illustration of Yahweh's direct activity in punishing deliberate rebellion against God. In describing Achan's sin as 'acting treacherously' or 'unfaithfully' (*mā'al*), the Chronicler introduces one of his key expressions that is found numerous times throughout the book. It was because they had acted 'unfaithfully' that the northern tribes were

---

13. See Mark A. Throntveit, 'The Relationship of Hezekiah to David and Solomon in the Books of Chronicles' in *The Chronicler as Theologian: Essays in Honor of Ralph W. Klein*, eds. M. Patrick Graham, Steven L. McKenzie and Gary N. Knoppers (London: T & T Clark, 2003), pp. 105-21.

sent into exile (1 Chron. 5:25-26). Towards the end of the
introduction, the term appears in 1 Chronicles 9:1 where, in
the case of Judah, they also found themselves exiled in Babylon
on account of their 'unfaithfulness', a point emphasised once
more in the final chapter of the book (2 Chron. 36:14). At the
beginning of the second main section of Chronicles, God's
activity is very pronounced in the downfall of Saul, who, like
Er, was 'killed' by Yahweh on account of his 'unfaithfulness'
(1 Chron. 10:13-14). The one doing this is 'the God of Israel'
(1 Chron. 4:10; 5:26) who, according to the Sinai covenant,
blesses those who seek Him and brings curses on those who are
unfaithful and who forsake Him (Lev. 26:3-42; Deut. 28:10-68;
2 Chron. 7:12-22; 34:24). Yahweh acts both to reward loyalty
and to punish unfaithfulness.

In all this activity, God's absolute authority and supreme
governorship of the entire world is revealed. The kings of the
earth do His bidding both as instruments of God's judgment
as well as vehicles of hope. It was God who 'stirred up' the
spirit of the Assyrian king (1 Chron. 5:26) to deport the
northerners and who later 'stirred up' the spirit of Cyrus to
bring about a return from exile (2 Chron. 36:22).

But far from operating in any automatic and simplistic
way, God's retributive justice is shown by the Chronicler
to have been accompanied by His mercy so that warnings
of impending judgment are given, and where repentance
occurs, then catastrophe is averted. Only when threats are
rejected does punishment fall. The Chronicler also indicates
that sin does not always bring the kind of disaster that is
deserved and he shows Yahweh's patience and kindness even
to those whom the book of Kings considers the worst of rulers.
Manasseh is an obvious example, for though he was severely
punished for his apostasy, Chronicles reveals that the king
was returned to his kingdom when he humbled himself and
expressed a true repentant spirit (2 Chron. 33).[14]

14. See Brian E. Kelly, 'Retribution and Eschatology in Chronicles,' *Journal
for the Study of the Old Testament* (JSOT) Sup. 211 (Sheffield: Sheffield Academic
Press, 1996), pp. 29-110; '"Retribution' Revisited; Covenant, Grace and Restoration"
in *The Chronicler as Theologian*, pp. 206-27; Donald F. Murray, 'Retribution and
Revival: Theological Theory, Religious Praxis, and the Future in Chronicles,'
Journal for the Study of the Old Testament 88 (2000), pp. 77-99.

Two passages summarise the Chronicler's teaching concerning God's justice. First, in 1 Chronicles 21:13, David confesses after his sin: 'Let me fall into the hand of Yahweh, for his mercies are very great'; and the second is 2 Chronicles 7:14, where Yahweh declares: 'If my people who are called by my name will humble themselves ... then I will hear from heaven and will forgive their sin and heal their land'. God is shown to be gracious and merciful (2 Chron. 30:9). Hope and well-being are held out to a sinful nation and to individual sinners who turn and seek God.

God's people
In 1 Chronicles 2:1-2, the twelve tribes of Israel are named, with Leah's sons mentioned first and those of her slave-girl, Zilpah, last. Rachel's sons and those of her slave-girl, Bilhah, are given a central position with Bilhah's sons, Dan and Naphtali, placed either side of Rachel's two, Joseph and Benjamin. The genealogical tribal lists that follow (1 Chron. 2–8) are ordered so as to give prominence to Judah, Levi and Benjamin. These were the tribes most loyal to the Davidic king and to the Jerusalem temple, and citizens from these three tribes figure prominently in the post-exilic period as the final introductory chapter makes clear (1 Chron. 9:2-34). Even more importantly, it was from Judah that the Davidic dynasty arose; it was from the tribe of Levi that the temple staff, including the priests, musicians and gatekeepers, were appointed, and it was the tribe of Benjamin that produced the first king of Israel. But though Judah, Levi and Benjamin are given a prominent position, it is significant that other tribes associated with the northern rebellion are not placed in a separate block but dispersed among the three leading tribes associated with the southern kingdom. By this means, Chronicles indicates from the start that Israel includes all twelve tribes and it is a viewpoint that is emphasised throughout the work.

The tribal lists conclude with the note that 'all Israel was enrolled by genealogies' (1 Chron. 9:1). This is the first of many references in Chronicles to 'all Israel'. It is an all-inclusive expression that is not limited either to the northern or southern tribes but emphasises that both north and south are part of 'Israel'. The book highlights that people from all twelve tribes belong to the covenant community and to add weight to this position their illustrious ancestor, Jacob, is always called 'Israel', the covenant name given him by God (1 Chron. 1:34; 2:1-2; 5:3; 7:29; etc.).[15] The division that occurred after Solomon's death did not mean the northern tribes had no place among God's people. For the Chronicler, the schism was never meant to be permanent or an encouragement to apostasy. The northern kingdom is viewed as politically and religiously illegitimate and for that reason, unlike Kings, the lives of its kings are ignored for the most part and only mentioned when they directly affected the south (see especially 2 Chron. 18; 21:5-7; 22). Nevertheless, the people themselves who lived there are regarded as part of Israel and told by prophets like Shemaiah not to fight against their 'brothers' (2 Chron. 11:4; see also 2 Chron. 28:10-15). During Asa's reign, many northerners came over to him because they saw that God was with him (2 Chron. 15:9). After the Assyrians destroyed the northern kingdom, Hezekiah encouraged those from the north to keep the Passover in Jerusalem, and while many mocked, there were some from Asher, Manasseh and Zebulun who humbled themselves and came to Jerusalem, and such 'remnants' are also mentioned during Josiah's reign (2 Chron. 30:10; 34:9,21; 35:18). The Chronicler considered these examples as encouraging pointers to the prophetic hopes for the reunification of Israel.

Another interesting aspect of the Chronicler's work is his depiction of the people's involvement in the affairs of the kingdom.[16] They are constantly consulted and encouraged, especially in support of the temple worship in Jerusalem. The identical form of the verb 'to consult' is used of David, Jehoshaphat and Hezekiah when each conferred with their people before taking action (1 Chron. 13:1; 2 Chron. 20:21; 32:3). Solomon, likewise, at the very beginning of his reign, involved 'all Israel' in his activities (2 Chron. 1:2-3). In addition, the Chronicler shows how, on many occasions, all the people came together as an 'assembly' (qāhāl), united in enthusiastic

---

15. See H. G. M. Williamson, *Israel in the Books of Chronicles* (Cambridge: Cambridge University Press, 1977).

16. S. Japhet, *The Ideology of the Book of Chronicles* (Frankfurt: P. Lang, 1989), pp. 417-27.

expressions of joy in support of the temple and in their worship of God (1 Chron. 29:9; 2 Chron. 7:10; 30:25-26).[17] It was a clear encouragement to the Chronicler's original readership for them to be wholeheartedly and unanimously involved as an assembly in the temple worship and in providing for its upkeep and for those who were involved in its ministry. This emphasis on the 'assembly' congregating together also provides the background to the New Testament church.

The Chronicler also highlights the contribution of wives, mothers, sisters and foreigners to the nation's life as the people of God. Even little ones and children are mentioned as standing with their mothers as part of the 'assembly', when Jehoshaphat made his desperate prayer to God in the face of grave danger (2 Chron. 20:13; see also 2 Chron. 31:18 for 'little ones'). Daughters are not overlooked in the genealogical lists, especially when no sons are produced and we read of a descendant of Judah giving his daughter to his Egyptian servant in marriage (1 Chron. 2:30, 32, 34-35). Such examples follow the early reference to Tamar, Judah's daughter-in-law, who gave birth to one who was in direct line to David (1 Chron. 2:4). David's sisters and their children are also highlighted and it is noted that one of the sisters married an Ishmaelite who had been absorbed into the Israelite community (1 Chron. 2:16-18; see 2 Sam. 17:25). Attention is also drawn to the place of women in the conquest of Canaan. In Manasseh's genealogy a number of women are mentioned, among them Zelophehad's daughters and an Aramean concubine (1 Chron. 7:14-19). Intriguingly, it is recorded that a woman of the tribe of Ephraim built three cities and had one named after her (1 Chron. 7:24).[18] Furthermore, these and other references indicate that the background to Israel involved intermarriage with those from a variety of

17. The term 'assembly' (qāhāl, often translated ekklēsía, 'church', in the LXX) is used many times by the Chronicler in such contexts. David and Solomon gathered the people together as 'church' and other good kings like Jehoshaphat and Hezekiah and the high priest Jehoiada followed them (1 Chron. 13:2,4; 28:8; 29:1,10,20; 2 Chron. 1:3, 5; 6:3, 12, 13; 7:8; 20:5, 14; 23:3; 24:6; 28:14; 29:23, 28, 31-32; 30:2, 4, 13, etc.; 31:18).

18. See 'Observations on Women in the Genealogies of 1 Chronicles 1–9,' in Ehud Ben Zvi, History, Literature and Theology in the Book of Chronicles (London: Equinox, 2006), pp. 174-94.

nations, including a Canaanite, an Ishmaelite, an Aramean, two Egyptians and a Moabite. From this, it is clear that the Chronicler is keen to show how foreigners were absorbed not only into Israel in general but into the family of Judah with no hint of disapproval (1 Chron. 2:3, 17, 34, 55).

Writing as he was, in the first instance, for the post-exilic community where marrying foreign women was prohibited, the Chronicler's emphasis might at first have appeared counter to the reforms of Ezra and Nehemiah and the prophetic message of Malachi (Ezra 10:7-17; Neh. 13:23-29; Mal. 2:10-12). However, there was all the difference between foreigners who left their foreign gods to become worshippers of Israel's God and those in the post-exilic era whose women brought their own gods with them. Nehemiah 13:26 actually refers to the sin of Solomon in this regard. Protecting the purity of their religion was important, surrounded as the Jews were by all kinds of pagan religions and substitutes of their own religion by those who had even built temples such as the one on Mount Gerizim or at Elephantine. The Chronicler was as forceful as Nehemiah in his denunciation of people who acted unfaithfully (*ma'al*; see Nehemiah 13:27). However, like the psalmists and the book of Jonah, he encouraged an openness to the wider world where male and female, Jew and Gentile, the advantaged and disadvantaged, would be part of the one covenant community (see Gal. 3:26-29). Luke's Gospel has numerous references to poor and needy sinners, widows, mothers with babies in arms coming to Jesus and finding a welcome, while a repentant, dying criminal is assured of paradise (2:8-12; 4:16-21; 7:11-15; 10:38-41; 13:10-17; 18:15-17; 23:26-31, 39-43).

God's king

Half of Chronicles is given over to recounting the reigns of David and Solomon and the introduction prepares the reader for this arrangement by calling attention to the tribe of Judah and the genealogy of the Davidic kings (1 Chron. 2:3–4:23). Saul's family line is introduced in readiness for the account of his tragic end and that of his sons which led to the rise of David (1 Chron. 9:35-44; 10:1–12:40). Nothing is reported of Saul's promising start or of David's troubles with Saul such as is found in the Samuel text. The result is that the Chronicler's depiction of Saul's kingship acts as a kind of foil or contrast to the true king of God's people.

Chronicles does not deliberately gloss over the sins and failings of David and Solomon but assumes familiarity with what is recounted in Samuel–Kings (see 2 Chron. 10:4, 10-15). Rather than uncovering again their private lives, attention is drawn to their public actions, especially those that have a bearing on the temple and God's kingdom. Nothing, for instance, is said about David's adultery with Bathsheba and the devious plan to kill her husband, of Absalom's rebellion or of David's physical frailty in old age. As for his son, Solomon, no reference is made to the intrigue surrounding his succession to the throne or to the foreign wives who turned Solomon away in his old age from wholly following Yahweh (see 1 Kings 1:1-2; 11:1-11). The only reason for mentioning David's sin in counting the people and where more space is actually given to it than in the 2 Samuel 24 account, is to draw special attention to its association with the site of Solomon's temple (1 Chron. 21:26-28; 2 Chron. 3:1).

The Chronicler also chose to include God's judgment on Uzza because of the improper way the ark was carried (1 Chron. 13; 15:13-15), for this again had to do with the ark's association with the Jerusalem temple and the proper respect and procedure that was due to Yahweh by the Levites in their sacred service. In addition, Chronicles stresses that David was prevented from building the temple because he was a man of war and had shed much blood (1 Chron. 22:8; 28:3). On the other hand, Solomon is shown to be a man of peace and rest who fulfilled the divine decree to be the chosen king of his people and to build Yahweh's temple (1 Chron. 17:11-15; 22:9-10; 28:6-7, 10).

Both reigns are important and complement one another. David is pictured as the one who provided the settled conditions for building the temple and who made the necessary preparations both for its erection and worship, while Solomon was appointed to construct it and set in place all the elements for worship. The Chronicler joins the two reigns together to form an unbroken union that is centred around the temple. This is emphasised in three passages unique to the Chronicler. Where 1 Kings 8:66 speaks of the people returning

to their homes after the dedication of the temple, joyful for
Yahweh's goodness shown to David and Israel, the Chronicler
adds 'to David and Solomon' (2 Chron. 7:10). The best part
of Rehoboam's reign is summarised as a time when Judah
'walked in the way of David and Solomon' (2 Chron. 11:17).
Again, in 2 Chronicles 35:4, the Levites are instructed to
prepare themselves for the Passover following the written
instructions 'of David king of Israel' and 'of Solomon his son'.

The relationship between father and son is so close that
the succession is portrayed as seamless. Before the usual
notice concerning the new king reigning in place of his father
(1 Chron. 29:28; see 2 Chron. 9:31; 12:16), the text highlights
that, prior to David's death, Solomon reigned and 'all Israel'
obeyed him (1 Chron. 29:23), while a few verses later, it is
stated that David 'reigned over all Israel' (v. 26). In addition to
being chosen by God, both had the unanimous support of the
people (1 Chron. 10:14b-11:3; 28:6; 29:1, 23) and both reigned
for forty years (1 Chron. 29:27; 2 Chron. 9:30). The two reigns
are joined to form a union that centres on the temple and its
worship. To understand why the Chronicler is so concerned
to focus such attention on the David–Solomon kingship and
the temple, another important factor needs to be added.

The Davidic kingship in Israel is linked to Yahweh's rule
on earth. This is emphasised by the Chronicler in a number
of places and is especially obvious when comparing the
passages in Chronicles that find a parallel in Samuel–Kings.
For instance, instead of referring to David's dynasty and
kingdom (2 Sam. 7:16: 'your house and your kingdom'), it
speaks of Yahweh's house and kingdom (1 Chron. 17:14: 'in my
house and in my kingdom'). Again, in the Queen of Sheba's
praise of what she had witnessed, she refers to Solomon
having been placed on God's throne whereas, in the earlier
account, Solomon is said to have been set 'on the throne of
Israel' (1 Kings 10:9; 2 Chron. 9:8). Other passages unique to
the Chronicler press home this close connection between
Yahweh's throne and that of David's. David states that God
had chosen his son, Solomon, 'to sit on the throne of the
kingdom of Yahweh over Israel' and then later, the Chronicler
comments that 'Solomon sat on the throne of Yahweh as
king instead of David his father' (1 Chron. 28:5; 29:23). The

two reigns are not only viewed as one, but both represent Yahweh's rule on earth.

This period is recalled later in the way in which Hezekiah's reign is depicted. The many parallels between both David and Hezekiah and Solomon and Hezekiah indicate that the Chronicler was concerned to present Hezekiah as a second David and a second Solomon. Hezekiah's reign kept alive the hope of a Davidic son who would more than realise the idyllic picture of the David–Solomon era, especially after recounting the intervening reigns from Rehoboam to Ahaz. Even the best of them is seen to have fallen short of the ideal. As for the situation following Hezekiah's reign, the Chronicler clearly wished to indicate a break in the presentation of the remaining kings of Judah by no longer naming the queen mother in the accession formulae and omitting any reference to the city of David in the burial notices. The emphasis is on exile, sorrow and judgment with Manasseh presented as an example of one who repented and returned from exile and Josiah's Passover celebration providing a further pointer to a new exodus and redemption that the Cyrus Edict prefigured.

Despite their failures, the kings of Judah still represented Yahweh's kingship on earth. King Abijah reminded Jeroboam and the breakaway northern tribes that in fighting against Judah they were seeking to resist 'the kingdom of Yahweh which is in the hand of the sons of David' for Yahweh, the God of Israel, had given the dominion over Israel to David for ever, to him and his sons by a covenant of salt (2 Chron. 13:5, 8). Davidic kingship in Israel is seen as the earthly representation of divine kingship over the whole cosmos. That divine kingship is emphasised by David himself in his praise of Yahweh: 'Yours, Yahweh, is the greatness, the power and the glory, the victory and the majesty; for all that is in heaven and in earth is yours; yours is the kingdom, Yahweh, and you are exalted as head over all' (1 Chron. 29:11). Likewise, King Jehoshaphat prays to Yahweh, 'Yahweh God of our fathers, are you not God in heaven and do you not rule over all the kingdoms of the nations, and in your hand is there not power and might, so that no one is able to withstand you?' (2 Chron. 20:6). That lasting covenant that God made with David is secure come what may, for the Davidic throne is God's throne. The future of God's rule on earth is secure because it belongs to Yahweh not to humans.

This was an important truth for the first readers and the truth that Yahweh is king is emphasised especially in Book Four of the Psalter (Psalms 90–106). Though they were back in the land of promise and had a temple built in Jerusalem for worship, they were still under foreign rule with no Davidic monarch reigning over them. Haggai and Zechariah had seen in the governorship of Zerubbabel, who was of the Davidic line, a pointer to the restoration of the Davidic dynasty, but nothing further had materialised. It was the Chronicler's concern to keep alive this sure and certain hope by stressing that God had not abdicated and that there was no possibility of God changing His mind with regard to His promises to David. In the genealogical list of David's royal line, he focuses on the continuing line of sons belonging to Jeconiah (Jehoiachin) the last Judaean king who was taken captive to Babylon as well as on Zerubbabel's family (1 Chron. 3:17-24). Chronicles also follows the compiler of the completed Psalter in encouraging the post-exilic people to remember that Yahweh is still king even though there was no king in Israel but to look to the fulfilment of those promises to David in one who would rule the world in righteousness. Such prophecies and psalms that speak of a future David and a son of David like Solomon can be better appreciated in the light of the Chronicler's work (Ezek. 37:24; Hosea 3:5; Amos 9:11; Ps. 72; Luke 1:30-33).[19]

God's Temple

The Chronicler presents the temple and its worship as of central importance and, as the theme of God's king has already indicated, the temple is closely associated with the Davidic king. David made the preparations for its construction in accordance with divine revelation and Solomon saw the building completed. The best of the Davidic kings who followed, such as Asa, Jehoshaphat, Hezekiah and Josiah, were concerned for temple renovations and worship reform after periods of neglect and apostasy.

---

19. See Brian E. Kelly, 'Messianic Elements in the Chronicler's Work' in *The Lord's Anointed*, eds. Philip E. Satterthwaite, Richard S. Hess, & Gordon J. Wenham (Carlisle: The Paternoster Press, 1995), pp. 249-64.

As with the other main themes, the temple, the ark, the priests and the Levites, as well as the worship conducted in the temple, are all introduced initially in the first nine chapters. With the rebuilding of the temple in Jerusalem after their return, the Jews' continued faithfulness to the worship at this God-ordained sanctuary would have been for the Chronicler and his first readers a sure indication of their identity with pre-exilic Israel as the true covenant community. To this end, Chronicles stresses more clearly than Kings the uniqueness of the Jerusalem temple as the means of access to God. The kings of Judah were frequently assessed on the basis of their attitude toward the temple. In view of the attempts during the exile and after, such as the Jewish temple at Elephantine in Egypt and the one built by the Samaritans on Mount Gerizim, it was necessary for the Chronicler to draw attention to the exclusive claims concerning the Jerusalem temple.

In the main part of the work, much is recorded of how David established the music side of the temple worship under the direction of three Levitical families and this is again first brought to our attention in the introduction (1 Chron. 6:31-32). In these chapters, as well as later, the temple is often called 'the house of God' or 'the house of Yahweh' and a very strong link is made between the temple and the original tabernacle. There are references to the temple as 'the tabernacle of the tent of meeting' or the 'the tabernacle of the house of God' (1 Chron. 6:31-32[16-17], 48[33]). In chapter 9, the temple is referred to using a variety of phrases such as 'house of God' (vv. 13, 26, 27), 'tent' and 'camp of Yahweh' (v. 19), 'tent of meeting' (v. 21), and 'the house of the tent' (v. 23). Chapter 9 especially records the post-exilic priests together with the various duties of those Levites who acted as gatekeepers, servers and singers ready for the work in the post-exilic temple. The Chronicler's particular interest in the non-priestly Levites is evident throughout. He records how David appointed many of them to be temple gatekeepers and musicians, officers and judges (1 Chron. 23–26) and indicates the involvement of the priests and Levites in bringing up the ark to Jerusalem and then in the newly erected temple (1 Chron. 16:4-5; 2 Chron. 7:6; 8:14-15). They are shown to support Rehoboam (2 Chron. 11:13-14; 13:9-10). The Levites generally as well as the Levitical priests had an important role as judges during Jehoshaphat's reign besides leading praise to God and exhorting the people (2 Chron. 19:8, 11; 20:14, 19). They were key in the overthrow of Athaliah, in collecting for temple repairs, in cleansing the temple and in other religious reforms during the reigns of Joash, Hezekiah and Josiah (2 Chron. 23; 24:5-6, 11; 29-31; 34-35).

Though the Chronicler does not give the same amount of space to the construction of the temple as in the parallel account in Kings, he does give far more detail concerning all the events that led up to the building and dedication of the temple. David himself is seen as engaging in conquests that are important in relation to the construction of the temple (1 Chron. 18:8) and David's census is included to stress the actual site of the temple, which is more precisely defined as Mount Moriah (2 Chron. 3:1), and attention is given to David's detailed preparations for its construction. The account of Solomon's reign is then dominated by the building, furnishing and dedication of the temple and Yahweh's presence at the sanctuary is made even more obvious. In comparison with Kings, 'The Chronicler's interest in the temple,' Selman remarks in his excellent commentary, 'has less to do with its physical appearance than with its meaning.'[20] Chronicles stresses more than Kings the close relationship between the temple and the Davidic king (see 1 Chron. 22:6-13; 28:2-10; 2 Chron. 6:4-11, 14-17; 13:4-12). Solomon's address to Israel presses home the point that Yahweh has fulfilled His promise that Solomon sits on the Israelite throne that David once occupied and has built the temple for the name of Israel's God (2 Chron. 6:10).

While the second temple was a poor substitute for Solomon's, in the providence of God the Persian king had not only agreed for it to be built but had gone out of his way to assist the enterprise. Continuity with Solomon's temple is maintained through its erection on the old site, through the resumption of the Aaronic priesthood and the other workers belonging to the tribe of Levi and through the return of the

20. Martin J. Selman, 1 Chronicles, Tyndale Old Testament Commentaries (Leicester: Inter-Varsity Press, 1994), p. 56.

temple vessels which had been taken to Babylon when the temple was destroyed.[21]

But God clearly had more for His people, for there were some missing elements in the situation after the exile. The three most obvious differences were that the ark of the covenant was missing, no glory cloud had filled the sanctuary on its completion and there was no king of David's lineage reigning. As with other important themes, the ark is mentioned in the introduction (1 Chron. 6:31-32 [16-17]) and it is in Chronicles, not Kings, that the ark is called the 'footstool of our God' (1 Chron. 28:2; see Pss. 99:5; 132:7; Isa. 66:1; Lam. 2:1) and is also uniquely described as 'the holy ark' (2 Chron. 35:3). Though Jeremiah 3:16 had prophesied that the original ark would be thought of no more, the Chronicler, living in the post-exilic period, encouraged his people to remember what the ark had stood for and to look, not for a lost ark, but for what the ark symbolised. What represented God among His people was fulfilled when the apostles saw the glory of God in the face of Jesus (Luke 9:32; John 1:14; 2 Cor. 4:6). In the Messiah, who according to the flesh was of the seed of David, all the fulness of God dwelt bodily (Col. 2:9). Later, the Jerusalem church was filled with the Holy Spirit and local churches and even individual Christians become temples where God dwells by His Spirt (John 14:23; Acts 2:4; 4:31; 1 Cor. 3:16-17; 6:19).

God's City

At first sight, Jerusalem seems to be no more important to the Chronicler than the compilers of Samuel-Kings and many of the references are paralleled in the earlier work. But there are in fact twenty per cent more references to the city in Chronicles than Samuel–Kings. However, it is not so much the number of times the place is mentioned, but how it is used and in what contexts, that is significant. Zion is another name often associated with Jerusalem and found many times in the psalms and the prophetic literature, particularly Isaiah, as a synonym for Jerusalem and especially for the worshipping company of God's people at the temple and symbolic of the eschatological, utopian city of God. In Chronicles, however,

---

21. Peter Ackroyd, 'The Temple Vessels,' pp. 166-81.

the name 'Zion' only occurs twice and in both cases it refers to the Jebusite fortress called 'the stronghold of Zion' that David captured and where he established his royal residence (1 Chron. 11:5, 7; see 2 Sam. 5:7, 9; 2 Chron. 5:2; 1 Kings 8:1). Chronicles presents the conquest of Jerusalem as David's first major royal act. It was from this city that David and the Davidic kings that followed ruled over God's people and it becomes a major focus of attention throughout the whole of Chronicles. This was the place where Yahweh chose to dwell among His people in the temple that Solomon built and the Chronicler even refers to Yahweh as 'the God of Jerusalem' (2 Chron. 32:19; see also Ezra 7:19). The book ends by recounting not only the burning of the temple and the destruction of Jerusalem's walls by the Babylonians but Cyrus's desire to build a temple to Yahweh in Jerusalem and his encouragement to God's people to 'go up' (2 Chron. 36:19, 23). This ending is anticipated in the introduction which alludes to the city a number of times in the genealogical lists (1 Chron. 3:4-5; 6:10, 15, 32 [5:36, 41; 6:17]; 8:28, 32) and closes by focusing on the various tribes who actually returned from exile to Jerusalem (1 Chron. 9:2-34). Furthermore, in that closing section, there are several references to the temple and those involved in its worship and the whole is bracketed by the phrase 'they lived in Jerusalem' (9:3, 34).

Jerusalem is more often than not the place where the Davidic king assembled the people and generally, such gatherings had a religious connotation. These assemblies (qāhāl) in Jerusalem united king and people in their devotion to Yahweh. This is first evident in the decision to bring the ark to Jerusalem and in David's address and prayer concerning the temple (1 Chron. 13:2, 4, 5; 15:3; 28:1, 8; 29:1, 10, 20). In Chronicles, Solomon's initial act as king was to assemble the people and to worship in front of the bronze altar where the Mosaic tabernacle was situated in Gibeon. When the temple was built, Solomon assembled the representatives of the people to bring the ark to its place in the inner sanctum of Yahweh's house and then praised Yahweh and prayed in the presence of 'all the assembly of Israel' (2 Chron. 1:3, 5; 5:2; 6:3, 12-17). The temple dedication merged with the Festival of Tabernacles for which a 'very great assembly' gathered (2 Chron. 7:8). Following the division of the kingdom and Rehoboam's attempt to muster the people in order to restore the kingdom (2 Chron. 11:1), three notable situations are recorded where the people were assembled in Jerusalem at the temple, two in the context of serious threats to the king and nation in the time of Jehoshaphat and Joash, and the third during the reforms of Hezekiah (2 Chron. 20:5, 14; 23:3; 24:6; 29:23, 28, 31, 32; 30:2, 4, 13, 17, 23, 24, 25; 31:18). Jerusalem is also central to the reign of Josiah. He purged the city of its pagan associations (2 Chron. 34:3, 5, 7) and in addition to his gathering of a great assembly in Jerusalem to renew the covenant, which is also recorded in Kings, Chronicles gives a detailed account of a Passover in Jerusalem, the like of which had not been celebrated since the days of Samuel (2 Chron. 35:18).

In such ways, the Chronicler drew attention to the prestige and significance of Jerusalem with its temple to Yahweh. It would have encouraged more Jews in the post-exilic period to return to Jerusalem, to support the security of the city and to assemble together to praise, pray and hear God's Word read and proclaimed (see Ezra 10:1, 7-8, 12, 14; Neh. 5:13; 8:1-2, 17; 13:1). The references to Jerusalem also provide the background to many of the psalms. The gathering together of the people within the gates of Jerusalem and its temple was a sight that God loved (Ps. 87). In Psalm 51:18, David pleads that God would build the walls of Jerusalem in the sense that He would provide for the safety and prosperity of the city (see Ps. 147:2-3). Other psalms speak enthusiastically of Jerusalem and, like Chronicles, would have encouraged the post-exilic community to look with faith beyond what the physical eye could see to God's promises concerning that city which has foundations whose builder and maker is God (Pss. 122; 125:1-2; 137; 147:1-2, 12; Isa. 26:1-2; Heb. 11:10; 12:22; Rev. 21:1-14). But for the Chronicler, it is the earthly, rather than the heavenly, city that is the centre of his attention. It was to this poor ruined city that the Persian king encouraged the exiles to 'go up' to build 'a house in Jerusalem' to the God of heaven (2 Chron. 36:23) in order to bring to realisation God's purposes concerning the Davidic dynasty.[22]

22. See Isaac Kalimi, 'The View of Jerusalem in the Ethnographical Introduction of Chronicles (1 Chron. 1-9),' *Biblica* 83 (2002), pp. 556-61; 'Jerusalem – The Divine City' in *The Chronicler as Theologian: Essays in Honor of Ralph W. Klein*, eds.

Of all the New Testament writers, it is Luke who draws particular attention to the significance of this historical city. It was to Jerusalem and the temple that Jesus was brought as a baby to be dedicated to the Lord and it was the prophetess Anna, from the tribe of Asher, who spoke about Jesus to all who were waiting for 'the redemption of Jerusalem' (Luke 2:22, 36-38). Every year, His parents 'went up' to Jerusalem at Passover time and at the age of twelve Jesus lingered in Jerusalem and was found in the temple (Luke 2:41-51). A significant point was reached in His ministry when Jesus 'set his face to go to Jerusalem' and Luke keeps emphasising that, in all His journeyings, Jerusalem was His goal (Luke 9:51, 53; 13:22, 33; 17:11; 18:31; 19:11, 28). Friend and foe were found in Jerusalem when Jesus was crucified (Luke 23:7, 26, 49; 24:13, 18) and it is Luke who tells us that at Jesus' transfiguration Moses and Elijah spoke of His 'exodus' which He was about to accomplish 'in Jerusalem' (Luke 9:31). The final true exodus and redemption took place in Jerusalem when Jesus died, rose bodily from the tomb and ascended into heaven. Jesus explained that it was necessary that the Messiah should suffer and rise and that repentance and forgiveness should be proclaimed to all nations 'beginning from Jerusalem' (Luke 24:46-47). It is Luke who reports how, after Jesus' ascension, the disciples followed His command and 'returned to Jerusalem' with great joy. In his second volume, he indicates how, following the gift of the Holy Spirit at Pentecost, His followers began witnessing in Jerusalem and from there to the whole world, again in fulfilment of Jesus' command (Luke 24:48-53; Acts 1:8, 12; 2:1-11). Chronicles prepares us for this focus on the actual city of Jerusalem in God's purposes.

Personal Piety

The Chronicler not only reveals an interest in the temple and its worship with the aim of encouraging his own people to continue to worship there and for the temple staff to maintain the ministry set up by Moses and David, but he clearly

Graham, McKenzie and Knoppers, JSOT Suppl. Series 371 (London: T & T Clark International, 2003).

wished that their worship contained a humble and prayerful dependence on God. There are some fifteen recorded prayers in Chronicles with many other incidental references to prayer and again, it is the introduction section that provides the initial examples of both individual and corporate prayer.[23] As the Chronicler deals with Judah's family line, he pauses to single out Jabez, whose start in life was not promising and yet Yahweh was pleased to answer his petition (1 Chron. 4:9-10). Jabez prayed on the basis of God's word concerning blessings in the land for obedience and curses for disobedience (Deut. 11:22-28; 30:19-20).

The second reference to prayer in the introduction is in 5:18-22 and, as with Jabez, the Chronicler once more encourages his people to be committed to God, to trust Him to give success and to pray especially in times of need, convinced that He really does hear and answer prayer. There are many other examples of God coming to the aid of His people when there are crisis situations and battles are often said to be 'of God' (1 Chron. 5:22; 2 Chron. 14:11-13; 18:31; 20:5-13, 15; 32:8, 20; 33:13, 19). In this connection, key words and phrases like to 'seek' God, to 'trust' or 'rely' on God and to experience God's 'help' occur throughout the book (1 Chron. 5:20; 12:18; 15:26; 22:19; 2 Chron. 7:14; 11:16; 12:14; 19:3; 25:8; 26:7, 15; 32:8).

In encouraging the people to seek God in prayer, wholehearted devotion to the Lord is stressed throughout. David urged his son, Solomon, to worship with a whole heart and a willing spirit and prayed that the people and his son would have a heart religion (1 Chron. 28:9; 29:18-19). It is said of Hezekiah that in all his reforms he did everything 'with all his heart' (2 Chron. 31:21). The Chronicler clearly emphasised how heart religion was even set above ritual rules of purification (2 Chron. 30:18-20). Enthusiastic worship is evidenced in the demonstrations of joy that are often mentioned. Joy was expressed by David, the captains and elders of the people in bringing up the ark to Jerusalem, then by the people themselves in their free will offerings as well as in their celebration of God's goodness at the time of the dedication

---

23. Philip H. Eveson, 'Prayer Forms in the Writings of the Chronicler,' unpublished M.Th. dissertation (University of London, 1979).

of the temple. The people also rejoiced when Athaliah, the usurper, was slain and joy characterised the people's worship when the temple was cleansed under Hezekiah, and later when the Passover festival was observed (1 Chron. 15:25; 29:9, 17, 22; 2 Chron. 7:10; 23:21; 29:30; 30:26). Along with prayer, the written word of God was also important for the Chronicler. God had revealed His will in the Mosaic law and through the writing of the prophets (1 Chron. 15:15; 2 Chron. 20:20; 34:14-33). Prayer, knowledge of God's written word, humbling oneself before God, trusting God and obedience to His word became important elements of Jewish piety leading up to the New Testament period and became even more significant in the context of the New Testament Church and individual believers (Luke 1–2; 24:52-53; Acts 2:42-46).

Future Hope
By focusing on the twelve tribes and examples of northerners coming back to the Davidic king and to the Jerusalem temple, the Chronicler encouraged his people to look for a future where God's people would be a united 'assembly' in worship as in the David–Solomon era. The restoration of Jerusalem was a first but important step in God's plan in the restoration of all things through God's Son, Jesus the Messiah, the ultimate descendant of David. Cyrus, the world ruler, is likened to a second David who is associated with a new exodus and with a concern for Yahweh's temple in Jerusalem. The Chronicler's work must be taken with the canonical prophets, all of whom were looking to the full realisation of these token blessings, where there would be the true Davidic king, who would build a new temple for a new Jerusalem, and where all God's Israel would be assembled together worshipping sincerely and joyfully the one true and living God (Rev. 21:1–22:5). That future is already present and anticipated in the New Testament Church (Acts 2:36-47; 4:10-13; 9:31; Gal. 4:22-28; 6:14-16; Eph. 2:19-22; Heb. 12:18-29).

PART ONE:
Israel's Roots
(1 Chronicles 1:1–9:34)[1]

While modern readers find these seemingly unending registers of names boring and of little interest, they were considered most valuable in the ancient world and were particularly prized by the people of God in the Old Testament era. For the Chronicler, these family trees and the incidental comments that he occasionally makes not only enabled him to cover a vast period of time as briefly as possible, but they provided him with a means of drawing attention to themes that are developed in the rest of Chronicles. In particular, they indicate the unfolding of a divine plan in which Israel is shown to be God's chosen means of bringing blessing to the whole of humanity.[2]

At the time when the Chronicler was writing, the outlook was not promising for the nation. After the Babylonian exile, the people of Israel had been reduced to a comparatively small community in and around Jerusalem, and though they

---

1. Among the commentaries from which I have benefited are these more recent ones: Gary N. Knoppers, *1 Chronicles 1-9, A New Translation with Introduction and Commentary,* Anchor Bible 12A (New York: Doubleday, 2004); *1 Chronicles 10–29, A New Translation with Introduction and Commentary,* Anchor Bible 12A (New York: Doubleday, 2004); Ralph W. Klein, *1 Chronicles* (Minneapolis: Augsburg Fortress Press, 2006); Ralph W. Klein, *2 Chronicles* (Minneapolis: Augsburg Fortress Press, 2012).

2. See M. D. Johnson, *The Purpose of the Biblical Genealogies: with Special Reference to the Setting of the Genealogies of Jesus,* 2nd edition (Cambridge: Cambridge University Press, 1988); Roddy Braun, *1 Chronicles,* Word Bible Commentary 14 (Waco: Word Books, 1986), pp. 1-12.

had been given certain freedoms by the Persians, they still considered themselves in bondage under foreign rule. God, however, had not abandoned His people and had raised up prophets like Haggai, Zechariah and Malachi to encourage them not to be despondent but to realise that God had made promises that were yet to be fulfilled. The messages of hope in the pre-exilic and exilic prophets were not to be dismissed and the prophetic writer of Chronicles, like the final compiler of the Book of Psalms, played his part in urging God's people to trust Yahweh and to be true to Him.

Interestingly, after his introductory genealogical lists in 1:1–2:2, the Chronicler orders his material by placing the tribe of Judah first (2:3–4:23), Benjamin last (8:1-40) and Levi in the middle (6:1-81), and it is to these tribes he devotes most attention. They are the ones that made up the bulk of the post-exilic community and, as it happened, they were the ones that Chronicles shows remained true to David and the Jerusalem temple in the pre-exilic period. This did not mean that the other tribes had no part in the covenant community and, to indicate this, they are placed each side of Levi but surrounded by Judah and Benjamin. The concluding chapter nine focuses on the post-exilic community before preparing for the next main section of the work.

I

Adam to Israel
(1:1–2:2)

In this whistle-stop tour from the creation of the first human to the twelve tribes of Israel, the Chronicler sets Israel in the context of the nations of the world. In particular, the lists draw attention to a special family line and highlight significant moments important to the compiler's overall aim. The genealogical tables found in Genesis are followed closely with ten names recorded of the chosen line from Adam to Noah (vv. 1-4a; Gen. 5) and ten from Shem to Abram (vv. 24-27; Gen. 11:10-26). Similar genealogical lists are found in Ancient Near Eastern texts.[1] It is unlikely that this family tree was meant to be a means of working out the precise date when Adam was created. Like the three sets of fourteen generations in Matthew's Gospel 1:1-17, where we know that Uzziah was not Joram's son (Matt. 1:8) but his great, great, grandson (see 2 Kings 8:25; 11:2; 14:1, 21; 1 Chron. 3:11-12), the symmetry of the two sets of ten generations suggests that they are not an unbroken chain of generations from Adam to Noah and on to Abram.

Some parts of the lists, of course, must be taken as continuous. Seth is the actual son of Adam and Lamech is the father of Noah and grandfather of Shem. Likewise, Nahor is the father of Terah and grandfather of Abram. But

---

1. See T. Jacobsen, *The Sumerian King List* (Chicago: University of Chicago Press, 1939).

in other cases 'son' can mean 'grandson' or even 'descendant', and 'father' can mean 'grandfather', 'ancestor' or 'founder', depending on the context. This was common practice throughout the Ancient Near East. Kenneth Kitchen presents an extreme example from Egypt where King Tirhakah honours his 'father', Sesostris III, who lived 1,200 years earlier.[2] If we compare the lists in Ezra 7:1-5 and 1 Chronicles 6:3-14, it is clear there are a number of omissions. It may well be that someone like Reu (1:25) fathered a son from whom Serug (1:26) was a direct descendant.

Two types of genealogies are found: linear and segmented. A linear genealogy, presenting a clear line of descent from one generation to another, is produced in 1:1-4a and 1:24-27. It is like the main trunk of a tree with only one son of each family named. In Genesis and Chronicles, it is used to indicate the central family line. Adam had many sons and daughters, including Cain and Abel, but in the genealogy only Seth is named. The same is true of Seth's children, for only Enosh is named, and so it continues down to Noah. Between the two linear genealogies of the elect line, in 1:4b-23, a segmented genealogy is found. This is more complex and, like the various branches from the main trunk, it separates off in all directions to present details of other family members.

The chapter is divided according to the principal characters: Adam, Noah, Abraham, Isaac and Jacob. As in Genesis, the descendants of non-elect lines appear before the elect: Ishmael's family is listed before Isaac's, and Esau's before Jacob's. Both Genesis 1–50 and 1 Chronicles 1:1–2:1 begin with Adam, God's son, before narrowing the divine choice to Israel, God's son.[3]

Adam to Noah (1:1-4a)

1:1. Adam, Seth, Enosh, 2. Kenan, Mahalalel, Jared, 3. Enoch, Methuselah, Lamech, 4. Noah,

Without any word of introduction, the Chronicler begins by listing the ten names of the chosen line as found in

---

2. Kenneth A. Kitchen, *Ancient Orient and Old Testament* (London: Tyndale Press, 1966), pp. 36-39.

3. See William J. Dumbrell, *The Faith of Israel* (Leicester: Apollos, 1989), p. 273.

Genesis 5:3-32 but lacking any of the details concerning their ages, the connection between them or, as in the case of Enoch, their spiritual standing with God. Numbers in the Bible often have symbolic significance and ten is a naturally round figure like the number of fingers on a person's hands. It symbolised totality or completion (Gen. 16:3; 18:32; 1 Chron. 6:61; 2 Chron. 4:6, 7, 8; 14:1b [13:23b]). These names are all real people and the Chronicler goes back to the very beginnings of human history. He expects his readers to be familiar with what is written in Genesis concerning these individuals.

From the initial ten names, a number of points are evident. The first is that the whole human race is descended from the one man, Adam, who was created in God's image and became a living being through God's life-giving breath which He personally breathed into Him. Humanity was created to rule as God's viceroys on the earth and to have fellowship with God (Gen. 1:26-28; 2:7-8; 3:8; 2 Chron. 6:18). By commencing with Adam, readers are also reminded of that initial disobedience to God's command which led to divine punishment and the tragic consequences for the rest of humanity. He is the first 'son' in a long line of 'sons' who were exiled; they included Israel and the Davidic kings who disobeyed God. Nothing is said of Adam's firstborn son, Cain, who murdered his brother Abel. Instead, Chronicles refers only to Seth, the one 'appointed' by God to replace Abel (Gen. 4:25). From the outset, the Chronicler indicates what he will illustrate many times during the course of his work, that God fulfils His purposes despite setbacks and false starts. He substitutes others to take the place of those who seemed to be the obvious choices. At the beginning of the main part of the Chronicler's work, David's appointment as king instead of Saul is the clearest example (1 Chron. 10:13-14).

By tracing Israel's family line back to Adam, the Chronicler has a universal perspective in mind and this fits with his overall interest in people of various nations who became part of Israel. The nations of the world belong to God and Chronicles indicates how they are used to fulfil God's purposes for His people.

Noah's descendants (1:4b-23)

Noah's sons (1:4b)

1:4. Shem, Ham and Japheth.

An unusual feature in verse 4 is the way Noah's sons are introduced. They are named in straight succession one after the other in exactly the same way as all the other names from Adam to Noah. It is as if Japheth were the son of Ham and Ham the son of Shem. The Chronicler, as always, expects readers to know their biblical history and it becomes more obvious in what follows that Shem, Ham and Japheth are brothers whose father was Noah. Typical of the Septuagint, this ancient Greek translation makes the text clearer by adding after Noah, 'sons of Noah,' before mentioning the three sons.

Noah's family of eight, which included his three sons and their wives, are the only ones who escaped the universal Flood. Though the event is not mentioned, the Chronicler wishes his readers to pause and remember that catastrophe, for the text does not immediately continue with the elect line of descent through Shem. The main trunk of the tree is abandoned for a moment in order to introduce some of the chief branches. Here again, a universal note is detected in the Chronicler's arrangement of his material. Israel and all the other nations of the world are descended not only from Adam, but from Noah's three sons. It is not an exhaustive list but a symbolic round figure of seventy names and it represents the entire world of nations and people groups. It reads like a verbal 'map of the world'.[4] One commentator notes that the only material the Chronicler omits from Genesis at this point is the genealogy of Cain (Gen. 4:17-24) and suggests that this is because the Flood 'meant a completely fresh start in the spread of mankind'.[5]

Descendants of all three of Noah's sons are named and they call to mind the nations of the world that spread out over the earth after the tower of Babel incident (Gen. 10:1–11:9). As

---

4. Gary N. Knoppers, 'Shem, Ham and Japheth,' in *The Chronicler as Theologian: Essays in Honor of Ralph W. Klein*, eds. M. Patrick Graham, Steven L. McKenzie and Gary N. Knoppers (London: T & T Clark, 2003), p. 30.

5. H. G. M. Williamson, *1 and 2 Chronicles*, The New Century Bible Commentary (London: Marshall, Morgan & Scott, 1982), p. 41.

in Genesis 10:2-29, Japheth's descendants are mentioned first
(vv. 5-7), then Ham's (vv. 8-16) and finally Shem's (vv. 17-23). In
this whole section, 'sons' is better translated 'descendants' for
the term can mean not only literal sons like Canaan, Arphaxad
and Joktan, but people groups like Kittim and Rodanim.

The descendants of Japheth (1:5-7)

> 1:5. The sons of Japheth: Gomer and Magog and Madai and
> Javan and Tubal and Meshech and Tiras. 6. And the sons of
> Gomer: Ashkenaz and Diphath and Togarmah. 7. And the sons
> of Javan: Elishah and Tarshishah, Kittim and Rodanim.

The list of Japheth's family line is the shortest (vv. 5-7) with
seven sons recorded and seven descendants from just two
of his sons, Gomer and Javan, again following the Genesis
account. There are minor variations in spelling between the
two lists but this need not indicate copying errors for both
forms can be equally original. The descendants of Japheth
came to occupy areas to the north and west of Israel. Gomer
is connected with the Cimmerians who, by 670 B.C., had taken
control of central Anatolia (modern Turkey). Among the
descendants of Gomer are Ashkenaz, who lived in the area
of Armenia (Jer. 51:27). Togarmah is closely related to other
brothers of Gomer such as Tubal and Meshech who are also
from the Anatolian region (Ezek. 27:13-14; 38:3-6).

Javan (see Ezek. 27:13; Isa. 66:19) is associated with the
Ionians who lived in the Aegean area, but it came to be the
name for all the Greeks (Dan. 8:21; 10:20; 11:2). Among his
descendants are Elishah and Kittim, both of whom are linked
with Cyprus (Ezek. 27:6-7; Num. 24:24; Isa. 23:1). Tarshishah
or Tarshish (Gen. 10:4) cannot be identified with certainty.
Suggestions include Phoenician colonies, either in Spain or
Carthage in North Africa. Clearly, it was west of Canaan
and reached by ships crossing the Mediterranean (Jonah 1:3;
1 Kings 10:22; Ezek. 27:12). Rodanim (or Dodanim in Gen. 10:4)
may refer to the island of Rhodes in the Aegean or some other
northern part of the Mediterranean around Greece.[6] Japheth's
descendants included nations furthest away to the north and

---

6. For more details concerning all the names, see Gordon J. Wenham, *Genesis
1-15*, Vol. 1, Word Biblical Commentary (Waco: Word Books, 1987), pp. 216-22.

west from Israel, but ones who would eventually be found in great numbers among God's people (Gen. 9:27).

The descendants of Ham (1:8-16)

1:8 The sons of Ham: Cush and Mizraim, Put and Canaan. 9. And the sons of Cush: Seba and Havilah and Sabta and Raamah and Sabteca. And the sons of Raamah: Sheba and Dedan. 10. And Cush fathered Nimrod; he began to be a mighty one in the earth. 11. And Mizraim fathered Ludim and Anamim and Lehabim and Naphtuhim, 12. and Pathrusim and Casluhim, from whom came the Philistines, and Caphtorim. 13. And Canaan fathered Sidon his firstborn 14. and Heth, and the Jebusite and the Amorite and the Girgashite 15. and the Hivite and the Arkite and the Sinite 16. and the Arvadite and the Zemarite and the Hamathite.

Ham's family line is much fuller than the other sons (vv. 8-16) and it suited the Chronicler's purpose to keep exactly to the similar list found in Genesis with only what was considered unnecessary omitted (Gen. 10:5, 9-12, 18b-20). Attention is particularly drawn to this genealogy for, unlike Japheth's descendants, many of the people groups mentioned were among Israel's closest neighbours, while others represent foreign forces that would threaten the very existence of God's people as Chronicles will show. Four sons of Ham are named (v. 8) but, like Genesis, only the offshoots of three of them are presented: Cush (vv. 9-10), Mizraim (vv. 11-12) and Canaan (vv. 13-16). Their descendants represent people groups to the south of Israel. Cush (v. 9), often translated Ethiopia as in the Septuagint, covers black-skinned tribes who lived to the south of Egypt in modern-day northern Sudan (Jer. 13:23). His descendants also lived on the shores of the Red Sea and Arabia including 'Seba' (Ps. 72:10; Isa. 43:3), 'Havilah' (Gen. 2:11; 25:18; 1 Sam. 15:7), 'Raamah' (Ezek. 27:22), 'Sheba' (1 Kings 10:1-13; 2 Chron. 9:1; Ps. 72:10, 15) and 'Dedan' (Jer. 49:8; Ezek. 25:13; 27:15).

'Mizraim' (v. 11) is the Hebrew word for Egypt, its dual ending indicating the country's division into two, Upper and Lower Egypt. A descendant of Judah was given in marriage to an Egyptian servant, while toward the close of Chronicles, it was an Egyptian pharaoh who brought about the death of Josiah, an event that precipitated Judah's exile (1 Chron. 2:34-35;

2 Chron. 35:20-24). All the names belonging to Mizraim have plural endings indicating tribal groups associated in some way with Egypt (vv. 11-12). Included is a reference to the 'Philistines' (v. 12) who later figured in the Chronicler's first major narrative when king Saul was killed (1 Chron. 10) and who continued to invade and capture territory belonging to Israel through to the days of king Ahaz (1 Chron. 11:13-16, 18; 14:8-16; 18:1, 11; 20:4-8; 2 Chron. 21:16; 26:6-7; 28:18). They are associated with the 'Caphtorim' from Crete (Deut. 2:23; Amos 9:7; Jer. 47:4) and the unknown 'Casluhim'. The Philistines probably came to Egypt by way of Crete. 'Put' (v. 8) is the only one of Ham's line not given descendants. The name is closely associated with Cush (Jer. 46:9; Ezek. 30:5; 38:5; Nahum 3:9) and is identified as Libya.

In the Genesis account, there is a lengthy piece describing 'Nimrod' and his exploits but in Chronicles this is much reduced and readers are expected to be acquainted with the fuller version (Gen. 10:8-12). The comment about Nimrod's prowess is significant (v. 10) for, as Genesis reveals, he is associated with some of the ancient civilisations, including Babylon and Assyria. Assyria was to be the superpower that would lead to the downfall of the northern kingdom of Israel and to Manasseh's exile (1 Chron. 5:6, 26; 2 Chron. 30:6; 33:11), while Babylon would carry Judah into exile (1 Chron. 6:15; 9:1; 2 Chron. 36:6-13).

'Canaan' (v. 13) has the closest association with Israel, hence the amount of space given over to this son of Ham on whom Noah pronounced a curse (Gen. 9:25-27). That curse was fulfilled when God used Israel to enter the land of Canaan and destroy its inhabitants. The peoples and places named indicate an area from the northern borders of Egypt to the regions of Phoenicia and Syria. This appearance of Canaan among the Hamites is seen by many as surprising but it is clear that the early Canaanites were non-Semitic. 'Sidon' became the name of one of Phoenicia's most ancient and important ports. 'Heth' is associated particularly with those Hittites who occupied land in Canaan from the days of Abraham. As in Genesis, this is the most comprehensive list of inhabitants occupying the promised land before Israel entered under Joshua's leadership. Some of the names such as the Jebusite, Amorite, Girgashite and Hivite (vv. 14-15a) are well-known from other lists (Gen. 15:21; Exod. 13:5; Deut. 7:1), whereas Arkite, Sinite and Zemarite are only found here and in Genesis. These latter peoples are probably in the same general area as the Arvadite and Hamathite, who, as their names imply, are inhabitants respectively of Arvad, the most northerly Phoenician city (Ezek. 27:8,11) and Hamath in Syria which lay beside the Orontes river (see Num. 34:8; 1 Kings 8:65). The 'entrance to Hamath' is mentioned in the Old Testament as the northern border of Canaan (Num. 13:21; Josh. 13:5). Interestingly, Canaan and all his descendants mentioned add up to twelve, probably to parallel the twelve tribes of Israel.

The descendants of Shem (1:17-23)

> 1:17. The sons of Shem: Elam and Asshur and Arpachshad and Lud and Aram and Uz and Hul and Gether and Meshech. 18. And Arpachshad fathered Shelah, and Shelah fathered Eber. 19. And to Eber were born two sons: the name of the first was Peleg, for in his days the earth was divided, and his brother's name was Joktan. 20. And Joktan fathered Almodad and Sheleph and Hazarmaveth and Jerah, 21. and Hadoram and Uzal and Diklah, 22. and Ebal and Abimael and Sheba, 23. and Ophir and Havilah and Jobab. All these were the sons of Joktan.

This list again conforms to the one in Genesis 10:22-29, but it omits all details considered unnecessary to the Chronicler's purpose, such as the introduction and the concluding summary (Gen. 10:21, 30-32). As in Genesis, the elect line of Shem is treated last, but nothing special is said at the start to mark his chosen position in the line from which Abraham will emerge (see v. 17 and Gen. 10:21). That is rectified by the linear genealogy that immediately follows (see vv. 24-27).

Shem's genealogy first names nine 'sons' but as we learn from Genesis, only five are immediate descendants, the final four are 'sons of Aram' (see Gen. 10:23), but, as in verse 4, the Chronicler expects his readers to know the original biblical source. It is Arpachshad's line that is significant and four generations are listed, closing with Eber's son, Joktan, and his many descendants. Again, it is the non-elect line of Joktan rather than Peleg's that is introduced first. Joktan's descendants are the ancestors of the tribal groups in the Arabian Peninsula.

'Elam' (verse 17) became an ancient nation with its capital at Susa, in what is now the Iranian province of Khuzestan. Chedorlaomer was a powerful king of Elam in the days of Abram and Lot (Gen. 14) and Jeremiah issued an oracle against the Elamites (Jer. 49:35-39). They did not speak a Semitic language but clearly, from an early period, there were Semites in the area. Much later, the Assyrians deported Israelites to Elam (Isa. 11:11; Ezra 4:9). 'Asshur' may refer to the Assyrian people of northern Mesopotamia. It was also the name of its old capital city on the river Tigris (Gen. 2:14; 10:11). Like Elam, these non-Semitic peoples (see vv. 11,13) also had Semites among them. Another possibility is that 'Asshur' refers to an Arab tribe descended from Abraham and Keturah that settled in northern Sinai (Gen. 25:3, 18; Num. 24:22). 'Aram' is the ancestor of the Arameans, and the Israelites were taught a confessional statement that began, 'A dying' or 'wandering Aramean was my father' (Deut. 26:5), which was a reference to Jacob's exile in the service of his mother's brother, 'Laban the Aramean' (Gen. 25:20; 28:5; 31:20). It served the Chronicler's purpose to include the descendants of Aram because of their connections with Jacob, the father of the nation, and the contacts that the Arameans, or Syrians as they are often called, had with Israel in the subsequent history (1 Chron. 18:6-8; 2 Chron. 1:17; 16:2-7; 18:10, 30; 22:5-6; 24:23-24; 28:5, 22-23). There is guesswork over the identity of the other descendants of Shem in verse 17.

As in Genesis 10:25, the Chronicler slows down to stress the significance of 'Eber', a personal name related to the word 'Hebrew' and used by others to describe Abraham and the Israelites (Gen. 14:13; Exod 1:15, 19; 2:7). Also included is a historical note that probably refers to the language confusion and the scattering of the peoples after the tower of Babel incident (Gen. 11:1-9). 'Peleg' means 'division' and there is a word-play on his name using the verbal form ('be divided') from the same three root letters (*p-l-g*). In Psalm 55:9 [10], it is employed for confusing the enemy's speech. It served the Chronicler's purpose to include this piece of information for it draws attention to the different languages and people groups of the world and their relationship to the ancestors of Israel.

Application

The post-exilic community needed to be reminded through this representative list of seventy nations that the whole of humanity, including Israel, is descended from one stock: from Adam and then through Noah and his three sons (see Acts 17:26). Many of these nations would have an impact for good or ill on Israel's subsequent life and history. The book of Chronicles ends by naming a foreign monarch who is described as having been given by Yahweh, Israel's God, 'all the kingdoms of the earth' (2 Chron. 36:23). This first chapter gives an idea of those kingdoms that stretched from southern Russia in the north to Ethiopia in the south and from Spain in the west to India in the east. Though God is not mentioned in this first chapter, these are the nations that are under God's sovereign control and are used to serve His purposes. The post-exilic prophet, Malachi, likewise reminded the people that God is a great king and His name is to be great among the nations and to be feared among them (Mal. 1:11,14b).

Though Satan, the usurper, could rightly say that all the kingdoms of the world were his to give to Jesus if He would but worship the evil one, Jesus resisted the temptation and won those of every tribe and nation, having redeemed them to God by His blood. Through the cross and resurrection, Jesus judged the ruler of this age and, as a result, a world of lost sinners is drawn to the Saviour (Matt. 4:8-10; John 12:31-32; Rev. 5:9). Luke traces Jesus's ancestry back to Adam, indicating that he, like Adam, was a real human being who had come to redeem Adam's fallen race and, as the last Adam, to form a new humanity. Interestingly, as Cyrus, the head of the world superpower, was used to bring God's people back from exile and to encourage them to rebuild their temple, another world empire (in the form of the Romans) was used to facilitate the kind of death appropriate for God's prophecies and purposes concerning the Messiah to be fulfilled for the freeing of God's people from their slavery to Satan and the building of God's new temple.

Shem to Abram (1:24-27)

1:24. Shem, Arphaxad, Shelah, 25. Eber, Peleg, Reu, 26. Serug, Nahor, Terah, 27. Abram, who is Abraham.

From the great mass of nations and people groups set out in verses 5 to 23, the list returns to Noah's son Shem (see vv. 17, 24) in order to draw attention to the elect line that would eventually lead to Israel. The linear genealogy of ten names that highlighted the elect line from Adam to Noah now traces that line from Shem to Abram, again with ten names through Eber's son Peleg (see v. 19 and Gen. 11:10-26). Nothing else is known of 'Reu' other than that given in Genesis (Gen. 11:18-21). It may be a shortened form of Reuel ('friend of God'; see v. 35 and Exod. 2:18). 'Serug', 'Nahor' and 'Terah' are all found in cuneiform texts either as place or personal names in northern Mesopotamia. 'Nahor' fathered Terah and is not to be confused with Abram's brother of the same name whose granddaughter was Rebekah, Isaac's wife (see Gen. 11:26; 22:20-23). Unlike the genealogies in Genesis 11:26-27, attention is not drawn to Terah's significance as the head of various branches of the family that included Lot and Laban, Bethuel and Rebekah, and unlike the case with Noah where the three sons are mentioned (v. 4; Gen. 5:32), only Terah's son Abram is named (vv. 26-27).

There is a short pause at this point in order for the Chronicler to indicate Abram's name change – 'Abram who is Abraham' (v. 27). It draws attention to God's covenant with Abraham, which included the promises that he would be 'a father of many nations', that from him kings would come and that he and his descendants would be given Canaan (Gen. 17:4-8). To suggest with some modern commentators that the Chronicler is not particularly interested in Abraham is hardly credible, seeing that his name appears more times than any other in this first section (vv. 27, 28, 32, 34).[7] The figures prominent in the list thus far are Adam, the founder of the human family, then Noah and his three sons, from whom all the nations of the world have their origins, and finally

7. See, for instance, H. G. M. Williamson, *1 and 2 Chronicles*, pp. 40, 43; Michael Wilcock, *The Message of Chronicles*, The Bible Speaks Today (Leicester: Inter-Varsity Press, 1987), pp. 27-28.

Abraham, the ancestor of Israel and to whom God promised that through him and his descendants all the nations of the world would be blessed (Gen. 12:1-3, 7; 15:16-21).

Abraham's descendants (1:28-34a)

> 1:28. The sons of Abraham: Isaac and Ishmael. 29. These are their generations: the firstborn of Ishmael is Nebaioth then Kedar and Adbeel and Mibsam, 30. Mishma and Dumah, Massa, Hadad and Tema, 31. Jetur, Naphish and Kedemah. These are the sons of Ishmael. 32. And the sons of Keturah, Abraham's concubine: she bore Zimran and Jokshan and Medan and Midian and Ishbak and Shuah. And the sons of Jokshan: Sheba, and Dedan. 33. And the sons of Midian: Ephah and Epher and Henoch and Abida and Eldaah. All these are the sons of Keturah. 34. And Abraham fathered Isaac.

The parallels with Genesis in this paragraph are not quite as close as in the previous ones. It begins by following the pattern set earlier – 'The sons of Abraham ... The sons of Isaac' (vv. 28, 34b; see vv. 5, 8, 17) and, as in Genesis, it is the non-elect family lines of Ishmael and Keturah that are treated before the elect. No mention is made of Abraham's sons by Keturah in verse 28 because, as in Genesis, only Isaac and Ishmael are named together and it was only these two who received special promises. The introductory phrase 'These are their generations' (v. 29) parallels the wording of Genesis (Gen. 25:13) and is a reminder of the distinctive headings found in that first book of the Torah (Gen. 2:4; 5:1; 6:9; etc.). It is the first of nine occurrences of the term 'generations' in 1 Chronicles (see 5:7; 7:2, 4, 9; 8:28; 9:9, 34; 26:31) and is related to the verb 'to bear' or 'to father' and could be translated 'these are what they produced'. The term does not appear in 2 Chronicles or Ezra-Nehemiah.

Ishmael's twelve sons (vv. 29-31; Gen. 25:13-16a) parallel the twelve sons of Israel and are in fulfilment of promises made by God to Abraham (Gen. 17:20). Their names are associated with northern Arabia. Before Isaac is mentioned, Abraham's descendants through his second wife Keturah are also listed as in Genesis 25:2-4, except that the three sons of Dedan are omitted. Keturah, Abraham's wife (Gen. 25:1), is considered to be his 'concubine' by the Chronicler and there is support for this in Genesis 25:6. It is very likely that Abraham had married her long before Sarah's death. Her name is associated

with spice or incense and some of her family who settled in
Arabia were involved in the spice trade. Of her six sons, only
the descendants of Jokshan and Midian are listed (vv. 32-33).
Midian is the father of the Midianites, a desert people who
were also traders. Moses married one of their women but
later they became a problem to Israel (Gen. 37:28, 36; Exod. 3:1;
18:1-24; Num. 25; Judg. 7–8).

'And Abraham fathered Isaac' (v. 34a; Gen. 25:19) forms the
conclusion to the paragraph relating to Abraham's sons and
prepares for the detailed treatment of the elect line through Isaac.

Isaac's descendants (1:34b-54)

1:34b. The sons of Isaac: Esau and Israel. 35. The sons of Esau:
Eliphaz, Reuel and Jeush and Jalam and Korah. 36. The sons of
Eliphaz: Teman and Omar, Zephi and Gatam, Kenaz and Timna
and Amalek. 37. The sons of Reuel: Nahath, Zerah, Shammah
and Mizzah. 38. And the sons of Seir: Lotan and Shobal and
Zibeon and Anah and Dishon and Ezer and Dishan. 39. And the
sons of Lotan: Hori and Homam, and Timna *was* Lotan's sister.
40. The sons of Shobal: Alian, and Manahath and Ebal, Shephi
and Onam. And the sons of Zibeon: Aiah and Anah. 41. The
sons of Anah: Dishon. And the sons of Dishon: Hamram and
Eshban and Ithran and Cheran. 42. The sons of Ezer: Bilhan and
Zaavan, Jaakan. The sons of Dishan: Uz and Aran.

43. Now these *are* the kings that reigned in the land of Edom
before a king ruled for the sons of Israel: Bela the son of Beor;
and the name of his city *was* Dinhabah. 44. And Bela died, and
Jobab the son of Zerah from Bozrah ruled in his place. 45. And
Jobab died, and Husham from the land of the Temanites ruled
in his place. 46. And Husham died, and Hadad the son of Bedad,
who smote Midian in the field of Moab, ruled in his place; and
the name of his city *was* Avith. 47. And Hadad died, and Samlah
from Masrekah ruled in his place. 48. And Samlah died, and
Shaul from Rehoboth on the river ruled in his place. 49. And
Shaul died, and Baal-hanan the son of Achbor ruled in his place.
50. And Baal-hanan died, and Hadad ruled in his place; and the
name of his city *was* Pai; and his wife's name *was* Mehetabel, the
daughter of Matred, the daughter of Me-zahab. 51. And Hadad
died. And the chiefs of Edom were: chief Timnah, chief Aliah,
chief Jetheth, 52. chief Aholibamah, chief Elah, chief Pinon, 53.
chief Kenaz, chief Teman, chief Mibzar, 54. chief Magdiel, chief
Iram. These are the chiefs of Edom.

The introduction, 'The sons of Isaac', follows the previous pattern (v. 34b; vv. 5, 8, 17, 28). There are a couple of unusual features to note in this genealogy. First, the non-elect Esau is named before his brother Jacob (v. 34b), whereas a little earlier, the elect Isaac, who is not the first-born, is placed before Ishmael (v. 28). Although we find Esau mentioned after his brother in Genesis 28:5 and elsewhere, probably in recognition of Jacob's birthright status and divine election (Josh. 24:4; Heb. 11:20; Mal. 1:2-3), the Chronicler's sequence at this point is not haphazard but indicates that he is being guided by what is found in the Genesis narrative. His order follows the wording in the account of Isaac's burial where Esau is named before his brother (Gen. 35:29 – 'and his sons Esau and Jacob buried him'). It parallels the previous case where, in reference to Abraham's sons, the Chronicler again follows the Genesis order at Abraham's burial where Isaac is named before Ishmael (v. 28; Gen. 25:9 – 'his sons Isaac and Ishmael buried him').

Secondly, instead of the name 'Jacob' the text reads 'Israel'. The Chronicler's method of introducing Jacob is different to his treatment of Abraham. Both were given new names by God but, whereas Abraham's original name is mentioned and the change noted (v. 27), this is not done in Jacob's case. Even though the parallel passage in Genesis has 'Jacob' (Gen. 35:29), the Chronicler, without any comment, refers to him by his new name 'Israel'. This conforms to the Chronicler's consistent policy of substituting the name 'Israel' for 'Jacob' (1 Chron. 2:1; 5:1, 3; 6:38; 7:29; 29:10, 18; 2 Chron. 30:6).[8] Only in 1 Chronicles 16:13, 17 is Jacob's original name retained since it is in parallel with Israel (see Ps. 105:6, 10). The Chronicler is concerned to emphasise to the post-exilic community that, despite the divisions that had occurred throughout their history and the curse of exile, they still belonged to Israel, the one people of God that included descendants of all twelve tribes.[9]

As was the case when listing Abraham's offspring, the descendants of the non-elect line of Esau are mentioned first. There are parallels with Genesis 36, but the Chronicles' text

---

8. The Septuagint retains the name Jacob but this is no cause for emending the Masoretic Text.

9. See H. G. M. Williamson, *Israel in the Books of Chronicles* (Cambridge: Cambridge University Press, 1977).

is much more condensed, and as in previous examples, there are numerous variations in spelling.[10] Esau's wives are not mentioned when listing his five sons beginning with Eliphaz (v. 35; see Gen. 36:4-5, 10). After listing the five sons of Eliphaz, Timna and Amalek are named as if they also were sons (v. 36). But as we find from Genesis, Timna was a concubine of Eliphaz and she bore Amalek (Gen. 36:12; also v. 39). The Chronicler expects readers to know the details from Genesis (see v. 4 for a similar omission of relationships). And this is true when the 'sons of Seir' are listed (v. 38; see Gen. 36:20-30 for their relationship to Esau).

Chronicles retains the Genesis note about the kings of Edom who 'reigned in the land of Edom before a king ruled for the children of Israel' (v. 43). 'Edom' is used both for Esau and the people who descended from Esau in addition to the country in which they lived (Gen. 36:1, 9, 31). Giving prominence to Esau in this chapter prepares for the numerous references to Edom in the subsequent history that the Chronicler relates. It was David who subdued Edom. Later, Edom rebelled after the division of the kingdom and further wars between Judah and Edom ensued (1 Chron. 18:11-13; 2 Chron. 21:8-10; 25:11-20; 28:17). For the post-exilic community, the very name Edom was associated with all that was opposed to God and His people (Ezek. 25:12; 35:5). Their unbrotherly activity at the time of the Babylonian invasion could not be forgotten. God's people are reminded that though the Edomites may have originally increased rapidly and organised themselves into a nation with rulers long before Israel, God did not forget His promises to Israel, and the Chronicler makes it clear that the kingship that counts is the one associated with David.

The listing of kings and chiefs of Edom keeps close to the Genesis text (vv. 43b-54; see Gen. 36:32-43a), the one major exception being the addition 'And Hadad died' (v. 51). While this Hadad may well have been alive when Moses wrote,[11] the Chronicler can now add his death following the pattern set,

---

10. The surname of my own ancestors has been spelt and even pronounced differently over the centuries from Evison and Everson to Eveson (pronounced Eve's son), but all belonging to the same family line!

11. Philip Eveson, *The Book of Origins: Genesis simply explained* (Darlington: Evangelical Press, 2002), p. 467.

thus bringing the list of Edomite kings to a satisfying close. The conclusion to Esau's descendants parallels that in Genesis, 'These are the chiefs of Edom' (v. 54b), but without the extended note concerning settlements and possessions (Gen. 36:43).

Israel's sons (2:1-2)

> 2:1. These are the sons of Israel: Reuben, Simeon, Levi and Judah, Issachar and Zebulun, 2. Dan, Joseph and Benjamin, Naphtali, Gad and Asher.

As expected, after presenting the descendants of the non-elect Esau, the Chronicler records the names of Isaac's grandsons through his elect son: the twelve 'sons of Israel' (see 1:34b). If the treatment of Esau's descendants seemed unending, it is short compared with the eight-chapter coverage of the chosen line which now follows! These verses not only form the conclusion to the genealogical lists of chapter one, they provide the introduction to the great family tree of the Israelite nation that follows (2:3–9:1a). The Chronicler may well have had Genesis 35:23-26 in mind for he lists, without mentioning Jacob's wives, the names of Leah's sons first and then those of her slave-girl, Zilpah, last. Rachel's sons and those of her slave-girl, Bilhah, are given central place as in the Genesis passage, but uniquely, Bilhah's two sons, Dan and Naphtali, are placed either side of Rachel's two, Joseph and Benjamin (v. 2). It may be that the Chronicler, on the basis of Genesis 30:1-6, considered Dan to be Rachel's adopted son who was born before she herself had any sons of her own.[12] If this is the case, then Chronicles certainly follows the order of Genesis 35. Again, it will be noticed that whereas Genesis speaks of the 'the sons of Jacob', Chronicles, true to form, has 'the sons of Israel' (see 1:34b).

Application

'Who do you think you are?' became a popular programme on British television where well-known people discovered something of their family history. Some were able to trace their

---

12. See John D. Currid, *Genesis*, Vol. 2, EP Study Commentary (Darlington: Evangelical Press, 2003), p. 89.

ancestry back to royal figures of the past while others were awed that they had come from very humble circumstances. The first readers of Chronicles were somewhat disheartened after the initial flourish of excitement over the return from exile. They seemed to have suffered from a loss of identity and lacked a sense of purpose now that they were back in their own land but still under foreign domination. By taking God's chosen people back to their roots, the Chronicler reminds them of their place among the nations in order to be a blessing. Israel did not emerge out of a vacuum but is purposefully set within the context of a large family of nations and is chosen, not because of anything special about them, but because God freely set His love on them in order that they might be of benefit to all the nations as God promised Abraham (Gen. 12:3; 22:18; Deut. 7:7-8).

The way the Chronicler has positioned the family records means that it is the genealogical line that leads to Israel and therefore to the Messiah that is prominent. Without mentioning God or His electing grace in this opening section, the Chronicler witnesses to the greatness of Yahweh who is working out His purposes for the whole world through His people Israel. For the post-exilic community in the first place, the compiler helps to keep alive the hope first proclaimed in the Law, then preached by the prophets and expressed in the psalms.

It may be questioned why Edom is given so much prominence but when it is remembered that the Chronicler selected his material with his first readers particularly in mind, it is not unremarkable. When Jerusalem was being destroyed by the Babylonians, the Edomites were on the side of the invaders. They acted as informants, cut off escape routes, engaged in looting and even entered Judah's vacated land (Obad. vv. 10-14). At the time when Malachi was prophesying, the Nabateans had begun to move into Edomite territory and yet Edom proudly boasted it would rebuild its ruined cities and country. Malachi made it clear, however, that the future lay with Jacob's line and not Esau's, and that the proud boast of Edom would come to nothing: 'I love Jacob but Esau I hate' (Mal. 1:2-3). The post-exilic prophets speak of Judah 'the holy land' (Zech. 2:12), whereas Edom is called 'the wicked country' (Mal. 1:4). The Chronicler, likewise, emphasises that the future lies with Israel not Esau. The fact that God promised certain blessings to the non-elect like Ishmael and Esau, and even gave them kings long before Israel had any, served as an encouragement to Israel that God's purposes concerning Israel would be fulfilled. Edom, like Babylon, became symbolic of world opposition to God and His people (see Obadiah and Ps. 137:7; Rev. 18:1-19:5).

2

Israel's Descendants

(2:3–8:40)

The various sons of Israel and their descendants are listed in a particular order. In central position is the holy tribe of Levi (6:1-81 [5:27–6:66]), with the two southernmost tribes (2:3–4:43) and the Transjordanian tribes (5:1-26) positioned first with the northern tribes bringing in the rear (7:1-40). Looking at the material from another angle, Judah (2:3–4:23) and Benjamin (8:1-40) frame the genealogical lists of Israel's descendants. It was they, along with the central tribe of Levi, who formed the bulk of the southern kingdom of Judah after the split and who lived in the Persian district of Yehud (Judea) following the exile.

Southern tribes (2:3–4:43)

Judah (2:3–4:23)
In the first block of genealogies, the universal history began with Adam and climaxed with Israel (1 Chron. 1:1–2:2). The Chronicler now indicates what the name Israel meant in terms of the twelve tribes (1 Chron. 2–8). He begins with Judah, the tribe that rose to pre-eminence with David and that made up the bulk of the post-exilic community. Judah's name actually forms an *inclusio*[1] around the genealogical

---

1. A literary device in which a word or phrase is used to frame a section in the text. The same material is found at the beginning and end of a paragraph or section so as to bracket or envelop all that is between.

lists of Israel's tribes beginning with his offspring through a Canaanite and ending with Judah's captivity to Babylon due to unfaithfulness (1 Chron. 2:3; 9:1).

Unlike the initial genealogical lists in chapter one, the Chronicler's ordering of names becomes much more complicated. While some of the material corresponds to what is found in Genesis, and 2 Samuel, the bulk finds no parallel in any biblical source. What is clear is that the arrangement and length of this segment is meant to give prominence to Judah and his sons and to the significance of King David who appears at the centre of this genealogy. For instance, it is Judah's initial sons, Er, Onan and Shelah, who frame this family history (2:3 and 4:21-23). Even the introduction to Reuben's descendants draws attention first to Judah and to the fact that a ruler will emerge from this quarter: 'Judah grew strong among his brothers, and a ruler came from him' (1 Chron. 5:2). This is in keeping with one of the Chronicler's main concerns throughout his work and summed up later, where David is quoted as saying that Yahweh 'chose me ... to be king ... For he has chosen Judah to be a leader' (1 Chron. 28:4). David's family line actually takes centre stage (3:1-24) with the various descendants of Judah either side (2:3-55; 4:1-23) yet all eventually having some connection with David.

1. Judah's family tree (2:3-8)

2:3. The sons of Judah: Er and Onan and Shelah: three were born to him from the daughter of Shua the Canaanitess. But Er, Judah's firstborn, was evil in the eyes of Yahweh, so he put him to death. 4. And Tamar his daughter-in-law bore for him Perez and Zerah. All the sons of Judah *were* five. 5. The sons of Perez: Hezron and Hamul. 6. And the sons of Zerah: Zimri and Ethan and Heman and Calcol and Dara: five of them in all. 7. And the sons of Carmi: Achar, the troubler of Israel, who acted unfaithfully in the devoted thing. 8. And the sons of Ethan: Azariah.

Verses 3-5 find a parallel in Genesis 46:12 and Genesis 38. Judah's five sons are named. The first three are by 'the Canaanitess', 'the daughter of Shua' or 'Bathshua', and it is only the third son, Shelah, who survived to produce offspring (see 1 Chron. 4:21-23). Although Judah's second son, Onan,

and his evil actions and death are not mentioned, it served the
Chronicler's purpose to refer only to 'Er', the eldest son, and to
his serious sin and swift punishment. The same wording 'so
he put him to death' is used of Saul's end (see 1 Chron. 10:14).
It is in reference to Er's death that the Chronicler, for the first
time in his work, makes an explicit reference to God using
His covenant name 'Yahweh'. This is also the first of many
examples in Chronicles where sin is seen to lead to divine
retribution. Judah's other two sons, the twins 'Perez and
Zerah', are the result of his liaison with 'Tamar his daughter-
in-law' (Lev. 18:15; 20:12). No further comment was deemed
necessary over these illicit relationships and the genealogy
of Judah will reveal further examples of intermarriage with
foreigners (1 Chron. 2:17, 34-35; 3:2; 4:17, 22).

After mentioning the sons of Perez in verse 5, it is the non-
elect line of Zerah that is briefly listed first (vv. 6-8). Of the five
named 'sons', it is a descendant of Zimri's son Carmi, 'Achar'
(meaning 'trouble'; see Josh. 7:25-26) and better known as
Achan, who is brought to our attention (Josh. 7:1, 10-12, 18).
Achan's 'unfaithful act' concerned taking for himself some
of the spoil of that first successful military campaign on the
West Bank of the Promised Land. They were items that were
'put under the ban', meaning that these things along with the
rest of Jericho were to be devoted to God for destruction. This
descendant of Judah had defrauded God of His rights. It was a
breach of faith and indicated unfaithfulness to Israel's covenant
relationship with God. Both the verb 'to act unfaithfully' and
the noun 'unfaithful act' are used frequently by the Chronicler
(see 1 Chron. 5:25; 9:1; 10:13; 2 Chron. 12:2; 26:16, 18; 28:19, 22;
29:6, 19; 30:7; 33:19; 36:14). Chronicles proclaims that Judah's
descendants, who ended up in exile due to unfaithfulness
(1 Chron. 9:1), showed evidence of this same serious sin from
the very beginning of their history, and in each case it led
to Yahweh's fierce wrath falling on them (vv. 3, 7). The other
descendants, such as Ethan, Heman, Calcol and Dara (v. 6),
may well be the wise men of the east named in 1 Kings 4:31
and must not be confused with the Levitical musicians of the
same names (1 Chron. 15:19; Pss. 88–89). The Hebrew reads
'sons of Carmi' and 'sons of Ethan' even though only one is
named in each case (vv. 7-8), which suggests that the phrase

'sons of' has become a conventional formula irrespective of the number of names listed.

Application

The Chronicler's message for the post-exilic community indicates how the firstborn son is often by-passed in God's plan and those who are not originally of the chosen line are used to fulfil God's purposes and are included among God's people. Matthew 1 shows how, in the providence and purposes of God, those illegal relationships are part of the genealogy of Jesus the Messiah. He is born into a race and family of sinners of every type to become the sinner's friend and to stand in the place of such sinners and receive the just punishment that they deserve.

The paragraph presents both a warning and an encouragement. All sin is an affront to God's honour and deserves the severest punishment. There were those who, despite their associations with the elect line, did not belong to the people of God. Their actions indicated either wilful disinterest in the promised 'seed', as in the case of Er, or displayed outrageous sin that showed a complete disregard for God's covenant, as in the case of Achan. Similarly, the New Testament points to others, like Cain or Esau, to warn Christians of the dangers of apostasy. Swift judgment for flagrant sin is seen in the lives of professing Christians like Ananias and Sapphira, as well as of opponents like Herod (Acts 5:1-11; 12:1-23). On the other hand, unwitting sins or sinful activities that nevertheless demonstrated a concern for the promised line are treated with leniency as Tamar's incestuous relationship with Judah indicates. We are also taught that outsiders become members of God's covenant people as in the case of Bathshua the Canaanitess and Tamar. In Jesus Christ, Gentile believers, 'who once were far off have been brought near by the blood of Christ' and are no longer strangers and foreigners (Eph. 2:13, 19).

2. Hezron's descendants (2:9-55)
The descendants of Judah through Perez's son, Hezron, are broken down into various family groupings. They include

Ram's line (2:9-17), Caleb's line (2:18-20), further descendants of Hezron (2:21-24), descendants of Jerahmeel (2:25-41), and further descendants of Caleb (2:42-55).

> 2:9. And the sons of Hezron, who were born to him: Jerahmeel and Ram and Chelubai. 10. And Ram fathered Amminadab and Amminadab fathered Nahshon, leader of the sons of Judah. 11. And Nahshon fathered Salma and Salma fathered Boaz 12. and Boaz fathered Obed and Obed fathered Jesse 13. and Jesse fathered Eliab his firstborn, then Abinadab the second and Shimea the third, 14. Nethaneel the fourth, Raddai the fifth, 15. Ozem the sixth, David the seventh. 16. And their sisters *were* Zeruiah and Abigail. And the sons of Zeruiah: Abshai and Joab and Asahel, three. 17. And Abigail bore Amasa and the father of Amasa *was* Jether the Ishmaelite.

Nothing is said of Perez's other named son, Hamul (v. 5); it is Hezron's family tree that is all-important (v. 9; see Gen. 46:12; Num. 26:21) for it is this line that leads to King David and to other names associated with him. A linear genealogy of Ram is first presented down to David and his family (vv. 10-17) with the descendants of Chelubai (v. 9), also called Caleb (vv. 18-24, 42-55), enveloping the descendants of Jerahmeel, Hezron's firstborn son (vv. 25-41). This is a different Caleb to the spy who, with Joshua, brought back a good report (Num. 13:6; 1 Chron. 4:15).

For verses 10-12, see Ruth 4:19-22, with the leadership of Nahshon mentioned in Numbers 2:3. David is described as the 'seventh son' (v. 15) which is the sum of all Jesse's sons named. But there was another son, Elihu, who, although omitted here, is mentioned in 1 Chronicles 27:18 and this resolves the difference with 1 Samuel 16:10-13 and 17:12 where David is the 'eighth' son. The Chronicler may be using the number seven symbolically for the ideal family of sons (Job 1:2; 42:13; 1 Sam. 2:5), while the Samuel text, on the other hand, could be following a Semitic idiom found in other parts of the Old Testament where the eighth is treated as part of the seven (Eccles. 11:2; Micah 5:5; Rev. 17:11).[2] Jesse's daughters are also

---

2. See D. T. Tsumura, *The First Book of Samuel*, The New International Commentary on the Old Testament (Grand Rapids: Eerdmans, 2007), pp. 420-21; G. K. Beale, *The Book of Revelation*, The New International Greek Testament Commentary (Grand Rapids: Eerdmans, 1999), pp. 877-78.

named and his grandsons 'Abshai' (spelt 'Abishai' in Samuel), Joab and Asahel, the sons of Zeruiah, are well known from the Samuel account as well as Amasa, his daughter Abigail's son (2 Sam. 17:25; 19:13 [14]). Again, it serves the Chronicler's purpose to state that Amasa's father was an Ishmaelite.

> 2:18. And Caleb the son of Hezron fathered through Azubah *his* wife, and through Jerioth, and these are her sons: Jesher, and Shobab, and Ardon. 19. Then Azubah died and Caleb took for himself Ephrath, and she bore to him Hur. 20. And Hur fathered Uri and Uri fathered Bezaleel.

Having reached David and the family members associated with his kingship, Caleb's line is introduced and taken as far as Bezalel, who had an important task in relation to the construction of the tabernacle and its furnishings (Exod. 31:2; 35:30; 36:1-2; 37:1; 38:22; 2 Chron. 1:5). By positioning the genealogies of Ram and Caleb next to each other and ending Ram's line with David and his relatives and Caleb's line with Bezalel, the Chronicler draws attention to the important connection between the Davidic kingship and the central sanctuary, a theme that will become more obvious later. Ephrah, called also 'Ephrathah' (v. 19; see vv. 24, 50), is the name associated with Bethlehem where Benjamin was born and Rachel died (Gen. 35:16, 19; 48:7). David is called the son of the 'Ephrathite of Bethlehem-Judah' (1 Sam. 17:12) and it is there the future messianic ruler would be born (Micah 5:2).

The Hebrew text of verse 18 is difficult. It is clear from verse 19 that Azubah was Caleb's wife and not his daughter. Jerioth may therefore have been a concubine or Azubah's maid and in the phrase 'these are her sons' the reference is to Azubah, as she is the one mentioned again in verse 19. If perhaps Jerioth was Azubah's maid and had given birth to one or more of the three sons, Azubah would have regarded them as her own (see verse 2 concerning Rachel and Dan). A less likely view is that Jerioth is the daughter of Caleb and Azubah and the mother of the named sons.

> 2:21. And afterward, Hezron came to the daughter of Machir, Gilead's father, whom he took when he *was* sixty years old, and she bore to him Segub. 22. And Segub fathered Jair, who had twenty-three cities in the land of Gilead. 23. But Geshur and

Aram took from them Havvoth-jair with Kenath and its villages, sixty cities. All these *were* the sons of Machir, Gilead's father. 24. And after Hezron's death in Caleb-Ephrathah, then Abijah, Hezron's wife, bore to him Ashhur, the father of Tekoa.

This paragraph shows a connection between the tribes of Judah and Manasseh through the marriage of Hezron to Machir's daughter, Abijah, and why it is placed as a sequel to Caleb's line (see v. 24). Machir was Manasseh's firstborn, one of the grandsons of Joseph (Gen. 50:23), and he fathered Gilead, the ancestor of the Gileadites who were allotted the northern Transjordan 'land of Gilead' (Num. 26:29; Deut. 3:15; Josh. 17:1). 'Jair' is a descendant of Hezron and Abijah and he had numerous cities in Gilead, but the name first appears as one of the sons of Manasseh who gave his name to 'Havvoth-Jair' ('villages of Jair'; Num. 32:41; Deut. 3:14). In the days of the Judges there was yet another Jair from the region who kept up the tradition of his predecessors (Judg. 10:3-4). Aram and Geshur became neighbouring kingdoms that were eventually absorbed into the Aramean kingdom of Damascus. As for 'Kenath' it became known as Nobah (see Num. 32:42).

There are uncertainties over the original text in verse 24 so that Ashhur the father of Tekoa (see 1 Chron. 4:5) is either the son of Hezron and Abijah as the Hebrew text suggests or of Caleb and Ephrath, as supported by the Septuagint. The emendation would read: '... Caleb went to Ephrathah (and Hezron's wife was Abijah) and she bore him Ashhur ...'. Until further light is forthcoming, it is better to stay with the more difficult Masoretic Text. It may well be that Ashhur was brought up by Caleb and Ephrath(ah) on account of Hezron's death, as happened in the case of Lot whom Abraham and Sarah reared.

2:25. And the sons of Jerahmeel the firstborn of Hezron were Ram the firstborn, and Bunah and Oren and Ozem, Ahijah. 26. And Jerahmeel had another wife whose name *was* Atarah. She was the mother of Onam. 27. And the sons of Ram the firstborn of Jerahmeel were Maaz and Jamin and Eker. 28. And the sons of Onam were Shammai and Jada. And the sons of Shammai: Nadab and Abishur. 29. And the name of the wife of Abishur *was* Abihail, and she bore to him Ahban and Molid. 30. And the sons of Nadab: Seled and Appaim, but Seled died without sons. 31. And the sons of Appaim: Ishi. And the sons of Ishi: Sheshan. And the sons of Sheshan: Ahlai. 32. And the sons of Jada the brother of Shammai: Jether and Jonathan; and Jether died without sons. 33. And the sons of Jonathan: Peleth and Zaza. These were the sons of Jerahmeel.

34. Now Sheshan had no sons only daughters. And Sheshan had an Egyptian servant whose name *was* Jarha. 35. And Sheshan gave his daughter to Jarha his servant as a wife and she bore to him Attai. 36. And Attai fathered Nathan and Nathan fathered Zabad. 37. And Zabad fathered Ephlal and Ephlal fathered Obed. 38. And Obed fathered Jehu and Jehu fathered Azariah. 39. And Azariah fathered Helez and Helez fathered Eleasah. 40. And Eleasah fathered Sismai and Sismai fathered Shallum. 41. And Shallum fathered Jekamiah and Jekamiah fathered Elishama.

The descendants of Jerahmeel, Hezron's first-born, are set out in two parts: a segmented genealogy (vv. 25-33) and a linear one (vv. 34-41). Apart from a mention of Jerahmeelites occupying the Negev on Judah's southern border (1 Sam. 27:10; 30:29) nothing is known of the individuals named in the genealogies. The first genealogy (vv. 25-33) shows how the line continued despite the extinction of some branches ('died without sons': vv. 30, 32). More attention is paid to the descendants by Jerahmeel's second wife 'Atarah' than his first wife whose name may well be 'Ahijah' rather than being the fifth son (vv. 25-26).[3]

The second genealogy (vv. 34-41) takes up the line from Sheshan, mentioned in the previous list as having 'Ahlai' (v. 31), who is perhaps a daughter or grandson, judging by verse 34. In verse 31, the phrase 'sons of' is a conventional formula as in 2:8 for offspring whether one or many, male or female. An additional note explains how Sheshan, who had no sons, gave in marriage one of his daughters to his Egyptian servant, Jarha, in order to continue his line (vv. 34-35). This is similar to situations recorded in Genesis and the Mosaic law where servants are used to obtain offspring for the master and his wife (see Gen. 16:2; 30:1-13; Exod. 21:4). The Chronicler is keen to show how foreigners were absorbed not only into

3. The *mem* at the end of the previous name 'Ozem' perhaps belongs to the following word to give 'from Ahijah' or maybe a second *mem* has been dropped through haplography.

Israel in general, but into the family of Judah (see also 2:3). Canaanites and Egyptians, male and female, are found within the people of God and there is no hint of disapproval. There is no means yet of ascertaining who Elishama was, but clearly it was thought important to indicate the legitimacy of his pedigree.

> 2:42. And the sons of Caleb the brother of Jerahmeel: Mesha his firstborn; he was the father of Ziph. And the sons of Mareshah, the father of Hebron. 43. And the sons of Hebron: Korah and Tappuah and Rekem and Shema. 44. And Shema fathered Raham, the father of Jorkeam; and Rekem fathered Shammai. 45. And the son of Shammai: Maon, and Maon *was* the father of Beth-zur. 46. And Ephah, Caleb's concubine, bore Haran and Moza and Gazez; and Haran fathered Gazez. 47. And the sons of Jahdai: Regem and Jotham and Geshan and Pelet and Ephah and Shaaph. 48. Caleb's concubine, Maachah, bore Sheber and Tirhanah. 49. She also bore Shaaph the father of Madmannah, Sheva the father of Machbenah and the father of Gibea; and the daughter of Caleb: Achsah. 50. These were the sons of Caleb.
>
> The son of Hur, the firstborn of Ephratah: Shobal the father of Kirjath-jearim, 51. Salma the father of Bethlehem, Hareph the father of Beth-gader. 52. And Shobal the father of Kirjath-jearim had sons; Haroeh, half of the Menuhoth. 53. And the families of Kirjath-jearim: the Ithrites and the Puthites and the Shumathites and the Mishraites. From these came out the Zorathites and the Eshtaolites. 54. The sons of Salma: Bethlehem and Netophathite, Atroth-beth-joab and half of the Manahathites, the Zorites. 55. And the families of the scribes who resided at Jabez: Tirathites, Shimeathites, Sucathites. These are the Kinites, the ones who came from Hammath, the father of the house of Rechab.

This section continues the family tree of Caleb (see 2:18-24) and is in two parts: verses 42-50a and verses 50b-55, with the first part beginning and ending similar to the segmented genealogy of Jerahmeel (vv. 25, 33). The first list names Caleb's descendants presumably from his main wife (vv. 42-45), then from his concubines: first Ephah (vv. 46-47) and then Maacah (vv. 48-49). A significant feature is the number of geographical place-names mentioned such as Ziph and Maon (see Josh. 15:55; 1 Sam. 23:24), Beth-zur (Josh. 15:58), Mareshah (Josh. 15:44; Micah 1:15), Hebron (Gen. 13:18; Josh. 15:13, 54) and Tappuah (Josh. 16:8; 17:8). All the place names that can be identified are associated with the territory given to the tribe of Judah (see Josh. 15). In particular, Beth-zur, Ziph, Mareshah and Hebron are among the strategic cities that Rehoboam fortified (2 Chron. 11:7-10). In some occurrences, 'father' may be translated 'founder', while in other cases, the person may be called after the place-name. The noun 'father', as in 'father of Ziph' (v. 42) must not be confused with the verb 'to father' or 'beget' as, for example, in verse 44: 'Shema fathered Raham'. As an appendage, we are told that 'the daughter of Caleb was Achsah' (v. 49b). This is the Caleb mentioned along with so many of the place-names in Joshua 15:16-17 and Judges 1:12-13, the faithful spy whose father was Jephunneh and who gave his daughter to Othniel, his brother or confederate. This more well-known Caleb was a descendant of the original Caleb the son of Hezron and brother of Jerahmeel.

The second part of the Caleb family line (vv. 50b-55) continues where it left off earlier with Hur's descendants (1 Chron. 2:19-20). Though the Masoretic Text has the singular ('son of Hur', v. 50b), the Septuagint and Vulgate interpret the idiom correctly by reading the plural ('sons of Hur'). The three sons mentioned are associated with important places: Shobal with Kiriath-jearim (Josh. 9:17; 15:9, 60; 18:14-15), the place where the ark of the covenant found a temporary home (1 Chron. 13); Salma with Bethlehem, the birth-place of David (Ruth 4:11-22; 1 Sam. 17:12-15); and Hareph with Beth-gader (v. 51). It is clear as the list continues that we are not always dealing with individuals but with groups of people like the Ithrites who belonged to David's mighty men (v. 53; see 2 Sam. 23:38; 1 Chron. 11:40), with 'families' or 'clans' (v. 53) and with guilds or professions such as the 'scribes' (v. 55; 1 Chron. 4:14, 21, 23). The phrase 'half of Menuhoth' (v. 52) again means we are dealing with a group, the other half of which is referred to as 'the Manahathites' (v. 54). As for the name 'Haroeh' (meaning 'the seer'; v. 52), it is probably a variant of 'Reaiah' ('seer of Yah'; 1 Chron. 4:2). The singular 'Netophathite' (v. 54), and without the definite article, is used as a collective noun both here and in 1 Chronicles 9:16 (see also Neh. 12:28). The Netophathites were people from Netophah, a place three miles (4.8 kilometres) southeast of Bethlehem (Ezra 2:21-22;

Neh. 7:26). Two of David's mighty men came from there
(2 Sam. 23:28-29; 1 Chron. 11:30; 27:13, 15).

The final statement concerns the Kinites. This is the only
occurrence in the Old Testament of this plural spelling for
the well-known Midianite tribe of Kenites. Their connection
with the Rechabites is somewhat enigmatic. It is possible, as
in previous instances, that 'house of Rechab' could be a place-
name Beth-rechab (see 'Beth-marcaboth' at 1 Chron. 4:31)
and Hammath would be the founder of the group living
there. But the verb 'came from' is not used of genealogical
descent but in the sense of motion 'to come from a place'
and thus Hammath is associated with a nomadic Kenite
tribe from whom the nomadic Rechabites are descended (see
2 Kings 10:15-23; Jer. 35:1-19). One of those who returned from
exile who played a prominent role in rebuilding Jerusalem is
Malchijah the son of Rechab (Neh. 3:14), which may be one of
the reasons for the Chronicler's mention of Rechab. Kenites
are associated with Moses and the wilderness wanderings
as well as the conquest of Canaan. Some lived for a time
among the Amalekites (Exod. 2:16-18; Num. 10:29; Judg. 1:16;
4:11; 1 Sam. 15:6; 27:10; 30:29).

Application

Hebron and Bethlehem are prominent in these lists and
prepare for the Chronicler's main focus on David who lies
at the centre of Judah's genealogy. David, the son of Jesse
(v. 13-15), came from the city of Bethlehem and it was at
Hebron that Israel came to make him king (1 Sam. 16:4-13;
1 Chron. 11:1-3, 16-18). It was prophesied that Yahweh's
true anointed one would come from Bethlehem Ephrathah
and be a 'rod' or 'branch' from the stem of Jesse (Isa. 11:1;
Micah 5:2; Matt. 2:4-6).

Again, we note the Chronicler's openness to outsiders.
There was no need to have mentioned them but he draws
attention specifically to instances of Judahites who married
foreigners, including a Canaanite, an Ishmaelite and an
Egyptian, yet without any word of condemnation. While it
was necessary for the post-exilic community to refrain from
relationships with pagans and those who were in a religiously

compromised position (see Ezra–Nehemiah), the Chronicler introduces these non-Israelite converts to encourage his people to look to the time when people from all the nations of the world would be one with Israel in worshipping the true and living God. In this, Chronicles draws attention to a theme expressed by prophets and psalmists (Isa. 19:24-25; 56:6-8; Zech. 2:11; 8:20-23; Mal. 1:11; Pss. 87; 117; see Rom. 15:1-13).

3. The Descendants of David (3:1-24)

Having already given prominence to David through his descent from Ram (1 Chron. 2:10-17), Chronicles moves on to David's own descendants, first by naming nineteen of his children (vv. 1-9), then by means of a linear genealogy from Solomon's son Rehoboam to Josiah (vv. 10-14) and finally by a segmented genealogy from Josiah's sons through the time of exile and down possibly to the period when the Chronicler was writing (vv. 15-24).

> 3:1. And these were the sons of David that were born to him in Hebron: the firstborn Amnon by Ahinoam the Jezreelitess; second, Daniel by Abigail the Carmelite; 2. the third, Absalom the son of Maacah the daughter of Talmai king of Geshur; the fourth, Adonijah the son of Haggith; 3. the fifth, Shephatiah by Abital; the sixth, Ithream by Eglah his wife. 4. Six were born to him in Hebron and he reigned there seven years and six months, and thirty-three years he reigned in Jerusalem. 5. And these were born to him in Jerusalem: Shimea and Shobab and Nathan and Solomon, four by Bathshua the daughter of Ammiel; 6. also Ibhar and Elishama and Eliphelet 7. and Nogah and Nepheg and Japhia 8. and Elishama and Eliada and Eliphelet, nine. 9. All *were* David's sons, beside sons of concubines; and Tamar *was* their sister.

The Chronicler returns to give further details concerning David's family line immediately after mentioning people and places associated with David such as Hebron, Ephrathah and Bethlehem (2:42-43, 50-51, 54). It consists of two parts, each with a heading: the first gives the sons born in Hebron (vv. 1-4a; 2 Sam. 3:2-5) and the second names the sons born in Jerusalem (vv. 5-8; 2 Sam. 5:14-16), with a statement concerning the duration of David's reign joining the two parts (v. 4b; 2 Sam. 5:5). In 1 Chronicles 14:4-7, the list of sons born in

Jerusalem appears again with minor variations in spelling. David's second son 'Daniel' is also called 'Chiliab' (2 Sam. 3:3). It was not unusual for a person to have two names, such as Reuel, who was also known as Jethro, and Solomon, who was also called Jedidiah. Absalom's mother was a foreigner from Geshur, an Aramaean city, and she seems to have been named after the Aramaean state of Maacah north of Manasseh's territory in Transjordan (Deut. 3:14; 2 Sam. 3:3; 15:8).

The conclusion (v. 9) includes an additional note concerning other children by concubines and to David's daughter Tamar, who is deliberately referred to as 'their sister'. It draws attention to how she was raped by Amnon who was in turn murdered by Absalom and to David's reactions to the whole sorry affair (2 Sam. 5:13; 13-14). By naming Amnon first and Tamar last (vv. 1, 9), the Chronicler emphasises the cloud that surrounded David's offspring. David's wife, Bathsheba, is here given a different spelling – Bathshua (meaning 'the daughter of Shua', v. 5; see Judah's wife in 2:3), but she was actually 'the daughter of Ammiel' (spelt 'Eliam' in 2 Samuel 11:3). Of her four sons named, Solomon is mentioned last not because he was the fourth to be born but to give him prominence and to associate Bathsheba more closely with him and all the sad events that had preceded his birth (2 Sam. 12:24-25). While the account of David's reign in Chronicles is generally presented in idealistic terms, the introduction makes clear that in reality all was not sweetness and light. When the whole list of David's sons is taken into account, Solomon is again seen to be the central figure. Nine of David's sons are named before Solomon (vv. 1-5) with a further nine sons listed after him (vv. 6-8).

> 3:10. And the son of Solomon, Rehoboam, Abijah his son, Asa his son, Jehoshaphat his son, 11. Joram his son, Ahaziah his son, Joash his son, 12. Amaziah his son, Azariah his son, Jotham his son, 13. Ahaz his son, Hezekiah his son, Manasseh his son, 14. Amon his son, Josiah his son. 15. And the sons of Josiah: the firstborn Johanan; the second Jehoiakim; the third Zedekiah; the fourth Shallum. 16. And the sons of Jehoiakim: Jeconiah his son; Zedekiah his son. 17. And the sons of Jeconiah: Assir, Shealtiel his son 18. and Malchiram and Pedaiah and Shenazzar, Jecamiah, Hoshama and Nedabiah. 19. And the sons of Pedaiah:

Zerubbabel and Shimei. And the son of Zerubbabel: Meshullam
and Hananiah, and Shelomith their sister; 20. and Hashubah
and Ohel and Berechiah and Hasadiah and Jushab-hesed, five.
21. And the sons of Hananiah: Pelatiah and Jeshaiah, the sons
of Rephaiah, the sons of Arnan, the sons of Obadiah, the sons of
Shecaniah. 22. And the sons of Shecaniah: Shemaiah. And the
sons of Shemaiah: Hattush and Igal and Bariah and Neariah and
Shaphat, six. 23. And the son of Neariah: Elioenai and Hizkiah
and Azrikam, three. 24. And the sons of Elioenai: Hodaviah
and Eliashib and Pelaiah and Akkub and Johanan and Delaiah
and Anani, seven.

The genealogy first lists those who occupied the Davidic throne
after Solomon where son follows father, through to Josiah
(vv. 10-14). Already notice is given of what will be stressed
later, that Solomon belongs with David in a separate category.
The genealogy therefore does not begin with Solomon, David's
son, but with Rehoboam, the son of Solomon. In this way
attention is also drawn to the new situation that existed after
the David–Solomon era. It was under Rehoboam's leadership
that the kingdom was divided (2 Chron. 10). Following Josiah,
the pattern changes suggesting that his death marked another
significant moment ('sons of Josiah … sons of Jehoiakim …'
etc., vv. 15, 16, 17, 19, 21, 22, 23, 24). Chronicles indicates that
following the tragic death of Josiah, the exilic age commenced
(2 Chron. 36:4, 6, 10, 20). Descendants of David are seen to
continue through the exile until the Chronicler's time in the
post-exilic period (vv. 17-24). No mention is made of Athaliah,
Ahab's daughter, who usurped the Davidic throne for a time
(2 Kings 11; 2 Chron. 22:10-12). The throne name 'Azariah'
is used rather than his more familiar name Uzziah (v. 12;
2 Kings 15:13, 30; 2 Chron. 26; Isa. 1:1; 6:1). Four sons of Josiah
are named, three of whom followed him on the throne (v. 15).
Johanan is unknown perhaps because he died before he
could become king. Jehoiakim, the throne name of Eliakim
(2 Kings 23:34), was Pharaoh Necho's choice in place of
Josiah's other son, Shallum, whose throne name was Jehoahaz
(2 Kings 23:30-34; Jer. 22:11). He is probably placed last because
of his brief reign. Jeconiah, the son of Jehoiakim, is sometimes
shortened to Coniah and is also known as Jehoiachin (v. 16;
2 Kings 24:8,12; Jer. 22:24, 28; 24:1; 29:2; 37:1). The 'third' son

of Josiah, whose name was Mattaniah but changed by the Babylonians to Zedekiah, was the last Davidic king to rule in Jerusalem (2 Kings 24:17; 25:7; 2 Chron. 36:10-11). This Zedekiah is not to be confused with the otherwise unknown grandson of Jehoiakim who was probably named after his older relative (v. 16).

The conventional formula, 'the sons of' before 'Jeconiah' (v. 17), introduces only one name, Assir (see 2:8, 31 for previous examples). Others bearing this name include a son of Korah (Exod. 6:24; see also 1 Chron. 6:22-23, 37 [6:7-8,22]). Some scholars assume that the word *assir* is not a person's name but an adjective describing Jeconiah as 'captive', which of course he did become throughout the days of Nebuchadnezzar (2 Kings 24:15; 25:27). Against this conjecture is the fact that in no other case is such a title found in these lists. It is prophesied of Jeconiah: 'Write this man down as childless' (Jer. 22:30) but as that prophecy goes on to indicate it was in the sense that he would have no son to succeed him on the throne.

Shealtiel is the most significant of the seven named sons of Assir (vv. 17-18) and is elsewhere said to be the father of Zerubbabel (Ezra 3:2, 8; 5:2; Neh. 12:1; Hag. 1:1, 12, 14; 2:2, 23; Matt. 1:12; Luke 3:27). In this list, Zerubbabel is the son of Shealtiel's brother Pedaiah. A possible solution is that Shealtiel died childless and Pedaiah took his brother's widow to raise up descendants according to the levirate marriage custom (Deut. 25:5-10). Another idea suggested in Jewish sources is that he was indeed the son of Shealtiel but brought up by his brother. Like David, Zerubbabel's sons[4] are in two groups (vv. 19-20; see vv. 4-8). Perhaps the first two were born before the return from exile with the other 'five' born after the restoration. Their names certainly convey the renewed hope of the people in contrast to Zerubbabel's name ('Offspring of Babylon'): Hashubah ('Thought about'); Ohel ('Tent'), Berechiah ('Yahweh blesses'); Hasidiah ('Yahweh has steadfast love'); Jushab-Hesed ('May steadfast love return'). Another indication of this hope is the naming of Zerubbabel's daughter, Shelomith ('Peace'), a feminine form from the

---

4. The MT reading has the idiomatic singular 'son' but the *Sebir* and some Hebrew MSS read the plural, as does the LXX.

same word-family as the name Solomon. Though she is not elsewhere known, judging by the references to other women mentioned in the genealogical lists (see 2:16, 49; 3:9), she may well have been a significant person at the time of the return from exile.

It is difficult to be certain how many generations the Chronicler intends after Zerubbabel. Some, on the basis of the Septuagint text of verse 21, have reckoned Shecaniah to be the sixth generation from Hananiah, meaning that Pelatiah alone was the son of Hananiah. On the basis of the traditional Hebrew text, it seems more likely that the 'sons of Hananiah' include not only Pelatiah and Jeshaiah but the sons of Rephaiah, Arnan, Obadiah and Shecaniah, making all six belong to the same generation. The following verse 22 is also problematic. It concerns the number 'six' after naming only five sons of Shecaniah. But it is possible that 'sons' of Shecaniah is used in the sense of 'descendants' so that Shemaiah and his five sons bring the total to six descendants.

To the final name in the list of David's descendants, 'Anani' (v. 24), the Targum adds, 'he is the king Messiah who will be revealed' and some ancient Jewish commentators associate the Hebrew consonants ('*nni*) with the Aramaic word for 'clouds of' in the phrase 'clouds of heaven' in Daniel 7:13.[5] Also of interest is that, as David was placed as the seventh son of Jesse (1 Chron. 2:15), so Anani is the seventh son of Elioenai (v. 24) as if to direct us to a new David.

Application

Mentioning Zerubbabel calls to mind the promises made to him as one who typified the coming Messiah (see Hag. 1–2 and Zech. 4). Further, the promises of God made to David concerning his 'son' may well be the reason why Solomon is given prominence in this list. Solomon becomes symbolic of the future 'son of David' who will sit on God's throne ruling God's kingdom for ever (see 1 Chron. 17:10-16). The names given to Zerubbabel's children indicate the people's

---

5. Matthew Henry mentions it as an example of Jewish Messianic hope. See also Thomas Willi, *Chronik*. Biblischer Kommentar, Altes Testament XXIV/1 (Neukirchen-Vluyn: Neukirchener Verlag, 1991) p. 120.

continued belief in God's covenant promises concerning the future, while Anani is seen as a final tangible indication of the Davidic hope. Both Matthew and Luke show how those various strands stemming from the son of Jesse and through Zerubbabel, come together in Jesus the Messiah.

It was not only from Solomon that our Lord descended (Matt. 1:6) but from Bathsheba's son, Nathan (Luke 3:31). Among the many solutions that have been proposed to account for the differences between the two Gospels, one possibility is that Matthew records the 'official' royal line while Luke records the actual physical genealogy, with both lines converging at two points, first with Shealtiel and Zerubbabel and then with Joseph.[6]

4. Further descendants of Judah (4:1-23)

Following the list of David's descendants, the Chronicler returns to other families of Judah and includes records that find no parallel in other parts of the Bible. They give information concerning the founders of some of the cities in Judah (vv. 3, 4, 5, 11, etc.) and add interesting details relating to craft guilds (vv. 14, 21, 23). In addition, the Chronicler reveals one of his main ongoing concerns, namely, the importance of prayer (vv. 9-10). This genealogy together with the earlier one (see 2:3-55) form a frame around David and his descendants, and by so doing draws attention to the importance of the Davidic line of kings.

4:1. The sons of Judah: Perez, Hezron and Carmi and Hur and Shobal. 2. And Reaiah the son of Shobal fathered Jahath, and Jahath fathered Ahumai and Lahad. These *were* the families of the Zorathites.

3. And these are the father of Etam: Jezreel and Ishma and Idbash; and the name of their sister *was* Hazelelponi. 4. And Penuel the father of Gedor, and Ezer the father of Hushah. These *are* the sons of Hur, the firstborn of Ephratah, the father of Bethlehem.

5. And Ashur, the father of Tekoa, had two wives, Helah and Naarah. 6. And Naarah bore to him Ahuzzam and Hepher and Temeni and Haahashtari. These *were* the sons of Naarah. 7. And the sons of Helah: Zereth, Zohar and Ethnan. 8. And Koz

---

6. Matthew Henry accepts this interpretation.

fathered Anub and the Zobebah, and the families of Aharhel the son of Harum.

9. And Jabez was more honourable than his brothers, and his mother called his name Jabez, saying, 'Because I bore him in pain'. 10. And Jabez called to the God of Israel, saying, 'Oh that you would really bless me and enlarge my territory, that your hand might be with me, that you would act contrary to the evil so as not to pain me.' And God brought about that which he had requested.

The Chronicler retraces his steps and begins again with Judah's son, Perez (see 2:4). The accompanying names are not brothers of Perez so that the phrase 'sons of' should be translated in this context, 'descendants of.' Thus like the names from Adam to Noah (1 Chron. 1:1-4), a linear genealogy covers the descendants of Judah from Perez through Hezron to Hur and Shobal (see 2:5, 19, 50). The name 'Carmi' may be a variant of either Caleb or Chelubai (see 2:7,9) but the details are unclear. Another short linear genealogy takes the family line from Shobal to the brothers Ahumai and Lahad (v. 2). The latter two names are unique but 'Jahath', their father, was a common name among the Levites (1 Chron 6:20; 23:10-11; etc.). 'Reaiah' is a variant form of Haroeh (see 2:52). The place-name 'Zorah' lay in the lowlands of Judah (Josh. 15:33), the home of Manoah the father of Samson (Judg. 13:2). It was the site of one of Rehoboam's fortifications (2 Chron. 11:10) and was re-occupied after the Babylonian exile (Neh. 11:29). The inhabitants of Zorah are called 'the Zorathites'. It is questionable whether they are the same as the 'Zorites' (2:54).

More supplementary material is found here concerning Hur's family (2:19, 50), with Hur being as much the 'father of Bethlehem' as his son Salma (2:51). 'Gedor' is in Judea lying between Hebron and Etam (Josh. 15:58) and is associated both with Penuel (v. 4) and Jered (v. 18). The Masoretic Text, 'And these *are* the father of' (v. 3), is difficult, but could mean that Jezreel, Isham and Idbash were the joint founders of Etam, a place in the hill country of Judah near Bethlehem and Tekoa and the site of another one of Rehoboam's fortifications (Judg. 15:8; 2 Chron. 11:6). Following the Septuagint, the NIV and ESV read 'sons of' in place of 'father of' while the AV adds '*were of*' before 'the father of' and the NKJV has 'the sons *of the father* of.'

Tekoa (v. 5) is best known as the home of the prophet Amos (Amos 1:1). It was also the place from where Joab brought a wise woman to speak to David on behalf of his son Absalom (2 Sam. 14:1-20). It lay about ten miles (sixteen kilometres) south of Jerusalem. Ashur (see 2:24), who was either the father or founder of Tekoa, had two wives. Of the children whom his wife Naarah bore, we know nothing, apart from Hepher (v. 6). This is quite a common name especially in Manasseh (Num. 26:32-33; 27:1; Josh. 17:2-3) but a king of Hepher is named immediately after the king of Tappuah (Josh. 12:17; see also 1 Chron. 2:43; 1 Kings 4:10), two places linked with Hebron and Caleb. The name 'Haahashtari' (v. 6) may be translated 'the Ahashtarites' and 'Coz' (v. 8) is probably a fourth son of Ashur by his wife Helah (vv. 5, 7).[7] 'Zohar' (v. 7) is the Qere reading and to be preferred to the Kethibh, 'Izhar' (see Gen. 46:10; Exod. 6:15). The name 'Anub' (v. 8) may be identified with the city of Anab near Debir (Josh. 15:50).

Following the example of Moses when he broke off the genealogical listing to comment on Enoch's personal relationship with God (Gen. 5:22,24), the Chronicler pauses in this part of Judah's family line to single out Jabez as a person whose prayers the Lord was pleased to answer (vv. 9-10). It is the first of a number of instances in the Chronicler's work that seeks to encourage the people of God to persevere in prayer (see 1 Chron. 5:20-22; 17:16-27; 21:26; 2 Chron. 14:11-12; 30:18-20, 27; 32:20-23, 24; 33:13, 18-19).

Who was Jabez? A city with that name was mentioned earlier in connection with Caleb's descendants and the Kenites (1 Chron. 2:55). The names of his parents are not given but we are told that it was his mother who gave him his name (see also 1 Chron. 7:16). Jabez (*ya'bēṣ*) involves a play on the word for 'hurt' or 'painful labour' (*'ōṣeb*) with the second and third root letters reversed (*'bṣ* to *'ṣb*). There may be an allusion to God's judgment on Eve '… in pain you will bear sons' (Gen. 3:16), where a similar word (*'eṣeb*) is used for

---

7. It is possible that 'and Coz' stood at the end of verse 7 and was lost through haplography.

'pain'.[8] The word-play is continued in Jabez' prayer '... not to pain me' (*'oṣbî*, v. 10).

Names were sometimes given to express the circumstances relating to a child's birth (Gen. 25:25-26). Others were prophetic (see Gen. 10:25). Some names turned out to relate both to the birth of the children and to their characters (Gen. 27:36). Rachel died in childbirth and named her child 'son of sorrow' (Ben-oni) but Jacob called him Benjamin ('son of the right hand'; see Gen. 35:18). How could a man like Jabez live down such an unfortunate name and be respected more than his unnamed brothers when people might have believed that nothing good was destined for him? The answer is associated with his piety. First, he 'called to the God of Israel'. While his mother 'called' him by this unpleasant name, Jabez countered this by praying to the God who is able to change things for the better. For the first time in Chronicles the epithet 'God of Israel' is found. Even though it is used in the context of an individual from the tribe of Judah praying to God, the Chronicler wished to indicate that this was the kind of prayer that the whole nation of Israel could pray, individually and corporately, and especially appropriate for the post-exilic community.

As for the prayer itself, it contains four requests but it could be that the first request is spelt out in the other three petitions. Divine blessing is often associated with fruitfulness and success, and that is what is implied in Jabez's prayer. In his opening request, the particle (*'im*) often introduces a conditional clause ('if ...') but here it expresses a wish ('Oh that ...'; see Ps. 139:19).[9] The translation 'really bless' tries to catch the force of the Hebrew infinitive absolute used with the imperfect verb (literally 'blessing you would bless me'; see Gen. 22:17). The blessing he desired included territorial expansion, and this clearly meant that he saw himself having a future in terms of many descendants. He also pleaded for the presence of God's 'hand', which suggests that Jabez was looking for God to intervene in his situation and act out of His

8. See Japhet, *I & II Chronicles*, p. 109.

9. W. Gesenius, *Hebrew Grammar*, ed. Krautzsch, translated by Cowley (second edition Oxford: Oxford University Press, 1910) §151e, p. 477.

infinite resources. This is a great blessing (Isa. 66:14) and the very opposite of having God's hand against someone which would mean being cursed by God (1 Chron. 21:17; Isa. 1:25; 5:25). In the final petition, Jabez prays that God would so act that the 'evil' or 'distress' associated with his name would not be his lot in life.[10]

The Chronicler adds that the prayer of Jabez was effective. Israel's God is the true and living God who hears and answers prayer (Ps. 65:2[3]). His petition concerning territory is not out of keeping with the geographical references in the genealogy. At a time when, perhaps unlike Othniel, his brothers were not interested in possessing more of the promised land (Josh. 15:17; 1 Chron. 4:13), Jabez prayed on the basis of God's word through Moses which spoke of blessings in the land for obedience and curses for disobedience (Deut. 11:22-28; 30:19-20).

Application

Though his start in life was not promising, Jabez trusted the true God who had made promises to His people concerning the land of Canaan and concerning a royal descendant from the tribe of Judah who would defeat the snake (Gen. 3:15; 49:10). It spoke to the post-exilic community especially after the pain of exile and the hardships they experienced on their return. God was still the God of Israel, the one who had blessed Abraham and their ancestors, and the prayer of Jabez would have been an encouragement to go on trusting God and praying to the God who hears and answers the prayers of His people. That same encouragement is for the Israel of God today. The Book of Psalms likewise gave similar reassurances (Ps. 102:17).

Jabez's situation and the answer to his prayers reminds us of the Lord's Suffering Servant, who was despised and cursed yet eventually prospered resulting in fruitfulness and expansion of territory (Isa. 42:13; 53:3-4, 10; 54:1-3). What

---

10. The preposition *min* has the sense of 'without regard to' in the phrase translated 'that you would act contrary to the evil' (literally 'that you would act from evil'). The English versions unjustifiably translate the verb 'do' or 'act' as 'keep'. It is also suggested that in this context the verb 'to do' means 'turn', and so to read 'turn yourself from evil', but this is not necessary; cf. D Winton Thomas, 'Translating Hebrew, *'ASAH'* in *The Bible Translator* 17 (1966), p. 193.

seems impossible with humans is possible with God and we are called to be involved in God's work.

The context indicates that the prayer of Jabez is not to be used to encourage selfish requests for personal advantage in this world.[11] Christians are often seen by the world as foolish and weak, yet God has chosen such people to shame the wise, so that all the glory may go to God. The Lord's people are called to be faithful by living obedient lives and seeking to bear fruit, not only in terms of personal maturity in Christlikeness (Gal. 5:22-23) but also through active involvement for the advancement of Christ's kingdom (John 15:1-17). It is in that context that we are urged to pray in the name of Jesus, who promises that 'whatever you ask the Father in my name, he may give you' (John 15:7-8, 16; 16:23-28). He also urged His followers by means of a parable not to faint but always to pray (Luke 18:1). We are assured by James that the earnest prayers of the righteous are effective (James 5:16-18).

4:11. And Chelub the brother of Shuah fathered Mehir, who *was* the father of Eshton. 12. And Eshton fathered Beth-rapha and Paseah and Tehinnah the father of Ir-nahash. These *are* the men of Rechah.

13. And the sons of Kenaz: Othniel and Seraiah; and the sons of Othniel: Hathath. 14. And Meonothai fathered Ophrah and Seraiah fathered Joab, the father of Ge-harashim, for they were craftsmen. 15. And the sons of Caleb the son of Jephunneh: Iru, Elah and Naam and the sons of Elah and Kenaz.

16. And the sons of Jehallelel: Ziph and Ziphah, Tiria and Asarel. 17. And the son of Ezrah: Jether and Mered and Epher and Jalon; and she conceived Miriam and Shammai and Ishbah the father of Eshtemoa. 18. And his Judahite wife bore Jered the father of Gedor, and Heber the father of Soco, and Jekuthiel the father of Zanoah. And these *are* the sons of Bithiah, the daughter of Pharaoh whom Mered took. 19. And the sons of Hodiah's wife, the sister of Naham, the father of Keilah the Garmite and Eshtemoa the Maachathite. 20. And the sons of Shimon: Amnon and Rinnah, Ben-hanan and Tilon. And the sons of Ishi: Zoheth and Ben-zoheth.

21. The sons of Shelah the son of Judah: Er the father of Lecah and Laadah the father of Mareshah, and the families of the house of linen workers of Beth-ashbea; 22. and Jokim and

---

11. See, for instance, *The Prayer of Jabez* by Bruce Wilkinson which became a best-seller (Colorado Springs: Multnomah Books, 2000).

the men of Cozeba, and Joash and Saraph who ruled in Moab, and Jashubilehem (and the records *are* ancient). 23. They *were* the potters, and the inhabitants of Netaim and Gederah. They dwelt there with the king in his work.

All the names in the short genealogy of Chelub are unknown (vv. 11-12). Some scholars have tried to identify Chelub with Chelubai (1 Chron. 2:9) and see both as variants of Caleb, but there is nothing to verify this.[12] Despite support from the Septuagint, there is no certainty that Rechah should be emended to Rechab.

Verses 11-15 are a genealogical fragment, which is perhaps all that the Chronicler could find. Probably a name is missing before 'and Kenaz'.[13] Caleb was mentioned earlier (1 Chron. 2:19,49). He was closely related to Othniel (Josh. 15:17; Judg. 3:9,11) who married Achsah, the daughter of Caleb (Judg. 1:13). They both belonged to the Kenizzites ('sons of Kenaz'; Num. 32:12; Josh. 14:6, 14) who were one of the groups in Canaan before the Israelite conquest (Gen. 15:19). By emphasising the name Kenaz, the Chronicler is keen to show that Canaanite clans were absorbed into Judah. The name 'Ge-harashim' means 'the valley of craftsmen' (see Neh. 11:35).

The genealogical fragments of Judah's descendants in verses 16-20 are not easy to unravel and there are a number of textual problems. What Jehallelel's connections are to the main family line is not given. A 'Ziph' has been mentioned earlier as a descendant of Caleb's son Mesha' (1 Chron. 2:42) and is the name of one of the cities fortified by Rehoboam (2 Chron. 11:8). There are many suggestions concerning who 'she' refers to in verse 17.[14] Though we think of 'Miriam' as a girl's name (v. 17; see Exod. 15:20), here it seems to be that of a man. 'Shammai' is a common Judean name (1 Chron. 2:28, 44-45). The name

12. Cf. Klein, *1 Chronicles*, p. 133 and H. G. M. Williamson, *1 and 2 Chronicles*, p. 60.

13. It is unlikely that the name was Ukenaz. A popular suggestion is that the original text read as a summary statement, 'These are the sons of Kenaz.' In a text without the vowel point, the pronoun 'these' is the same as the personal name Elah. But this would involve transposing the text and dropping the 'and' before Kenaz.

14. One suggested reconstruction follows the LXX to produce 'and Jether fathered Miriam ...' Another solution is to transpose the clause from verse 18b to read, 'These are the sons of Bithiah the daughter of Pharaoh whom Mered took and she conceived ...' The LXX is no real help as it has its own textual problems.

'Eshtemoa' (v. 17) appears again in verse 19. It is also the name of a city twenty miles (thirty-two kilometres) south of Hebron (Josh. 21:14; 1 Sam. 30:28). An unknown man's wife, a Judean (it is unlikely that 'Jehudijah' refers to her personal name; v. 18) gave birth to three sons, who became the founders of ('father of') Judean cities: Gedor, Soco and Zanoah (Josh. 15:34, 35, 48, 58). It seems strange that the wife of Hodiah (v. 19) is not recorded whereas her brother Naham is. The name Keilah is a city of Judah that David saved from the Philistines but whose inhabitants were ungrateful (Josh. 15:44; 1 Sam. 23:1-13).

The marriage of Mered to Pharaoh's daughter (v. 18) calls to mind Solomon's marriage to an Egyptian princess (1 Kings 3:1). Scholars have made heavy weather of the likelihood of an ordinary Israelite marrying the daughter of an Egyptian king. Stranger things have happened and we have no reason to be sceptical. As he has done in the previous lists, the Chronicler has deliberately included this note concerning a marriage to a foreigner and again adds no comment of disapproval.

The genealogy closes by returning to Shelah, the third son of Judah and Bath-shua (v. 21; 1 Chron. 2:3). As in the case of Ram, Er is named after his uncle whom God punished (1 Chron. 2:3, 9, 25). The 'father of Mareshah' (v. 21) suggests that Laadah was the founder of the well-known place that became another of those cities that Rehoboam fortified (Josh. 15:44; 2 Chron. 11:8), but we know of no city of Judah named Lecah. There is a Mareshah listed as a descendant of Caleb and as a 'father' or founder of Hebron (1 Chron. 2:42). The phrase 'families of the house of linen workers' refers to a 'guild' of linen workers at an unknown place called Beth-ashbea. The word for this fine white Egyptian cloth 'byssus' (*buṣ*, 'linen') is common in Aramaic and Akkadian and appears five times in Chronicles as well as in other later biblical books (1 Chron. 15:27; 2 Chron. 2:14[13]; 3:14; 5:12; Ezek. 27:16; Esther 1:6; 8:15). A more common biblical synonym is *šeš* which is of Egyptian origin (Gen. 41:42; Exod. 26:1, 31, 36; etc.). Another family of skilled workers were 'potters' who settled in Netaim and Gederah (vv. 22-23; Josh. 15:36). As in more modern times, professions or trades tended to be kept within families.[15]

15. R. L. Braun, *1 Chronicles*, Word Bible Commentary 14 (Waco: Word, 1986), p. 60.

It is difficult to know whether Jashubilehem (v. 22) is a person's name or to be understood with the Targum and Vulgate as inhabitants of Moab who 'returned' (*j/yashub* from the verb 'to return' *šûḇ*) to Lehem, short for Bethlehem. The phrase, 'who ruled in Moab' could be translated 'married into Moab' or 'worked for Moab',[16] and either of the latter options would be more in keeping with the context and similar to the story of Naomi and Ruth. The Chronicler had ancient records to prove the authenticity of his material (v. 22b).

The information concerning the ancient craftsmen in Israel is of particular interest. There were skilled manual workers involved in the construction of the tabernacle (Exod. 36:1-2) and reference has already been made to the 'valley of the craftsmen' (v. 14). Such craftsmen were employed by David in preparation for the building of the Jerusalem temple and by Joash and Josiah for the temple repairs. Skilled men were also involved in rebuilding the temple after its destruction by the Babylonians (1 Chron. 22:15; 29:5; 2 Chron. 24:12; 34:11; Ezra 3:7).

Application

The comment by the Chronicler concerning the antiquity of the records (literally 'the words are ancient') emphasises, as in Luke's account of Jesus, the care and attention paid in obtaining accurate information (Luke 1:1-4). As Michael Wilcock has stated, 'the setting of the book is factual not fictional.'[17] Though there are many gaps in our knowledge, the author has brought to our attention significant places associated with real people some of them with skills that were used for the benefit of the nation and its communal worship. It would have served as yet more encouragement to the people to whom he first wrote. In the church of Jesus Christ all our abilities and gifts are to be brought into the service of the King of kings for the advancement of His kingdom and the honour of His name.

---

16. The verb *bā'alû lᵉ* ... ('they ruled/married in') could be a dialectical variant of *pā'alû lᵉ* ... ('they worked for'). Cf. M. Dijkastra, 'A note on 1 Chr IV 22-23,' *Vetus Testamentum* 25 (1975), 671-74; H. G. M. Williamson, *1 and 2 Chronicles*, p. 61.

17. Wilcock, '1 and 2 Chronicles' in *New Bible Commentary*, eds. D. A. Carson, R. T. France, J. A Motyer, G. J. Wenham (Leicester: Inter-Varsity Press, 1994), p. 392.

These final genealogical fragments of Judah's line (4:1-23) also form an *inclusio* with the beginning of that line (2:3-55) so that attention is especially drawn to the centre with its genealogy of David and his descendants (3:1-24). In this way, the Chronicler reminds his people of the prophecy made by Jacob (Israel) that the sceptre would not depart from Judah (Gen. 49:10) and of God's covenant with David concerning the permanence of his dynasty (1 Chron. 17:10-14), an important element in the prophetic messages of hope (Isa. 9:7; 55:3; Jer. 30:8-9; 33:15, 17, 22; Ezek. 34:23f.; Hosea 3:5; Amos 9:11; Zech. 12:7-10). Both Matthew and Luke draw our attention to the fulfilment of these promises in the birth of Jesus who 'according to the flesh' is a descendant of David (Matt. 1:1-17; Luke 1:32,69; Rom. 1:3).

At the same time, the Chronicler is pointing out that not only Israel as a whole had foreign elements within her, but even Judah contained Canaanite and Egyptian blood. The election of Abraham, Israel and David was with a view to blessing all the nations of the world as was emphasised in the Abrahamic covenant and some of these nations are represented even in the line that leads to the promised 'seed'. Like the Chronicler, Matthew is quick to point out the universal significance of Messiah's coming by referring to Tamar, Rahab the Canaanite, Ruth the Moabitess, Bathsheba who was the wife of a Hittite, as well as to the worship of the Magi from the East.

Simeon (4:24-43)

The tribe of Simeon was closely related to Judah. Both Judah and Simeon had Leah as their mother (Gen. 29:33, 35) and Simeon's inheritance lay within the borders of Judah's deep south (Josh. 19:1-9). Because Simeon collaborated with Levi in the treacherous massacre of Shechem's inhabitants, their descendants were allotted no separate portion of land (Gen. 34:25-30; 49:5-7). Judah and Simeon worked closely together to claim their allotted territory (Judg. 1:3). Though many areas associated with Simeon were treated as belonging to Judah (see v. 33; Josh. 15:28-32; 19:2-8), there were people as well as places like Beersheba linked with the northern tribes long after the division of the kingdom under Rehoboam (see v. 41; Amos 5:5; 8:14; 2 Chron. 15:9; 34:6).

The section begins with Simeon's genealogy which is much
shorter than Judah's and is set out differently (vv. 24-27).
Unlike its more influential partner, the tribe did not increase
greatly and this is specially noted (v. 27). The second part
of the section deals with Simeon's territory (vv. 28-33),
tribal princes (vv. 34-38) and expansion (vv. 39-43). In some
respects, the Chronicler's depiction of Simeon resembles the
situation of Jabez (1 Chron. 4:9-10) for they both began at a
great disadvantage and yet contrary to expectation they were
blessed with descendants and gained territory (Gen. 48:5-7;
1 Chron. 4:27, 38-43).

> 4:24. The sons of Simeon: Nemuel and Jamin, Jarib, Zerah, Shaul;
> 25. Shallum his son, Mibsam his son, Mishma his son. 26. And
> the sons of Mishma: Hammuel his son, Zaccur his son, Shimei
> his son. 27. And Shimei had sixteen sons and six daughters; but
> his brothers did not have many sons, neither did all their family
> multiply like the sons of Judah.

The names of Simeon's sons are identical in Genesis 46:10
and Exodus 6:15, but in Numbers 26:12-14, Ohad is omitted
and likewise here in Chronicles. This may be due to the clan
having died out.[18] Comparing the census at the end of the
wilderness period with the one taken at the time of the exodus
(Num. 1 and 26), Simeon's population dropped by nearly two-
thirds. Chronicles agrees with Numbers in reading Nemuel in
place of Jemuel, which may be a pronunciation difference, and
Zerah (zrḥ) instead of Zohar (zhr), which in the consonantal
text may be due to metathesis, the transposition of the last
two letters. As in Numbers, Chronicles omits the note that
Shaul, which in Hebrew is spelt the same as Israel's first king,
was the son of a Canaanite woman. Only in Chronicles is the
name Jarib found; the other three lists read Jachin.

The remaining names are unique to the Chronicler but
Shallum is a common name (see 1 Chron. 2:40; 3:15; 6:12;
7:13; etc.), while Mibsam and Mishma appear together in
the genealogy of Ishmael (1 Chron. 1:29-30) and it might be
that some Ishmaelite clans, who settled in the Negev were

18. Timothy R. Ashley, *The Book of Numbers*, The New International
Commentary on the Old Testament (Grand Rapids: Eerdmans, 1993), p. 535.

incorporated into Simeon as happened with Canaanite clans into Judah (1 Chron. 2:55; 4:12-13).

We probably have a linear genealogy of seven generations, with Shallum being the son of Simeon's son Shaul and ending with Shimei, whose importance is revealed in the number of his offspring. While the population of Simeon decreased rapidly during the wilderness wanderings unlike Judah's descendants, Shimei bucked the trend (v. 27). In the post-exilic era, when the Chronicler wrote, Judah was the main tribe.

> 4:28. And they dwelt in Beersheba, and Moladah and Hazar-shual 29. and in Bilhah and in Ezem and in Tolad 30. and in Bethuel and in Hormah and in Ziklag 31. and in Beth-marcaboth and in Hazar-susim and in Beth-biri and in Shaaraim. These *were* their cities until David reigned. 32. And their villages *were* Etam and Ain, Rimmon and Tochen and Ashan, five cities, 33. and all their villages that *were* round about these cities as far as Baal. This *was* their settlements, and their genealogical record belonged to them.

The cities named in verses 28-33 follow closely Joshua 19:2-8 with changes in spelling probably due to the passing of time from Joshua's day to the post-exilic period: Bilhah for Balah, Tolad for Eltolad, Bethuel for Bethul, Hazar-susim for Hazar-susah, Beth-biri for Beth-lebaoth and Shaaraim for Saruhen. Shema/Sheba is omitted in the traditional Hebrew text (see Josh. 15:26; 19:2).[19] Beersheba (see Gen. 21:31; 1 Chron. 21:2; 2 Chron. 30:5)[20] in the southernmost part of Canaan is the only place that can be precisely located and suggests that Moladah and Hazar-shual are in the same general region (Neh. 11:26-27). Excavations in the Beersheba region have unearthed inscriptions that name Ezem and Tolad. Interestingly, Beth-marcaboth means 'house of chariots' and Hazor-susim 'village of horses'. Both Simeon and Judah are credited with 'utterly destroying' Zephath so that it was called 'Hormah' (Judg. 1:17).[21] Ziklag (see Neh. 11:28) came under the rule of Achish the Philistine who gave it to David

---

19. The LXX includes it. See M. H. Woudstra, *The Book of Joshua*, The New International Commentary on the Old Testament (Grand Rapids: Eerdmans, 1981), pp. 280-1.

20. See Currid, *Genesis*, vol. 1, p. 384.

21. See verse 41 below for the use of the verb from the same root letters.

during the time he was being hunted by King Saul (1 Sam. 27:6; 1 Chron. 12:1). The text of Samuel states that Ziklag 'has belonged to the kings of Judah to this day' and details are also given of other cities in the south taken by David (1 Sam. 27:6; 30:26-31). This probably accounts for the Chronicler's note that these cities, no longer held by the Simeonites, were officially recognised as Judean when David became king (v. 31).

Perhaps the phrase 'and their villages' (v. 32)[22] should be taken with the previous sentence and refer to the Simeonite villages that surrounded the cities (see Josh. 19:6) rather than as an introduction to the ones that follow. The five named places are not unwalled 'villages' (Lev. 25:31) but 'cities'. Etam (see v. 3) is not included in the Joshua account, hence the reference there to four cities (Josh. 19:7). Tochen is perhaps a variant of Ether and both may be variants of Athach (1 Sam. 30:30).[23] Ain and Rimmon are listed as two separate cities (v. 32; see Josh. 15:32; 19:7) and it is possible that one of them is the post-exilic city of En-rimmon (Neh. 11:29). Other cities mentioned here that were inhabited by the returning exiles included Moladah, Hazar-shual, Beersheba and Ziklag (Neh. 11:26-28).

After the cities are named, reference is made to the surrounding villages that reached 'as far as Baal' (v. 33). At this point, the Chronicler breaks off the rest of the sentence found in his source (compare Joshua 19:8 'as far as Baalath-beer, Ramah-negeb'). This Baal(ath) seems to be identified with Ramah-negeb ('Ramah of the South') and is one of the original cities of the Simeonites to which David sent gifts (1 Sam. 30:27).

In keeping with his general policy, the Chronicler does not speak of the 'inheritance' of Simeon (see Josh. 19:8; compare also verse 28, 'And they dwelt in ...,' with Josh. 19:2, 'And their inheritance was in ...'), but of 'their habitations' or 'settlements'. The stress is on Israel living in the land 'from time immemorial' rather than conquering and receiving it by lot.[24] This approach is appropriate to the post-exilic period when God's people

---

22. The personal pronoun is masculine, referring to the Simeonites, while the corresponding 'their' in Joshua 19:6 is feminine, referring to the villages surrounding the cities.

23. See David T. Tsumura, *The First Book of Samuel*, p. 648.

24. See S. Japhet, 'Conquest and Settlement in Chronicles,' *Journal of Biblical Literature* 98, 1979, pp. 205-18.

were seeking to reclaim their settlements.[25] There may be 'an eschatological hint' in verse 33 that God's promises to Abraham would be fulfilled (Gen. 15:18-21; see Neh. 9:8).[26]

The phrase 'genealogical record' (v. 33) translates a verb meaning 'be enrolled by genealogy' or 'enrol oneself' (*hiṯyaḥeś*). It is one of the Chronicler's key terms which he uses fourteen times (1 Chron. 5:1, 7, 17; 7:5, 7, 9; 9:1, 22; 2 Chron. 12:15; 31:16-19). Apart from five other occurrences in Ezra-Nehemiah, it is found nowhere else in the Bible. A noun from the same root meaning 'genealogy' (*yaḥaś*) is used in Nehemiah 7:5. There is an unusual emphasis on the third person plural pronoun which may indicate the Chronicler's desire to stress the separate identity of the Simeon tribe in view of the dominance of Judah in the region.[27]

> 4:34. And Meshobab and Jamlech and Joshah the son of Amaziah 35. and Joel and Jehu the son of Joshibiah, the son of Seraiah, the son of Asiel, 36. and Elioenai and Jaakobah and Jeshohaiah and Asaiah and Adiel and Jesimiel and Benaiah 37. and Ziza the son of Shiphi, the son of Allon, the son of Jedaiah, the son of Shimri, the son of Shemaiah – 38. these, the ones entered by names, *were* princes in their families: and the house of their fathers increased greatly.

Without any introduction, thirteen names are listed in verses 34-37 and it seems likely that we are to understand the 'these' in verse 38 to refer to these names. What relationship the 'princes' or 'heads' of families were to the previous list in verses 24-27 is not clearly apparent, unless Shemaiah (v. 37) can be identified with Shimei (v. 27). It is clear that the Chronicler is using a written record of their names ('entered by name,' v. 38). Only three are given prominence: the father of Joshah is named (v. 34); Jehu is traced back over three generations (v. 35); but pride of place goes to Ziza, the last named, who has five generations of ancestors recorded (v. 37). Though generally they may not have multiplied like Judah

---

25. See Gregory Goswell, *A Study Commentary on Ezra-Nehemiah* (Darlington: Evangelical Press, 2013) on Nehemiah 11:25-36, which includes some of the names mentioned by the Chronicler.

26. As suggested by Klein, *1 Chronicles*, p. 150.

27. Williamson, *1 and 2 Chronicles*, p. 62.

(v. 27), these Simeonites 'increased greatly' (see Exod. 1:12) and this led to their move westward and eastward.

> 4:39. And they went to the entrance of Gedor, as far as the east of the valley, to seek pasture for their flocks. 40. And they found fertile and good pasture; and the land was spacious and quiet and peaceful; because those who dwelt there formerly were of Ham.
>
> 41. And these, written by name, came in the days of Hezekiah king of Judah, and struck their tents, and the Meunim who were found there, and utterly destroyed them to this day. And they dwelt in their place because there was pasture there for their flocks. 42. And some of them, five hundred men of the sons of Simeon, went to Mount Seir, and Pelatiah and Neariah and Rephaiah and Uzziel, the sons of Ishi, were at their head. 43. And they struck the remnant of the Amalekites that had escaped, and they have dwelt there to this day.

An increase in population involved an increase in the flock and this led to the Simeonites migrating in two different directions. There were those who expanded in a more westerly direction and this took them to Gedor (v. 39), a place that cannot be precisely identified.[28] As Abraham and Lot were forced to separate on account of their flocks so these Simeonites moved to find better grazing areas[29] in land once held by Egyptians, Canaanites or Philistines and referred to here as 'of Ham' (v. 40; see 1 Chron. 1:8, 12; Gen. 10:6, 14). There were a few places considered 'quiet and peaceful' such as Laish before the Danites attacked it (Judg. 18:7, 27; see Jer. 49:31).

A military campaign occurred in the time of King Hezekiah (v. 41) when, possibly, a census was held ('written by name'; see v. 38) in preparation for the battle (see 2 Kings 18:8). A nomadic group associated with the Philistines, 'the Meunim' (see 2 Chron. 26:7)[30] who had been making use of the pastureland, were caught up in the battle and all were 'utterly destroyed' just as Israel had done to many of the Canaanites in the days

---

28. Many scholars emend with the LXX to 'Gerar' (Gen. 20:2; 26:1), but this is doubtful. 'Gedor' is a common name (see 1 Chron. 4:4, 18; 8:31).

29. The word for 'fertile' is 'fat', 'stout' or 'rich' (see Num. 13:20; Neh. 9:25, 35, for its use in describing land), while 'spacious' translates 'broad of hands'.

30. The Qere reading is 'Meunim' while the Kethibh is 'Meinim'. The Targum followed by the Vulgate has 'dwellings'.

of Joshua. The verb used means to 'put under the ban' or 'devoted to destruction' (*ḥrm*; see the name 'Hormah' in v. 29 above; Lev. 27:28-29; Josh. 6:17-18, 21). The phrase 'to this day' (v. 41) probably refers to the time when the original record was made (see v. 43 below). It is not without significance that the Chronicler draws attention to this event taking place in the time of King Hezekiah, a ruler who trusted Yahweh in times of crisis and who is later depicted as another example of the ideal monarch (2 Chron. 29–32).

Mention is made of a second military campaign connected with the Simeonite expansion (vv. 42-43), which possibly took them in an easterly direction into Edomite territory ('Mount Seir') that lay in the southern part of the Negeb (see 2 Chron. 20:10, 22-23). The relationship of the Amalekites and Edom is due to a descendant of Esau, Eliphaz, producing a son named Amalek by Timna his concubine (Gen. 36:10-12; 1 Chron. 1:35-36). The 'remnant of the Amalekites' will be those who escaped the defeats by Saul and David (1 Sam. 14:48; 15:1-7; 2 Sam. 8:12). These descendants of Simeon who defeated the Amalekite remnants with five hundred men calls to mind David's battles against the Philistines and Amalekites with between four to six hundred men (1 Sam. 22:2; 23:13; 30:1-3, 16-17). It is not clear whether the final comment 'to this day' (v. 43) refers to the Chronicler's own time which is possible in this context (see 1 Chron. 5:26) or, as earlier (v. 41), to the period found in the Chronicler's sources (see 1 Chron. 4:41; 13:11; etc.).

Some of those who returned after the exile and who claimed descent from Simeon, yet recognised as relatives of the Judahites, may very well have occupied land to the south of the official Persian province of Judah. The Book of Nehemiah certainly mentions the reoccupation of cities listed here (Neh. 11:26-30).

Application

Simeonite exploits in the past are an encouragement to Israel in the Chronicler's own day not to lose heart. Israel during the period of Persian supremacy, like Christians in today's world, may seem a people of no importance, but they are to hold on to God's promises. Canaan is a picture or type of the new creation to which all God's people are encouraged to look forward when they will take possession of the whole earth. The promise is that the meek will inherit the earth (Ps. 37:11; Matt. 5:5).

The references to Simeonite occupation of pastures that were fertile and of land that was spacious, quiet and peaceful is a reminder of the ideal picture of life in Canaan (Deut. 8:7-10; 12:9-10; 25:19; Josh. 21:44; 23:1), and thus of the new earth. Seen in the context of Jabez and other examples provided later, the Chronicler is perhaps suggesting that Simeon's successes were due to faithfulness to Yahweh and dependence on Him in spite of the odds stacked against them.[31] This is his message both to his first readers and to Christians today in a world opposed to the living God and His elect ones.

Transjordanian tribes (5:1-26)

This section deals with the tribes on the East Bank, from Reuben in the south to Gad in the middle and the half of Manasseh in the north (see Josh. 13:8-31). These tribes were part of Israel in the past and, though they were punished for their apostasy with an exile that continued through to the Chronicler's own day, they are not forgotten and there is the prospect of a future for them.

Reuben (5:1-10)

> 5:1. And the sons of Reuben the firstborn of Israel (for he *was* the firstborn, but because he defiled his father's bed his birthright was given to the sons of Joseph the son of Israel, but not to be in the genealogical enrolment according to the birthright. 2. For Judah became strong among his brothers, and a ruler *came* from him; but the birthright belonged to Joseph).

As Judah continued to be a focus of attention in dealing with Simeon so in introducing Reuben, Judah's prominence is still emphasised (vv. 1-2). Three points are made clear.

First, much is made of the 'birthright', a term that appears three times in these two verses. The rights of the firstborn

---

31. See Brian E. Kelly, *Retribution and Eschatology in Chronicles*, Journal for the Study of the Old Testament Supplement Series 211 (Sheffield: Sheffield Academic Press, 1996), pp. 65-66.

should have gone to Reuben but, on account of his gross sexual misconduct with his father's concubine, he forfeited that right (Gen. 29:31-32; 35:22).[32] This is the reason why Reuben did not 'excel' (Gen. 49:3-4) and one reason for Judah being placed at the head of the genealogical list rather than Reuben.

Secondly, a further piece of information is attached that makes explicit what is assumed elsewhere, that the status of the firstborn passed from Reuben to Joseph's sons, Ephraim and Manasseh, who were regarded as full sons, like Jacob's first two sons, Reuben and Simeon (Gen. 48:5). The birthright belonged to Joseph who received the double share (see Deut. 21:17) and this resulted in his sons being reckoned as two distinct tribes. It is interesting to find 'the open attitude toward the north' shown by the Chronicler, in view of the conflict with the Samaritans in the post-exilic period.[33] As far as Chronicles is concerned Ephraim and Manasseh have not forfeited their ancient privileges (see 2 Chron. 28:5-15; 30:1-12).[34]

Thirdly, in the phrase that includes one of the Chronicler's favourite terms, 'genealogical enrolment' (v. 1; see 1 Chron. 4:33; 5:7), it is not clear whether the reference is to Reuben the firstborn or Joseph the birthright holder, but the main point is to indicate why neither occupy first place in the Chronicler's own genealogical list (2:3–9:1). It was the tribe of Judah that became pre-eminent among his brothers as Jacob's prophecy indicated (Gen. 49:8, 10), but it was Joseph's life that previewed the future king promised to Judah when his brothers bowed down to him in fulfilment of his God-given dreams (Gen. 42:6; 43:26, 28). Also, as the genealogy has already shown, it is from Judah that David's royal line has descended and it is from this same tribe that the one greater than David will come (Micah 5:2).

5:3. The sons of Reuben the firstborn of Israel: Hanoch and Pallu, Hezron and Carmi. 4. The sons of Joel: Shemaiah his son, Gog

32. See Martin J. Selman, 'Comparative customs and the patriarchal age,' in A. R. Millard and D. J. Wiseman (eds.) *Essays on the Patriarchal Narratives* (Leicester: Inter-Varsity Press, 1981), pp. 113-14, 126.

33. Klein points this out in *1 Chronicles*, p. 160.

34. Martyn J. Selman, *1 Chronicles* (Leicester: Inter-Varsity Press, 1994), p. 105; H. G. M. Williamson, *Israel in the Books of Chronicles* (Cambridge: Cambridge University Press, 1977), pp. 89-95.

his son, Shimei his son, 5. Micah his son, Reaiah his son, Baal his son, 6. Beerah his son, whom Tilgath-pilneser king of Assyria, carried into exile. He *was* prince of the Reubenites. 7. And his brothers, according to his families, enrolled according to their generations: Jeiel the chief, and Zechariah, 8. and Bela the son of Azaz, the son of Shema, the son of Joel, who dwelt in Aroer, and as far as Nebo and Baal-meon: 9. and eastward he dwelt to the beginning of the wilderness that reaches to the river Euphrates, because their cattle had multiplied in the land of Gilead. 10. And in the days of Saul they made war with the Hagrites, who fell by their hand; and they dwelt in their tents throughout all the *region* east of Gilead.

Verse 3 resumes after the parenthesis (vv. 1b-2) by repeating the opening words of verse 1a. The use of the name 'Israel' rather than Jacob (vv. 1, 3) is a reminder of the Chronicler's general policy throughout the work (see 1 Chron. 1:34). In this way, he taught those for whom he first wrote that though the northern tribes broke away they were still to be regarded as part of Israel. Likewise, the repetition of Reuben's place as the 'firstborn' indicated that while the rights of the firstborn had been taken from him, his biological priority was to be respected.

The sons of Reuben are placed in pairs exactly as they are listed in Exodus 6:14 (compare Gen. 46:9; Num. 26:5-7). What relation Joel is to Reuben's family is not stated but we are given a linear genealogy down to Beerah, a leader or 'prince' of the Reubenites, who was carried into captivity by the 'king of Assyria', Tilgath-Pilneser III (745-727 b.c.) at the time of the Syro-Ephraimite war around 732 b.c. (2 Kings 15:29; see v. 26), eleven years before the fall of Samaria. The four different spellings of the Assyrian king's name found in the Hebrew Bible are probably due to various ways of transliterating the Assyrian. His name is usually spelled Tiglath-Pileser.[35] His exile was a foretaste of what was to befall the north first and then later the southern kingdom. The seven names from Shemaiah to Beerah give a sense of completeness, but it is nowhere near a comprehensive list as many more generations would be needed to take us from patriarchal times to the exile.

---

35. See Alan R. Millard, 'Assyrian Royal Names in Biblical Hebrew,' *Journal of Semitic Studies* 21 (1976), p. 7.

Though there is support from the versions for reading 'their families' in place of 'his families' (verse 7), the harder reading should be retained.[36] It is referring to other Reubenite clans and the word 'brothers' or 'kinsmen' is probably a reference back to Beerah rather than Joel. Three relatives are named: Jeiel the chief, Zechariah and Bela who is the great-grandson of perhaps another Joel. The places named, 'Aroer ... Nebo and Baal-meon' (verse 8), are mentioned as part of Reuben's tribal inheritance (Num. 32:38; Josh. 13:15-17). They were lost to Moab toward the end of the Omri dynasty as the Mesha stela indicates (see also Jer. 48:1, 19, 22-23).

The Reubenites' eventual loss of land is contrasted with their activity at an earlier period in which they expanded eastward to the edge of the desert. As with the Simeonites, it was on account of the increase in their livestock that new grazing ground was sought. From the time of Moses, the tribe of Reuben, along with the tribe of Gad, had acquired a vast number of livestock (Num. 32:1). An additional note refers to Reubenite activity 'in the days of Saul' when 'they made war with the Hagrites' who once inhabited the area they conquered (v. 10; see vv. 18-22). This tribal group is closely associated with the Moabites and Ishmaelites (see Ps. 83:6[7]) and in some way they may be related to Hagar, Abraham's concubine. Hagrites were found among David's officers (1 Chron. 11:38; 27:30-31). The area known as Gilead (vv. 9-10) can sometimes be used for the entire Transjordan area occupied by the two and a half tribes (Deut. 34:1; 2 Kings 10:33), whereas Gilead in the narrower sense stretched north and south of the river Jabbok (Deut. 3:10-12). Despite all the negative comments, the Reubenites were blessed with descendants, much livestock, increase of land and victory over enemies.

Application

The Chronicler is interested in all the tribes of Israel and this is made very clear with the amount of space devoted to the Reubenites. Reuben himself was punished for his wicked action but his descendants were not disinherited. Though disadvantaged from the beginning, they overcame and were

36. Both AV and NKJV emend without comment.

blessed, as was the case with Jabez and Simeon. The exile of one of the tribe's leaders by the Assyrians is a reminder of the original curse when God punished Adam and Eve for their sin by removing them from God's Garden. Nevertheless, at that very time, God announced the first gospel promise. Similarly, it is in the context of the curse on Reuben that hope is held out in a ruler of Judah's line. Jesus, the lion of the tribe of Judah, is the one who through becoming a curse himself has brought blessing to all the cursed families of the earth (Gal. 3:13-14; Rev. 5:5, 9-10).

Gad (5:11-22)

> 5:11. And the sons of Gad dwelt next to them in the land of Bashan as far as Salecah. 12. Joel the chief, and Shapham the second, and Janai and Shaphat in Bashan. 13. And their brothers according to the house of their fathers: Michael and Meshullam and Sheba and Jorai and Jacan and Zia and Eber, seven. 14. These *were* the sons of Abihail the son of Huri, the son of Jaroah, the son of Gilead, the son of Michael, the son of Jeshishai, the son of Jahdo, the son of Buz. 15. Ahi the son of Abdiel, the son of Guni *was* chief of the house of their fathers. 16. And they dwelt in Gilead in Bashan, and in her towns, and in all the pasturelands of Sharon to their borders. 17. All these were genealogically enrolled in the days of Jotham king of Judah and in the days of Jeroboam king of Israel.

Gad was the son of Jacob's concubine Zilpah, Leah's maid (Gen. 30:10-11). His descendants were given land 'next' (literally 'in front of', 'in the sight of') to the Reubenites. The Chronicler lays emphasis on a fertile region and for that reason a sensitive area that had come into Gad's possession on the north-eastern border of Israel. We read of the well-fed cattle of 'Bashan' (Ezek. 39:18; Amos 4:1) and of battles in that region between Israel and the Arameans of Damascus (see 1 Kings 22). The place-name, Sharon, is not the well-known plain along the Mediterranean coast but a place east of the Jordan also mentioned in the Mesha stela. Interestingly, the brief list of names, unique to this paragraph, is framed by reference to areas occupied by the Gadites (vv. 11,16). It is not clear how the three lists of names relate to each other (vv. 11-13). Another interesting note is the chronological reference pinpointing the time when a census was taken (v. 17; see v. 7). This will have been around the middle of the eighth century, toward the end of the northern king Jeroboam II's long reign, when Jotham ruled Judah as co-regent after his father Uzziah became a leper (2 Kings 15:5).

> 5:18. The sons of Reuben and the Gadites and the half-tribe of Manasseh had sons of valour, men who bore shield and sword and drew the bow and were skilful in battle, forty-four thousand seven hundred and sixty, who go out to war. 19. And they made war with the Hagrites, and Jetur and Nephish and Nodab. 20. And they were helped against them, and the Hagrites and all who were with them were given into their hand, for they cried out to God in the battle, and he granted their entreaty because they trusted in him. 21. And they took captive their livestock: fifty thousand camels and two hundred and fifty thousand sheep, and two thousand donkeys and a hundred thousand living persons. 22. For many fell slain because the battle *was* from God. And they dwelt in their place until the exile.

Before moving on to the half tribe of Manasseh, the Chronicler inserts this important battle account that involved all three tribes that lived in the Transjordan region. Whether this is a more detailed report of the brief statement in verse 10 or an entirely separate incident is hard to say.[37] It is probably more likely to have occurred during Saul's kingship or earlier when the central government was weaker. Alongside the Hagrites (v. 19) three names follow, two of which are probably sons of Ishmael (1 Chron. 1:31; see Gen. 25:15), while the third is unknown. They represent various Arab tribes in the area. In overcoming them, the Chronicler shows firstly how these Israelite tribes provided their best men for military action and with the most up-to-date armaments. Secondly, and most importantly, they prepared themselves spiritually. This is the reason why the incident is recorded. It emphasises the importance of commitment to God, of trusting Him and praying to Him in times of need. They 'cried out' to God in the battle and 'trusted in him'[38] to give success (see 2 Chron. 18:31;

---

37. Williamson *1 and 2 Chronicles*, p. 66, states: 'the likelihood of prolonged skirmishing between rival settlers in the region makes certainty about this impossible.'

38. This is the only place where the Chronicler uses the verb 'trust' (*bāṭaḥ*) apart from 2 Chronicles 32:10.

20:9; 32:20). The passive verbs 'they were helped' and 'they were given' is a way of indicating that God was behind the victory and this is made explicit by the comment that God 'granted their entreaty'[39] and that the enemy was routed 'because the battle was from God' (see 2 Chron. 26:7,15). As in the note concerning Jabez, the Chronicler encourages his people to pray to the living and true God of Israel who does hear and answer prayer (Ps. 65:2[3]).

The unusual phrase 'living persons' (*nepeš 'ādām*, literally 'soul of man', v. 21) occurs nine times in the Hebrew Bible, mostly in Numbers, and distinguishes people from animals (see, for example, Lev. 24:17; Num. 9:6-7; 31:35, 40, 46). Another reference to the exile brings this paragraph to a close (see v. 6) and prepares for the fuller statement in verses 25-26.

Application

Though we are not to despise natural gifts and talents but use them in God's service, we are to rely, not on them, but on divine power. We are urged to trust in the Lord and pray to Him for success, whether it be in the context of the church's conflict with the world in reaching the lost for Christ or in the Christian's personal warfare. Putting on the whole armour of God, we are to pray in the Spirit with all kinds of prayer and supplication (Eph. 6:18-19). There is a battle that God started in His judgment on the snake. It reached a decisive stage at the cross when Jesus gained the victory over the devil. Though now a defeated foe, the devil still wages war against God's people but his time is short and soon Satan will be crushed under our feet (Gen. 3:15; John 12:31-32; Rev. 12:9-12, 17; Rom. 16:20).

East Manasseh (5:23-26)

> 5:23. And the sons of the half-tribe of Manasseh dwelt in the land from Bashan to Baal-hermon and Senir and Mount Hermon. They were numerous. 24. And these *were* the heads of the house of their fathers: and Epher and Ishi and Eliel and Azriel and Jeremiah and Hodaviah and Jahdiel, valiant warriors, men of fame, heads of the house of their fathers.

---

39. The verb is '*āṭar*. See also 2 Chronicles 33:13,19.

As in the case of Gad, it is Manasseh's territory that is described first followed by a list of seven 'military commanders'.[40] As this tribe will be described further in chapter 7:14-19 no genealogical table appears here. The phrase 'They were numerous' needs to stand alone at the end of verse 23. It indicates the population growth of the Manassites in this area. The Hebrew text begins the list with 'and Epher' (v. 24) which though unusual is probably what the Chronicler intended. It suggests to some that a name has dropped out or that the Chronicler deliberately selected these final seven from a source that included more names. We know nothing further of these men or of their relationship to Manasseh, their ancestor. This half of Manasseh lived from the borders with Gad (Bashan, see v. 11) to the Mount Hermon range with Senir (Deut. 3:9) which is probably a peak in the same range.[41] Baal-hermon (Judg. 3:3) may be associated with 'Baal-gad under Hermon' (see Josh. 11:17; 12:7; 13:5).

> 5:25. And they acted unfaithfully against the God of their fathers, and committed prostitution after the gods of the people of the land, whom God had destroyed before them. 26. So the God of Israel stirred up the spirit of Pul king of Assyria, namely, the spirit of Tilgath-pilneser the king of Assyria, and he carried them into exile, as regards to the Reubenites, and to the Gadites, and to the half tribe of Manasseh, and he brought them to Halah and Habor and Hara, and the river Gozan, until this day.

The Chronicler not only shows that success comes through prayerful trust in God but that defeat and failure are due to unfaithfulness, which is another important feature of his work. What has been alluded to in previous verses (vv. 6, 22) is now mentioned more fully, namely, the removal from the land. The specific reason for the exile is the people's spiritual prostitution, a theme emphasised in Hosea's prophecy (see also Exod. 34:15; Deut. 31:16; Ezek. 16; etc.). They have left 'the God of their fathers', this phrase, or a similar one with 'your' in place of 'their', occurs twenty-seven times in

---

40. Williamson, *1 and 2 Chronicles*, p. 67.
41. Klein *1 Chronicles*, p. 169; see Song of Solomon 4:8.

Chronicles. Instead of being committed like a faithful wife to her husband, they had left the God of Israel to worship the gods of the Canaanites who were in the land before them. The comment applies not only to East Bank Manasseh but also to the Reubenites and Gadites.

The use of the verb 'to act unfaithfully' (*mā'al*) is a characteristic of the Chronicler (see 1 Chron. 2:7; 9:1; etc.). It has the idea of being deprived of one's rights. This judgment on the tribes and what happened to them follows the wording found in 2 Kings. The 'God of their fathers' is 'the God of Israel' (v. 26) and He has acted to punish His people. It is the same God who 'stirred up the spirit of' the Assyrian king to deport the people and who later 'stirred up the spirit of' the Persian king Cyrus to make a proclamation concerning the return of the people and the rebuilding of the temple (2 Chron. 36:22-23). The Hebrew text makes it clear that the Chronicler knew that Pul and Tilgath-Pilneser were one and the same person, for the verbs 'carried them into exile' and 'brought' are in the singular.[42] Pul is the personal name of Tiglath-Pileser III (see v. 6; 2 Kings 15:19,29) as suggested in extra-biblical sources.

These tribes were defeated and exiled during the time of Pekah, the son of Remaliah, king of Israel (see 2 Kings 15:29). This was ten years before the Assyrian king, Shalmanesser, finally overthrew the northern kingdom in 722/21 B.C. The apostasy of these two and a half tribes was typical of the northern kingdom as a whole and Chronicles uses phraseology associated with the taking of Samaria and the exile of its people to underline that the whole northern kingdom of Israel east and west of the Jordan were taken into captivity for exactly the same reason (see 2 Kings 17:6; 18:11). The probable areas where they were transported seem to be near the Tigris and Euphrates. 'Hara' is an unknown name not included in the text of Kings. As for the phrase 'until this day', it probably refers to the time when the Chronicler was writing in the post-exilic period, although many hold that it belongs to his source (see 2 Kings 17:23).

---

42. The translation 'namely' indicates an explicative use of *waw* as in Deuteronomy 9:8, 22; see Brown, Driver and Briggs (BDB), *A Hebrew and English Lexicon of the Old Testament* (Oxford: Clarendon Press, 1962), p. 252, 1b or c.

Application

The Chronicler provides his readers with early examples to inspire trust in God or to warn against apostasy. They are themes that occur frequently in the main part of the work. Divine help comes to those who call out to God in their trouble but disaster is the outcome of acting unfaithfully toward God. The final curse of exile is the result of apostasy. Like Adam, these northern tribes were removed from the land associated with God's presence. They are grim pictures of the final state of exile, away from all blessing and hope in that place reserved for the devil and his angels.

In order to punish His people, God used a Gentile pagan nation like Assyria, as He had used the Philistines in the days of Saul (1 Chron. 10). The God of Israel is the universal sovereign who raises up rulers and superpowers to accomplish His purposes. Isaiah and Habakkuk have much to say on this topic.

The tribe of Levi (6:1-53 [5:27–6:66])

The tribe specially set apart to minister at the central sanctuary is placed at the centre of the genealogical lists. This follows the arrangement of the tribes as they camped in the wilderness, with the Levites placed in the middle of the camp around the tabernacle (see Num. 1:52-53). It is also the Chronicler's way of indicating the importance of the tribe, just as the house of David was placed at the centre of the genealogy of Judah. Again, as was the case with Judah, the amount of space the Chronicler gives to the tribe of Levi is another indication of the tribe's special status. Interestingly, it is only the lines of David and Aaron that are traced from the patriarchs to the exile (see 1 Chron. 2:3-15; 3:1-24; 6:1-15), and this encourages the post-exilic community to continue to appreciate the future importance of Israel's royal and priestly offices.

The whole chapter falls into three main blocks: the genealogy of the Levites (vv. 1-30); the genealogy of the Levitical musicians and priests (vv. 31-53); and the Levitical cities (vv. 54-81). While the priests are given pride of place, the chapter does emphasise that the Levites have a position in their own right.

As for the first block, this can be divided into two sections: the list of high priests (vv. 1-15) and the three Levitical families (vv. 16-30).

High Priests (6:1-15 [5:27-41])

Aaron's line, like David's, is traced from patriarchal times to the exile (1 Chron. 2:1-17 and 3:1-24; 6:1-15). Since this is done with no other family, it indicates their significance and is a pointer to the future hope.

> 6:1[5:27]. The sons of Levi: Gershon, Kohath and Merari. 2[5:28]. And the sons of Kohath: Amram, Izhar and Hebron and Uzziel. 3[5:29]. And the sons of Amram: Aaron and Moses and Miriam. And the sons of Aaron: Nadab and Abihu, Eleazar and Ithamar.

Of the three sons of Levi (see Gen. 46:11; Exod. 6:16; Num. 3:17; 26:57), the focus is on Kohath and his position as the ancestor of the priestly line. Then the spotlight moves to Amram and his son Aaron with his four sons (see Exod. 6:18, 20, 23; Num. 3:2, 19; 26:60). Moses and his older sister Miriam are mentioned but they take second place in this context (see Exod. 15:20; Num. 12:1, 5; 26:59; Micah 6:4). The Hebrew word for 'sons' (v. 3) can have a wider meaning so that 'children' would be an appropriate translation in view of Amram's daughter Miriam.[43]

Of the sons of Aaron, only Eleazar and Ithamar survived after the incident that led to the premature deaths of Nadab and Abihu (v. 3 [5:29]; see Lev. 10:1-2).

> 6:4[5:30]. Eleazar fathered Phinehas, Phinehas fathered Abishua 5[5:31]. and Abishua fathered Bukki and Bukki fathered Uzzi 6[5:32]. and Uzzi fathered Zerahiah and Zerahiah fathered Meraioth, 7[5:33]. Meraioth fathered Amariah and Amariah fathered Ahitub 8[5:34]. and Ahitub fathered Zadok and Zadok fathered Ahimaaz 9[5:35]. and Ahimaaz fathered Azariah and Azariah fathered Johanan 10[5:36]. and Johanan fathered Azariah (he who served as priest in the house that Solomon built in Jerusalem).

A linear genealogy of Aaron's descendants now begins, starting with his son Eleazar (v. 4). He succeeded Aaron as

---

43. See BDB, p. 121, 2.

high priest (Num. 20:25-29) and was involved with Joshua in dividing up the land by lot to the tribes (Num. 34:17; Josh. 14:1). His son Phinehas was commended by God for his zeal (Num. 25:7, 11; Ps. 106:30) and he led the delegation that considered an alleged unfaithful act by the two and a half tribes (Josh. 22:13-16, 30-34). We know nothing of those mentioned from Abishua to Meraioth although they do appear in the list that records Ezra's priestly status (Ezra 7:1-5).

The genealogy is not a straightforward succession of high priests but a selective line from Eleazar to Jehozadak. Eli and his descendants, from Phinehas to Abiathar (see 1 Sam. 14:3; 22:20; 30:7), are deliberately omitted as the Chronicler probably had in mind the prophecy relating to the end of that family line (1 Sam. 2:27-36; 1 Kings 2:27). It is with Zadok and his descendants that the Chronicler is chiefly concerned (v. 8). Although Zadok's details are sketchy (2 Sam. 8:17; 1 Chron. 24:3), he served under David and was the one Solomon made sole priest after Abiathar sided with Adonijah, David's son, in his failed attempt to become king (1 Kings 1:5-7; 2:35). Ahimaaz, Zadok's son, is mentioned at the time of Absalom's rebellion (2 Sam. 15:27) and an Azariah, a 'son of Zadok', was one of Solomon's officials (1 Kings 4:2). Other names in this paragraph are unknown and the listing of two Azariahs (vv. 9-10) is no evidence that the Chronicler was confused.

It is suggested that the note concerning the priest who served in the temple ('house') built by Solomon (v. 10) should refer to Ahimaaz's son Azariah in verse 9, but it is without textual evidence. Another suggestion is that the second Azariah in verse 10 is the one who resisted King Uzziah's attempt to burn incense 'in the house of Yahweh' at the incense altar (see 2 Chron. 26:17-20),[44] although the note is better suited as a reference to the time when Solomon actually erected the temple than to a later period. All the priests named in verses 9-10 may have been active in the time of Solomon. Mentioning the house that Solomon built is significant in itself as the Jerusalem temple is one of the Chronicler's central concerns.

44. See J. Barton Payne, 'I and II Chronicles' in *The Wycliffe Bible Commentary*, eds. Charles F Pfeiffer & Everett F. Harrison (London: Oliphants, 1963), p. 373.

6:11[5:37]. And Azariah fathered Amariah and Amariah fathered Ahitub, 12[5:38]. and Ahitub fathered Zadok and Zadok fathered Shallum 13[5:39]. and Shallum fathered Hilkiah and Hilkiah fathered Azariah 14[5:40]. and Azariah fathered Seraiah and Seraiah fathered Jehozadak. 15[5:41]. And Jehozadak departed when Yahweh carried away Judah and Jerusalem into exile by the hand of Nebuchadnezzar.

As in the previous paragraph, it is clear from both Kings and 2 Chronicles that not all the high priests are named. This suggests that the verb 'fathered' or 'begat' does not always refer to the son but to a descendant. Missing from the list are some surprising names, such as Jehoiada, who was an influential high priest during the period when Athaliah usurped the Davidic throne and during Joash's reign (2 Kings 11:4-12:9; 2 Chron. 22:11-24:25). Azariah, who confronted King Uzziah when he entered the sanctuary to offer incense, is also omitted unless he is the one mentioned at the beginning of this paragraph. A further omission is another high priest named Azariah, referred to as 'the ruler of the house of God', who ministered during Hezekiah's reign (2 Chron. 31:10,13). Not surprisingly, no mention is made of Uriah (or Urijah) who acquiesced in King Ahaz's apostasy (2 Kings 16:10-16).

Of the names that are listed, Hilkiah will be the high priest who found the book of the law in the temple during the reign of Josiah (2 Kings 22:4–23:24; 2 Chron. 34:9-22; 35:8). Seraiah was high priest when king Zedekiah reigned in Jerusalem. At the time when Jerusalem and the temple were destroyed, he was taken along with Zephaniah the deputy high priest and other leaders to the Babylonian king at Riblah where they were executed (2 Kings 25:18-21; Jer. 52:24-27). The final name, Jehozadak (or Josedech/Jozadak) did not receive the same treatment as his father but went into captivity at the time of the Babylonian captivity. After referring earlier to the exile of the northern kingdom (1 Chron. 5:6, 22, 26), the Chronicler indicates that the southern kingdom of Judah received the same treatment, only this time by the Babylonian king Nebuchadnezzar in 587 B.C. Jehozadak was the father or ancestor of Joshua (or Jeshua) who was among the first batch of returning exiles and, as high priest, was a leader of the people alongside Zerubbabel (Ezra 2:2; 3:2; Hag. 1:1, 12, 14; 2:2, 4; Zech. 6:11).

The agent in the deportation of Judah and Jerusalem was the king of Babylon ('by the hand of Nebuchadnezzar') but it was 'Yahweh' who willed and initiated the carrying of the people into exile. By the same token, the return from exile was Yahweh's doing, but by means of Cyrus, the Persian king's edict.

Application

Though the priesthood had the task of offering sacrifice on behalf of the people to atone for their sins in the God-ordained Jerusalem sanctuary, this did not prevent the people being taken into exile. Not even the high priests were spared. As one writer comments: 'There is nothing mechanical about the cult in ancient Israel; the priests share in the captivity of their people'.[45] Outward acts of worship are no substitute for a life in tune with the living God. The pre-exilic prophets had much to say on this topic (Isa. 1:11-17; Jer. 7:21-23). For the post-exilic community it was still necessary to emphasise this point. The Lord had harsh words for the religious leaders and pronounced judgment on them for their unbelief (Mal. 1:6–2:16). It is a challenge to those who lead Christian communal worship as well as to their congregations.

The Levitical families (6:16-30 [6:1-15])

6:16[6:1]. The sons of Levi: Gershom, Kohath and Merari. 17[6:2]. And these *are* the names of the sons of Gershom: Libni and Shimei. 18[6:3]. And the sons of Kohath: Amram and Izhar and Hebron and Uzziel. 19[6:4]. The sons of Merari: Mahli and Mushi. And these *are* the families of the Levites according to their fathers: 20[6:5]. of Gershom: Libni his son, Jahath his son, Zimmah his son, 21[6:6]. Joah his son, Iddo his son, Zerah his son, Jeatherai his son. 22[6:7]. The sons of Kohath: Amminadab his son, Korah his son, Assir his son, 23[6:8]. Elkanah his son, and Ebiasaph his son, and Assir his son, 24[6:9]. Tahath his son, Uriel his son, Uzziah his son, and Shaul his son. 25[6:10]. And the sons of Elkanah: Amasai and Ahimoth. 26[6:11]. *As for* Elkanah, the sons of Elkanah *were* Zophai his son, and Nahath his son, 27[6:12]. Eliab his son, Jeroham his son, Elkanah his

45. William Johnstone, *1 and 2 Chronicles*, Vol. 1, *1 Chronicles 1–2 Chronicles 9, Israel's Place among the Nations*, Journal for the Study of the Old Testament Series (JSOT) Sup 253 (Sheffield: Sheffield Academic Press, 1997), p. 84.

son. 28[6:13]. And the sons of Samuel: the firstborn Vashni and
Abijah. 29[6:14]. The sons of Merari: Mahli, Libni his son, Shimei
his son, Uzzah his son, 30[6:15]. Shimea his son, Haggiah his
son, Asaiah his son.

The focus now turns from the line of high priests to the non-
priestly Levites. At the beginning of the chapter, the first
named son of Levi was spelled 'Gershon' (1 Chron. 6:1 [5:27]
as in Gen. 46:11; etc). However, 'Gershom' is the more normal
spelling in Chronicles (see vv. 17, 20, 43, etc.). The same list of
sons belonging to Levi's offspring (vv. 16-19a [1-4a]) is found
in Exodus 6:17-19 and Numbers 3:18-20.

The Levitical 'families' or clans are introduced with words
similar to Numbers 3:20 (v.19b [4b]). In the case of Gershom a
linear genealogy of seven generations is presented through
the line of the firstborn son from Libni to Jeatherai (vv. 20-21
[5-6]). A similar linear genealogy of seven generations applies
to Merari from his firstborn Mahli to Asaiah (vv. 29-30 [14-15]).
It is possible that the line ends during David's reign, as an
Asaiah (v. 30 [15]) is mentioned as one of the Levite leaders at
that time (1 Chron. 15:11).

With Kohath the situation is different and difficult
(vv. 22-28 [7-13]). The list can be compared with the genealogy
of the Kohathite musicians in verses 33-38 [18-23]. This was
the line that produced the priests and Kohath's pre-eminent
position is again made obvious by the amount of space
given to it here. As the high priestly line through Amram,
the firstborn, has already been given, another of Kohath's
sons is introduced, a name not accounted for elsewhere. It is
possible that Amminadab is another name for Izhar (named
after Aaron's father-in-law; see Exod. 6:23) whose son is called
Korah (v. 22 [7]; see vv. 37-38 [22-23]). This Korah is the one
who was severely punished by God for rebelling against
Moses and Aaron (Num. 16) and with whom the musical
guilds are associated (see Pss. 42–49, etc.). Elkanah and
Ebiasaph are brothers of Assir, all sons of Korah, rather than
his descendants (vv. 22-23 [8-9]; see Exod. 6:24) with the name
Assir repeated (v. 23b [9b]) to continue the linear genealogy
of seven generations from Amminadab (Izhar) the son of
Kohath to Shaul the son of Uzziah, and thus matching the
other two Levitical families (v. 24 [9]).

Having presented Assir's descendants, the list returns to Assir's brother, Elkanah and two of his 'sons' in the sense of 'descendants': Amasai and Ahimoth (vv. 23, 25 [8, 10]). This 'Ahimoth' is the same as Mahath the son of Amasai (see v. 35 [20]). Without stating that Ahimoth had a son called Elkanah, Elkanah's name is introduced abruptly in verse 26, followed by a linear genealogy of his descendants ('sons') down to another Elkanah, the son of Jeroham (vv. 26-27 [11-12]). Comparing this genealogy with the one in 1 Samuel 1:1, it is clear that this Jeroham was Samuel's grandfather (v. 27 [12]). It also means that Eliab is equivalent to Elihu or Eliel, Nahath to Toah or Tohu and Zophai to Zuph (vv. 26-27 [11-12]; see vv. 34-35 [19-20]). Samuel and his sons are also introduced abruptly without any direct reference to his father (see vv. 27-28 [12-13]). It is taken for granted that Samuel is Elkanah's son. 'Vashni' is either another name for Samuel's 'firstborn' son Joel (see v. 33; 1 Sam. 8:2) or to be emended to 'and the second' referring to Samuel's other son 'Abijah' with Joel's name supplied from verse 33 [18]. Some ancient versions support this reading of verse 13 [28]: 'The sons of Samuel: Joel the firstborn and Abijah the second'.

The main reason for the listing is to trace the genealogy of Samuel and to indicate that, though he was not of the high priestly line and though his father Elkanah came from Ephraimite territory (1 Sam 1:1.), he was of Levitical stock. His situation in some respects can be compared to the Levite who was from the family of Judah in Bethlehem (Judg. 17:7). During a most difficult period in Israelite history, Samuel was not only set apart to serve God under Eli, but he also later functioned as priest in addition to being a prophet and judge (1 Sam.1:1; 3:1; 3:19–4:1; 7:15-17; 8:2).

Application

Though Samuel is not given much attention in the Chronicler's work, he is not forgotten and his standing as a representative of the tabernacle worship is acknowledged. He becomes a second Moses who acted legitimately as a priest at a crucial moment in Israel's history. Moses was God's appointed leader when the Sinai covenant was established, while Samuel's ministry coincided with the introduction of the Israelite monarchy. Both Samuel and Moses resemble and foreshadow our Lord Jesus in His special status as priest who inaugurated the new covenant as well as in His role as prophet and ruler over God's people.

The Levitical musicians and priests (6:31-53 [6:16-33])

The passage divides into two parts: David's action in appointing the musicians from among the Levites (vv. 31-48 [16-33]) and the Mosaic appointment of the priests, particularly the high priests who alone could enter the holy of holies (vv. 49-53 [34-38]).

David's appointments (6:31-48 [16-33])

6:31[16]. And these *are the ones* whom David set over the service of song in the house of Yahweh, the ark having rested. 32[17]. And they were ministering with song before the dwelling-place of the tent of meeting until Solomon built the house of Yahweh in Jerusalem; and they stood over their service according to their custom.

33[18]. And these are the ones who served and their sons. Of the sons of the Kohathites: Heman the singer, the son of Joel, the son of Samuel, 34[19]. the son of Elkanah, the son of Jeroham, the son of Eliel, the son of Toah, 35[20]. the son of Zuph, the son of Elkanah, the son of Mahath, the son of Amasai, 36[21]. the son of Elkanah, the son of Joel, the son of Azariah, the son of Zephaniah, 37[22]. the son of Tahath, the son of Assir, the son of Ebiasaph, the son of Korah, 38[23]. the son of Izhar, the son of Kohath, the son of Levi, the son of Israel.

39[24]. And his brother Asaph, who stood on his right hand, *even* Asaph the son of Berechiah, the son of Shimea, 40[25]. the son of Michael, the son of Baaseiah, the son of Malchijah, 41[26]. the son of Ethni, the son of Zerah, the son of Adaiah, 42[27]. the son of Ethan, the son of Zimmah, the son of Shimei, 43[28]. the son of Jahath, the son of Gershom, the son of Levi. 44[29]. And on the left hand their brothers the sons of Merari: Ethan the son of Kishi, the son of Abdi, the son of Malluch, 45[30]. the son of Hashabiah, the son of Amaziah, the son of Hilkiah, 46[31]. the son of Amzi, the son of Bani, the son of Shemer, 47[32]. the son of Mahli, the son of Mushi, the son of Merari, the son of Levi. 48[33]. And their brothers the Levites were dedicated to all the services of the dwelling-place of the house of God.

The Chronicler distinguishes between the Levites that David appointed to this special musical role (vv. 31-47) and the rest of the Levites who served the tabernacle in more general ways (v. 48). They had originally been appointed by Moses to transport and guard the tabernacle and its furniture and assist the priests. Now that the ark had come to rest (v. 31), the duties associated with transporting it were no longer required (2 Sam. 6; 1 Chron. 16:1; 23:25-26). The phrase 'until Solomon had built the house of Yahweh' (v. 32) means that the Levitical musicians first appointed by David continued in this employment after Solomon's temple had been erected. Coupling David and Solomon in this way implies Solomon's approval of these Davidic appointments for the newly-erected temple worship.

David's musical interest extended from song writing to inventing and playing instruments (1 Sam. 16:18, 23; 18:10; 19:9; 2 Sam. 6:5; 22:1; Amos 6:5) so it is quite understandable that he was involved in the new arrangements for the Levites. Just as Israel's wisdom literature is especially associated with Solomon, the sanctuary music is linked to David.

The three musical leaders appointed by King David came from the three branches of Levi's family: Heman was a descendant of Kohath (vv. 33-38), Asaph, a descendant of Gershom (vv. 39-43) and Ethan, a descendant of Merari (vv. 44-47). In keeping with the prominence given to the Kohathites (Num. 4:1-20; 1 Chron. 6:2-15), even though Kohath was the second of Levi's sons (Num. 3:17; 1 Chron. 6:1), Heman had a central position, being given a much fuller genealogy that included Samuel and he alone is called 'the singer' (v. 33; see 2 Samuel 23:1 where David is called 'the sweet psalmist of Israel'), with Asaph the Gershonite on his right (v. 39) and Ethan the Merarite on his left (v. 44). Matthew Henry suggests that in making Heman the chief, David 'had some respect to his old friend Samuel'. How the ark was brought to Jerusalem and the part played by the Levitical musicians and priests is recorded in 1 Chronicles 15 and 16.

The rest of the Levites, as distinct from the priests, were 'dedicated' or 'wholly given' (see Num. 3:9; 8:16-19) to the remaining duties related to the tabernacle and later the temple (v. 48[33] and see 1 Chron. 26). For the post-exilic community, it was important to know who the rightly appointed officials were. Though not ordained by Moses, the musical leaders had the support of the two kings associated with establishing the permanent sanctuary in Jerusalem.

There are some key terms used by the Chronicler in this section. The first is 'to set' or 'appoint' (the *hiphil* of *'md*, verse 31[16]; 1 Chron. 15:16-17; 22:2; 2 Chron. 8:14; 19:5, 8; 20:21; 23:10; etc.). It is a term of 'royal authority' that includes not only putting into effect God's will through Moses but applying God's law to new situations (2 Chron. 30:5; 31:2; 34:32; 35:2).[46] Another key term is 'rest' (*nûah*; see 1 Chron. 22:9; 28:2) and numerous times we are informed that God gave 'rest' to His people (1 Chron. 22:9, 18; 23:25; 2 Chron. 14:6-7; 15:15; 20:30). Here, 'rest' applies to the ark which finds its resting-place or 'condition of rest' (*mānôah* v. 31[16]) in the Jerusalem sanctuary. The Chronicler has an interest in the one item that was not returned from Babylon if indeed it was not destroyed when Solomon's temple was razed to the ground (Jer. 3:16). Both the Davidic king and the ark no longer existed when the Chronicler wrote and yet he is concerned that his people appreciate their importance. The brief mention of the ark at this point also associates it with David and Solomon who are the ones who provided its resting place, first in the temporary tent (1 Chron. 13–16) and then in the temple (2 Chron. 5–6). In addition, the ark is also brought into close association with the Levites whom David and Solomon appointed to introduce music and singing into Israel's worship.

While the ark was placed in Jerusalem, the altar for burnt offerings remained at the sanctuary at Gibeon (2 Chron. 1:3). David's tent for housing the ark is described as 'the house of Yahweh' (v. 31[16]; see 'house of God,' verse 48[33]), a phrase generally employed for the temple (1 Kings 6:1-2; 8:6) but occasionally used for the tabernacle (Exod. 23:19; Deut. 23:18[19]; Josh. 6:24). The other, not so common, name for the wilderness tabernacle, 'dwelling-place of the tent of meeting' (v. 32[17]; see Exod. 39:32; 40:2, 6, 29) probably applies to the tent sanctuary at Gibeon rather than to David's tent erected for the ark (1 Chron. 16:39; 21:29; 2 Chron. 1:3,13). We read later that the

---

46. See Johnstone, *1 and 2 Chronicles*, Vol. 1, p. 89.

musicians were divided between the two sites, with the Asaph family ministering before the ark in Jerusalem and the Heman and Ethan (Jeduthun) families ministering alongside Zadok and the priests before the tabernacle at Gibeon (1 Chron. 16:37-42). This division of labour ceased when Solomon's temple was completed and all were together in the one holy complex in Jerusalem (2 Chron. 5:5–7:7).

The word 'dwelling-place' (*mišcān*, vv. 32, 48[17, 33]) is the usual term for the tabernacle, God's mobile home, during the wilderness period (Exod. 25:9; 26:1-35; 36:8-38; 40:2-38; Lev. 8:10; Num. 1:50-53; 3:23-38; 31:30, 47). It suggests a temporary place to settle. The glory cloud of Yahweh that had 'settled' on Mount Sinai, 'settled' over the 'dwelling-place' (Exod. 24:16; Num. 9:17, 18, 22). The name 'the dwelling-place/ tabernacle of the house of God' is only found here in the Bible but 'the house of God' is one of the Chronicler's favourite ways of referring to the temple (see, for example, 1 Chron. 9:13; 28:21; 22:2; 23:28; 2 Chron. 31:21; 33:7; 36:18-19). 'Tent' is another term for the wilderness tabernacle (Exod. 26:9, 11-14, 36) and is used, as here, in the phrase 'tent of meeting' (v. 32; AV 'tabernacle of the congregation'). The phrase suggests that this was to be the appointed meeting-place between God and His people (see Exod. 40:7,12, etc.).

Application

The Chronicler spends a considerable amount of space focussing on the music of the sanctuary, and in this preface to his work, he introduces the three main musical families. Under the new covenant in Christ, the emphasis moves from choirs and soloists to the whole assembly of God's people teaching and admonishing one another in song (Eph. 5:19; Col. 3:16). In the world to come, the victorious people of God will sing the song of Moses and of the Lamb (Rev. 15:1-4). The glory of God that settled on the tabernacle and temple of old was seen in Christ, the Son of God, who tabernacled among us (John 1:14; 17:21; Col. 1:19). God has seen fit to show His glory among His people, who are described as temples of the Holy Spirit (Eph. 2:22; 3:10-11). We long that this would be more evident to people but we look forward to the day of the new creation when 'the tabernacle of God is with men and he will dwell with them' and when the whole eternal city will be God's temple (Rev. 21:2-3, 22).

The Mosaic appointments (6:49-53 [34-38])

6:49[34]. But Aaron and his sons made sacrifices on the altar of burnt offering and on the altar of incense, for all the work of the holy of holies and to make atonement for Israel, according to all that Moses, the servant of God, commanded. 50[35]. And these are the sons of Aaron: Eleazar his son, Phinehas his son, Abishua his son, 51[36]. Bukki his son, Uzzi his son, Zerahiah his son, 52[37]. Meraioth his son, Amariah his son, Ahitub his son, 53 [38]. Zadok his son, Ahimaaz his son.

While the whole of Aaron's family was set apart for the priesthood, only those of Eleazar's line through his son Phinehas were to function as high priests. The earlier list of high priests took the genealogy down to the Babylonian exile (1 Chron. 6:4-15), whereas this paragraph lists the same names but closes with Ahimaaz, the son of Zadok, who served during the David–Solomon era. These two lists of high priests form a frame around the other lists of Levites (vv. 16-30, 31-48). The main priestly duties are highlighted which involve making sacrifices smoke at the large bronze altar and at the incense altar next to the most holy place. Only the high priest went into 'the holy of holies' on the Day of Atonement (Lev. 16). All was done according to the Mosaic Law (v. 49; see Lev. 1–7; Num. 18:5), which is another of the Chronicler's emphases as he preaches to the post-exilic community.

Moses (see 1 Chron. 6:3) is described as 'the servant of God' (2 Chron. 24:9; Neh. 10:29, with 'the servant of Yahweh' being the more usual form in the Bible as in 2 Chron. 1:3; 24:6), a title of honour that God often uses to describe those in his service. It is both a privileged and responsible position and is applied to individuals like Job, Joshua and David, as well as to Yahweh's true prophets and collectively to the nation Israel.

Application

For the worshipping community of Israel, God ordained those who were to function as priests and offer the God-appointed sacrifices. They were divine visual aids until the coming of the Messiah who fulfilled the types by becoming the true high priest to offer Himself as the one real, sufficient end-time sacrifice. Jesus said to the Samaritan woman that her religion was not true, even though there were some similarities to the Jerusalem temple worship, stating that 'salvation is of the Jews'. But he went on to explain that even the Jerusalem sanctuary would soon be redundant (John 4:20-26).

The Levitical cities (6:54-81 [6:39-66])
Details are given of the cities allotted to the priests and Levites together with some indication of the cities of refuge. The list is similar to Joshua 21:1-40 but adapted to suit the Chronicler's purpose. By his omissions and rearrangements, he is reflecting the situation in the David–Solomon era as well as emphasising the importance of the cities given to the descendants of Aaron which were in the southern half of the land belonging to the tribes of Judah, Simeon and Benjamin (vv. 54-60, 65). It was within this area that the post-exilic province of Judah was situated.

The passage divides as follows: Aaronite cities (vv. 54-60; see Josh. 21:10-19); summaries (vv. 61-65; see Josh. 21:5-9); Kohathite cities (vv. 66-70; see Josh. 21:20-26); Gershonite cities (vv. 71-76; see Josh. 21:27-33); Merarite cities (vv. 77-81; see Josh. 21:34-40).

6:54[39]. Now these are their dwelling-places according to their encampments in their borders: to the sons of Aaron, from the family of the Kohathites, for the lot was theirs, 55[40]. to them they gave Hebron in the land of Judah and its pasture lands around it, 56[41]. but the fields of the city and its villages they gave to Caleb the son of Jephunneh. 57[42]. And to the sons of Aaron they gave the cities of refuge, Hebron; and Libnah and its pasture lands, and Jattir, and Eshtemoa and its pasture lands, 58[43]. and Hilez and its pasture lands, Debir and its pasture lands, 59[44]. and Ashan and its pasture lands, and Beth-shemesh and its pasture lands. 60[45]. And from the tribe of Benjamin, Geba and its pasture lands, and Alemeth and its pasture lands, and Anathoth and its pasture lands. All their cities throughout their families were thirteen cities.

61[46]. And to the remaining sons of Kohath from the family of the tribe from half of a tribe, the half of Manasseh, ten cities by lot. 62[47]. And to the sons of Gershom, according to their families, from the tribe of Issachar, and from the tribe of Asher, and from the tribe of Naphtali, and from the tribe of Manasseh in Bashan, thirteen cities. 63[48]. To the sons of Merari, according to their families, from the tribe of Reuben, and from the tribe of Gad, and from the tribe of Zebulun, twelve cities by lot. 64[49]. So the sons of Israel gave the Levites the cities and their pasture lands. 65[50]. And they gave by lot from the tribe of the sons of Judah, and from the tribe of the sons of Simeon, and from the tribe of the sons of Benjamin, these cities that they called them by name.

66[51]. And some of the families of the sons of Kohath had cities for their territory out of the tribe of Ephraim. 67[52]. And they gave to them the cities of refuge, Shechem in the hill country of Ephraim and its pasture lands; and Gezer and its pasture lands, 68[53]. and Jokmeam and its pasture lands, and Beth-horon and its pasture lands, 69[54]. and Aijalon and its pasture lands, and Gath-rimmon and its pasture lands; 70[55]. and from the half-tribe of Manasseh, Aner and its pasture lands, and Bileam and its pasture lands, for the family of the sons of Kohath who remained.

71[56]. To the sons of Gershom from the family of the half-tribe of Manasseh, Golan in Bashan and its pasture lands, and Ashtaroth and its pasture lands; 72[57]. and from the tribe of Issachar, Kedesh and its pasture lands, Daberath and its pasture lands, 73[58]. and Ramoth and its pasture lands, and Anem and its pasture lands; 74[59]. and from the tribe of Asher, Mashal and its pasture lands, and Abdon and its pasture lands, 75[60]. and Hukok and its pasture lands, and Rehob and its pasture lands; 76[61]. and from the tribe of Naphtali, Kedesh in Galilee and its pasture lands, and Hammon and its pasture lands, and Kiriathaim and its pasture lands.

77[62]. To the sons of Merari who remained, from the tribe of Zebulun, Rimmono and its pasture lands, Tabor and its pasture lands; 78[63]. and across the Jordan from Jericho, on the east side of the Jordan, from the tribe of Reuben, Bezer in the wilderness and its pasture lands, and Jahzah and its pasture lands, 79[64]. and Kedemoth and its pasture lands, and Mephaath and its pasture lands; 80[65]. and from the tribe of Gad, Ramoth in Gilead and its pasture lands, and Mahanaim and its pasture lands, 81[66]. and Heshbon and its pasture lands, and Jazer and its pasture lands.

The list with its geographical details presses home the understanding that the land belongs to Yahweh. Unlike the other tribes, the Levites were not given territories. Instead they were allotted cities with their pasture lands throughout the whole country in accordance with the prophecy of Jacob (Gen. 49:7) and God's command through Moses (Num. 35). The Levites claimed their rights by lot (vv. 54, 61, 63, 65; Josh. 21:4-6, 8, 10, 20, 40) and although no mention is made of God's command through Moses as in Joshua 21:2, 8, the Levitical entitlement to cities was understood. The Israelites gave the Levites forty-eight key centres (vv. 60-64). With the whole tribe of Levi spread out and settled throughout the land, the Chronicler's 'all Israel' theme is thus reinforced. In addition, with these priests and Levites, as representatives of the whole of Israel and ministers of God at the sanctuary, the Chronicler prepares for another of his major themes concerning the central place of worship.

Again, the priests, the descendants of Aaron, are given a prominent position (vv. 54-60). They were allotted thirteen cities all in the south of the land west of the Jordan in territory belonging to Judah, Benjamin and Simeon. Only eleven are listed, as the Chronicler omits Juttah and Gibeon. The supplementary information about Caleb 'the son of Jephunneh' is included to indicate that although Hebron with its pasture lands was given to Aaron's descendants, the fields and surrounding villages belonged to Caleb (v. 56; Josh. 14:6-15; 21:12; 1 Chron. 4:15).

For the remaining Kohathites, they received ten cities with their pasture lands in the territories of Ephraim, Dan and the western half of Manasseh (vv. 61, 66-70; see Joshua 21:5, 23-24). The text of verse 61 is difficult as the AV indicates with its many words in italics. Only eight of the ten cities are listed. Omitted are Elteke and Gibbethon in Danite territory (Josh. 21:23). Aijalon and Gathrimmon, though originally belonging to Dan, are listed as if they belonged to Ephraim (v. 69; see Josh. 21:23). The Danites had probably ceased holding this land by David's time. During the Judges period they had moved from the lowland region next to Judah to the very north of the country (Josh. 19:40-48; Judg. 18; 1 Sam. 3:20; 1 Chron. 21:2).

The descendants of Gershom received thirteen cities from the eastern half of Manasseh and from Issachar, Asher and Naphtali. In this case alone, all thirteen cities are listed (vv. 71-76). As for the Merari family of Levites, they received twelve cities. The cities listed from the territories of Reuben and Gad all tally with Joshua 21. As for those in Zebulun, whereas Joshua names four cities, only two are listed by the Chronicler and they are different, although Rimmono may be equivalent to Dimnah (Josh. 21:35) but in place of Nahalal (Josh. 21:35; see Josh. 19:15) we have Tabor (see Josh. 19:12). While the names of the cities in the Chronicler's list often differ from that in Joshua 21, this may be due to alternative pronunciations and spellings, varying traditions or to changes resulting from the lapse of time. It is very likely that the omission of Danite territory is deliberate as the tribe is missing from all the genealogical lists of chapters 1–9; only Dan himself is named as one of Jacob's sons (2:1-2).

The Chronicler assumes an understanding of the cities of refuge for unintentional and unpremeditated killing (Josh. 20:3), as, unlike the Joshua text, there is no mention of 'for the manslayer' (vv. 57, 67; Josh. 21:13, 21, 27, 32, 38). Only two out of an original six (see Num. 35:13-14; Josh. 20:7-8) are called cities of refuge: Hebron and Shechem (vv. 57, 67; Joshua 21 names five) although the others are listed and appear as the first city for their particular tribe: Golan (v. 71), Kedesh (v. 76), Bezer (v. 78) and Ramoth in Gilead (v. 80). Having mentioned the first two as asylum cities, the Chronicler saves space by assuming a knowledge of the other four. For this reason, the plural 'cities of refuge' is used in each case, not because the Chronicler considered the place names that follow in his text were asylum cities, but to indicate that there were other refuge cities apart from the two he named.

Application

The 'dispersion' of the Levites throughout Israel 'reflects something of the sojourner's status which the patriarchs had while in Canaan' (Gen. 23:4; 35:27; see Deut. 18:6).[47] The sojourner (*gēr*) was a resident alien and dependent on the goodwill of the people as the Law of Moses directed. Israel was to remember that they too had been resident aliens in Egypt (Exod. 22:21; Deut. 10:19). In fact, Yahweh tells His people that the promised land belongs to Him and they are resident

---

47. See précis of K. Gutbrod's suggestion in Woudstra's commentary on *The Book of Joshua*, p. 304.

aliens and sojourners in it (Lev. 25:23). The Chronicler will later remind his people of their status through David's prayer 'For we are aliens and pilgrims before you, as were all our fathers ...' (1 Chron. 29:15; see Ps. 39:12[13]). It is a reminder to Christians that this present world order is not our permanent residence. We look for an enduring home (Heb. 11:10; 12:28; 13:14; 1 Pet. 2:11).

To these Levites who received no inheritance of land like the other tribes (see Josh. 13:14, 33), the children of Israel readily gave some of their cities and pasture lands (vv. 55-57, 64). No mention is made of the command of God as in Joshua 21:3. A willingness to offer freely, without compulsion, of one's goods or land for God's work, especially in relation to the central sanctuary, is another concern of the Chronicler as he preaches to the people to whom he writes (see 1 Chron. 29:10-20). Paul expresses the same concern as he writes about financial giving (2 Cor. 8–9). Christians are also encouraged to give in support of those who labour in preaching the gospel and pastoring God's people (1 Cor. 9; Gal. 6:6; 1 Tim. 5:17-18).

Ideally, the Levites, scattered as they were throughout Israel in every tribe east and west of the Jordan, were to benefit the people by teaching them God's law (Deut. 33:10). Chronicles will later give examples of Levites preaching and teaching the people (2 Chron. 17:8-9; 20:14-17; 30:22; 35:3). Such ministry was expected of the priests in the post-exilic period (Mal. 2:6-7). Local churches throughout the countries of the world need preachers and pastors to instruct and exhort God's people (Col. 1:28; 1 Tim. 2:2). Is this not an encouragement for churches to invest financially in the support of training men called to the ministry of God's Word?

Northern tribes (7:1-40)

After giving pride of place to Levi, the Chronicler now continues with the second half of the Israelite tribal genealogies. The first half dealt with the southern and Transjordanian tribes and now the central and northern tribes are set out. Again, the Chronicler's own period and concerns are evident. Compared with the Levites, the six tribes listed are treated in a much briefer way, although Benjamin will figure again in greater detail in the following chapters. In addition to genealogical lists, it is possible that the Chronicler used military census returns for the tribes of Issachar, Benjamin and Asher (as is likely in 1 Chron. 5:24). As for Manasseh and Ephraim, instead of military terminology, more personal and geographical material is included. In the Masoretic Text, the Dan and Zebulun tribes are completely missing from this section with only a brief mention of Naphtali. By placing Issachar first and Asher last (compare 1 Chron. 2:1-2), it is possible that the Chronicler wished to indicate that the whole of the north was included in his understanding of Israel even though he does not list every tribe.

Issachar (7:1-5)

> 7:1. And as for the sons of Issachar: Tola and Puah, Jashub and Shimron, four. 2. And the sons of Tola: Uzzi and Rephaiah and Jeriel and Jahmai and Ibsam and Shemuel, heads of their fathers' house, *that is* of Tola, valiant warriors of their generations, their number in the days of David *were* twenty-two thousand six hundred. 3. And the sons of Uzzi: Izrahiah. And the sons of Izrahiah: Michael and Obadiah and Joel, Isshiah, five, all of them heads. 4. And with them, by their generations, according to the house of their fathers, thirty-six thousand troops of an army for war, for they had many wives and sons. 5. And their brothers belonging to all the families of Issachar, eighty-seven thousand valiant warriors in all by their genealogical enrolment.

While many of the names are unique to this passage, Issachar's four sons are those of Genesis 46:13 and Numbers 26:23-24, except that Puvah is spelt Puah and Jashub is spelt Job in Genesis 46:13. A judge from the same tribe is also called Tola, a son of another Puah (Judg. 10:1), which indicates the popularity of the ancestral names. Tolah's six sons are heads of ancestral clans with only the descendants of Uzzi taken further. The five 'heads' or 'chiefs' include Izrahiah as well as the four descendants named (v. 3). This further reference to David's reign (v. 2; see 1 Chron. 4:31; 6:31) calls to mind the military census that he called for and that resulted in divine punishment (1 Chron. 21). There may have been other occasions during David's reign when legitimate counts were taken of 'the valiant warriors'. The more specialised word 'troops' (see 1 Chron. 12:18, 21; 2 Chron. 22:1; 25:9-10, 13; 26:11) is employed for those members of Uzzi's descendants who were able soldiers. The large difference in the military census figures for Uzzi's descendants of 36,000 compared with the 22,600 of Tola's line, are due to the 'many wives and sons'. The fighting men from all the families or clans of Issachar number 87,000, which is probably meant to include Tola and Uzzi.[48]

The Chronicler does not mention Zebulun in this present list. This is probably on account of the two tribes, Issachar and Zebulun, being closely linked, sharing as they did the same mother and a common frontier (see Gen. 30:17-20; Josh. 19:10-23). Though Issachar was born before his younger brother, it is often Zebulun who is mentioned first (Gen. 49:13-15; Deut. 33:18-19; Josh. 19:10-23; Judg. 5:14-15). It is in Numbers 2:5-8 and 26:23-27 that the order of birth is observed. Though Zebulun gained an ascendancy over his brother due to his brother's laziness and indifference (Gen. 49:14-15), the Chronicler restores Issachar to his rightful place and makes him Zebulun's representative.

Benjamin (7:6-12)

7:6. Benjamin: Bela and Becher and Jediael, three. 7. And the sons of Bela: Ezbon and Uzzi and Uzziel and Jerimoth and Iri, five; heads of fathers' house, valiant warriors; and their genealogical enrolment was twenty-two thousand thirty-four. 8. And the sons of Becher: Zemirah and Joash and Eliezer and Elioenai and Omri and Jeremoth and Abijah and Anathoth and Alemeth. All these were the sons of Becher. 9. And their genealogical enrolment according to their generations, heads of their fathers' house, valiant warriors, was twenty thousand two hundred. 10. And the sons of Jediael: Bilhan. And the sons of Bilhan: Jeush and Benjamin and Ehud and Chenaanah and Zethan and Tarshish and Ahishahar. 11. All these were the sons of Jediael, according to the heads of the fathers, valiant warriors, seventeen thousand and two hundred, who go out *as* an army for battle. 12. And Shuppim and Huppim, the sons of Ir, Hushim, the sons of Aher.

---

48. It is unlikely that Chronicles is intending us to add up the three figures to make 145,600 or even the final two figures to make 123,000. In Numbers 26:25, the total for Issachar is 64,300.

This tribe plays a key role in the Chronicler's presentation, being the territory in which Jerusalem, the capital of the Davidic kingdom, was situated and where the temple was built, and having the honour of producing Saul, the first king of Israel (1 Chron. 8:1–9:44). It is included here as part of the Chronicler's purpose to stress the tribe's military might and in this respect Benjamin can be compared to Issachar. The names bear little resemblance to those in the following two chapters. Only Bela, the firstborn, is the same, but the names of his sons are quite different in the two texts. The term 'sons' should therefore probably be taken to mean 'descendants' (v. 7). One of the names is identical with the place, Anathoth, one of the Levitical cities in Benjaminite territory and from where Jeremiah came (verse 8; Jer. 1:1). Interestingly, there is a 'Hushim' (v. 12) mentioned as a Danite in Genesis 46:23, which may indicate that the Benjamin tribe lying immediately to the east of Dan appropriated some of the land following Dan's migration north. Altogether the Benjaminites' total is 59,434 compared with 45,600 in Numbers 26:41.

Naphtali (7:13)

> 7:13. The sons of Naphtali: Jahziel and Guni and Jezer and Shallum, the sons of Bilhah.

The territory of Naphtali lay in the far north of Canaan. Apart from spelling differences, the Chronicler follows the text of Genesis 46:24-25 and Numbers 26:48-50. No territory is mentioned and there are no totals of the population's strength. It suggests that its most northerly location led to the tribe's increasing isolation and detachment from Israel. But the brief genealogy does include the mother's name, Bilhah, Rachel's maid. By means of the plural 'sons of Bilhah', the Chronicler may well be presupposing her other son Dan, who is passed over in silence. It seems to have been a deliberate policy of the Chronicler to omit Dan (see 1 Chron. 6:61-69), perhaps on account of the tribe's idolatry as well as its move from the original settlement west of Benjamin to the far north of the country beyond Naphtali (Josh. 19:40-48; Judg. 18:1-31; 1 Kings 12:28-30). If Naphtali is barely mentioned, how can Dan be included?

Application

As the Chronicler has informed us that the tribes on the east bank of the Jordan had many valiant men who were able to wage war against their enemies (1 Chron. 5:18-22), so for Issachar he indicates that they had even more able soldiers ready to fight for Israel. Even though this tribe was no longer an entity in the post-exilic period, the Chronicler's people, though few in number and under foreign rule, were to consider Issachar's important contribution in the past to the well-being of Israel and from this to gain encouragement for the future. It was another factor in keeping alive the hope of a future glory for the entire nation (Ezek. 37:15-28).

Benjamin too, despite being the smallest of the tribes, is seen to have increased in population size and produced able fighters. Revelation shows how the elect of God, under the symbolic total of 144,000, are numbered like an army, using language reminiscent of a military census (Num. 1:2-3, 18, 20, 21, 23, etc.; 26:2-4).[49] They conquer through the blood of the Lamb (Rev. 7:4-8, 13-14; 14:1-5).

Like Lot and Esau, Dan moved beyond the land allotted to the people of God. Dan is missing for the same reasons from the list of tribes in Revelation 7:5-8.[50] John, like the Chronicler, is pointing to a future where idolatry and apostasy will have no part in the life of the elect people of God. All is not lost however, for Matthew quotes Isaiah to show how Jesus fulfils prophecy by beginning His public ministry in Galilee, in that despised area of Zebulun and Naphtali (Isa. 9:1-2; Matt. 4:12-17). The last book of the Bible sees all the elect from every tribe and nation gathered in, as does Paul (Rom. 11:25-27; Rev. 7:9-10).

West Manasseh (7:14-19)

7:14. The sons of Manasseh: Asriel, whom she bore; his Aramean concubine bore Machir the father of Gilead. 15. And Machir took a wife for Huppim and for Shuppim. His sister's name

---

49. R. J. Bauckham, *Climax of Prophecy: Studies in the Book of Revelation* (Edinburgh: T. T. Clark, 1993), pp. 217-29; Beale, *Revelation*, pp. 422-23.

50. In Jewish tradition, Dan, who is likened to a snake in Jacob's prophecy (Gen. 49:17), is associated with the devilish snake in Eden (Gen. 3).

was Maachah and the name of the second Zelophehad: and
Zelophehad had daughters. 16. And Maachah the wife of
Machir bore a son, and she called his name Peresh; and the
name of his brother *was* Sheresh; and his sons *were* Ulam and
Rakem. 17. And the sons of Ulam: Bedan. These were the sons
of Gilead, the son of Machir, the son of Manasseh. 18. And his
sister Hammolecheth bore Ishhod and Abiezer and Mahlah. 19.
And the sons of Shemida were Ahian and Shechem and Likhi
and Aniam.

The part of the Manasseh tribe living on the east bank of the
Jordan has already been given (5:23-26). This genealogy of the
west bank section includes people associated with the eastern
sector, which suggests that the Chronicler wished to encourage
his readers to view the tribe as a whole. As he proceeds, he
introduces pieces of information in elliptical form so that
it is difficult sometimes to piece together the meaning. The
word 'sons' must be understood in the sense of descendants
of Manasseh. In the fuller genealogy (Num. 26:31), Asriel is
the son of Gilead and, as was mentioned earlier, Machir is the
father of Gilead (1 Chron. 2:21, 23; Num. 36:1; Josh. 17:1). Machir
was Manasseh's firstborn through his Aramean concubine.
The phrase 'whom she bore' is there for emphasis to indicate
that Asriel, the great-grandson of this Aramean concubine
is of mixed race, which again indicates the Chronicler's
concern to show how foreigners were integrated into Israel
apparently without disapproval (see 1 Chron. 2:3; 2:34; 3:2;
4:17). Under the administration of Ezra and Nehemiah, such
mixed marriages were outlawed.

    Machir's wife was Maachah (v. 16), but he seems also to
have had a sister of that name (v. 15) unless 'sister' means
'relative'. Huppim and Suppim have been mentioned earlier
in the Benjamin genealogy (v. 12).

    Another grandson of Manasseh was Zelophehad who had
died in the wilderness leaving no son to inherit his portion
of the land. The story of how his five daughters pleaded
for a possession in the land and the satisfactory outcome
is recorded in some detail (see Num. 26:33; 27:1-11; 36:1-12;
Josh. 17:3-6). Chronicles assumes this background knowledge.

    After naming some descendants of Gilead, his sister,
Hammolecheth, is introduced together with her offspring

(v. 18). Gideon is from Abiezer's family (Judg. 6:11, 15, 24, 34; 8:2). The name Hammolecheth means 'the one who reigns' and it is interesting in this connection that Israel wanted Gideon to reign over them, which is what Abimelech, his son, attempted to do for a time (Judg. 8:22-23; 9:22). It is clear in verse 19 that 'sons' cannot mean actual sons (see Num. 26:29-33; Josh. 17:1-2). All the names including the more well-known Shechem are mentioned to show the various clans belonging to Manasseh and his descendants. Some names, otherwise unknown to us, may be due to pronunciation and spelling differences, as in the case of Likhi, whom many scholars identify with Helek, the second son of Gilead (Num. 26:30; Josh. 17:2).

Instead of the military interest of the previous west bank tribes, with their valiant fighters, this genealogy highlights the women. Five are mentioned: the Aramean concubine (v. 14), Machir's wife and sister Maacah (vv. 15-16), Zelophehad's daughters (v. 15) and Hammolecheth (v. 18). Some have taken this striking feature that is in marked contrast to the mighty warriors of Issachar as a sign of military weakness and vulnerability. On the other hand, the Chronicler may be stressing that women and children do have rights in the land and it is to be noted that he makes a point of mentioning women and children on a number of other occasions (see for example 2 Chron. 20:13; 31:18).

Application

Again, the Chronicler indicates that Israel's past included outsiders from enemy and menial backgrounds like Manasseh's Aramaean concubine. Zelophehad's daughters were also a reminder to the post-exilic community of how important the preservation of Israel's inheritance was (Num. 36:1-13). This earthly inheritance was in anticipation of the future eternal inheritance that is reserved for all God's people of whatever race, colour, sex, age and background in the new creation (Matt. 5:5; Heb. 11:13-16; 1 Pet. 1:4). 'Fear not little flock', said Jesus to His disciples, 'for it is the Father's good pleasure to give you the kingdom' (Luke 12:32; 22:29-30). The mention of so many women and children in this paragraph also reveals God's concern for the weak and vulnerable. It is picked up especially by Luke as he shows Jesus' compassion for such people (Luke 7:11-17; 8:1-3; etc.). But the New Testament also indicates the importance of women in the work of the gospel as fellow workers with Paul and others and who have special roles in the local church (Acts 18:18,24-26; Rom. 16; Phil. 4:2-3; 1 Tim. 5).

Ephraim (7:20-29)

7:20. And the sons of Ephraim: Shuthelah and Bered his son and Tahath his son and Eleadah his son and Tahath his son 21. and Zabad his son and Shuthelah his son. And *as for* Ezer and Elead, the men of Gath, who were born in the land, killed them because they came down to take away their cattle. 22. And Ephraim their father mourned many days, and his brothers came to comfort him. 23. And he went in to his wife and she conceived and bore a son, and he called his name Beriah, because evil was in his house. 24. And his daughter was Sheerah, and she built both Lower and Upper Beth-horon and Uzzen-sheerah. 25. And Rephah his son and Resheph and Telah his son and Tahan his son, 26. Ladan his son, Ammihud his son, Elishama his son, 27. Non his son, Joshua his son.

28. And their possessions and settlements were Bethel and its towns, and eastward Naaran, and westward Gezer and its towns, and Shechem and its towns, as far as Ayyah and its towns. 29. And along the borders of the sons of Manasseh, Bethshean and its towns, Taanach and its towns, Megiddo and its towns, Dor and its towns. In these dwelt the sons of Joseph the son of Israel.

Ephraim was Joseph's younger son and both he and Manasseh were adopted by Jacob as full sons, receiving the birthright that Reuben forfeited (1 Chron. 5:1-2). They became two tribes, each with their own separate inheritance in the land. Ephraim, though younger than his brother, received Jacob's firstborn blessing (Gen. 48). Two genealogies are included (vv. 20-21a; 25-27), together with some historical and geographical notes. Clearly the Chronicler's desire was to indicate the ancestry of Joshua the son of Nun (spelt 'Non' in verse 27) who led Israel into Canaan. Conquest, inheritance and occupation of the promised land are important themes in Chronicles (see 1 Chron. 4:38-43; 5:8-10, 18-22; 6:54-81; etc.) as he sought to encourage the post-exilic community.

There are numerous difficulties understanding the text and only tentative solutions can be offered given our present knowledge. The first part (vv. 20-21a) appears like a linear genealogy of six generations from Shuthelah I to Shuthelah II. This, however, is unlikely especially if, as many think, the genealogy continues in verses 25 to 27. Some commentators understand the first list of names as brothers, all of them sons of Ephraim with 'his son' meaning Ephraim's son in each case. This is a unique but not uncommon feature in Chronicles. Support for this is Numbers 26:35, which gives the first three sons as Shuthelah, understood as Shuthelah I, Becher understood as a variant spelling of Bered and Tahan a variant of Tahath.

Ezer and Elead, presumably brothers (v. 21), have also been thought of as sons of the initial tribal leader, Ephraim, but this is unlikely. The interesting tribal incident has been considered by some to have occurred during the early years of Israel's time in Egypt before they became slaves. On the other hand, as Poole[51] suggests, the name Ephraim may stand patronymically for a successor of Ephraim. In this case, the raid by these Ephraimites on the cattle belonging to 'the men of Gath' most probably took place after the conquest under Joshua. These men are described as an indigenous people, 'born in the land' (v. 21), separate from both the Philistines who occupied that area and the Israelites who had recently entered Canaan (compare Joshua 11:22).[52] As the father mourned the loss of his sons, 'his brothers', or in this context 'his relatives', came to console him. To this Ephraimite and his wife another son was born who is given the relatively common name of Beriah (Gen. 46:17; 1 Chron. 8:13-16; 23:10-11). As earlier with Jabez (1 Chron. 4:10), there is a pun on his name. The made-up word for 'evil' or 'calamity' (bᵊrā'āh, using the preposition bᵊ and the noun rā'āh 'evil') sounds like Beriah (bᵊrî'āh).

While Beriah's name points to the disaster that befell the tribe, Sheerah, who is either Beriah's sister or his daughter, speaks of blessing. Her claim to fame concerns the cities she founded particularly Uzzen-sheerah ('Sheerah's ear'), which

51. Matthew Poole, *A Commentary on the Holy Bible*, Vol. 1 (Edinburgh: The Banner of Truth Trust, 1962), p. 787.

52. In support of the later occasion is the use of 'came down' rather than 'came up' to describe the raid, an unlikely verb if Israel was in Egypt.

is named after her. While we read of men who built cities (Gen. 4:17; 10:11; etc.) this is the only example in the Bible of a woman building cities. Again, as with the descendants of Manasseh, attention is drawn to the place of women in the conquest of the land. While Uzzen-sheerah's location is unknown, Lower and Upper Beth-horon are in the south of Ephraim's territory.

Judging by the names of Joshua's father, grandfather and great-grandfather, whose names are found in the earlier records (Num. 1:10; Josh. 1:1), the second genealogy is a linear descent from Rephah to Joshua (vv. 25-27). In mentioning their 'possessions and settlements', the Chronicler alludes to Joshua's conquest of the Ephraimite territory to which he himself belonged (see Josh. 16:5-10). Gezer lay to the southwest of the boundary and Naaran to the southeast near Jericho (Josh. 16:7), with Shechem in the north and Bethel and Ayyah (possibly Ai) lying on the southern border. Because the Manasseh towns of Beth-shean, Taanach, Megiddo and Dor are mentioned, the final verse links Ephraim and Manasseh together as the descendants of Joseph ('sons of Joseph', v. 29). The Chronicler also adds 'the son of Israel' not only as a reminder that Joseph was Jacob's favourite son but to stress the significance of the Joseph tribes in the subsequent history of Israel. Although they were by-passed in favour of Judah and broke away from their brothers in the south, the Chronicler still considers them an integral part of Israel and encourages the post-exilic community to appreciate the unity of God's people (see Pss. 77:15; 80:1-2). To this end Jacob is again referred to as 'Israel' as is customary in Chronicles (see 1 Chron. 2:1).

Application

In the Old Testament, Ephraim and Manasseh often represent the whole of the northern kingdom as do Judah and Benjamin the southern (2 Chron. 31:1). Ephraim alone, the more prominent of the Joseph tribes as Jacob's blessing indicates (Gen. 48:19), is frequently used as a synonym for the Israelite north. This tribe experienced setbacks that seemed to counter the promises made, but, as Matthew Henry comments, 'when they do so, they really magnify the promise, and make the performance of it, notwithstanding, so much the more illustrious.' As with the violent death of Ephraimite sons and the blessings that follow a new son, God does make up for the losses Christians endure both in this life and especially in the life to come (Mark 10:28-30). 'Beriah' is a reminder that 'evil' in the form of trouble and calamity is the lot of humans in this life but we are encouraged to pray with Moses that times of affliction and evil would be compensated by similar periods of gladness (Ps. 90:15). Joshua was the one who was used by God to bring about the conquest and settlement of the tribes in Canaan. But one greater than Joshua, the son of Nun, has appeared to destroy the works of the devil and to bring to reality the promises and types for the benefit of all the tribes of the earth. As very few would have thought in those days that a woman would build cities, so God works through those considered weak to fulfil His purposes. Mary was blessed to give birth to the one to whom every knee will one day bow. The stone that smashed in pieces the kingdoms of this world became a mountain that filled the earth. It is through the weakness and foolishness associated with the cross of Jesus that God has ordained to save lost people and to set up a kingdom that will not perish (1 Cor. 1:18–2:5).

The province of Samaria lay within the old inheritance of Ephraim. It was in God's plan that Jesus should pass that way and engage in conversation with the Samaritan woman which led to a whole village confessing Jesus as the Saviour of the world. Jesus later commissioned His disciples to be witnesses also in Samaria (John 4:1-42; Acts 1:8).

Asher (7:30-40)

> 7:30. The sons of Asher: Imnah and Ishvah and Ishvi and Beriah and Serah their sister. 31. And the sons of Beriah: Heber and Malchiel, who was the father of Birzaith. 32. And Heber fathered Japhlet and Shomer and Hotham and Shua their sister. 33. And the sons of Japhlet: Pasach and Bimhal and Ashvath. These are the sons of Japhlet. 34. And the sons of Shemer: Ahi and Rohgah and Hubbah and Aram. 35. And the son of Helem his brother: Zophah and Imna and Shelesh and Amal. 36. The sons of Zophah: Suah and Harnepher and Shual and Beri and Imrah,

37. Bezer and Hod and Shamma and Shilshah and Ithran and Beera. 38. And the sons of Jether: Jephunneh and Pispa and Ara. 39. And the sons of Ulla: Arah and Hanniel and Rizia. 40. All these were the sons of Asher, heads of the house of fathers, select valiant warriors, heads of the princes. And their number enrolled by genealogy for army *service* in battle was twenty-six thousand men.

While the whole of the Chronicler's arrangement from chapters 2 to 8 is enveloped by the two royal tribes of Judah (1 Chron. 2:3-4:23) and Benjamin (1 Chron. 8:1-40), Simeon and Asher balance each other in that Simeon represents the southernmost tribe (1 Chron. 4:24-43) and Asher the most northerly, lying to the northwest on the sea coast. As we find in Genesis 46:17 (see Num. 26:44-46), four sons of Asher are named together with their sister and two grandsons by Beriah (v. 30). The Chronicler makes a point of not forgetting Asher's daughter, Serah (Num. 26:46), as well as Shua, a daughter of Heber (v. 32; see 1 Chron. 7:14-18,24). Perhaps military census lists (v. 40; see vv. 1-5, 6-12) provided the Chronicler with the other names mentioned. As with Issachar only one family line, that of Beriah, is followed throughout. It is enough to indicate that Asher is not lacking descendants to occupy the area allotted to them. Shemer (v. 34) is perhaps the same as Shomer (v. 32), Helem (v. 35) the same as Hotham (v. 32), Jether (v. 38) the same as Ithran (v. 37) and Ulla (v. 39) the same as Ara (v. 38) but there can be no certainty.

Unique to this tribal list are the references to the 'chiefs' or 'heads of the princes' and 'select' warriors (v. 40). Again, the Chronicler is concerned to indicate that this tribe on the periphery of Israel is not to be despised but is as much a part of Israel as Ephraim or Judah. It did not lag behind militarily as it possessed the choicest of fighting men. They had, as noted later, 'experienced troops ready for battle' (1 Chron. 12:36).

Application

For northern Israel west of the Jordan, the Chronicler has placed Issachar first and Asher last, both of them on the peripheral of the promised land and the area no longer part of the post-exilic community. Nevertheless, they are given due attention with the aim of broadening the vision of the post-exilic community. It prepares us for the realisation of all God's promises to the patriarchs associated with Messiah. The prophetess Anna was of the tribe of Asher and it is significant that she was in the Jerusalem temple at the time of Jesus' dedication. She gave thanks to God and spoke of Him to all who were awaiting the redemption of Jerusalem (Luke 2:36-38). The name 'Asher' means 'blessing' and blessing is certainly what this daughter of Asher received (Gen. 49:20; Deut. 33:24-25).

Benjaminite families (8:1-28)

The brief genealogy of Benjamin (1 Chron. 7:6-12) is resumed with this much fuller treatment of Benjaminites associated with the southern kingdom and that balances the very long genealogy of Judah (1 Chron. 2:3-4:23) to form an *inclusio*. These two tribes are given special attention not only because they produced kings for Israel but they are the two that remained loyal to David and Jerusalem when the kingdom was divided and, in addition, they were the two main tribes that returned from Babylonian exile (Ezra 1:5). The Levites were also strongly represented after the exile and they have already been given a prominent central position in these family lists (1 Chron. 6:1-81).

The section falls into two parts: the descendants of Bela and Ehud (vv. 1-7); and the descendants of Shaharaim and Elpaal (vv. 8-28). Only verses 1-5 bear any comparison with Genesis 46:21 and Numbers 26:38-41.

> 8:1. And Benjamin fathered Bela his firstborn, Ashbel the second, and Aharah the third, 2. Nohah the fourth, and Rapha the fifth. 3. And Bela had sons: Addar and Gera and Abihud 4. and Abishua and Naaman and Ahoah 5. and Gera and Shephuphan and Huram. 6. And these are the sons of Ehud (these ones were heads of fathers belonging to the inhabitants of Geba, and they carried them into exile to Manahath): 7. and Naaman and Ahiah and Gera who exiled them and fathered Uzza and Ahihud.

Bela, Benjamin's first, is the only name that links all the lists of Benjamin's descendants (Gen. 46:21; Num. 26:38; 1 Chron. 7:6). Some of the differences in names may be due to variant pronunciations and spellings, for example: Addar and Ard;

Aharah and Ahiram. However, we are probably not to think so much of direct family connections but of descendants and clan groupings. The Chronicler's way of presenting tribal relationships do not necessarily follow modern western practices. At times the material is also very compressed.

Brought to our attention in this paragraph is Ehud. Although the name is spelt differently, it is probably to be taken as the Benjaminite judge whose father was Gera (Judg. 3:15; 1 Chron. 7:10). The phrase 'and Abihud' is possibly not introducing another person's name but to be translated: 'even the father of Ehud' (v. 3). Gera would then be a descendant not an immediate son of Bela and he, or a second Gera, is said to have sent into exile some Benjaminites. This followed a previous exile by inhabitants of Geba to Manahath, which is either the one in Judah, three miles (five kilometres) south west of Jerusalem (1 Chron. 2:52,54) or in Edom (1 Chron. 1:40). The time of these 'exiles' or perhaps in these contexts, local tribal movements or 'migrations', was when the Moabites were oppressing Israel. The phrase 'heads of fathers' (v. 6) is one that occurs often in Chronicles and refers to ancestral heads of households (see 1 Chron. 9:9, 13, 33-34). Geba was a Levitical city and an important Benjaminite centre, six miles (9.6 kilometres) north of Jerusalem, near Bethel, where king Asa carried out building works (1 Kings 15:22; 2 Chron. 16:6). The southern kingdom of Judah is described as from Geba to Beersheba and where local shrines were situated (2 Kings 23:8). It continued to be an important city after the Exile (Neh. 11:31; 12:29). Uzza and Ahihud were probably descendants of Gera living at the time when this genealogy was compiled.

8:8. And Shaharaim fathered in the field of Moab, after he had sent away his wives, Hushim and Baara. 9. And from Hodesh his wife he fathered Jobab and Zibia and Mesha and Malcam 10. and Jeuz and Sachia and Mirmah. These were his sons, heads of fathers. 11. And from Hushim he fathered Abitub and Elpaal. 12. And the sons of Elpaal: Eber and Misham and Shemed (he actually built Ono and Lod and its daughter towns), 13. and Beriah and Shema (they were the heads of the fathers belonging to the inhabitants of Aijalon; they were the ones who put to flight the inhabitants of Gath), 14. and Ahio, Shashak and Jeremoth 15. and Zebadiah and Arad and Eder, 16. and Michael and Ishpah and Joha, the sons of Beriah. 17. And Zebadiah and Meshullam and Hizki and Heber 18. and Ishmerai and Izliah and Jobab, the sons of Elpaal. 19. And Jakim and Zichri and Zabdi 20. and Elienai and Zillethai and Eliel 21. and Adaiah and Beraiah and Shimrath, the sons of Shimei. 22. And Ishpan and Eber and Eliel, 23. and Abdon and Zichri and Hanan 24. and Hananiah and Elam and Anthothijah 25. and Iphdeiah and Penuel, the sons of Shashak. 26. And Shamsherai and Shehariah and Athaliah 27. and Jaareshiah and Elijah and Zichri, the sons of Jeroham. 28. These were the heads of the fathers, heads according to their generations. These dwelt in Jerusalem.

It is the name Elpaal that stands out in this section (vv. 11-12,18). Its connection with the preceding paragraph is probably through Ehud and the Moabites. Shaharaim was an ancestor of a family of Benjaminites that included Elpaal who had lived in Moab. In the Judges' period we read of other families exiled in Moab including ancestors of king David (Ruth 1) and it was he who asked permission of the king of Moab for his parents to stay there while he was a fugitive from Saul (1 Sam. 22:3-4). Concerning Shaharaim (v. 8), the text would suggest that he divorced two of his wives and emigrated to Moab where he married Hodesh. The children of this marriage included 'Mesha', a name associated with Moab for it was also the name of the Moabite king whose 'Moabite Stone' commemorated his revolt against Israel (compare 2 Kings 3:4-5).

It is from the rejected Hushim that Shaharaim's descendants are traced through Elpaal (v. 11). Working backwards from verse 27, it can be seen that the families of some of the sons of Elpaal are set out: Beriah (v. 13 in vv. 15-16); Shema also spelt Shimei (vv. 13, 21 in vv. 19-21); Shashak (v. 14 in vv. 22-25); Jeremoth also spelt Jeroham (vv. 14, 27 in 26-27). Other sons of Elpaal are interspersed among his sons' relatives but with no descendants named (vv. 12, 17-18). Elpaal's third son, Shemed, engaged in building work at the ancient cities of Ono, seven miles (eleven kilometres) southeast of Joppa, and Lod (Lydda of New Testament times), a further four miles (6.5 kilometres) south east of Ono. They are listed among the places inhabited by the returned exiles (Ezra 2:33; Neh. 7:37). These places are outside the territory originally assigned to Benjamin and together with the reference to Aijalon, which was originally assigned to Dan, and the dispersal of the inhabitants of Gath (v. 13), there is clear evidence of Benjaminite expansion westwards perhaps during the reigns of David and Rehoboam (2 Chron. 11:10; 28:18).

At the later time, when this genealogy was compiled, these Benjaminite families lived 'in Jerusalem' (v. 28), which lay on the border between Judah and Benjamin and associated with both tribes (Josh. 15:8, 63; 18:28; Judg. 1:21). The reference to Jerusalem is in preparation for the fuller treatment of the city's inhabitants in chapter 9. Verse 28 provides the conclusion to this Benjaminite section and is very similar to the one that summarises the Levitical families (1 Chron. 9:34). Interestingly, both summary statements appear immediately before listing Saul's genealogy and family (8:29-40; 9:35-44).

Application

The passage indicates some measure of blessing for Benjamin (v. 12) witnessed by their expansion westward and their building projects (see 1 Chron. 7:24; 8:12). This would have been an encouragement to the post-exilic community who settled in these areas made up as it was of many from this tribe (Ezra 2:33; Neh. 7:37; 11:35). The passage also reveals that, among the Benjaminites, there was a racial mix of people who came to settle in Jerusalem. Psalm 87 speaks of representatives of the nations as born in Jerusalem and like Chronicles encourages a belief in a city made up of God's people from every nation. This is the spiritual Jerusalem described in many parts of the New Testament.

Saul's family (8:29-40)

8:29. And in Gibeon dwelt the father of Gibeon; and his wife's name *was* Maacah. 30. And his firstborn son *was* Abdon; then Zur and Kish and Baal and Nadab 31. and Gedor and Ahio and Zecher. 32. And Mikloth fathered Shimeah. And these also lived opposite their brothers in Jerusalem, with their brothers.

33. And Ner fathered Kish, and Kish fathered Saul, and Saul fathered Jonathan and Malchishua and Abinadab and Eshbaal. 34. And the son of Jonathan *was* Merib-baal; and Merib-baal

fathered Micah. 35. And the sons of Micah: Pithon and Melech and Tarea and Ahaz. 36. And Ahaz fathered Jehoaddah, and Jehoaddah fathered Alemeth and Azmaveth and Zimri; and Zimri fathered Moza. 37. And Moza fathered Binea; Raphah *was* his son, Eleasah his son, Azel his son. 38. And Azel had six sons and these are their names: Azrikam, Bocheru and Ishmael and Sheariah and Obadiah and Hanan. All these were the sons of Azel. 39. And the sons of Eshek his brother: Ulam his firstborn, Jeush the second, and Eliphelet the third. 40. And the sons of Ulam were valiant warrior men, archers, having many sons and grandsons, one hundred and fifty. All these were from the sons of Benjamin.

This segmented genealogy, much of which is repeated in 1 Chronicles 9:35-44, links the family of King Saul, the Benjaminite, with the cities of Gibeon and Jerusalem. It divides into three parts: verses 29-32; 33-34; 35-40.

Verses 29-32 present a genealogical list from 'the father of' in the sense of 'patriarch of' or 'founder of' Gibeon to Shimeah (called Shimeam in 1 Chron. 9:38). From the parallel passage (1 Chron. 9:36-37) we learn that Mikloth, who fathered Shimeah, was the youngest of the sons. Only the patriarch's wife, Maacah, is given here but we learn later that his name was Jeiel (1 Chron. 9:35). The emphasis on 'in Gibeon' is striking, which in the Hebrew is placed first in the sentence (v. 29; see also 1 Chron. 9:35) immediately after 'in Jerusalem' (v. 28; 9:34). Gibeon lay six miles (9.5 kilometres) northwest of Jerusalem and was part of Benjaminite territory (Josh. 18:25). After the exile, men from the city assisted Nehemiah in rebuilding the walls of Jerusalem (Neh. 3:7). Much is made by the Chronicler of the close association of Gibeon and Jerusalem especially as places of worship (1 Chron. 16:39; 21:29 in addition to 2 Chron. 1:1-6,13//1 Kings 3:4,15). There is also some stress on these Gibeonites living in Jerusalem alongside other Benjaminites and Israelites from other tribes (v. 32; 1 Chron. 9:38). After the exile there was reluctance at first to repopulate Jerusalem (Neh. 7:4; 11:1-2).

Verses 33-34 present a linear genealogy from Ner to Saul, at which point four of his sons are named. This then allows for Saul's son Jonathan and his descendants to be given some prominence. Instead of siding with Saul against

David, Jonathan chose to help his close friend escape from his father's evil intentions. Jonathan died at the hands of the Philistines together with his father and brothers, Malchishua and Abinadab, but Ishbaal, who is also known as Ishvi, Eshbaal or Ishbosheth, survived (see 1 Sam. 14:49; 2 Sam. 2:8; 1 Chron. 10:2). Ner's relationship to the family is not entirely clear but it seems he is father to Abner, Saul's uncle and military leader, and grandfather to Saul (1 Sam. 14:50-51). Kish, Saul's father, was the son of Ner and a 'son of' or 'descendant of' Abiel (see 1 Sam. 9:1; 14:51). Merib-baal (v. 34), the son of Jonathan, is called in the earlier history Mephi-bosheth (2 Sam. 4:4; 9:1-13, where *bosheth* 'shame' is substituted for *baal* on account of its idolatrous associations; see similarly Eshbaal/Ishbosheth).

Verses 35-40 name descendants of Saul that are nowhere else referred to in the Bible (apart from 1 Chron. 9:41-44), but these twelve representative generations after Saul are probably meant to bring the line down to the exile, as witnessed in the high-priestly line (1 Chron. 6:1-15). Against any suggestion that David had murderous intentions against Saul and his family, as originally suggested by Shimei the son of Gera, the Chronicler devotes a large amount of space to Jonathan's descendants. It is a reminder of David's pledge to Jonathan on account of his kindness toward him (1 Sam. 20:15, 23, 42) and the care he took to respect the bodily remains of Saul and Jonathan (2 Sam. 21). The final verse recalls the earlier military census lists and Benjaminites who served their country well (see 1 Chron. 7:2, 5, 7, 9, etc.).

Application

The genealogy reveals that the ancestry of Saul, the first king of Israel, included some Canaanite blood, as the Gibeonites were Canaanites who deceived Israel into thinking they had come from a far country (Josh. 9). As has been noted already, numerous Gentiles become part of Israel, a preview of God's purpose all along that the Israel of God should include people of all nations. Many of Saul's family perished in the battle against the Philistines (1 Chron. 10:1-7). Later, justice was seen to be done on account of Saul's sin against the

Gibeonites when David handed over seven members of Saul's family to be executed (2 Sam. 21:1-14). Despite this, Saul's descendants flourished through his son Jonathan and his lame grandson Merib-baal or Meri-baal with valiant warriors and numerous descendants (see 1 Chron. 9:40). Again, this was an encouragement to the post-exilic generations to be faithful and trust God for the future and not to despair. What seemed like total disaster for Saul's family had a sizeable and prosperous outcome.

If there was a future and forgiveness for Saul's family then the post-exilic community could rest assured that God's great promises to David would materialise in the end. But as that future for Saul's family only came through Jonathan's fellowship with David, so the future for God's people lay in the Davidic covenant. Gabriel's words to Mary concerning Jesus renewed the expectations (Luke 1:30-33) and as a result of Jesus' atoning work repentance and the remission of sins are preached in His name to all nations beginning in Jerusalem (Luke 24:44-49). Paul was of the tribe of Benjamin and considered himself to be the chief of sinners, having been instrumental in the persecution and death of many Christians, yet God had mercy on him. The only hope for sinners is in knowing David's Son, King Jesus, the Saviour of the world.

3

Israel's Future
(9:1-34)

This chapter concludes the genealogical records relating to Israel (verse 1a) and lists the people who resettled after the exile (verses 1b-34).

All Israel Enrolled and Judah exiled (9:1)

9:1. So all Israel was enrolled by genealogies; and there they are, written in the Book of the Kings of Israel. And Judah was taken into exile to Babylon because of their unfaithfulness.

This verse is a summary of the lists from chapters 2 to 8 and prepares for what follows. It includes some of the Chronicler's significant wording. The first occurrence in Chronicles of the phrase 'all Israel' appears here and recalls Israel's twelve sons named at the beginning (1 Chron. 2:1-2). Throughout Chronicles, the phrase is used extensively to stress that all the tribes belong to God's people and not simply Judah, Benjamin and Levi who made up the bulk of the post-exilic community. The deep rift that occurred when the kingdom was divided in the days of Rehoboam did not mean that the northern tribes had no future as God's people. Like Ezekiel (see Ezek. 37:15-28), the Chronicler looks forward to the day when north and south would be once again under the Davidic ruler. The phrase 'enrolled by genealogies' is a reminder of the previous family and military lists (1 Chron. 4:33; 5:1, 7, 17; 7:5, 7, 9). Outside of Chronicles, it is only used in Ezra and Nehemiah.

The Chronicler names his source, deliberately referring to it as 'the Book of the Kings of Israel' (elsewhere only at 2 Chron. 20:34) rather than the more usual '... Kings of Israel and Judah' (2 Chron. 27:7; 35:27; 36:8).[1] Again, he probably does this to emphasise the unity of Israel at this point. Mention has already been made of the captivity of the northern tribes by the Assyrian king (1 Chron. 5:25-26) and also of Judah's captivity by Nebuchadnezzar (1 Chron. 6:15). This fresh reference to Judah's exile at the end of the Chronicler's genealogical introduction provides a more exact parallel to the northern kingdom's exile in 1 Chronicles 5:25-26 than the one in 1 Chronicles 6:15 and anticipates the account of the Babylonian exile in the final chapter (2 Chron. 36:20). The reason for the exile is noted with another of the Chronicler's key terms, 'unfaithfulness', employed (see 1 Chron. 10:13). The related verbal form 'to break faith' or 'transgress' was used earlier (see 1 Chron. 2:7; 5:25). In the final analysis, the kingdom of Judah turned out to be no different to its northern neighbour in its disregard of God and His commandments and deserved the same punishment of removal from the land as the final curse of the Sinai covenant indicated (1 Chron. 5:25-26; see Lev. 26:40-41).

Jerusalem repopulated (9:2-34)

The structure of the first part of Chronicles moves from the world at large made up of the Gentile nations in chapter 1, to the tribes of Israel and their territories in chapters 2–8 and closes with Jerusalem and its inhabitants, its sanctuary and staff in chapter 9. It is this city and temple that become the main concern of the Chronicler for the remainder of his work. There are echoes of Nehemiah 11:3-19 in the way the list is assembled, but the differences are substantial enough to suggest that if a common source were employed in each case, it has been used selectively and perhaps with some updating according to the purpose of each work.

---

1. The pointing in the MT makes 'and Judah' the subject of a new sentence. The AV follows the LXX and Vulgate in connecting 'and Judah' with Israel to give the more common rendering 'the Book of the Kings of Israel and Judah'. But unless a second 'Judah' has been omitted through haplography, some word is needed to begin the second half of verse 1. The AV adds 'who' before 'was taken into exile' in order to make sense.

After the general statement (v. 2), the section that follows is framed by the phrase 'in Jerusalem' (vv. 3, 34) and is divided into three segments: the lay population (vv. 3-9); the priests (vv. 10-13); and the Levites (vv. 14-34).

General statement (9:2)

> 9:2. Now the first settlers who were in their possessions in their cities were Israel, the priests, the Levites, and the Nethinim.

Before detailing the inhabitants of Jerusalem (vv. 3-34), the Chronicler lists the four kinds of people who dwelt in the land of promise after the exile. They included 'Israel', here used for all the lay people, then the priests and Levites (see Ezra 10:25) and finally the 'Nethinim', often translated 'temple servants'. This latter group are only mentioned here in Chronicles but the term occurs frequently in Ezra–Nehemiah (see Ezra 2:43, 58, 70, etc.; Neh. 7:46, etc.). As the Levites were given to support the priests (Num. 3:9; 8:16, 19) so these 'Nethinim' were given to serve in the sanctuary.[2] They are perhaps descendants of the Gibeonites (see Josh. 9:27) or of the Midianites who had been captured (Num. 31:47). Some of the names of the Nethinim, such as Rezin, Meunim and Nephusim, would indicate foreign origin (Ezra 2:48, 50). They are to be distinguished from the 'gatekeepers' who belonged to the descendants of Levi (Ezra 2:70; 7:7). It was David who appointed these Nethinim (Ezra 8:20) and they are associated with the descendants of Solomon's servants (Ezra 2:58). In the post-exilic period their numbers were quite considerable and they had their own leaders (Ezra 7:24; Neh. 7:60; 11:21).

It speaks of these first settlers as occupying 'their possessions', which is a reference to their own landed property. In the jubilee year, the Mosaic Law allowed the dispossessed to return to take possession of their ancestral land (Lev. 25:10, 13, etc.). The idea of the jubilee proclamation is suggested at the end of the book in 2 Chronicles 36:22. Similarly, Moses encouraged the two and a half tribes of the Transjordan region to return to the land of their possession when the rest of Israel had settled in Canaan (Josh. 22:4). By using this term 'possession', the Chronicler indicates the continuity with the past.

---

2. The term 'Nethinim' is related to the verb 'to give' (*ntn*).

The lay population (9:3-9)

9:3. And in Jerusalem dwelt some of the sons of Judah, and some of the sons of Benjamin, and some of the sons of Ephraim and Manasseh: 4. Uthai the son of Ammihud, the son of Omri, the son of Imri, the son of Bani, from the sons of Perez the son of Judah. 5. And from the Shilonites: Asaiah the firstborn and his sons. 6. And from the sons of Zerah: Jeuel and their brothers, six hundred and ninety. 7. And from the sons of Benjamin: Sallu the son of Meshullam, the son of Hodaviah, the son of Hassenuah, 8. and Ibneiah the son of Jeroham and Elah the son of Uzzi, the son of Michri, and Meshullam the son of Shephatiah, the son of Reuel, the son of Ibnijah; 9 and their brothers, according to their generations, nine hundred and fifty-six. All these men were heads of fathers according to the house of their fathers.

Judah and Benjamin are mentioned in Nehemiah 11:4 but not 'Ephraim and Manasseh'. These latter two tribes are used to represent the whole of northern Israel (see 2 Chron. 30:1, 5, 10; 31:1; 34:9 and compare Judg. 10:9; Hosea 5:13-14; 11:3, 8, 12) in the same way that the former two stand for the southern part. As with his use of 'all Israel', by placing Ephraim and Manasseh together with Judah and Benjamin, he is stressing the unity of Israel. Those who had taken up residence in Jerusalem included representatives from both north and south and this was a small pointer to the realisation of Ezekiel's vision of Jerusalem with its gates named after the tribes of Israel (Ezek. 48:30-35).

No specific descendants of the northern tribes are highlighted and only a few are noted from the south. In the case of Judah, descendants ('sons') of three of his sons, Perez, Shelah and Zerah, are to be found in the city (vv. 4-6; see Num. 26:20). The name Shilonites (see Neh. 11:5) is not a reference to people from Shiloh. It is probably a variant spelling or pronunciation of Shelah (1 Chron. 2:3; 4:21; see Gen. 38:5). Perez and Zerah were sons of Judah's daughter-in-law Tamar (1 Chron. 2:4-6; see Gen. 38:11-30). While Nehemiah 11:6 gives a total only for the Perez line of four hundred and sixty-eight, the Chronicler's figure of six hundred and ninety is for those of the three clans.

Application

The reference to the exile at the conclusion of Israel's tribal genealogies calls to mind the original exile experienced by

Adam (1 Chron. 1:1). But just as there was a future for Adam and his posterity after that initial transgression, so there was for Israel after the Babylonian exile in order for God's purposes to be realised. It is a reminder of God's declaration to the evil one that through the woman's seed victory would be won over the snake.

The unity of Israel witnessed by the representatives from north and south in post-exilic Jerusalem is one of the themes Chronicles aims to highlight. Along with Ezekiel 48:30-35, it symbolises the completeness of God's people in the temple-city of God, the new Jerusalem described by John in his visions (Rev. 21:10-14). He not only refers to twelve gates, each with the name of one of the twelve tribes of Israel but to twelve foundation stones each bearing the name of one of the apostles. This gives the fuller picture of the unity and oneness of God's people of Old and New Testament times. The symbolic number of 144,000 (12,000 x 12) that John had previously heard, presents the totality of the elect who will inhabit the future city-state, and which the apostle then saw as an innumerable company from every nation, tribe and language (Rev. 7:1-17).

The priests (9:10-13)

> 9:10. And of the priests: Jedaiah and Jehoiarib and Jachin, 11. and Azariah the son of Hilkiah, the son of Meshullam, the son of Zadok, the son of Meraioth, the son of Ahitub, the leader of the house of God; 12. and Adaiah the son of Jeroham, the son of Pashhur, the son of Malchijah, and Maasai the son of Adiel, the son of Jahzerah, the son of Meshullam, the son of Meshillemith, the son of Immer; 13. and their brothers, heads belonging to the house of their fathers, one thousand seven hundred and sixty, valiant warriors for the work of the service of God's house.

The priests are descendants of Aaron who had the task of offering sacrifices on behalf of the people. Closely paralleling Nehemiah 11:10-14, six priestly clans are listed (five if Jehoiarib/Joiarib is the father of Jedaiah; see Neh. 11:10): Jedaiah, Jehoiarib, Jachin (v. 10; 1 Chron. 24:7,17; Neh. 12:6, 19), Azariah (v. 11), who is not, as some suggest, the same person as the Seraiah of Nehemiah 11:11 (see Ezra 7:1), Adaiah and Maasai (v. 12). The latter two are associated with

two of the post-exilic families, Pashhur and Immer (see Ezra
2:37-38; 10:20, 22; Neh. 7:40-41). Azariah belongs to the family
of Zadok (v. 11; see 1 Chron. 6:12-14; Ezra 7:1-2). The term
for 'leader', which can also be translated 'ruler' or 'prince'
(1 Sam. 9:16; 1 Chron. 5:2), is used here for Ahitub the high
priest (1 Chron. 6:11-12; 2 Chron. 31:10,13; Jer. 20:1). In the time
of Zerubbabel, Joshua (Jeshua) was high priest of the same
Zadokite stock (Hag. 1:1; Zech. 3; Ezra 3:2; 5:1-2). An updated
total for the priests is given as 1,760 whereas the Nehemiah
figures adds up to 1,192 (822+242+128) but as Selman points
out 'they are considerably fewer than the 4,289 who returned
initially'.[3] Some of the slight differences in names found
in Nehemiah may be due to pronunciation or spelling (e.g.
Maasai is identified with Amashsai and Meshillemith with
Meshillemoth (v. 12; Neh. 11:13). Both Adiel and Jahzerah
may be equivalent to Azarel and Ahzai (v. 12; Neh. 11:13) as
the Hebrew letters more clearly suggest. The phrase 'valiant
warriors' (v. 13; see Neh. 11:14), while it does not mean they
had military duties, conveys the idea that they were men of
strength and ability ready for their onerous tasks in 'the work
of the service of God's house'. Offering the various sacrifices
each day could be quite demanding and, along with the other
Levites, they needed to be strong enough to withstand temple
gate-crashers (1 Chron. 26:6; 2 Chron. 23:4; 26:17, 20).

There is no evidence of a Zadokite faction in the exilic
or post-exilic period over-against other claimants to the
priesthood. Zadok sided with David's son Solomon and was
appointed to be chief priest in place of Abiathar who had
supported Adonijah (1 Sam. 2:27-36; 3:11-14; 1 Kings 1:5-8, 26,
32-40; 2:26-27, 35).

Application

While Jesus fulfils the priestly role, God does give to His
church on earth overseers and pastors to lead and teach. As
there were leaders in the post-exilic community qualified
for the task of serving in God's temple so Paul, while
acknowledging his own insufficiency and inadequacy, speaks
of being made sufficient by God to be a reliable and competent

3. Selman, *1 Chronicles*, p. 127.

minister or emissary of the new covenant (2 Cor. 3:1-6). Every elder and preacher-pastor, as a servant of Christ, is required to be found trustworthy (1 Cor. 4:1-4).

The Levites (9:14-34)

The Levites were given various duties that included leading the singing, guarding the sanctuary, and maintaining its equipment and supplies. In the wilderness period, Levites were in charge of guarding the sanctuary, assisting the priests in their duties and carefully wrapping and carrying the tabernacle and its furnishings through the wilderness. An even wider range of duties fell on the Levites in David's time (see 1 Chron. 23:4-5). Verses 14-16 introduce some Levites who were from musical families and ties up with verse 33 which may also be referring to them, with verse 34 providing a summary statement. The intervening verses list a special group of gatekeepers who likewise included those with a musical background (vv. 17-18) but particularly stressed their important work of guarding the entrances to the temple (vv. 19-27) and maintaining the purity of the sanctuary (vv. 28-32).

> 9:14. And of the Levites: Shemaiah the son of Hasshub, the son of Azrikam, the son of Hashabiah, of the sons of Merari; 15. And Bakbakkar, Heresh and Galal, and Mattaniah the son of Mica, the son of Zichri, the son of Asaph; 16. and Obadiah the son of Shemaiah, the son of Galal, the son of Jeduthun, and Berechiah the son of Asa, the son of Elkanah, who dwelt in the villages of Netophathites.

First, the Chronicler mentions the Levites who were singers or musicians. It has some close parallels with Nehemiah 11:15-18 where only three families are named: Shemaiah, Mattaniah and Abda. Here, attention is drawn to four families: Shemaiah, Mattaniah, Obadiah and Berechiah. Shemaiah belonged to the Merari clan, which was one of the three original Levitical clan leaders, the other two being Kohath and Gershom (1 Chron. 6:37,43,47). The other three names – 'Bakbakkar, probably the same as 'Bakbukiah' (Neh. 11:17), Heresh and Galal' – are separate individuals who assisted in the musical side of temple worship. 'Mattaniah' is a descendant of Asaph the musician in the time of David who belonged to the Gershom clan. Zichri, one of his ancestors, is probably the same man called Zabdi in Nehemiah 11:17.[4] Obadiah is a descendant of Jeduthun, another of David's chief musicians (1 Chron. 25:1, 3, 6, etc.; 2 Chron. 5:12-14; 35:15; the headings to Psalms 39, 62 and 77). As for 'Berechiah', he probably belonged to the Kohathite clan (see 1 Chron. 6:33-38). Though he lived in the villages of the Netophathites to the south of Jerusalem, about three miles (4.8 kilometres) from Bethlehem, he along with other singers are associated with the inhabitants of Jerusalem, probably because that is where they resided when on duty (see vv. 25, 33).[5] Earlier the Chronicler lists the Netophathites next to Bethlehem as descendants of Salma (1 Chron. 2:54). Singers from Netophah were among those present when the walls of Jerusalem were dedicated (Neh. 12:28).

> 9:17. And the gatekeepers: Shallum and Akkub and Talmon and Ahiman and their brothers. Shallum was the chief, 18. and until now *were* in the king's gate on the east. These were the gatekeepers belonging to the camps of the sons of Levi. 19. And Shallum the son of Kore, the son of Ebiasaph, the son of Korah, and his brothers belonging to his father's house, the Korahites, *were* in charge of the work of the service, guardians of the thresholds of the tent; their fathers *had been* over the camp of Yahweh, guardians of the entrance. 20. And Phinehas the son of Eleazar was leader over them previously; Yahweh *was* with him. 21. Zechariah the son of Meshelemiah was gate-keeper of the entrance of the tent of meeting. 22. All these, chosen to be gatekeepers at the thresholds, were two hundred and twelve. They were enrolled by their genealogy in their villages, whom David and Samuel the seer established in their office of trust.
>
> 23. So they and their sons had the oversight of the gates of the house of Yahweh – of the house of the tent – as guards. 24. The gatekeepers were on the four sides, east, toward west, toward north and toward south. 25. And their brothers in their villages to come from time to time for seven days to be with these, 26. for in their position of trust these four valiant gatekeepers were Levites and they were over the chambers and over treasuries of the house of God. 27. And they lodged the night around the

---

4. There was often confusion over both the Hebrew letters b (*beth*) and k (*kaph*) and d (*daleth*) and r (*resh*).

5. Leslie C. Allen, 'The First and Second Books of Chronicles' in Volume 3 of *The New Interpreter's Bible*, ed. I. E. Keck (Nashville: Abingdon, 1999), p. 362.

house of God, because the guard-duty was theirs, and they had charge of opening it each morning.

Unlike the brief reference to 'gatekeepers' in Nehemiah 11:19, a long section is given over to describing the duties of the temple 'gatekeepers', sometimes translated 'porters' or 'doorkeepers'. The term for 'gatekeeper' (šōʿēr) is brought to our attention in the books of Chronicles and Ezra–Nehemiah. Elsewhere in the Old Testament, this particular Hebrew word is only found twice and used for city and not temple gatekeepers (2 Sam. 18:26; 2 Kings 7:10-11). For the Chronicler, living in the post-exilic period, these temple gatekeepers were clearly important and he wished to emphasise the continuity between them and earlier occupants of the position. There were four 'chief' gatekeepers (vv. 17-18, 26) who were on permanent sentry duty around the temple, guarding the rooms and the treasury and responsible for opening the temple each morning (vv. 26-27). Others ('their brothers' or 'relatives') were appointed to assist them (vv. 17, 22-23, 25). Because of the apparent shortage of Levites in the post-exilic period (see Ezra 8:15-20; Neh. 13:10-11),[6] the Chronicler encourages all the Levites to be active as temple servants by highlighting the faithfulness of these Levitical temple gatekeepers.

In the original tabernacle erected in the wilderness, there was only one main entrance into the courtyard where the bronze altar and laver were situated and one entrance into the tabernacle itself where only the priests were allowed. Both faced east. It is difficult to work out precisely the number of gates associated with the courts of Solomon's temple. Apparently, there were gates on the four sides of the temple area: the important east gate (2 Chron. 31:14; Ezek. 11:1), one facing south (2 Kings 11:19; 16:18; Jer. 38:14), a third facing north (Ezek. 8:14; 9:2) and a fourth on the west side (1 Chron. 26:16). In the post-exilic settlement, as the present paragraph indicates, the four 'chief' Levitical gatekeepers were each assigned to one of the four sides of the temple area (v. 24) similar to the situation instituted by David (1 Chron. 26:13-16).[7] The

---

6. Selman, *1 Chronicles*, p. 129.

7. In Ezekiel's vision of the new temple, there are three outer gates (Ezek. 40:5-16, 20-27) and three inner gates (Ezek. 40:28-37) facing north, east and south.

military term 'valiant' (v. 26; see v. 13) is used in this context to describe their position as the 'chief' men for the job. They did need to be strong men to keep out robbers and other intruders, much like security guards or bouncers today. The Chronicler also describes these special Levites as 'gatekeepers in the thresholds' (*šō'ᵃrîm bassippîm*, v. 22; see 2 Chron. 23:4, 19).[8] The 'threshold' was the sill raised above the floor of an entrance to help prevent water from streaming through. It was found in domestic houses and palaces as well as the temple (1 Kings 14:17; Esther 2:21; 6:2; Zeph. 2:14).

Nehemiah 11:19 refers by name only to two of the Chronicler's 'four' (vv. 17, 24, 26) gatekeepers: Akkub and Talmon, although Shallum's name was included earlier among the six sons of the gatekeepers (Neh. 7:45; see also Ezra 2:42).[9] Ahiman, however, is not found elsewhere.

In order to indicate beyond doubt Shallum's position as 'head' or 'chief' porter who was stationed at the main east gate, now called the 'king's gate' (see Ezek. 8-11; 43:1-5; 44:1-3), his pedigree is traced back not only to the time of Samuel and David (v. 22) but to Korah who belonged to the Kohathite clan, the same major branch of Levi's family as Aaron the high priest (vv. 19, 31-32; see Exod. 6:18-24). Even the language in this paragraph is reminiscent of the early period. The term 'tabernacle' or 'tent' (*'ōhel*) which is applied both to the sanctuaries of the David–Solomon period and the post-exilic temple (see vv. 19,23), and the Chronicler's use of 'camp' (vv. 18-19) recall the wilderness situation. Similarly, the exact phrase 'entrance of the tent of meeting' (v. 21) that is found in Numbers 25:6 is employed here with reference to Zechariah of the Davidic period (1 Chron. 26:2,14).[10] This 'tent' is probably the one that David erected in Jerusalem to house the ark before the temple was built (1 Chron. 16:1) rather than the sanctuary at Gibeon (1 Chron. 16:39; 2 Chron. 1:2-6). The Chronicler also uses the phrase 'the camp of Yahweh' (v. 19) to refer to the temple courts (see 2 Chron. 31:2). Interestingly, the

---

8. Elsewhere the singular 'threshold' (*sap̲*) is found (e.g. 2 Kings 12:9[10]; 22:4; 23:4; 25:18; 2 Chron.34:9).

9. See also Nehemiah 12:25 where Talmon and Akkub are again mentioned and where Meshullam is probably to be identified with Sallum.

10. Selman, *1 Chronicles*, p. 129.

post-exilic temple which is called 'the house of Yahweh' is in the same breath described uniquely as 'the house of the tent' (v. 23) again emphasising the continuity of the sanctuary from the time of Moses to the present, in addition to the validity of the gatekeepers' office. During the wilderness wanderings, the Levites were instructed to pitch their tents around the tabernacle, to surround it as they marched forward and to guard it and its furnishings from intruders (Num. 2:17; 3:5-10).

Part of Samuel's service to Yahweh as a young man under Eli the priest was to open the doors of the house of Yahweh at Shiloh (1 Sam. 3:15) and knowing first-hand the importance of the task he may well have conveyed this to David at some point after he had anointed him king in that undercover ceremony (1 Sam. 16:1-13). Though Samuel was a Levite and acted as a priest and judge, he is here described as a 'seer' (1 Chron. 26:28; 29:29), a popular term that in some circles was regarded as outmoded (1 Sam. 9:9). It became synonymous with 'prophet', which was an equally ancient name. In the present context, David is mentioned first for he formally established the institution of gatekeeper (1 Chron. 23:5; 26:1-19; see also 1 Chron. 16:38). His gatekeeper, Zechariah, the son of Meshelemiah (v. 21), had responsibility for the north gate (1 Chron. 26:14) while his father, Meshelemiah or Shelemiah was stationed by lot at the important east gate.[11]

It is most probably to strengthen the position of the present gatekeepers, that Chronicles has associated them with 'Phinehas, the son of Eleazar' who was high priest toward the close of the wilderness period. The Law of Moses specified that the Levities were to be the guardians or keepers of the tabernacle and Eleazar the son of Aaron as high priest had the oversight of them (Num. 1:53; 3:32). It is his son, Phinehas, however, who is highlighted (v. 20). The comment that immediately follows – 'Yahweh was with him' – probably indicates the reason for mentioning him. God had praised him for his zeal for Yahweh and made him a promise, guaranteeing a future priestly line to make atonement for the people (Num. 25:6-13; Ps. 106:28-31).

---

11. Meshelemiah or Shelemiah may also have been called Shallum (the same root letters are found in both names).

The four gatekeepers, named earlier (v. 17), had the responsibility of guarding the entire temple day and night (v. 33) including the various rooms and treasuries (vv. 26-27; see 1 Chron. 26:15, 17, 20-22) and lived on site while relatives from the villages came for seven-day periods to support them (v. 25; see v. 16). In all, there were 212 gatekeepers (v. 22). It is stressed that these four 'valiant' gatekeepers were Levites (v. 26) probably to distinguish them from other high-ranking temple staff in pre-exilic times (2 Kings 25:18; Jer. 52:24). They were in a responsible office of 'trust' (vv. 22, 26) and their duties are summarised in verse 27 including being 'over the opening' (literally 'over the key') of the temple.[12]

> 9:28. And some of them were over the utensils of service, for by number they brought them in and by number they took them out. 29. And others of them were appointed over the utensils, and all the holy vessels, also over the fine flour and the wine and the oil and the incense and the spices. 30. And some of the sons of the priests made the spice-ointment mixture. 31. And Mattithiah, one of the Levites, who was the firstborn of Shallum the Korahite, was in the position of trust over the making of the flat cakes. 32. And some of their brothers, ones from the sons of the Kohathites, were over the rows of bread, to prepare it each Sabbath.

It was part of the gatekeepers' duty to guard and count all the temple vessels and to take charge of the offerings in kind received from the people. Some English versions translate 'furniture' for 'utensils' in verse 29 to distinguish them from the other 'holy vessels'. These utensils would have been very valuable and attractive to thieves and enemies. We read of the large quantity of gold and silver vessels taken by Nebuchadnezzar to Babylon when the temple was destroyed and brought back by the returning exiles by order of Cyrus (Ezra 1:9-11; Dan. 1:2; 5:2-3). Vessels belonging to Solomon's temple are mentioned on a number of occasions and provide one of a number of references to the Chronicler's 'continuity' theme (see 1 Chron. 28:13-17).

A distinction is clearly made within the tribe of Levi between those who served as priests in the temple to offer

---

12. The word for 'key' is used elsewhere only in Judges 3:25 and Isaiah 22:22.

sacrifices and to prepare the spices for the incense (vv. 10-13, 30), and the rest of the Levites who assisted the priests (vv. 28, 31-32; see Ezek. 44:10-16). Moses had offered the first sacrifices and prepared the initial anointing oil and spices (see Exod. 30:22-38), but it became the duty of the high priest to have general management of the sanctuary and its vessels along with overseeing the preparation of the temple lights, incense, anointing oil and grain offering (Num. 4:16). Thus, while it was forbidden for the Levites in general to prepare the holy oil and incense and to offer sacrifice, some were allowed to help in making the 'flat cakes' for the cereal offering and in the preparation of the weekly holy loaves of bread for the sanctuary table that were replaced every Sabbath (vv. 31-32). These 'rows of bread' (literally 'bread of the row'), which Tyndale, following Luther's German, translated as 'showbread' was so-called because the loaves were placed in rows on the table (see Lev. 24:6-7; 1 Chron. 23:29; 28:16; 2 Chron. 13:11; 29:18; Neh. 10:33). 2 Chronicles 4:19 uses the synonymous Hebrew phrase 'bread of the presence' (literally 'bread of the faces'; Exod. 35:13; 39:36).

Mattithiah, the eldest son of the chief gatekeeper, Shallum (v. 31; see vv. 17, 19), was responsible for the 'flat cakes' or 'bread-wafers' (*ḥaḇittîm*, a word only found here) which were most probably the ones baked on the griddle (Lev. 6:19-23) and made of 'fine flour' (v. 29). Some of the relatives ('brothers') of the Kohathites, to whom the Korahites belonged (v. 31-32; Num. 3:17, 19, 27), had the important task of preparing the 'showbread'.

> 9:33. And these were the singers, heads of the fathers belonging to the Levites, in the chambers, set free *from other work*, for they were on duty day and night. 34. These were the heads of the fathers belonging to the Levites, heads according to their generations. These dwelt in Jerusalem.

This additional comment about the singers (v. 33; see vv. 14-16) is possibly introduced to indicate that though some of the Kohathites were involved in preparing the 'showbread', the majority were singers who were exempt from such service (see 1 Chron. 6:33; 2 Chron. 20:19). Theirs was a full-time task ministering to Yahweh in song by night as well as by day (see Ps. 134:1).

Apart from 'belonging to the Levites', the summary statement in verse 34 repeats the words of 1 Chronicles 8:28. In doing so, it fulfils a dual purpose. It first provides a conclusion to the Levitical families (vv. 14-33) and indicates that those from this tribe, like the other tribes, 'dwelt in Jerusalem' (see v. 3). In addition, it prepares for a return to the genealogy of Saul that was first given in 1 Chronicles 8:29-38.

The Chronicler was keen to point out that Jerusalem was the place where they should reside, even though some Levites lived in the surrounding villages (see vv. 16, 22, 25). There is a chiasmus arrangement[13] that draws attention to this emphasis on Jerusalem: in verse 3, the Hebrew text begins, 'And in Jerusalem they dwelt' while in verse 34, the text closes with 'these dwelt in Jerusalem'.[14] Thus the introduction to Chronicles ends by encouraging representatives of the old tribes of Israel and even former foreigners to be part of the new Israel centred on the temple 'in Jerusalem'. Jerusalem was first named in the genealogy of David (1 Chron. 3:4,5), then in the genealogy of Levi with reference to Solomon's temple and the priest exiled by Nebuchadnezzar (1 Chron. 6:10, 15, 31-32[5:36, 41; 6:16-17]). In the final two chapters of the introduction, dwelling 'in Jerusalem' appears at three key points (1 Chron. 8:28; 9:3, 34). This is the Jerusalem that King David would capture and make his home and where he would bring the ark of the covenant and where he would make the necessary preparations for the temple that Solomon would build.

Application

Jerusalem is central to the Chronicler's work but only because of its associations with David and the temple. It becomes symbolic of the Israel of God from all nations gathered together with David's greater Son in the new Jerusalem where God dwells among them (Rev. 21).

The duties of the Levites in guarding the temple are a reminder of the cherubim that guarded the entrance to the

---

13. A chiasmus is a literary or rhetorical device where words or phrases are repeated in the reverse order, like a mirror image.

14. Japhet, *I & II Chronicles*, p. 218.

garden after the Fall. No intruders were allowed into God's temple. It is only on account of the righteous life and atoning death of our great high priest, Jesus the Messiah, that we sinners can enter the heavenly sanctuary as God's servants. The Levites who gave unstinted service night and morning are a reminder of the heavenly reality, where the living creatures 'do not rest day or night' in worshipping God (Rev. 4:8). It becomes an encouragement to all Christians to be faithful in the work that God gives them to do, however menial and difficult, especially in support of their local gospel churches.

Though the translation 'door-keeper' may be too specific in Psalm 84:10 for the Hebrew phrase 'standing at the entrance', it certainly includes the gatekeepers mentioned here and David encourages them and all God's people that being involved even at the entrance to God's house is far better than dwelling within 'the tents of wickedness'. It made a great impression on me, when as a child collecting up the hymnbooks after the service, my minister quoted the words of Psalm 84:10.

The concern of the Chronicler to show that post-exilic worship followed a tradition stretching back to Moses who first set out God's will for His people, draws attention to an important principle. While regulations for Christian communal worship are less prescriptive and confining than Old Testament worship, certain directives are set out in Scripture for the Church of Jesus Christ. They include Scripture reading, prayer, singing spiritual songs, preaching and teaching God's Word, administering the sacraments, disciplining the wayward, counteracting false teaching and showing a loving concern for fellow members. Those called and set apart to care for God's flock are to guard against all that is false and wrong. Such Scriptural principles are important for today's church to continue to follow. To the independent Christians of Corinth, Paul makes these appeals: 'if one is inclined to be contentious, we have no such procedure, nor do the churches of God' and 'for God is not one of confusion but of peace, as in all the churches of the saints' (1 Cor. 11:16; 14:33).

PART TWO:
The David–Solomon Kingdom
(I Chron. 9:35–2 Chron. 9:28)

With the move from genealogies and lists of names to narrative, the Chronicler continues to stress the themes that he introduced in the first nine chapters. This whole block of material, covering the history of the united monarchy under David and Solomon, is of central concern to the Chronicler as he preaches to his own post-exilic community. That united period in Israelite history, however, actually began with the divine appointment of Saul as the first king of all Israel. What is said of him provides the backdrop to the Chronicler's presentation of David and Solomon.

4

The tragic end of Saul

(9:35–10:14)

By way of introduction to David's reign, the genealogy of Saul's family is reproduced (9:35-44), followed immediately by the account of his death and that of his sons (10:1-7) and the treatment of their corpses by the Philistines and the people of Jabesh Gilead (10:8-12). The section concludes with a theological reflection unique to the Chronicler (10:13-14).

Saul's family (9:35-44)

9:35. And in Gibeon dwelt Jeiel, the father of Gibeon and his wife's name *was* Maacah: 36. And his firstborn son: Abdon, then Zur and Kish and Baal and Ner and Nadab 37. and Gedor and Ahio and Zechariah and Mikloth. 38. And Mikloth fathered Shimeam. And these also dwelt opposite their brothers in Jerusalem, with their brothers.

39. And Ner fathered Kish and Kish fathered Saul and Saul fathered Jonathan and Malchishua and Abinadab and Eshbaal. 40. And the son of Jonathan was Merib-baal and Meri-baal fathered Micah. 41. And the sons of Micah: Pithon and Melech and Tahrea. 42. And Ahaz fathered Jarah and Jarah fathered Alemeth and Azmaveth and Zimri. And Zimri fathered Moza, 43. and Moza fathered Binea and Rephaiah his son, Eleasah his son, Azel his son. 44. And Azel had six sons, and these are their names: Azrikam, Bocheru and Ishmael and Sheariah and Obadiah and Hanan; these were the sons of Azel.

The Chronicler reproduces the genealogy of Saul's family found in 1 Chronicles 8:29-40 with a few slight changes and without repeating the final two verses of that chapter (vv. 39-40). Repetition is one means of emphasising a passage's importance. Whereas in chapter 8, it concludes the genealogy of the Benjaminites and notes their places of residence, here, it is used to introduce the account of Saul's downfall in chapter 10 and to show that the first king of all Israel came from good Benjaminite stock. His genealogy is traced back four generations. The genealogy also indicates that despite his own unfaithfulness Saul's descendants were not all cut off from Israel. Only Saul's royal line was eliminated in battle (1 Chron. 10:6). Twelve generations of Saul's descendants are listed ending with Azel and his sons, living perhaps around the time of the exile. Azel's six sons were an indication of Yahweh's blessing on the family (Ps. 127:3) and provided encouragement to those after the Babylonian exile that there is hope with each new generation.

Unlike the earlier genealogy, this version gives the name of Gibeon's father as Jeiel (v. 35) and adds Ner (v. 36) and Mikloth (v. 37) to the list of his sons, all missing in the Masoretic Text of 1 Chronicles 8:29, 30, 31. Interestingly for understanding the Chronicler's way of working, while the name of Ahaz is missing here from the sons of Micah (v. 41; see 1 Chron. 8:35) it is mentioned in the next breath as the person who fathered Jarah/Jehoaddah (v. 42). Many suppose that a copyist mistakenly left it out due to haplography, but it is more likely that the Chronicler deliberately omitted it. Omissions have been made previously where we know the Chronicler was not unaware of the names. Again, not uncommon in Chronicles, names are spelled differently from the earlier list: Zechariah for Zecher (v. 37; 8:31); Shimeam for Shimeah (v. 38; 8:32); Tahrea for Tarea (v. 41; 8:35); Jarah for Jehoaddah (v. 42; 8:36); and Rephaiah for Raphah (v. 43; 8:37). Unlike the earlier list, where Merib-baal's name is repeated exactly, in this passage the Hebrew drops the first *beth* (*b*) when repeating the name to read Meri-baal (v. 40; see 1 Chron. 8:34). All these slight differences between the two lists are helpful in showing the Chronicler's faithfulness to his sources and how one passage is useful in interpreting another. This is better than supposing copyist errors, which even Matthew Henry too readily accepts with regard to this whole paragraph.

Application

Though Saul proved unfaithful and was punished, this did not mean the extermination of his entire family. God was merciful and blessed his descendants, especially Azel. Though God's punishments can last some three or four generations toward those who hate Him, His enduring love is shown toward thousands of generations of those who love Him (Exod. 20:5-6). It is a reminder of God's amazing grace and patience toward His people.

The death of Saul and his sons (10:1-7)

There are twenty-three chapters in 1 Samuel devoted to the reign of Saul (1 Sam. 9–31) and the Chronicler assumes we are familiar with them. Having provided an appropriate introduction with his family tree (1 Chron. 9:35-44), he has purposefully chosen to include only what is found in the final chapter of 1 Samuel relating to Saul's death. There are a few stylistic differences between the two accounts with more significant changes in verses 6 and 7.

> 10:1. Now the Philistines fought against Israel and each one of Israel fled from before the Philistines, and fell slain on Mount Gilboa. 2. And the Philistines pursued closely after Saul and after his sons; and the Philistines killed Jonathan and Abinadab and Malchi-shua, Saul's sons. 3. And the battle was heavy against Saul and the archers with the bow found him, and he was wounded by the archers. 4. Then Saul said to his armour-bearer, 'Draw your sword, and thrust me through with it lest these uncircumcised come and ridicule me.' But his armour-bearer was not willing for he was very afraid. Then Saul took the sword and fell on it. 5. And when his armour-bearer saw that Saul was dead, he too fell on the sword, and died. 6. So Saul died and his three sons, and all his house together died. 7. And when everyone of Israel who was in the valley saw that they had fled, and that Saul and his sons were dead, then they abandoned their cities and fled, and the Philistines came and dwelt in them.

The narrative moves quickly from the scattering of Saul's army to the death of his sons and climaxes with Saul's own sad end.

It is the king's death that is the main focus (vv. 5-6) with the flight of the people of Israel, both soldiers and inhabitants, mentioned in verses 1 and 7.

The Philistines (see 1 Chron. 1:12) had been Israel's great enemy from the time of Samson (Judg. 10:7; 13:1). They were defeated under Samuel (1 Sam. 7:13) and under Saul's leadership (1 Sam. 14:31), but at Mount Gilboa they were victorious. Taking the mountain that overlooked the Jezreel valley meant the Philistines were able to overrun the cities below. From routing the Israelite army, the Philistines were determined to put an end to Saul and his family. King Saul was, after all, the one divinely chosen to defeat them (see 1 Sam. 9:16; 13-14). On this occasion, they killed three of his sons and, as happened later with Ahab by the Aramaeans (2 Chron. 18:30,33), an arrow badly wounded the king, this despite the Benjaminites' own noted ability at shooting arrows (1 Chron. 12:2). The weapons in which they trusted and boasted are used to their own destruction.

Contrary to the false report by the Amalekite (see 2 Sam. 1:6-10) concerning Saul's death, of which the Chronicler makes no mention, the narrative presents what actually happened. Saul's armour-bearer, himself a soldier, remained faithful to the end. His fear would seem to be a godly one, not wishing to slay the Lord's anointed. This was David's reason for not killing Saul when he had the opportunity and interestingly, David himself had first entered Saul's service as his armour-bearer (1 Sam. 16:21; 24:6; 26:11). Saul's worry about the 'uncircumcised' Philistines mocking him was a real one, as we see in Samson's case (Judg. 16:25). The refusal of the trusted armour-bearer to kill Saul led to his own suicide when he saw that the king had killed himself. In death, as in life, Saul remained self-centred and an ungodly example to others. Suicides or assisted suicides in the Bible are rare (Abimelech in Judges 9:54; Ahithophel in 2 Samuel 17:23; Zimri in 1 Kings 16:18 and Judas in Matthew 27:5) and betray a desperation to escape earthly repercussions.

The Chronicler's concern is to stress the death of Saul and his whole dynastic house and that, with Saul's death, his royal line died with him. The Hebrew of verse six is framed by the verb for 'died' (wayyāmot...mētû). For the Chronicler,

the fact that Eshbaal survived to rule for a short period
(2 Sam. 2:8-4:12) or that descendants of Saul's son Jonathan
remained (1 Chron. 9:39-40) was of no consequence. As far as
Israelite kingship was concerned, Saul's line was at an end.
As for the reference to the Philistine occupation of the 'valley'
(v. 7), this may be shorthand for the whole lowland area from
Esdraelon to the Jordan (see 1 Sam. 31:7).

The treatment of the corpses (10:8-12)

10:8. And it happened on the following day, when the Philistines
came to strip the slain, that they found Saul and his sons fallen
on mount Gilboa. 9. So they stripped him and took his head and
his armour and sent word throughout the surrounding land of
the Philistines to tell good news to their idols and to the people.
10. Then they put his armour in the temple of their gods, and
fastened his skull in the temple of Dagon. 11. And all Jabesh
Gilead heard what the Philistines had done to Saul, 12. so all
the valiant men arose and took the body of Saul, and the bodies
of his sons, and brought them to Jabesh, and buried their bones
under the terebinth in Jabesh, and fasted seven days.

The paragraph opens and closes with a time reference: 'the
following day' (v. 8) and 'seven days' (v. 12). Two contrasting
scenes are presented, the one focusing on the Philistines and
their desecration of Saul's corpse and the other on the noble
action of the people of Jabesh Gilead who risked their lives
to retrieve the royal bodies and give them a decent burial.

Saul's suicide to avoid disgrace and ridicule did not
prevent the enemy from using his remains to humiliate him
and to provide tangible evidence of their astounding victory.
Unlike Yahweh, heathen gods needed to be told the outcome
of the battle by their worshippers! The verb 'bring good news'
(v. 9) is used of heralding God's salvation (Isa. 40:9; 52:7) and
is so used in its only other occurrence by the Chronicler in
1 Chronicles 16:23. The plural 'gods' (v. 10) is used in place of
the plural 'Ashtoreth' found in Samuel (1 Sam. 31:10). Ashtoreth
or Astarte in Greek script was a Canaanite mother goddess
of fertility and war. Often, it would seem in the Hebrew
Bible, plural forms of both Baal and Ashtoreth stand for gods
and goddesses in general (Judg. 2:13; 10:6; 1 Sam. 7:3-4; 12:10;
1 Kings 11:5; 2 Kings 23:13). Interestingly, however, we find

the Chronicler replacing the singular 'Asherah' by 'idol' in
2 Chronicles 33:7 (see 2 Kings 21:7).

As Goliath's sword which had been taken by David was
eventually placed in the sanctuary at Nob (1 Sam. 17:54; 21:9),
so Saul's armour was placed in a Philistine pagan sanctuary.
His skull, on the other hand, was fastened in one of Dagon's
temples (see Judg. 16:23; 1 Sam. 5:2-5), while the rest of his
body, as the Samuel account indicates, was pinned to the
wall of Bethshan (1 Sam. 31:10). The Chronicler probably
wished readers to see the contrast between the present
situation and what happened to Dagon's head when the
ark of the covenant was placed in his temple (1 Sam. 5:4). It
also contrasts sharply with the flight of the Philistines after
David's victory over Goliath and the removal of his head to
Jerusalem (1 Sam. 17:51-54).

At the beginning of his reign, Saul had proved his position
as king by rescuing the people of Jabesh Gilead from the
Ammonites (1 Sam. 11:1-11). It is understandable that they
should be the ones to express loyalty toward their king.
The Chronicler assumes the background knowledge and
provides a shortened version of their brave and pious activity
(see 1 Sam. 31:11-13). They took the corpses of Saul and his
sons and buried their bones, the Chronicler preferring not
to mention the burning of their bodies. The burning is
presumed when 'body' (12a) is replaced by 'bones' (12b). Why
they were burnt is unknown. Perhaps it was a local custom.
That their bones were not burnt to dust is interesting in the
light of Moab's transgression in burning to lime the bones
of the king of Edom (Amos 2:1). In Israel, death by fire was
restricted to particularly repugnant sexual acts (Gen. 38:24;
Lev. 20:14; 21:9). Achan's sin also deserved this punishment
(Josh. 7:15, 25). Leaving the dead bodies of executed criminals
in the open overnight was not allowed under the Mosaic Law
(Deut. 21:22-23). However bad the character, every person's
bodily remains were to be treated with dignity and decency.
This was based on the principle that every human being was
created in the image of God (Gen. 1:27; 9:6). The seven-day
fast may be in conjunction with a period of mourning (see
2 Sam. 12:17-19) as well as with the period of uncleanness
arising out of touching dead bodies (Num. 19:11).

The theological reflection (10:13-14)

10:13. Thus Saul died because of his unfaithfulness, acting unfaithfully against Yahweh, concerning the word of Yahweh, which he did not keep, and also for consulting a medium, to seek *guidance*. 14. And he did not seek Yahweh so he killed him and turned the kingdom over to David the son of Jesse.

In the Samuel account, the narrative ends with the seven-day fast by the people of Jabesh Gilead with no concluding statement such as we find here. It is meant to be read in the context of what was prophesied earlier (1 Sam. 28:16-19). Because the Chronicler has not provided this background, he adds his own evaluation of the tragic end of Saul but it clearly incorporates the substance of Samuel's words that came when Saul consulted the medium of Endor. Not only does the indictment include a reference to the medium but it mentions Saul's disobedience to God's word (see 2 Chron. 34:21). Again, Samuel's prophecy of the kingdom being torn out of Saul's hand and given to David (1 Sam. 28:17) is echoed in the words 'turned the kingdom over to David'.

Saul's kingship is assessed using two of the Chronicler's favourite terms: 'unfaithfulness' or 'to act unfaithfully' (see for example 1 Chron. 2:7; 5:25; 2 Chron. 36:14) and 'seek'/'not seek' (for example 1 Chron. 16:11; 28:9; 2 Chron. 12:14; 34:3). The infidelity that led to Saul's death and the loss of his kingship was the sin that led to the exile in Babylon (1 Chron. 9:1). Chronicles never uses the term for the David–Solomon period but introduces it once more in connection with events in Rehoboam's reign (2 Chron. 12:2). Saul's unfaithfulness was seen in his disobedience to Yahweh's word (v. 13; 2 Chron. 34:21; see 1 Sam. 13:13-14; 15:22-24) and in the incident with the medium.

It is in the context of consulting a medium that a further accusation is levelled against Saul: 'He did not seek Yahweh' (v. 14). Chronicles proclaims that seeking Yahweh is more than looking for a specific word from God; it is a life of devotion to Him and this was the missing element in Saul's life and why he resorted to a forbidden means of guidance (Lev. 20:6). The verb 'to seek', added at the end of verse 13, draws out the contrast between seeking a medium and seeking

Yahweh. The Samuel text records that when Saul enquired of
Yahweh, He did not answer Him 'by dreams or by Urim or by
prophets' (1 Sam. 28:6). His life as a king indicated his basic
unfaithfulness which, for the Chronicler, was synonymous
with not seeking Yahweh. If his heart was right with God,
he would not have even contemplated resorting to a medium
but would have continued seeking God. One of the great
messages of this book, as is clearly indicated later to king
Asa, is that 'Yahweh is with you while you are with him. If
you seek him, he will be found by you, but if you forsake him,
he will forsake you' (2 Chron. 15:2).

The stark statement 'so he killed him' only highlights the
prophecy of Samuel that the battle of Gilboa would end with
the death of the king and his sons (1 Sam. 28:19). Saul's own
suicide is the secondary cause of their deaths, but primarily,
this is a judgment by God. Here, as elsewhere, the Chronicler
is keen to stress, especially in his treatment of the individual
kings, the close connection between disobedience and divine
punishment yet without it being thought of in mechanical
and simplistic terms.

Chronicles makes clear that it was Saul's rejection of
Yahweh's word that resulted in his kingship being given to
David. Saul could have received an enduring dynasty but
was rejected for being disloyal to God. All this together with
the statement about the kingdom being transferred to David
echoes the Samuel text (1 Sam. 13:13-14; 15:26-28) but, as it will
become more evident later, the Chronicler is at great pains to
show that kingship in Israel is equated with God's rule. It is
fundamentally Yahweh's kingdom and the Israelite king sits
on Yahweh's throne (1 Chron. 28:5; 29:23). This 'turning over'
or 'bringing round' (v. 14) of the kingdom to David was as
crucially important as the 'turn' that led to the great cleavage
under Rehoboam. Both events were brought about by God
(see 2 Chron. 10:15).

Application

It is interesting that the Chronicler begins the narrative part
of his work with an account of war and death, of an enemy
victorious and the people of God and their king defeated. It

was a state of affairs similar to the events surrounding the Babylonian exile and its aftermath. How appropriate to the circumstances in which the Jews who first read these words found themselves. Like Israel after Saul's death, they were without a king and they were under foreign domination! Hope lay with what God would do next through the Davidic king.

The sovereignty of God is very evident in the passage. God's purposes are fulfilled through divine providence in the judgment on Saul and the appointment of David as king. It is a reminder of Peter's words concerning the crucifixion. Lawless human hands put Jesus to death but it was in the pre-ordained plan of God that he should suffer (Acts 2:23). In the same way, Judas was responsible for Jesus' betrayal but it was determined by God (Luke 22:22).

The Chronicler had started his prophetic history with Adam. Saul was, like the first man, appointed to rule but he disobeyed God's word and was punished. By God's grace another was appointed to rule in Saul's place. David becomes a type of the last Adam (Gen. 3:15) to gain victory over the snake and his offspring but it would involve an exile far worse than anything Israel experienced in her history.

5

David's reign
(11:1–29:30)

Yahweh's rule through his chosen servant David occupies the remainder of 1 Chronicles. The significant moments are the establishment of Jerusalem as the capital city, the unity of Israel, international recognition, the transfer of the ark of God to Jerusalem, God's promises to David, enemies defeated and peace won, the temple site chosen and acquired, preparations made for the building and organisation of the temple and the seamless transfer of rule to David's son Solomon.

David's rise to power (11:1–12:40[41])
The section commences with David made king at Hebron (11:1-3) and closes with the celebrations at Hebron (12:38-40[39-41]). A chiastic structure is discernible with David at Hebron the main focus in 11:1-47 and 12:23-40[24-41]. In between, the narrative first takes us back in time to David at Ziklag in 12:1-7 and 12:20-22 and then, at the centre, there is a reminder of David in the wilderness stronghold in 12:8-15 and 12:16-18.[1] Much of the material is also found in 2 Samuel, but in Chronicles it is used to emphasise the unity of all Israel in the appointment of David as king (11:1-3; 12:38-40), the fulfilment of Yahweh's word (11:3; 11:10; 12:23), the taking of Jerusalem as David's first major act as king (11:4-9) and David's strong military support (11:10-12:40[41]).

---

1. Williamson, *1 and 2 Chronicles*, pp. 96-97, 105.

The section divides into six parts: David is anointed king of all Israel (11:1-3); David conquers Jerusalem (11:4-9); David's valiant warriors (11:10-47); David's early tribal support (12:1-22[23]); David's army at Hebron (12:23-37[24-38]); and celebrations at Hebron (12:38-40).

King of all Israel (11:1-3)

> 11:1. Then all Israel gathered together to David to Hebron, saying, 'We really are your bone and your flesh. 2. Also, in time past, even when Saul was king, you brought out and brought in Israel and Yahweh your God said to you, "You will shepherd my people Israel and you will be prince over my people Israel".' 3. So all the elders of Israel came to the king to Hebron and David made a covenant with them in Hebron before Yahweh, and they anointed David king over Israel according to the word of Yahweh by the hand of Samuel.

This paragraph closely follows 2 Samuel 5:1-3 but, in the light of the Chronicler's statement at the end of chapter 10, the details of the seven-year, six-month reign in Hebron over Judah (see 1 Chron. 3:4) as well as Ishbosheth's attempt to rule in the north (2 Samuel 2–4) are not mentioned as those events did not serve his purpose, although he will have expected them to be known. The focus is on the final outcome that had been determined by God. Some important matters are considered.

Firstly, in preaching his overall message to the post-exilic community, he calls attention not to the divisions but to the unity of Israel (v. 1). Though Judah had anointed David king over them at Hebron seven years earlier, Chronicles indicates that all the tribes and elders came to David to anoint him king over the whole nation of Israel. At Hebron they 'gathered together' (*qāhal*) for this first of many significant assemblies highlighted by the Chronicler (1 Chron. 13:2; 2 Chron. 15:9-10; 20:4; etc.). The unity is also cemented by means of a covenant initiated by David with the people in a religious ceremony ('before Yahweh,' v. 3; see 2 Chron. 23:1-3). There was, under David, to be no despotic rule in Israel. This covenant would have set out the terms of kingship and would have included the people's acceptance (see 2 Chron. 10; 23:16). The anointing by the elders was a public recognition that David was king over Israel and that they accepted the terms of the covenant he had made with them. The Samuel text had made mention of two other occasions when David was anointed (1 Sam. 16:13; 2 Sam. 2:4), the first accompanied by God's Spirit giving him a leadership charisma. It did not suit the Chronicler's purpose to include such information and takes it for granted his readers are familiar with the previous anointings. He nevertheless gives the important reminder that the people's commitment to David was according to the divine plan (v. 3b). As for the endowment of God's Spirit, in Chronicles this is reserved for those uttering a prophetic word (see 1 Chron. 12:18).

Secondly, not only Judah or the northern tribes but 'all Israel', north and south, are part of David's family. There is a blood relationship ('your bone and your flesh', v. 1; Gen. 29:14; 2 Sam. 19:12-13). They are brothers together and belong to Israel their father (see Deut. 17:15).

Thirdly, David's previous exploits are remembered. The phrase 'in time past' translates a Hebrew idiom that literally reads 'also yesterday also three days ago' (v. 2; see Exod. 4:10). A king was needed to fight battles against enemies (1 Sam. 8:20) and David had fulfilled that role even when Saul was king. It suggests that the people had already concluded that David was destined to be the nation's leader.

Fourthly, David's kingship over all Israel was in fulfilment of God's word. The people themselves speak of an otherwise unknown divine oracle (v. 2b) that is similar to Nathan's words to David (2 Sam. 7:7-8; 1 Chron. 17:6-7). The Chronicler also adds his own summary by referring to a prophecy given through Samuel (v. 3). Again, no specific oracle is identified but Yahweh's word to Saul that he had given the kingdom to a neighbour, someone better than Saul (1 Sam. 15:28), would spring to mind, as well as the clandestine anointing of David the shepherd lad by Samuel (1 Sam. 16:1-13).

Finally, Israel belongs to God (v. 2b, where, compared with 2 Samuel 5:2, a second 'my people Israel' is added for emphasis) and David is God's appointed ruler over them. It is for the sake of Israel that David has been chosen. From shepherding sheep (1 Sam. 16:11; 17:15, 34-35), David is to 'shepherd' Yahweh's people (Ps. 78:71; 1 Chron. 17:7). This Ancient Near Eastern pastoral image of kingship is used in the Bible to describe God's caring rule over His people (Ps. 80:1) and David, like the subsequent rulers in Israel, was seen as shepherding the people on God's behalf (Jer. 23:1-4; Ezek. 34:1-10). Prior to the institution of the monarchy in Israel, the judges were commanded to shepherd God's people (1 Chron. 17:6/2 Sam. 7:7). The other term 'prince' or 'leader' was sometimes used for a military leader and, in the case of Saul and David, as a royal title before they actually began to reign (1 Sam. 9:16; 10:1; 13:14; 25:30; 1 Chron. 17:7/2 Samuel 7:8). During Saul's kingship, David was already the ruler designate or 'crown prince'. The Chronicler's use of the term 'king' in verse 3 is a reminder that Judah had already anointed David king at Hebron and that God Himself had turned the kingdom over to David on the death of Saul (1 Chron. 10:14).

Application

This presentation of David would have been an encouragement to the post-exilic community that God's purposes for His people through a Davidic monarch would eventually be realised. David can again be seen as a type of the Messiah (Luke 1:32-33). Jesus, God's anointed prince, is one with His people. Like us he is a flesh and blood person, made like His brothers and is not ashamed to call us brothers (Heb. 2:9-17). He is our shepherd king who fought the greatest battle of all as He laid down His life for His sheep. They are given to Jesus by the Father and He unites all His people into one flock under His leadership (John 10:14-16, 27-30). This is all in fulfilment of God's word through His prophet (Ezek. 34:23-24; 37:22).

Conquest of Jerusalem (11:4-9)

11:4. And David and all Israel went to Jerusalem, that is Jebus, and the Jebusites, the inhabitants of the land, were there. 5. And the inhabitants of Jebus said to David, 'You shall not come here,' but David captured the stronghold of Zion, which is the city of David. 6. Now David said, 'Anyone who smites a Jebusite first will be chief and commander.' And Joab the son of Zeruiah went up first and became a head. 7. Then David dwelt in the stronghold; therefore they called it the city of David. 8. And he built the city around about, from the Millo and up to all the area around, while Joab revived the rest of the city. 9. Then David continued becoming greater, for Yahweh of hosts was with him.

Like 2 Samuel 5:6-10, the account quickly moves to the capture of Jerusalem but does so in a much simpler way and introduces Joab and his part in the conquest. Again, the picture presented is of a united Israel under David's leadership with a neutral city established as a royal city and the nation's capital.

Instead of 'all his men' (2 Sam. 5:6), Chronicles indicates that representatives from 'all Israel' (v. 4; see 1 Chron. 11:1) were involved in securing this city. Jerusalem was an ancient city-state which Abraham knew as Salem when he met Melchizedek (Gen. 14:18). During the Israelite conquest of Canaan, its king had been executed and the tribe of Judah had captured it. However, it was within Benjaminite territory, and they were unable to dislodge the Jebusites who lived there (Josh. 10:1-5; 12:7, 10; 15:63; Judg. 1:8, 21) so that by the time of David the Jebusite inhabitants had become over-confident within their walled city on top of the hill of Zion (v. 5; 2 Sam. 5:6). The name 'Jebus' would appear to be a local name for the city to associate it with its Canaanite inhabitants (see Josh. 15:8; 18:28; 1 Chron. 1:13-14).

In the present context, the 'fortress' or 'stronghold of Zion' referred to the south-east corner of the old city overlooking the Kidron valley. After its capture, David made it his place of residence which is why it was called 'the city of David'. It was not unusual for cities to be named after persons just as the people who originally built Babylon wished to make a name for themselves (Gen. 4:17; 11:4). The Assyrian king Sargon called his city by his own name.[2]

Joab was one of the sons of David's sister Zeruiah (1 Chron. 2:16). Unlike the text of 2 Samuel 2–3, none of his exploits have been mentioned up to this point by the Chronicler, but now he adds some significant details about Joab not found elsewhere. It probably explains why Joab continued to be in David's service after he killed Abner (2 Sam. 3:26-27). David never forgot Joab's crime and expected God to punish him (2 Sam. 3:39; 1 Kings 2:5-6; 28-34). Perhaps David, believing that Joab would accept the challenge to be first to kill a Jebusite, considered that God would providentially use the occasion to

---

2. P. K. McCarter, 2 Samuel, Anchor Bible 9 (New York: Doubleday, 1984), pp. 140-1.

bring about his death (see 2 Sam. 11:14-25 for David's scheming mind). But Joab lived and David kept his word and this may well explain why he became 'head' and 'commander' (see 2 Sam. 8:16/1 Chron. 18:15; 2 Sam. 11:1/1 Chron. 20:1; etc.).

Having taken the city, David set about making it the capital of his kingdom. The 'Millo' (literally 'filling', v. 8; see Judg. 9:6,20; 2 Chron. 32:5) was perhaps the terraced structure in the old city built by the Jebusites to strengthen the eastern slope that needed constant repair as the archaeological evidence would suggest.[3] David improved the outward defences all round while Joab probably 'revived' in the sense of restored or repaired the rest of the city (see Neh. 4:2[3:34]). It is unlikely that the verb 'revive' or 'preserve alive' means that Joab kept alive the remainder of the city's population after his initial attack in verse 6.[4] Again, the Chronicler's additions to what is reported in the Samuel text would indicate that he had the concerns of the post-exilic community in mind. Their own rebuilding efforts after the destruction of Jerusalem, though small, should not lead them to despair but, in the light of that initial work under David, they should be encouraged to press on and look to the full realisation of God's purposes.

Verse 9 is a reminder that David's early successes in which his reputation increased greatly[5] were due neither to his own abilities or those of his 'commander' but to Yahweh's presence with him. The divine title 'Yahweh of Hosts', used sparingly by the Chronicler in contrast to the post-exilic prophets Haggai, Zechariah and Malachi,[6] indicates God's authority and power and, with its military overtones, is appropriate before listing David's mighty men. While 'hosts' can refer to the stars (Deut. 4:19; Isa. 40:26), Israel's armies (Exod. 6:26) or to angelic beings (Josh. 5:14-15; Ps. 103:21), the latter are probably in mind here. Yahweh is the God of the heavenly hosts.

3. K. M. Kenyon, *Digging up Jerusalem* (London: Ernest Benn Ltd., 1974).

4. See Williamson, *1 and 2 Chronicles*, p. 100.

5. The phrase uses the waw consecutive imperfect and infinitive absolute of the verb 'to go' plus the adjective 'great' to indicate advance or progress.

6. Japhet, *I and II Chronicles*, p. 242.

Application

For the first readers of Chronicles there was no king reigning over God's people in Jerusalem, but the prophetic compiler uses this historical event to encourage his people to look in expectation of a glorious future. David's capture of the stronghold of Zion, making it the place where he lived and reigned over God's people, provides the symbolism for the truth concerning David's descendant, of whom Yahweh could say, 'I have set my king on my holy hill of Zion' (Ps. 2:6). In John's vision we see Jesus, the Lamb of God, standing on Mount Zion with His elect people (Rev. 14:1-5).[7]

David's valiant warriors (11:10-47)

In 2 Samuel 23:8-39, the list of heroes forms part of the conclusion to David's reign whereas for the Chronicler it is an important part of his introduction to David's life. Comparing this roll of honour with the Samuel text there are numerous differences, notably the Chronicler's introduction and the list of sixteen names extending beyond that of Uriah. Following the preamble (v. 10), the list can be divided into four parts: two named heroes (vv. 11-14), the anonymous three (vv. 15-19), two named heroes (vv. 20-25), and a list of elite warriors (vv. 26-47). Twelve of those mentioned in verses 11-31 reappear in a later list of commanders (1 Chron. 27:2-15).

> 11:10. Now these are the heads of David's warriors, who strengthened themselves with him in his kingdom, with all Israel, to make him king, according to the word of Yahweh concerning Israel.

With these opening words, unique to the Chronicler, attention is drawn to the prophetic historian's own specific themes: the unity of Israel in supporting David's kingship ('all Israel'; see vv. 1, 4) and the emphasis on God's purposes being fulfilled (see 1 Chron. 10:14; 11:3; 12:23). The following list indicates that these warriors did not act in isolation; they worked on behalf of and together 'with all Israel' and for the good of Israel and thus fulfilled the divine plan. The verb 'to

---

7. See Philip H. Eveson, *Psalms Vol. 1*, Welwyn Commentary Series (Darlington: EP Books 2014), pp. 38-39.

strengthen oneself'[8] is one of the Chronicler's favourite terms
(1 Chron. 19:13; 2 Chron. 1:1; 12:13; 13:7, 20; etc.). It is used here
to show that the kingdom under David had strong support,
witnessed by the warriors who came from the various parts
of Israel and included foreigners. It is a summary statement
that applies not only to that initial moment when David was
made king over all Israel at Hebron but also to events both
before and after the coronation, events that helped to make
him the king of Yahweh's choosing for the benefit of His
people (see 1 Chron. 14:2).

> 11:11. And these are the number of the warriors whom David
> had: Jashobeam, the son of a Hachmonite, the head of the
> officers; he brandished his spear against three hundred killing
> *them* at one stroke. 12. And after him was Eleazar the son of
> Dodo, the Ahohite, who *was* among the three warriors. 13. He
> was with David at Pas-dammim when the Philistines were
> gathered there for battle. Now a portion of the field was full
> of barley and the people fled from the Philistines. 14. But
> they stationed themselves in the middle of the portion and
> defended it, and smote the Philistines; and Yahweh delivered
> by a great deliverance.

Instead of 'names', as might be expected (v. 11; 2 Sam. 23:8),
the term 'number' is found.[9] It may have been used to draw
attention to the additions to the Samuel list. Comparing
the names with the parallel list in Samuel has led some to
make wild suggestions of copying errors by the Chronicler.
However, many of the differences may be due to variations
in spelling and local pronunciation while other discrepancies
may be due to a person having a second name or to additional
material in the Chronicler's possession. There are also
difficulties with the Samuel text. Where problems cannot at
present be ironed out, it would be wise not to speculate but
to wait until further light is shed on the differences.

The numbers 'thirty' and 'three' occur often in this section
and it is not entirely clear to which group they are referring.
It becomes more complicated on account of textual problems
relating to these numbers. The numbers three and thirty may

---

8. The verbal form is the *hithpael* or T stem of *ḥzq*.
9. Johnstone, *1 and 2 Chronicles*, Vol. 1, p. 152.

be referring to military ranks and therefore the names need not add up to the precise figures. If the text is referring to actual numbers, thirty men are distinguished for their valour, three achieved exceptional honours while three more were also pre-eminent but they did not attain the distinction of the first three.

Many scholars assume that a piece about Shammah has been omitted due to haplography (see 2 Sam. 23:9-11). It is more likely, however, that the Chronicler has purposefully headed his list of worthies with just two named heroes rather than the three in the Samuel text. This balances the two named heroes in verses 20-25. The reference to the three heroes is retained in verse 12. Jashobeam, the son of a Hachmonite, probably came from an unknown place called Hachmon and had a father called Zabdiel (1 Chron. 27:2; see 27:32 for another Hachmonite). He was 'head' of the military 'officers'[10] and distinguished himself by slaying, on one occasion, three hundred belonging to an unnamed enemy. The Samuel text reads 'eight hundred' but as Firth suggests this might have happened 'through troop deployment rather than single combat, but as commander the credit would go to him'.[11]

Another of the three pre-eminent 'mighty ones' was Eleazar whose father is named. He probably came from a place called Ahoah.[12] There was however an Ahoah who was a descendant of Benjamin (1 Chron. 8:4). An example of Eleazar's heroic exploits pertains to an incident when David was employed by Saul. Pas-dammim is not mentioned in the Samuel text but it is probably the same place as Ephes-dammim where David had, on a previous occasion, met Goliath (1 Sam. 17:1). The account is similar to what is said of Shammah, only the victory over the Philistines took place in a barley rather than a lentil plot. While great courage and dogged determination are acknowledged, in the final analysis it was Yahweh who brought victory.

11:15. Now three of the thirty heads went down to the rock to David, to the cave of Adullam, and the camp of the Philistines

---

10. This is the *Qere* reading: *šālîsîm*; 'thirty' is the *Kethibh* and preferred reading supported by the LXX: *šᵉlôsîm*. If the *Kethibh* reading is followed then Jashobeam was head of the 'thirty' elite men.

11. See David G. Frith, *1 & 2 Samuel*, Apollos Old Testament Commentary (Nottingham: Inter-Varsity Press, 2009) p. 534.

12. See Klein, *1 Chronicles*, pp. 303-04.

settled in the valley of Rephaim. 16. And David was then in the stronghold, and the garrison of the Philistines was then in Bethlehem. 17. And David had a longing and said, 'Oh that someone would give me water to drink from the well of Bethlehem which is at the gate!' 18. So the three broke through the camp of the Philistines and drew water from the well of Bethlehem which is at the gate and lifted *it* up and brought *it* to David; but David would not drink it but poured it out to Yahweh. 19. And he said, 'Far be it to me from my God to do this. Shall I drink the blood of these men at the risk of their lives. For at the risk of their lives they brought it.' So he would not drink it. These things the three mighty did.

There are no textual uncertainties over the term 'thirty' in this paragraph. It concerns the bravery and commitment of three unnamed warriors from this elite group of soldiers listed in verses 26-40. The Philistines were again the enemy and the incident probably took place when David was in hiding from Saul in the cave of Adullam, at the stronghold in the wilderness hills between Gath and Bethlehem. It is however possible that the event took place early in David's reign (see 2 Sam. 5:17-25). David's craving for water from the well at Bethlehem's gate, his home town, symbolised a longing for free access to home and a return to normality.[13] It is unlikely that he was really expecting to have his thirst quenched in this way when he was about thirteen miles (21 kilometres) from Bethlehem with an enemy barring the way. As well as proving their heroism (v. 19), the reckless action of the three also demonstrated their devotion to David. The whole account has the effect of exalting David's own standing as a respected leader among his people.

David's refusal to drink the water was not a sign of ingratitude but recognition of their sacrificial action and his symbolic gesture was an act of worship 'to Yahweh'. The water represented the men's life blood. For David to drink the water would be like drinking the men's blood. The phrase 'at the risk of their lives' translates the Hebrew words 'with their souls'. The background to this thinking is the Mosaic law where the Israelites were forbidden to eat the blood of a slaughtered animal. The blood was treated with respect

13. Joyce Baldwin, *1 and 2 Samuel*, Tyndale Old Testament Commentaries (Leicester: Inter-Varsity Press, 1988), p. 293; Frith, *1 & 2 Samuel*, p. 535.

for it symbolised the God-given life of the animal and was to be poured out on the ground (Lev. 17:10-14; Deut. 12:16).[14] This action had no atoning significance and did not hold the same meaning as the pouring out of water before Yahweh in connection with the people's penitence (1 Sam. 7:6).

> 11:20. Now Abshai, the brother of Joab, he was head of the three; he brandished his spear against three hundred killing *them*, and he had a name among the three. 21. Of the three, he was more honoured among the two and he became their commander, but he did not attain to the three.
>
> 11:22. Benaiah the son of Jehoiada, the son of a valiant man from Kabzeel, doing great deeds, killed two of the powerful leaders of Moab. He also went down inside a pit and killed a lion on the day of the snow. 23. And he killed the Egyptian, a sizeable man, five cubits tall. Now in the Egyptian's hand *was* a spear like a weaver's beam, but he went down to him with a staff and snatched the spear from the Egyptian's hand and killed him with his spear. 24. These things Benaiah the son of Jehoiada did, and he had a name among the three valiant ones. 25. Among the thirty, he was indeed honoured but he did not attain to the three, yet David set him over his bodyguard.

These two named heroes, Abishai and Benaiah, together with their deeds, balance the two earlier heroes, Jashobeam and Eleazar (vv. 11-13). It would appear that they belonged to a second group of three who also distinguished themselves above the thirty, yet Benaiah fell short of a place among the three mentioned in verses 15-19 (vv. 24-25). David's nephew, Abshai (1 Chron. 2:16; 18:12; 19:11, 15 and spelt 'Abishai in the Samuel text), is identified as 'the brother of Joab' (1 Chron. 2:16) and commander of this second trio of heroes. The Chronicler omits the further identification found in the Samuel text ('son of Zeruiah,' 2 Sam. 23:18) having already referred to this detail earlier in the chapter (1 Chron. 11:6). Abishai had accompanied David on dangerous missions (1 Sam. 26:6-12; 2 Sam. 21:15-17) but his claim to fame was similar to the exploits of Jashobeam (v. 11).[15] Verse 21 is difficult as the literal translation indicates,

---

14. See Eveson, *The Beauty of Holiness*, pp. 226-28.

15. Some English versions read 'thirty' instead of 'three' following the evidence of the Syriac Peshitta, arguing that 'three' would seem to contradict verses 21-25. My translation of verse 20 also accepts the Qere which reads the preposition with

but it may be stating that of this second famous trio, Abshai, one of the two named heroes, outshone Benaiah and was the commander of the three. There is no justification, other than the Syriac, for emending the Hebrew text to read 'of the thirty' instead of 'of the three' (see 2 Sam. 23:19) or omitting 'among the two'.[16]

Benaiah, another valiant man, is given much space with three of his courageous deeds mentioned and concluding with his prominent position in charge of David's bodyguard (v. 25; see 2 Sam. 23:20-23), a position that David himself had held when Saul was king (1 Sam. 22:14). The bodyguard probably consisted of the Cherethites and Pelethites, a band of mercenary soldiers captained by Benaiah, who continued loyal to David when Absalom and Sheba rebelled against the king (1 Chron. 18:17; 2 Sam. 18; 20:7, 23). It is also recorded that he was captain of the third division of the army (1 Chron. 27:5-6). Later, Solomon ordered him to execute Joab for his disloyalty and appointed him commander in chief of the army in Joab's place (1 Kings 1–2). Benaiah originated from Kabzeel, a town in the south of Judah (Josh. 15:21; Neh. 11:25).

In the course of his many courageous actions, Benaiah killed two powerful Moabites. This may well have taken place when David invaded Moab (2 Sam. 8:2). The Hebrew for 'powerful leaders' is literally 'lion of god' ('*ʰrî'ēl*) which could be read as a proper name 'Ariel' (Ezra 8:16; see Isa. 29:1-2), but in this context, however, this seems improbable. The term 'god' probably expresses the superlative (see 'mountains of God' for 'mighty mountains' in Psalm 36:6[7]) with 'lion' used metaphorically to indicate two powerful military men of Moab. The 'lion' ('*ʰrî*) imagery in the word 'ariel' leads to a second heroic action which has no direct military significance: the killing of a lion in a pit on a snowy day. It is included as an illustration of Samson-like strength (see Judg. 14:5-6). The action was long remembered due especially to the day on which it occurred – it was the day it snowed – snow being comparatively rare in Canaan.

───────────────────────────────

the third person singular pronoun 'to him' (*lô*) rendered literally 'and to him a name' rather than the negative adverb 'not' (*lō'*) which would translate as 'and not a name'.

16. As is done in the English Standard Version.

In the third example of fearless courage by Benaiah that involved killing, the Chronicler clearly wished to remind his readers of David's encounter with Goliath by adding two details not found in the Samuel text. Firstly, the Egyptian's height is given as 'five cubits' (seven feet six inches; see 1 Samuel 17:4 for Goliath's height) and secondly, his spear is likened to a weaver's beam (see 1 Samuel 17:7 where Goliath's spear is similarly described). Like David, Benaiah's staff seemed no match for the giant's spear, yet he was able to overpower him and kill him using his opponent's own weapon (1 Sam. 17:48-51).

11.26. Now the valiant warriors were Asahel the brother of Joab, Elhanan the son of Dodo from Bethlehem, 27. Shammoth the Harorite, Helez the Pelonite, 28. Ira the son of Ikkesh the Tekoite, Abiezer the Anathothite, 29. Sibbecai the Hushathite, Ilai the Ahohite, 30. Maharai the Netophathite, Heled the son of Baanah the Netophathite, 31. Ithai the son of Ribai from Gibeah of the sons of Benjamin, Benaiah the Pirathonite, 32. Hurai from the brooks of Gaash, Abiel the Arbathite, 33. Azmaveth the Baharumite, Eliahba the Shaalbonite, 34. the sons of Hashem the Gizonite, Jonathan the son of Shagee the Hararite, 35. Ahiam the son of Sacar the Hararite, Eliphal the son of Ur, 36. Hepher the Mecherathite, Ahijah the Pelonite, 37. Hezro the Carmelite, Naarai the son of Ezbai, 38. Joel the brother of Nathan, Mibhar the son of Hagri, 39. Zelek the Ammonite, Naharai the Berothite, the armour bearer of Joab the son of Zeruiah, 40. Ira the Ithrite, Gareb the Ithrite, 41. Uriah the Hittite, Zabad the son of Ahlai, 42. Adina the son of Shiza the Reubenite, head of the Reubenites and thirty with him, 43. Hanan the son of Maacah, and Joshaphat the Mithnite, 44. Uzzia the Ashterathite, Shama and Jeiel the sons of Hotham the Aroerite, 45. Jediael the son of Shimri and Joha his brother, the Tizite, 46. Eliel the Mahavite, and Jeribai and Joshaviah the sons of Elnaam, and Ithmah the Moabite, 47. Eliel and Obed and Jaasiel the Mezobaite.

In place of 'the thirty' (see 2 Sam. 23:24) the Chronicler has 'the valiant warriors'.[17] The substitution is possibly due to the list being longer than the one in Samuel. The Samuel text begins by stating that Asahel belonged to the thirty and ends

17. It literally reads 'the mighty men of strengths' where both nouns in the construct chain are in the plural as in 1 Chronicles 7:5; see Gesenius-Kautzsch-Cowley, *Hebrew Grammar*, 2nd edition (Oxford: Clarendon Press, 1910) §124q.

with Uriah the Hittite. If those two names are omitted the total does add up to thirty, even though it is noted that there were 'thirty-seven in all' (2 Sam. 23:39). This has led to the suggestion that the term 'the thirty' in this context was not an exact figure but a military title or rank so that actual numbers could fluctuate. Asahel, David's sister's third son, lost his life early on in David's reign during the war with Ishbosheth (2 Sam. 2:18-32), while Uriah the Hittite was killed in battle under suspicious circumstances instigated by David himself (2 Sam. 11:17). As men were killed in action so others joined the ranks of this elite military group.

The list tends to be arranged geographically beginning with and centring on Bethlehem, David's hometown from where Elhanan came and presumably the place from where Asahel and Joab's mother, Zeruiah, David's sister, hailed (v. 26). Shammoth is probably the same person as Shamhuth or Shammah the Irahite or Zerahite (v. 27; 1 Chron. 27:8), a prominent Judean family descended from Zerah (1 Chron. 2:4, 6-8), who came from Haror or Harod near Mount Gilboa (Judg. 7:1). A city called Beth-Pelet is listed as belonging to Judah (Josh. 15:27; Neh. 11:26), making it likely that Helez the Pelonite or Paltite was originally from that area (v. 27; 2 Sam. 23:26; 1 Chron. 27:10). Ira came from Tekoa in Judah the hometown of Amos the prophet (v. 28; 1 Chron. 2:24; Amos 1:1). It lay a few miles south of Bethlehem. Abiezer was from Anathoth (v. 28), a Levite town where Jeremiah the prophet was born and was situated north of Bethlehem, about three miles (4.8 kilometres) northeast of Jerusalem. Husha lay west of Bethlehem while Ahoah is either a Benjaminite clan or a place name in Benjamin (v. 29; 1 Chron. 8:4; 11:12). Netophah, the hometown of Maharai and Heled, was probably located near Bethlehem (v. 30; 1 Chron. 2:54; Ezra 2:22). Ithai was from the Benjaminite city of Gibeah (v. 31), Saul's birthplace and again, north of Bethlehem, about three miles (4.8 kilometres) north of Jerusalem.

The list begins to name soldiers from further afield in Israel. Included is another Benaiah (v. 31; see vv. 22-25) who came from Pirathon, a city south of Shechem in the centre of the country from where judge Abdon hailed (Judg. 12:13-15). Further south were the wadies of Gaash in the hill country of Ephraim, the home of Hurai and near where Joshua was buried (v. 32; Josh. 24:30; Judg. 2:9). Abiel the Arbathite may be associated with Beth-arabah which is on the Judah-Benjamin border near Jericho (v. 32; Josh. 15:6,61; 18:22), while Azmaveth (v. 33) came from the Benjaminite city of Bahurim just northeast of Jerusalem (2 Sam. 16:5). Eliahba the Shaalbonite suggests he was from Shaalbon, probably Shaalabbin, a city in the valley of Aijalon east of Gezer belonging originally to Dan (Josh. 19:42; written Shaalbim in Judg. 1:35). Gizon and Harar are unknown (v. 34). 'Mecherathite' either means that Hepher (v. 36) came from an unknown place called Mecherath or that it is a variant of Maacathite, in which case he came from Maacah, an Aramean state bordering Manasseh in Transjordan (Deut. 3:14; Josh. 13:8-13; 2 Sam. 10:6; 1 Chron. 3:2) or perhaps was a descendant of a Judean clan (1 Chron. 2:48; 4:19). It is suggested that 'Ahijah the Pelonite' (v. 36; compare v. 27) is a corruption of 'Ahithophel the Gilonite' (see 2 Sam. 23:34; the suggestion is more plausible when viewing the Hebrew text) with 'Eliam the son of' having been dropped accidentally. Another suggestion[18] is that Chronicles and Samuel witness to two different men, one in each version, and may be a further indication that the list varied over the years of David's reign. Carmel, the home town of Hezro, lay south of Hebron in Judah (Josh. 15:55). 'Naarai the son of Ezbai' is probably the same as 'Paarai the Arbite' (v. 37; 2 Sam. 23:35) who came from Arab (Josh. 15:52). For stylistic reasons, 'son of Ezbai' is used in place of the gentilic 'Arbite' and the difference in names due to spelling.

Mentioning Joel's brother 'Nathan' (v. 38) may suggest that the Chronicler is referring to the well-known prophet of that name who ministered during David's rule but there can be no certainty. 'Mibhar the son of Hagri' may again be a stylistic change for the gentilic 'Hagrite'. The Hagrites were among Israel's traditional enemies from across the Jordan (1 Chron. 5:10,19-22; Ps. 83:6[7]). 'Zelek the Ammonite' (v. 39) is another representative from an enemy nation in Transjordan which was subdued by David (2 Sam. 8:12; 10:1-14; 12:26-31). 'Beeroth', a few miles north of Jerusalem, is Naharai's home

---

18. See Japhet, *I and II Chronicles*, p. 249.

town and from where the sons of Rimmon, Ishbosheth's killers, came (2 Sam. 4:3-12). Interestingly, Naharai is described as Joab's armour-bearer. This is the third reference to Joab, the son of Zeruiah, David's sister (vv. 20, 26, 39), in the list of valiant men. He is not mentioned in his own right probably because he was the commander in chief of the whole army including all the elite soldiers (v. 6). Ira and Gareb are both Ithrites, a group belonging to Kiriath-jearim (v. 40; 1 Chron. 2:53).

Unlike the prophetic writer of Samuel, it was not the Chronicler's concern to draw attention to Uriah the Hittite (v. 41) and so his name does not appear last in the series as in Samuel. Uriah was just one of many who made up David's elite band of soldiers.

The stylistic differences, such as the linking of names by 'and' and the pairing of names, together with the preponderance of place names from the eastern side of the Jordan probably indicate that the final six verses (vv. 42-47) come from a completely separate source, equally ancient and reliable, to the one found in the previous verses. Fifteen additional names are included to complete the Chronicler's register of David's special military force. The list is headed by 'Adina the son of Shiza' (v. 42) who is described as the leader of the Reubenites, one of the ancestral tribes given land in Transjordan (Josh. 13:15-23). The phrase 'and thirty with him' may suggest that an additional group of 'thirty' was 'recruited from the eastern tribes of Israel' and 'established some time during the reign of David'.[19] Only fourteen of the 'thirty' are named. 'Maacah' (v. 43) could be the place from where Hanan came in northern Transjordan (see v. 36). Ashteroth (v. 44) is a Levitical city east of the Jordan in Manasseh (1 Chron. 6:71[56]). Aroer lies east of the Dead Sea in Reubenite territory. It is suggested that 'Mahavite' (v. 46) could be another spelling of 'Mahanite' from 'Mahanaim', a city on the borders of Gad (1 Chron. 6:80).[20] From Moab, another Transjordan enemy nation conquered by David like Ammon (v. 39), came Ithmah (v. 46; 2 Sam. 8:2,12). These

---

19. Japhet, *I and II Chronicles*, p. 252.

20. James G. Murphy, *The Books of Chronicles* (Edinburgh: T. & T. Clark), p. 53; Japhet, *I and II Chronicles*, p. 252.

members are all the more surprising considering that the Ammonite and Moabite were not allowed to come near to worship at the tabernacle (Deut. 23:3). Whether Mezoba (v. 47) is the same as Zobah is uncertain. As for the other people associated with place names, like Mithnite and Tizite (vv. 43,45), nothing is known.

Application

Jesus the Messiah is worthy of the devotion and loyalty of all His people. He calls them into His service. The enemies of God make war on the Lamb and He conquers them. Those who belong to the Lamb, who fight the spiritual battles and overcome through Him are by His grace God's elite soldiers who are described as the 'called and chosen and faithful' (Rev. 17:14). As David had foreign soldiers of Hittite, Moabite and Ammonite origin, so the Son of David has people of all nations in His service.

Early tribal support (12:1-22[23])

> 12:1. Now these are those who came to David to Ziklag, while he was still restrained from before Saul the son of Kish; and they were among the warriors who helped *him* in war. 2. And they were equipped with bow, using both the right and the left hand *to sling* stones and *shoot* arrows with the bow; from brothers of Saul from Benjamin. 3. The head was Ahiezer, then Joash, the sons of Shemaah the Gibeathite; also Jeziel and Pelet the sons of Azmaveth; and Beracah and Jehu the Anathothite. 4. And Ishmaiah the Gibeonite, a warrior among the thirty, and over the thirty. 5. Then Jeremiah and Jahaziel, and Johanan, and Jozabad the Gederathite, 5[6]. Eluzai, and Jerimoth, and Bealiah, and Shemariah, and Shephatiah the Haruphite, 6[7]. Elkanah, and Isshiah, and Azarel, and Joezer, and Jashobeam, the Korahites; 7[8]. And Joelah and Zebadiah, the sons of Jeroham from Gedor.

This section concerning David's initial tribal backing (12:1-22[23]) has no parallel in Samuel or anywhere else in the Old Testament. In the middle of verse 4, the Hebrew text begins verse 5 and this means that there is a difference in the numbering between the English and Hebrew in the rest of the chapter. As part of the overall chiastic structure of 11:1–12:41 (see introduction to chapters 11–12), there are four

short paragraphs arranged as follows: A. Ziklag (vv. 1-7[8]):
B. stronghold (vv. 8-15[9-16]); B¹. stronghold (vv. 16-18[17-19]);
A¹. Ziklag (vv. 19-22[20-23]). The construction focuses attention
on the type of tribal assistance David enjoyed during that
most difficult period in his struggle with Saul. Even before
he was made king in Hebron, David is shown to have the
support of 'all Israel'. The 'help' theme that the Chronicler
often introduces is particularly noticeable throughout chapter
12 (verses 1, 17[18], 18[19] twice, 19[20], 21[22], 22[23]), besides
appearing in some of the names: Ahiezer, 'my brother helps'
(v. 3); Azarel, 'God has helped' and Joezer, 'Yahweh is help'
(v. 6 [7]); Ezer, 'help' (9[10]). This continues from two of the
names in the previous chapter: Eleazar, 'God has helped'
(11:12) and Abiezer, 'my father helps' (11:28).

The Chronicler wishes to stress that David, from the very
beginning, had support from Saul's own tribe, even while
he was restricted on account of Saul. This emphasis is more
striking when the Benjaminites are described as 'brothers of
Saul' in the sense of his 'kinsmen' or in some cases 'Benjaminite
residents' (v. 2; see v. 16 [17]). Though the majority remained
with Saul (v. 29[30]), twenty-three elite soldiers came over to
David. While the name 'Benjamin' means 'son of the right
hand' (Gen. 35:18), it is interesting that the tribe was noted for
many who could use their left hand effectively, especially in
long-range fighting with bow and sling (v. 2; Judg. 3:15; 20:16;
1 Chron. 8:40). All the place names that can be identified with
certainty are associated with Benjaminite territory, such as
Gibeah, Azmaveth, Gibeon and Anathoth. Special mention is
made of Ishmaiah of Gibeon as a warrior associated with 'the
thirty' (v. 4). He is not mentioned in previous lists that refer
to 'the thirty' in chapter 11. Either there were several troop
units known as 'the thirty'[21] or that members of the special
unit varied from time to time as did the leader over them.[22]
The Korahites (v. 6[7]) could refer to people originally from
Edom (Gen. 36:5, 14, 16, 18; 1 Chron. 1:35) or to descendants
of Levi (Exod. 6:21; 1 Chron. 6:22) or to Judeans belonging
to Caleb's descendants (1 Chron. 2:43), but with Elkanah

21. Japhet, *I and II Chronicles*, p. 261.
22. Murphy, *The Books of Chronicles*, p. 54.

(see 1 Chron. 6:23) appearing as the first of the five named Korahites and no further details given, it is most likely the Chronicler is thinking of the Levitical clan who were tabernacle gatekeepers and bakers and associated with some of the psalms (1 Chron. 9:19, 31; Pss. 42–49). It is a reminder that numerous Levite families lived in Benjaminite territory. Ziklag belonged originally to Simeon (Josh. 19:5), but had been taken by the Philistines. The Philistine king of Gath, Achish, had given the city to David in return for his loyalty (1 Sam. 27:6).

Application

The Chronicler indicates that God was providentially preparing the way for David to be king and it served as a spur to the Jews of the post-exilic period to await God's timing for God's promises concerning the Davidic king to be realised. At the same time, the defections from Saul's own tribe were an encouragement to David; they were tangible indications that all Israel would eventually acknowledge him. Jesus saw the Greeks who came seeking Him as a foretaste of what would happen as a result of His death and resurrection. The devil, who is described as the ruler of this world, lost his power as a result of Messiah's victory on the cross, enabling people of all nations to be drawn to the Lord Jesus (John 12:31-32). Isaiah could write of Him, 'He shall see of the travail of his soul and shall be satisfied' (Isa. 53:11). The day of Pentecost was another foretaste of the time when people groups the world over would acknowledge Jesus as Saviour and Lord. Jesus shall reign till all His enemies are under His feet. God has highly exalted Him that at the name of Jesus every knee shall bow (Phil. 2:9-11).

12:8[9]. And from the Gadites, there separated themselves to David at the stronghold in the wilderness valiant warriors, armed men for battle that could handle shield and spear, whose faces were like the faces of lions, and who were as swift as the gazelles on the mountains; 9[10]. Ezer the chief, Obadiah the second, Eliab the third, 10[11]. Mishmannah the fourth, Jeremiah the fifth, 11[12]. Attai the sixth, Eliel the seventh, 12[13] Johanan the eighth, Elzabad the ninth, 13[14]. Jeremiah the tenth,

Machbannai the eleventh. 14[15]. These from the sons of Gad
were heads of the military host: the one who was least was to
a hundred, and the greatest to a thousand. 15[16]. These are
they who crossed the Jordan in the first month, when it was
overflowing all its banks; and they put to flight all *those in* the
valleys, both to the east and to the west.

The Chronicler now gives an example of a small band of
brave, valiant men who came to David from the other side of
the Jordan. These Gadites from southern Gilead and much
further north than the other tribes mentioned, defected early
on in David's flight from Saul and before Ziklag, when he
was in the 'stronghold' at Adullam or, more likely, Engedi,
as this was the nearest spot to the Transjordan (1 Sam. 22:1;
23:29; 24:1).[23] The eleven courageous men named complement
the previously mentioned experts in long range warfare, by
their skill in close combat with 'shield and spear' (v. 8[9];
compare v. 2). Their fearful looks are compared to lions
(see 2 Sam. 1:23) and their speed and agility to gazelles (see
Song of Songs 2:8-9). By waxing so eloquently concerning
their military might, the Chronicler would have had in
mind the blessings and prophecies of Jacob and Moses
concerning Gad (Gen. 49:19; Deut. 33:20). Two further items
are mentioned to indicate their exceptional qualities: their
competence in commanding a large or small army (v. 14) and
their exceptional strength and determination in crossing
the Jordan when the river was in full flow and putting
to flight all those living in the valleys (v. 15). The Jordan
overflowed its banks during the first month of Israel's
religious calendar (March–April), due to the melting snow
from the mountains (see Josh. 3:15). Some scholars[24] emend
the verb 'they put to flight' to read 'it barred' or 'prevented'
to give the idea that the flooded Jordan made the valleys
impassable. Without further support, it is better to stick
with the traditional text even though it means in translation
supplying a subject such as 'those in' before the elliptical
'all the valleys'. Many take the cryptic expression of verse
14 to mean that these warriors were 'a match for' or 'equal

23. Allen, *The First and Second Books of Chronicles*, p. 379.
24. See Williamson, *1 and 2 Chronicles*, p. 107.

to' the task of overcoming few or many (see Lev. 26:8). The Targum of Chronicles on which this view is based is not as supportive as scholars have supposed.[25]

> 12:16[17]. And some of the sons of Benjamin and Judah came to the stronghold to David. 17[18]. And David went out before them, and answered and said to them, 'If you have come peacefully to me to help me, my heart will be united to you. But if you have come to betray me to my enemies, seeing there is no violence in mine hands, may the God of our fathers see and decide.' 18[19]. Then the Spirit clothed Amasai, the head of the officers: *'We are yours, David, and with you, son of Jesse!* Peace, peace to you, and peace to those helping you; for your God has helped you.' Then David received them and made them heads of the troop.

While men from Benjamin have been listed earlier (vv. 1-7[8]), the Chronicler has theological reasons for mentioning the tribe again in this context. Judah and Benjamin became the tribes faithful throughout David's kingship and dynasty and, along with Levi, made up the bulk of the post-exilic community. The genealogical lists have already drawn attention to their importance (1 Chron. 2:2–8:40). Here the Chronicler shows how, even during this early period, David chose loyal men from Judah and Benjamin to be troop leaders.

It was only strong leadership and faithfulness to the covenant that kept the tribes together. The divisions noted in the period of the judges were still evident at the time of Saul's death, especially between the northern tribes and those in the south, as the Samuel text indicates (2 Sam. 2–4). Sheba's rebellion that occurred during David's kingship (2 Sam. 20:1-2) again witnessed to the fragility of the united kingdom and this uneasy union led eventually to the permanent split after Solomon's death (1 Kings 12:16; 2 Chron. 10:16). Counteracting those who were later to oppose the Davidic rule, we have in this paragraph early expressions of loyalty from the two southern tribes who were to remain loyal, using language reminiscent of those negative slogans concerning the 'son of Jesse' but, on this occasion, in a positive way.

---

25. Selman, *1 Chronicles*, p. 145. The Targums are Aramaic paraphrases of the biblical text.

David's natural suspicions were understandable given the precarious position he was in, especially as Saul was a Benjaminite and even cities of Judah like Keilah and Ziph were willing to betray him (see 1 Sam. 23:10-12, 19-24). He gave them a pledge that, if they acted honourably in helping him, he would make them his close associates but, if they proved false when David himself was without fault ('though there is no violence in my hands'; see Job 16:17), then he called on the God they all worshipped ('the God of our fathers') to view the situation and make a judgment. The verb translated 'decide' (v. 17[18]) is used in legal disputes for giving judgment, settling disputes or setting someone right. In some contexts, the verb can be translated more specifically as 'rebuke' (see Gen. 31:42). Similar words were uttered by Israel's leaders when Moses and Aaron had met with Pharaoh: 'The Lord look upon you and judge' (Exod. 5:21).

God was gracious to David when he felt so vulnerable by giving him a prophetic message of assurance and encouragement. It came through the mouth of Amasai, the chief officer of this band of fighting men.[26] Apart from the name itself, there is no other indication for this Amasai to be identified with Absalom's army general (2 Sam. 17:25; 19:13). In place of any account of his ability as a soldier, the Chronicler fastens on Amasai's message of loyalty that came with divine authority and is the first of a number of such unique prophetic messages recorded in Chronicles.

Amasai was endowed with the Spirit (see 2 Chron. 24:20 for an almost exact parallel). The only other case in the Old Testament where this striking expression is used is in Judges 6:34. We read that the 'Spirit of Yahweh clothed Gideon' in his leadership position. In Chronicles it is employed when someone speaks with divine authority. A similar phrase 'the Spirit of God/Yahweh came upon' is found in 2 Chronicles 15:1; 20:14. The prophetic message in poetic form begins with reassuring words of loyalty and declares that it is God who has helped David. When disloyalty to David's dynasty is expressed, 'David' and 'the son of Jesse' are again

26. While the Qere reads 'officers', the Kethibh along with the LXX, Syriac and Vulgate has 'thirty'.

used in parallel (2 Chron. 10:16) and recalls Nabal's ungrateful
words and Sheba's call to rebel (1 Sam. 25:10; 2 Sam. 20:1).
Saul likewise used the label 'son of Jesse' in a disdainful way
(1 Sam. 20:27).

The threefold blessing of peace (*shalom*) picks up David's
use of the term in verse 17[18] and contains the idea of
prosperity and success to David and to those who had risked
all to join him. It is also recognised that help ultimately came
from the God whom David trusted and served.

Application

David does not contemplate taking vengeance on betrayers but
commits such cases for God to witness and judge. David, the
servant of the Lord, acted like the unique Servant of the Lord
who, when He had done no 'violence', committed Himself to
Him who judges justly (see Isa. 53:9; 1 Pet. 2:22-23). All who
unite themselves to the true David will not be disappointed,
for He will receive them into His royal service 'to follow
the Lamb wherever he goes' (Rev. 14:4). Our affection and
allegiance to the Lord Jesus must be similar to Amasai's
prophetic message. As Matthew Henry quaintly states: 'His
we must be without reservation or power of revocation. On
His side we must be forward to appear and act. To His interest
we must be hearty well-wishers … till he shall have put down
all opposing rule, principality, and power.'

While those endowed with the Spirit under the old
covenant are associated with special individuals particularly
in leadership positions, Jesus speaks of all His followers
being 'clothed with power from on high' (Luke 24:49).
This is associated with the promised Spirit, wished for by
Moses, prophesied by Joel and John the Baptist (Num. 11:29;
Joel 2:28-29; Mark 1:8) and again stressed by Jesus prior to
His ascension, where the baptism with the Holy Spirit is
associated with power to be witnesses to Jesus (Acts 1:5-8).

> 12:19[20]. And some from Manasseh defected to David when
> he came with the Philistines to battle against Saul; but they did
> not help them, for the rulers of the Philistines after consultation
> sent him away, saying, 'At the cost of our heads he will defect to
> his master Saul.' 20[21]. When he went to Ziklag, there defected

to him from Manasseh: Adnah, and Jozabad, and Jediael, and
Michael, and Jozabad, and Elihu, and Zillethai, heads of the
thousands who belonged to Manasseh. 21[22]. And they helped
David against the raiding band, for they were all valiant warriors
and were commanders in the army. 22[23]. Because at that time
day by day they came to David to help him, until there was a
great army, like the army of God.

Seven chiefs are named who defected from the tribe of Manasseh
toward the end of David's enforced exile to become officers in
his army. The Hebrew term for 'thousand' could be interpreted
as 'clan' in this context. The Chronicler often uses Manasseh
along with Ephraim to represent the north (see 2 Chron. 15:9;
30:1; 34:9). The original sons of Joseph were considered co-
equals and although Manasseh was the older brother it was
Ephraim who was given the firstborn rights (Gen. 48:5, 14).
Manasseh's territory on the west side of the Jordan lay to the
north of Ephraim (Josh. 17:1-12) which probably accounts for
the Chronicler's selection. It was a surprising defection from
such a northerly region (see Gad in verses 8-15[9-16]) but these
men used the opportunity when David accompanied Achish
to Aphek (1 Sam. 29:1-2). The text assumes a knowledge of
David's time in the service of Achish, king of Gath, and of the
Philistine lords' refusal to allow him to assist in the final battle
against Saul at Gilboa (v. 19; 1 Sam. 27:2-7; 28:1-2; 29:1-11). It also
assumes knowledge of David's victory over the Amalekite
'raiding band' who had burnt Ziklag and taken captive its
inhabitants (v. 21[22]; 1 Sam. 30). The mention of Ziklag enables
the Chronicler to bring his account back to where it started (see
v. 1) and the summary statement (v. 22[23]) then indicates the
measure and quality of the support David had on the eve of
Saul's defeat and death.

The 'help' theme is prominent in this paragraph
(vv. 19[20], 21[22], 22[23]). While 'help' came to David
from people within Israel, David and his men were, in the
providence of God, prevented from helping the Philistines
(v. 19). God's people were not to help Gentile or ungodly
nations in their military advances nor to expect them to
assist Israel (see 2 Chron. 19:2; 28:16, 23).

From the six hundred strong company that supported
David before he moved to Ziklag, numbers kept on flocking to

him on a daily basis so that he became a force to be reckoned with (v. 22[23]). The phrase 'an army' or 'camp of God' could be a way of expressing the superlative and translated 'a vast army' (see Genesis 23:6 where 'mighty prince' is literally 'prince of God' and 1 Samuel 14:15 'a very great trembling' is literally 'a trembling of God'). However, as the phrase is preceded by 'a great army/camp' it is better to translate it more literally and thus to indicate a comparison with God's army or camp (see Genesis 32:2[3] where the exact phrase, 'camp of God', occurs). In 2 Chronicles 14:13[12] king Asa's army/camp is the army of Yahweh. The word 'camp/army' is itself a reminder of Israel's 'camp' in the wilderness. In Numbers alone the word is found almost fifty times. It is used especially in the context of God's presence with His people against the might of Egypt and the Canaanites (Exod. 14:19-20; Josh. 1:11; 6:11,14; see also 1 Chron. 9:18-19 and 2 Chron. 31:2 where the term is used of the tent or temple area).

Application

Though the Manasseh chiefs 'shrewdly'[27] left it to the last minute to change sides, they were welcomed by David. Before the final day of reckoning comes, while it is still the day of grace, there is a welcome for all who defect from the devil's rule and seek to join the company over whom Jesus is the head. We are urged to turn from idols to serve the living and true God. In Jesus' parable of the labourers, those who came to work in the vineyard at the eleventh hour received the same wage as those who had toiled there the whole day (Matt. 20:1-16).

Throughout the whole paragraph, God's providential ways are evident in the way David was prevented from fighting against his own people and also in the encouragements David was given through the defections from Saul. David awaited God's time for the kingdom to be handed over to him. As one former minister's wife said to me at the beginning of my ministry, 'God's time is always the right time.'

From the beginning of His public ministry, our Lord was tempted to receive the homage of the nations by worshipping

27. Wilcock, *The Message of Chronicles*, p. 62.

the devil and thus to avoid the cross. But Jesus waited for the divine moment, for 'the hour' when the devil's grip over the nations would be broken, and victory accomplished, not through worldly might but through apparent weakness and death. As a result of His bodily resurrection and ascension to God's right hand, Jesus the Messiah was vindicated and His reign began. His people are to follow the example set. 'Fear not, little flock, it is your Father's good pleasure to give you the kingdom.'

David's army at Hebron (12:23-37[24-38])

12:23[24]. And these are the numbers of the heads equipped for war. They came to David at Hebron to turn over the kingdom of Saul to him according to the word of Yahweh. 24[25]. The sons of Judah bearing shield and spear, six thousand eight hundred equipped for war. 25[26]. From the sons of Simeon, valiant warriors for war, seven thousand one hundred. 26[27]. From the sons of Levi, four thousand six hundred. 27[28]. And Jehoiada, Aaron's leader, and with him three thousand seven hundred. 28[29]. And Zadok, a youth, a valiant warrior and his father's house, twenty-two officers. 29[30]. And from the sons of Benjamin, brothers of Saul, three thousand, until then most of them had kept loyal to the house of Saul. 30[31]. And from the sons of Ephraim, twenty thousand eight hundred, valiant warriors, men of renown, belonging to the house of their fathers. 31[32]. And from the half tribe of Manasseh, eighteen thousand, who were designated by name to come and make David king. 32[33]. And from the sons of Issachar who had an ability to understand the times, to know what Israel should do, two hundred heads, and all their brothers under their command. 33[34]. From Zebulun, fifty thousand, who went out for war, lining up for battle with all the battle weapons, to help with a single purpose. 34[35]. And from Naphtali, a thousand commanders, and with them thirty-seven thousand with shield and spear. 35[36]. And from the Danites, twenty-eight thousand six hundred lined up for battle. 36[37]. And from Asher, forty thousand who went out for war to line up for battle. 37[38]. And from the other side of the Jordan, from the Reubenites, the Gadites and the half tribe of Manasseh, with all the weapons of war for battle, a hundred and twenty thousand.

These verses return to the scene at Hebron when David was anointed king (1 Chron. 11:1-3) and before he made

Jerusalem his capital (1 Chron. 11:4-9). It presents evidence of the wholehearted support for David from every part of the nation by the tribal warriors, and especially at a time when there was still uncertainty in the north following Saul's death.

Though the word 'head' (verse 23[24]) often means 'chief' in military contexts, such a translation seems inappropriate as an introduction to the list that follows. A better translation would be 'division' or 'company' (see Judg. 7:16, 20; 1 Sam. 11:11; etc.). The verse picks up earlier phraseology where Yahweh 'turned over' Saul's kingdom to David just as 'the word of the Lord' had indicated through Samuel (1 Chron. 10:14; 11:3, 10). What God purposed when Saul was killed came to reality with this gathering at Hebron.

From the trickle in the early days of David's time as an outlaw, the Chronicler now indicates the overwhelming flood of support of armed men at his disposal from Simeon's area in the deep south to Dan in the far north (vv. 25[26], 35[36] – the Dan tribe having moved from its original place northwest of Judah, see Josh. 19:40-46, 47; Judg. 1:34-35; 13:2, 25; 18:1-31). To make the point clear that the whole of Israel united around David, every tribe is mentioned, including Levi and Joseph's two sons, with the two parts of Manasseh mentioned separately. This makes fourteen named tribal areas rather than the usual twelve. However, if the three Transjordanian tribes, which are grouped together and listed last, are treated as one, then the figure remains at twelve. Because of the Chronicler's special interest in Judah, Levi and Benjamin, they are mentioned first with Simeon closely associated with Judah. In comparison with the rest of Israel, the numbers mentioned from the south are not great and the small contingent from Benjamin is explained as being due to the tribe's loyalty to Saul's family (v. 29[30]). What is striking are the figures for the most northerly tribes and for Transjordan. Though Dan is absent from the genealogies in 1 Chronicles 2–8 they are well represented on this occasion. The Chronicler is emphasising that David had overwhelming military support even from the most distant parts of Israel.

Though the Levites had duties associated with the tabernacle and later the temple, they could still serve in the army. Even priests could be described as warriors (see 2 Chron. 26:17). Of particular interest is the naming of individuals from this tribe. Jehoiada (v. 27[28]) was 'leader' of the Aaronite warriors and not the high priest, for that belonged to Abiathar (see 1 Sam. 23:9). It is unlikely that he is the same person described as the father of Benaiah (1 Chron. 11:22-25; 2 Sam. 8:18; 1 Kings 1:8). On the other hand, Zadok (v. 28[29]; see 1 Chron. 6:12,50-53), who in his youth was a mighty warrior, later replaced Abiathar and became Solomon's high priest (1 Kings 1:7; 2:35). The reference to the twenty-two officers from his ancestral house may have been prompted by the twenty-two priestly heads of fathers' houses in the days of Jeshua and Joiakim (Neh. 12:1-7, 12-21).[28]

Also of note is the additional material relating to three of the northern tribes: Issachar, Zebulun and Naphtali (vv. 32-34[33-35]; see also v. 40[41]). Beside the thirty-seven thousand warriors, Naphtali had a thousand officers (v. 34[35]) while Zebulun's contingent was the largest number of warriors for any tribe (v. 33[34]). Emphasis is placed on their eager and well-equipped troops and the whole-hearted help[29] they gave David. The phrase 'with a single purpose' translates the Hebrew idiom 'with not a heart and a heart' meaning not having two intentions. It suggests unwavering loyalty. Only the number of Issachar's chiefs is provided but the phrase, 'all their brothers under their command' (v. 32[33]), suggests that the vast majority from that tribe was committed to David. They are characterised as having 'understanding of the times' which implies they had something of the perception and insight of Solomon (2 Chron. 2:12) and of the statesmen in the Persian court (Esther 1:13). There is no hint that they were astrologers. In this context, it may be indicating that the men of Issachar discerned that the house of Saul was doomed. Interestingly, these three tribes are specially mentioned for their faithfulness and willingness to risk their lives in support of Barak against the Canaanites (Judg. 4:6, 10; 5:15, 18).

If the figures for each tribe and group are counted then a grand total of 339,600 warriors plus a further 1,222 officers and

---

28. See Klein, *1 Chronicles*, pp. 323-24.

29. The Aramaic for 'help' is used rather than the Hebrew; compare Psalm 2:12 where the same phenomenon is found with the word for 'son'.

chiefs belonging to Levi, Issachar and Naphtali had assembled for military service. The total would be greater if the number of Issachar warriors had been given after the 200 officers, as is done with Naphtali. How are the numbers to be taken? Most agree that it is difficult to accept them at face value. But they are not numbers plucked out of the air. The Chronicler may be using the term 'thousand' and 'hundred' to designate military units (see 1 Chron. 13:1) or tribal and clan groups, as it sometimes does elsewhere (see Num. 10:36; Judg. 6:15; 1 Sam. 10:19; 29:5; 2 Sam. 4:2; Micah 5:1[2]), although that does not appear so obvious here.[30] Hyperbole cannot be ruled out in some cases (see 1 Chron. 5:21; 22:14) but again that seems unlikely here. Bearing in mind the Chronicler's use of 'army/camp of God' (v. 22), the large figures may be hinting that there was something supernatural about it.[31] Israel's armies are the battle-lines of 'the living God' (1 Sam. 17:26, 36). The hosts of heaven are associated with Israel's army by Deborah in her song of victory (Judg. 5:20).

The large numbers certainly indicate the vast size of David's army compared with the few who sided with him earlier and show that those furthest away were more eager in their support of David than those closer to him. All this agrees with the Chronicler's 'all Israel' theme, especially emphasising Israel's united military strength under David. It would have especially encouraged those in the post-exilic period, particularly those who were not of the dominant tribes, to become wholeheartedly involved in working for the future of the Judean province.

Application

The passage inspires united effort by God's people and wholehearted commitment to Jesus our Lord and Saviour. David's experiences were previews and pointers to the true realisation of God's purposes in David's greater son.

---

30. G. E. Mendenhall, 'The Census Lists of Numbers 1 and 26', *Journal of Biblical Literature* 77 (1958), pp. 52-66. See Klein, *1 Chronicles*, pp. 314-16, who also dismisses John Wenham's suggestion that 'thousand' can be revocalised to 'chief' (*'allûp*) in 'Large Numbers in the Old Testament,' *Tyndale Bulletin* 18 (1967), pp. 19-53.

31. See Selman, *1 Chronicles*, p. 147. The same may have been true of vast numbers recorded who came out of Egypt and travelled through the wilderness to Canaan.

As people from all the tribes joined David at Hebron, so people of all nationalities are drawn to the Messiah with individuals not lost in the crowd for the Lord knows each by name. The prophets look forward to this universal ingathering. Isaiah writes of the far north of Israel in particular experiencing the gospel light (Isa. 9:1-2). An innumerable company from every tribe, people group and language are viewed as belonging to King Jesus. They can be described symbolically as the one hundred and forty-four thousand of all the tribes of Israel (Rev. 7:4). The Church on earth is called the Church militant because we are in a war situation. As the hosts of heaven were associated in some mysterious way with Israel's armies so we must reckon with such heavenly activity on behalf of the Church. Paul speaks of the presence of angels at our gatherings for worship (1 Cor. 11:10) and John probably draws on the imagery of Daniel in his use of stars and angels as heavenly counterparts of the earthly local churches (Dan. 8:10-11; 10:20-21; 12:1, 3; Rev. 1:20). The Church on earth belongs to Mount Zion and comes to this heavenly city-state where countless numbers of angels are gathered (Heb. 12:22).

Celebrations at Hebron (12:38-40[39-41])

> 12:38[39]. All these men of war, helpers of the line-up, came with a perfect heart to Hebron to make David king over all Israel, and likewise all the rest of Israel were of one heart to make David king. 39[40]. And they were there with David three days, eating and drinking, for their brothers had provided for them. 40[41]. And also those who were near to them as far as Issachar and Zebulun and Naphtali were bringing food on donkeys, on camels, on mules and on oxen – abundant provisions of flour, fig cakes and bunches of raisins, and wine and oil and oxen and sheep, for there was joy in Israel.

The concluding verses of this section are a fitting end to the events surrounding the acceptance of David as the king over all Israel at Hebron. Having briefly described the covenant and coronation ceremony in 1 Chronicles 11:1-3 and having shown how warriors from the various tribes had forsaken Saul for David even before Saul was killed, the Chronicler returns to indicate the widespread relief and joyous nature of the occasion. Not only the military men who had helped David (v. 38[39];

see v. 33[34]), but 'all the rest of Israel' came with a 'perfect heart'. This is a favourite expression in Chronicles that conveys again the idea of wholehearted devotion or single-minded intent. The exact phrase also occurs in 1 Chronicles 28:9 and 2 Chronicles 19:9 and 25:2 (but see also 1 Chron. 28:9; 29:9,19; 2 Chron. 15:17). 'Brothers', in the sense of relatives, unable to be present, provided food in abundance. Even neighbouring tribes, 'those who were near to them', from as far away as the three northern tribes, Issachar, Zebulun and Naphtali (v. 40[41]; see vv. 32-34), brought an abundance of food and drink on every conceivable beast of burden. For a similar army menu, we have Abigail's supplies for David's men (1 Sam. 25:18).

The provisions that were given by the tribal areas witnessed to their generosity and were an expression of national unity and of their joy at David's coronation. Joy is another of the themes of Chronicles (1 Chron. 15:16; 29:9, 17, 22; 2 Chron. 6:41; 15:15; 20:27; 23:18; 24:10; 29:30, 36; 30:21, 23, 25, 26). Though David made a covenant with the people at Hebron (see 1 Chron. 11:3) nothing is said of any covenant meal and neither is there any reference to eating and drinking 'before Yahweh' as was done when Solomon was made king in Jerusalem (1 Chron. 29:22). At Hebron, there was no sanctuary and the ark at this stage was still in Kiriath-jearim. The following chapters deal with the ark and its transfer to the tent in Jerusalem.

Application

As 'help' came to David from within Israel so God more often than not helps Christian workers indirectly through others. Phoebe is especially mentioned by Paul as one who had given help to many including himself and he urges the church in Rome to assist her in whatever way was needed (Rom. 16:1-2). We are all called as Christians to support and help our church leaders in the cause of the gospel as well as each other in our own spiritual development.

The description of these events, especially the joyful united participation of 'all Israel', would have been an encouragement to the post-exilic community to work together and be committed to God and their leaders and at the same time to look with anticipation to the final realisation of God's promises to David and His people. Christians live in days of fulfilment and yet they await the grand consummation. Every time we meet on the Lord's Day to hear God's Word and to celebrate the Lord's Supper we do so in joyous anticipation of the final Day of the Lord when all His people will be together with King Jesus, who is both the root and descendant of David (Rev. 22:16). In the light of this, the Chronicler, like the apostle Paul, encourages us to live in a way that is worthy of our calling in Christ 'bearing with one another in love, eager to maintain the unity of the Spirit in the bond of peace' (Eph. 4:1-3).

David and the Jerusalem worship (13:1–17:27)

Now that David's position as king over all Israel has been underlined, the Chronicler moves on to describe another of his main interests, namely, David's desire to see the worship of God established at the heart of his kingdom. This section concerns a failed first attempt at transferring the ark to Jerusalem (1 Chron. 13) to a final joyous resolution of the situation (1 Chron. 15-16). Between these two narratives the Chronicler inserts important details concerning David's foreign recognition, family affairs and his defeated foes (1 Chron. 14). The whole section concludes with the account of God's promise to David indicating the close relationship between the Davidic king and the temple worship (1 Chron. 17). Much of the material is found in 2 Samuel 5–7 but with significant differences and variations. Helping to bind the whole section together is the 'house' theme whether in the sense of a palace, a household, a temple, or a dynasty (1 Chron. 14:1; 15:1; 16:43; 17:1-27).

First Attempt to Transfer the Ark (13:1-14)

While the event itself may have come later in David's kingship,[32] it is placed here as the most significant moment after the coronation of David and the capture of Jerusalem (1 Chron. 11:1-9). Similarly, in the subsequent history,

---

32. See E. H. Merrill, *Kingdom of Priests* (Grand Rapids: Baker, 1987), pp. 238-48; see Todd Bolen, 'The Date of the Davidic Covenant' (JETS 65, 2022), pp. 61-78.

Chronicles is eager to mention the religious reforms of both Hezekiah and Josiah right from the start of their reigns (2 Chron. 29:3; 34:3).

The Chronicler assumes knowledge of the ark including the references in the time of Samuel and its almost total neglect during Saul's reign (see 1 Sam. 4-7; 14:18). This coffin-like wooden box was covered in gold and contained the two stone tablets of the covenant inscribed with the Ten Commandments. Also associated with the ark were the pot of manna and Aaron's rod that budded (Num. 17:10[25]; 1 Kings 8:9; Heb. 9:4-5). On top of the ark was the golden lid called 'the mercy seat' or 'atonement lid' with a cherub at each end (Exod. 25:10-22). It was viewed as Yahweh's footstool (1 Chron. 28:2; Pss. 99:5; 132:7-8) and above it, between the cherubim, God ordained to speak. This visible object signified the presence of the invisible Holy One whose true throne was in heaven. It was associated with atonement and holiness (Lev. 16:16, 19).[33]

The account contrasts David's excitement at the beginning with his despair at the close. Nevertheless, the chapter ends on a note of hope. After the opening introduction (vv. 1-4), the chapter describes how the ark's journey began (13:5-8) and Yahweh's anger and subsequent blessing (vv. 9-14).

> 13:1. Then David consulted with the commanders of the thousands and the hundreds, in fact every leader. 2. And David said to all the assembly of Israel, 'If it seems good to you and from Yahweh our God, let us burst out and send to our brothers who remain in all the lands of Israel, and with them the priests and the Levites in their pasture land cities,[34] that they may be gathered to us. 3. And let us transfer the ark of our God to us, for we did not seek it in the days of Saul.' 4. Then all the assembly said to do so, for the thing was right in the eyes of all the people.

The opening verses are unique to Chronicles and stress the involvement of the whole assembly of Israel in David's desire to bring the ark to his capital city. Three of the Chronicler's themes stand out. First, David consulted and obtained the

---

33. See Deuk-Il Shin, *The Ark of Yahweh in Redemptive History* (Eugene, Oregon: Wipf & Stock, 2012); M. H. Woudstra, *The Ark of the Covenant from Conquest to Kingship* (Philadelphia: P & R, 1965).

34. It literally reads 'in their cities of their pasture lands'; for 'pasture lands, see 1 Chronicles 6:64, 67, 69-81[49, 52, 54-66].

support of the military commanders[35] and all the leaders of the people.[36] The words 'if it seems good to you' indicate that David's rule was not despotic. Likewise, Jehoshaphat and Hezekiah had the support of the people before making big decisions and precisely the same Hebrew form is used for 'consulted' (2 Chron. 20:21; 30:2, 23). Rehoboam and Amaziah, on the other hand, acted rashly on the advice of an ill-informed elite (2 Chron. 10:6-11; 25:17).

Second, the 'all Israel' theme is prominent in David's address to 'all the assembly of Israel'. To indicate that this meant more than the military men, reference is made to the 'priests and Levites' and 'the brothers who remain' who are not mentioned as having attended the coronation (see 1 Chron. 12:38[39]). The nation as a whole was encouraged to be concerned about the worship of God. This is the first of over thirty occurrences of the noun 'assembly' or 'congregation' (*qāhāl*; vv. 2, 4) in Chronicles, while Samuel–Kings has fewer than ten references. The term was used when Israel was first formed as the covenant people of God (Exod. 12:6; Deut. 5:22; 9:10; etc. See also Gen. 28:3; 35:11; 48:4). The verb from the same word family appears in verse 5 in association with 'all Israel' (see also 1 Chron. 11:1). David's idea was to have the widest possible acceptance which would indicate Yahweh's approval. Unique to Chronicles is the use of the plural when referring to the promised land as Israel's 'lands' (v. 2; 2 Chron. 34:33). It suggests separate entities that needed to be unified. Along with David's position as king reigning from Jerusalem, the ark, as the focal point of worship, helped to unify the people. In this connection, the emphasis on first person plural pronouns is quite noticeable ('our God ... let us ... our brothers ... to us ... let us ... our God to us ... we ...' [vv. 2-3]).

Third, the verb 'seek' is found again and is a reminder of Saul's failure to seek God for guidance (v. 3; see 1 Chron. 10:13-14). David includes himself and the people in their neglect of the ark during Saul's reign: 'we did not ...' (v. 3). Apart from one occasion when it was brought out to the

---

35. The 'thousands' and 'hundreds' probably refer to military units in this context.

36. See BDB, p. 514 5f(d), for the generalising force of the *lamedh*: 'namely', 'in brief', 'as regards', 'in fact'.

field of battle for a day, it remained in Kiriath-jearim in the
house of Abinadab, where his son Eleazar was consecrated
to have charge of it (1 Sam. 7:1; 14:18).[37] This chest that was
meant to be the visible sign of Yahweh's presence was side-
lined. Failure to 'seek' the ark meant, in effect, a failure to
seek Yahweh, which in turn indicated a lack of dependence
on Him. By contrast, there is now an eagerness on the part
of 'all Israel' to bring the ark to Jerusalem. They saw it as
the right thing to do.

Interestingly, the verb 'to break through' or 'burst out' (prṣ,
v. 2) prepares for its use in verse 11 and 1 Chronicles 14:11 and
15:13. There may also be a word-play in the Chronicler's use
of the verb 'to cause to turn' or 'transfer' (v. 3; literally, 'let us
bring round'; see 1 Chron. 10:14; 12:23[24] and 1 Sam. 5:8-10).
As Yahweh and the troops had transferred the kingdom
from Saul to David (1 Chron. 10:14; 12:23[24]) so now David
responds by transferring 'the ark of our God to us', from its
obscurity during Saul's time.[38]

> 13:5. So David assembled all Israel from the Shihor of Egypt
> and up to the entrance of Hamath, to bring the ark of God from
> Kiriath-jearim. 6. So David and all Israel went up to Baalah, to
> Kiriath-jearim which belongs to Judah, to bring up from there
> the ark of God, Yahweh who inhabits the cherubim, who is
> called Name. 7. And they carried the ark of God upon a new cart
> from the house of Abinadab, and Uzzah and Ahio were driving
> the cart. 8. And David and all Israel were merry-making before
> God with all their strength, and with songs and lyres and harps
> and tambourines and cymbals and trumpets.

The differences from the earlier account are revealing
(2 Sam. 6:1). Instead of using the word 'gathered', the Chronicler
employs his favourite term 'assembled' and in place of a
procession of thirty thousand chosen people of Israel, 'all
Israel' is here equated with the type of assembly from the
entire land that was witnessed at the climactic moment of
the David–Solomon era (see 2 Chron. 7:8). The southern and
northern borders of Israel are similar to the ones promised by
God to Joshua (Josh. 13:1-7; see also Num. 34:5, 7-9). 'Shihor'

---

37. See D. T. Tsumura, *The First Book of Samuel*, pp. 365-66.

38. See Williamson, *1 and 2 Chronicles*, p. 115.

('dark stream') has often been identified with the wadi or brook of Egypt' (modern Wadi El-Arish; 2 Chron. 7:8) but it may well be the easternmost branch of the Nile Delta (Isa. 23:3), while 'the entrance to Hamath' ('Lebo Hamath'), is probably modern Lebweh, nearly fifty miles (80 kilometres) north of Damascus. Uniquely, the Chronicler always works from south to north when referring to Israel's boundaries, as in the two references 'Beersheba to Dan' rather than 'Dan to Beersheba' (1 Chron. 21:2; 2 Chron. 30:5; compare 1 Sam. 3:20; 2 Sam. 3:10).

This crowd from the furthest extremities of Israel descended on Kiriath-jearim, which is also called Baalah, as well as Baalah-judah and Kiriath-baal (see 2 Sam. 6:2; Josh. 15:9, 60; 18:14), to bring the ark on its seven-mile (eleven kilometres) journey to Jerusalem. Attention is drawn, as in the Samuel text, to the ark's importance by referring to it as 'the ark of God' and to God's personal name 'Yahweh'. The 'name' of God is another theme the Chronicler emphasises (see 1 Chron. 16:2, 8, 29; 17:24; 21:19; 2 Chron. 6:5-6, 33). In this context, no military associations were deemed appropriate, hence the absence of the usual descriptive addition 'of hosts' to the name 'Yahweh' (see 1 Sam. 6:2). The unseen God of Israel, whom the highest heaven cannot contain (2 Chron. 6:18), is ordained to be with His people on earth by means of the ark, and especially present in that area above the mercy seat and between the two cherubim which lay either end on the ark (Exod. 25:22; see Gen. 3:24). The cherubim faced inwards and downwards demonstrating, like Isaiah's seraphim, creaturely humility and reserve before the Creator's awesome splendour. On the other hand, their wings soared upward, directing the observer to the heavenly reality. Ezekiel's vision gives a detailed description of the cherubim and on that occasion we are informed that above them something like a throne was seen on which God's glory was displayed in a form that resembled a human (Ezek. 1 and 10). The Chronicler, like the rest of Scripture, is reticent to actually say that God sat 'between' or 'on' the cherubim.[39] God

39. Literally translated, the phrase 'who inhabits the cherubim' is 'sitter of the cherubim' and often translated 'sits enthroned on' or 'sits between the cherubim' (see 1 Sam. 4:4; 2 Kings 19:15; Isa. 37:16; Ps. 80:1[2]). The epexegetical genitive defines the location of the sitting without specifically stating that God sits on or between the cherubim; see John N. Oswalt, *The Book of Isaiah Chapters 1-39*, The

condescended to dwell on earth in that most holy inner place of the tabernacle and later the temple where the ark was situated. It is that holy square rather than the ark itself that is spoken of as Yahweh's footstool (Ps. 99:1, 5; 1 Chron. 28:2; Isa. 60:13). Lest anyone should gain the idea that God was confined to such temples, Yahweh subsequently reminded His people that heaven was His throne and the earth His footstool (Isa. 66:1). The ark was no idolatrous representation of God but it was a way of stressing both God's transcendence and immanence.

On account of its religious significance, the ark also became a symbol of unity for the tribes, witnessed on this occasion as 'David and all Israel' expressed their worship 'before God' with jubilant merrymaking and music (v. 8). In addition to the trumpets that were generally used by the priests, the lyre, harp and cymbal are the usual instruments for accompanying singing. The 'tambourine', which was more like a hand drum than a modern tambourine, was generally used by women (Exod. 15:20; Judg. 11:34; Ps. 68:25[26]).[40] This is the only place in Chronicles where these tambourines appear.

The method by which they carried the ark is brought to our attention. They made use of 'a new cart', one not polluted through previous use, and drawn by oxen (v. 9). It would have been a reminder of the successful way the Philistines had sent the ark back to Israel after their disastrous experience with it (1 Sam. 6). By employing the verb 'to cause to ride' instead of 'to lift' or 'carry' as in the Samuel text, the Chronicler makes more obvious that this was not the appropriate way in Israel for the ark to be moved (Deut. 10:8; Num. 3:31; 1 Chron. 15:2,15). Uzzah and Ahio, 'sons' in the sense of descendants of Abinadab (2 Sam. 6:3), are introduced without comment. Again, the Chronicler assumes a knowledge of the details from the Samuel text.

13:9. When they came to the threshing floor of Chidon, Uzzah put out his hand to grasp the ark, for the oxen had stumbled. 10. And the wrath of Yahweh was kindled against Uzzah and he slew him because he had put out his hand on the ark and he died there before God. 11. Then David was angry because Yahweh had burst out an outburst against Uzzah, so he named that place Perez-uzza to this day. 12. And David was afraid of God on that day, saying, 'How can I bring the ark of God to me?' 13. So David did not remove the ark to himself, to the city of David but took it aside to the house of Obed-edom the Gittite. 14. So the ark of God remained with the household of Obed-edom in his house three months. And Yahweh blessed the household of Obed-edom and all that belonged to him.

'Chidon' (spelled Nachon in 2 Samuel 6:6) is either the name of the place or the owner of the threshing floor. Nothing else is known about either form of the name, but it is remembered on account of the tragedy that turned joy to anger and fear.

When the oxen stumbled, the natural reaction of Uzzah was to grasp the ark to stop it from sliding off the cart. Yahweh's wrath was aroused and Uzzah was immediately killed. In the very place where there had been joyous celebrations in God's presence ('before God,' v. 8), there was now a dead body in God's presence ('before God,' v. 10). The Mosaic law made it clear that if the ark and other holy things were touched or looked at by the Kohathite family of Levites or anyone else other than the priests they would die (Num. 4:15, 20). In addition, specific instructions were given on how the ark and the other tabernacle items were to be carefully covered and transported (Exod. 25:14; Num. 4:1-20; 7:9).

The expression of God's wrath in the death of Uzzah resulted in an angry David for the way Yahweh had 'burst out' against Uzzah's natural desire to steady the ark (v. 11). This verb (*pāraṣ*, 'to break out) along with the accompanying accusative noun (*pereṣ*) from the same word family provides an interesting parallel to David's concern for the ark when he 'burst out' to send to all Israel to lend their support (v. 2). The original place-name was changed to 'Perez-uzza' meaning 'the burst out against Uzzah'.[41] In the next chapter, David acknowledged that Yahweh had 'burst out' against the Philistines, where the same verb is used again and, as here,

---

41. The literal meaning of the place-name, 'Outbreak of Uzzah', has an objective genitive which means that Uzzah is the object of the outbreak.

the place was given a new name to remind the people of the 'break out' (1 Chron. 14:11).

David is not only angry but afraid. His was not a reverential fear of God on this occasion but a terror of the holy God whose anger he had provoked. David could not continue to bring the ark to his own city (1 Chron. 11:5, 7) under these circumstances. His question 'How can I bring the ark of God to me?' will be answered in chapter 15 when David follows the correct procedure as laid out in the Mosaic law.

Nothing is said about Israel's reaction to David's failure to bring the ark to Jerusalem. But it certainly must have turned out to be a public relations disaster for David as king, and a great embarrassment to him with so many people from all parts present. But for David and the Chronicler, the chief concern was the Lord's reaction and how best to house the ark. Though the ark was no representation of God, it was symbolic of the presence of the holy God among His people. What God had set apart as holy was to be treated as holy at all times.

The ark was thus taken to the home of a Gittite called Obed-edom. This person was probably the Levite mentioned later as a doorkeeper (1 Chron. 15:17-18, 24; 26:5). A 'Gittite' is an inhabitant of Gath (2 Sam. 15:18). Levites came from different tribal areas, so it is not inconceivable that Obed-edom hailed originally from the Philistine city of Gath but more probably he was from the Levitical city of Gath-rimmon (Josh. 21:23-24).[42]

The chapter ends on a note of hope. Yahweh blessed Obed-edom and his whole household, which would have encouraged David to believe that God's wrath was not on account of removing the ark from Kiriath-jearim and placing it elsewhere but for their incorrect transporting of it.

Application

This chapter was to be an encouragement to the post-exilic community to pull together and to place the communal worship of God at the centre of the nation's life. At the same time, it was a warning to the Chronicler's first readers and

---

42. Another Gath-rimmon near Shechem is mentioned in Joshua 21:25 and the Amarna Letters (see Woudstra, *The Book of Joshua*, pp. 310-11).

us that there is a right and wrong way of proceeding. Pagan practices, however meaningful and successful, were not to be followed. They were also reminded that even God's people, however sincere, cannot control God.

This account has been considered by liberal scholars and preachers as a clear example of the imperfect morality of the Old Testament. Kenneth Slack, onetime general secretary of the British Council of Churches, when discussing God's character referred to the circumstances of Uzzah's death as 'not only shocking but immoral' and that such a God was not 'the same God as the Father of Christ'. Martyn Lloyd-Jones, responding to the criticism, indicated that this striking intervention by God was a sign-post, warning and teaching us that He is to be worshipped and served in His way not ours.[43] It was on account of human rebellion against God that in His merciful love He struck down His own Son, Jesus Christ, who had willingly come for that very purpose to save His people from their sins.

David's kingship established and internationally recognised (14:1-17)

While 2 Samuel 6:1-23 relates the successful transfer of the ark to Jerusalem immediately after the initial aborted attempt, the Chronicler uses the three-month gap between the two episodes to introduce material that is paralleled in 2 Samuel 5:11-25. Though the events cover different periods of David's life, it serves the Chronicler's purpose to bring them together at this point in order to emphasise how God had blessed David by not only establishing him in Jerusalem and giving him offspring but by granting him victory over his enemies. In contrast to the Perez-uzza incident in the previous chapter, Baal Perazim becomes a reminder of an 'outbreak' by God against the formidable Philistines (14:11).

The chapter begins and ends with David's position as king internationally recognised (14:1-2; 17) with details of his large household (14:3-7) and his victories over the Philistines (14:8-16) sandwiched in between.

---

43. Iain H. Murray, *D. Martyn Lloyd-Jones, The Fight of Faith 1939-1981* (Edinburgh: Banner of Truth Trust, 1990), p. 319.

1. David's relations with Tyre (14:1-2)

14:1. Now Huram king of Tyre sent messengers to David and cedar trees, and masons and carpenters, to build a house for him. 2. And David knew that Yahweh had established him as king over Israel, for his kingdom was highly exalted for the sake of his people Israel.

Both Huram and Hiram are short forms of Ahirama.[44] From c. 979 B.C., Hiram I became king of the important Phoenician city of Tyre on the Mediterranean coast in what is today southern Lebanon. By that time, David was well-established in Jerusalem and Hiram was happy to assist David in the building of the king's palace (v. 1). This same king also provided Solomon with wood and skilled labour when Yahweh's palace was constructed (2 Chron. 2:3-16). Trading alliances and sharing of resources such as is found here, were significantly different from the disastrous marriage alliances entered into later by David's descendants.

The Chronicler indicates that not only was Obed-edom blessed (1 Chron. 13:14) but that David's reign had divine blessing, despite God's anger over Uzzah and the ark. The building of the palace in Jerusalem was a tangible indication that God had established him in Jerusalem as king of Israel. It is emphasised more strongly than in Samuel that David's kingdom had been especially exalted[45] by God for one very powerful reason: it was 'for the sake of' God's people Israel. It was not for self-aggrandizement but for the benefit of His people (v. 2; see 1 Chron. 11:10). The 'house' (v. 1) that was built for David is also seen later to be symbolic of the 'house' that Yahweh promises to build him (see 1 Chron. 17:10) and the next paragraph provides a pointer to this (vv. 3-7; see 1 Chron. 15:1).

Application

Officers in the church of Jesus Christ are chosen for the benefit of God's people not for their own private ambitions. In fact, Paul states that even rulers are appointed as ministers

---

44. The *Qere* reads Huram as in 2 Chronicles 2:3,11-12[2:2,10-11]; the *Kethibh* has Hiram followed by the LXX, Syriac and Vulgate.

45. *m'l* with *h locale* is used metaphorically for 'exceedingly' (BDB 2.c.(b), p. 752). It is a form only found in Chronicles (see 1 Chron. 22:5; 23:17; 29:3,25; etc.).

of God for the good of people under them (Rom. 13:4). More generally, as Matthew Henry comments, 'We are blessed in order that we may be blessings …. We are not born, nor do we live, for ourselves.' Christians are comforted by God that they may be able to comfort others who are afflicted with the comfort they themselves receive from God (2 Cor. 1:3-7).

2. David's household (14:3-7)

14:3. And David took more wives in Jerusalem, and David fathered more sons and daughters. 4. Now these are the names of the children whom he had in Jerusalem: Shammua and Shobab, Nathan and Solomon 5. and Ibhar and Elishua and Elpelet 6. and Nogah and Nepheg and Japhia 7. and Elishama and Beeliada and Eliphelet.

Chronicles continues largely to follow the narrative as in 2 Samuel 5:13-16 but does so for his own theological purposes. Only wives are mentioned; concubines are omitted. However, the two references to 'more' (v. 3) in connection with wives and children assume knowledge of the 2 Samuel 3:1-5 passage that mentions the sons born in Hebron as well as their mothers (see also 1 Chron. 3:1-4). The Chronicler is only interested at this point in those born in Jerusalem for the future of the kingdom lay there. Among these particular sons, Solomon appears, the one who would succeed David as king and to whom great promises are made. It is through Solomon that David's 'house' would be established for ever (1 Chron. 17:10-14).

Though the law forbad kings to possess many wives, polygamy was tolerated under the old Sinai administration (Deut. 17:17) and is not condemned by the Chronicler. Rather, the large number of sons born in Jerusalem indicates how blessed David was and it was a further sign that God had established his kingship.

His list of sons generally follows the earlier genealogy in 1 Chronicles 3:5-8 where thirteen names are given rather than the eleven in the Samuel text due to Elpelet or Eliphelet and Nogah being omitted. Where the spelling of the names in the two Chronicles' passages differs, the present passage agrees with the Samuel text in the case of Shammua (Shimea) and Elishua (Elishama). The penultimate name, 'Beeliada' is peculiar to this paragraph, as both 1 Chronicles 3:8 and

2 Samuel 5:16 read Eliada. Chronicles preserves at this point the original names which included the word 'Baal'. The change to 'El' had fewer negative associations. There are other cases where Chronicles keeps the original form (see 'Eshbaal' or 'Ishbaal' and 'Merib-Baal' in 1 Chron. 8:33-34), while 2 Samuel 2:8 and elsewhere replace 'baal' with 'bosheth' as in Ishbosheth. Jeremiah 3:24 and 11:13 indicate that the word 'bosheth' ('shame') was used as a substitute name for Baal when it referred to the Canaanite god.

3. David's victory over the Philistines (14:8-16)

14:8. Now the Philistines heard that David had been anointed king over all Israel, and all the Philistines went up to seek David, but David heard and went out to face them. 9. Now the Philistines came and made a raid in the valley of Rephaim. 10. And David asked God, 'Shall I go up against the Philistines? And will you give them into my hand?' Then Yahweh said to him, 'Go up, and I will give them into your hand.' 11. So they went up into Baal-perazim and David smote them there and said, 'God has burst through my enemies by my hand, like a bursting through of water'; therefore they called the name of that place Baal-perazim. 12. And they abandoned their gods there, and David ordered, and they were burned with fire.

13. And the Philistines yet again made a raid in the valley. 14. So David yet again asked God, and God said to him, 'You shall not go up after them; circle round about them and come to them in front of the Baca-trees. 15. And it shall be when you hear the sound of marching in the tops of the Baca-trees, then you will go out into the battle, because God has gone out before you to smite the camp of the Philistines.' 16. And David did as God commanded him, and they smote the camp of the Philistines from Gibeon to Gezer.

Much of the country was under the control of the Philistines after the death of Saul and, during the civil war period, the Philistines seem to have left David and Ishbosheth to fight it out between themselves. But now that 'all' Israel had acknowledged David as king, the Philistines recognised the need to destroy him. As in the parallel text in 2 Samuel 5:17-25, two battles against the Philistines are recorded where David obtained divine help and gained notable victories over this long-standing enemy.

The first battle (vv. 8-12) probably took place soon after the anointing ceremony at Hebron and therefore probably before David's capture of Jerusalem. David is shown to be fearless in seeking to confront them. When the Philistines made a raid in the Rephaim valley south of Jerusalem, David sought guidance from God and success was assured (v. 10). Guidance was probably obtained by means of the Urim and Thummim associated with the ephod (see 1 Sam. 14:41; 23:4-6; 28:6). The place where David defeated the enemy became known as Baal-perazim ('the Lord of breaking-through'; see *prṣ*, 1 Chron. 13:11), on account of David's confession that God had used him to break through the enemy lines like water bursting through a dam. The name Baal, meaning 'lord' or 'master', is applied here to Yahweh, not to the Canaanite or Phoenician god. In case anyone assumed from the Samuel text that David and his men kept as booty the costly statues of their gods that the Philistines had left behind, Chronicles makes clear that they were carried away to be burnt. David was faithful to the living God (see Deut. 7:5).

Though the actual site of the second battle (vv. 13-16) is not named, it may be assumed that it is in the same Rephaim valley, as indicated in the Samuel account. Again, David sought divine guidance and this time instead of direct assault, David and his men were instructed to circle around and make a surprise attack from the rear. The 'baca' are probably trees or shrubs, with many interpreters suggesting a variety of balsam or aspen but this is not certain. The singular form is found in the phrase 'valley of Baca' (Ps. 84:6[7]). On this occasion, God not only gave guidance to David but went before him into battle, the sign being the 'sound of marching' in the tree tops (v. 15). The word for 'marching' recalls Yahweh's awesome marching through the wilderness on behalf of His people (Judg. 5:4; Ps. 68:7[8]); see Deut. 33:2; Hab. 3:3, 12). There is a cosmic aspect to this battle. As a result, David was again victorious for he had obeyed God and went on to defeat the Philistines and push them back west as far as Gezer.

In this passage it is interesting to note the subtle differences between the Chronicler's text and the parallel passage in Samuel. Whereas Samuel uses God's covenant name 'Yahweh' consistently throughout, the Chronicler prefers

'God' (Elohim) apart from verse 10b. A similar phenomenon is found in the Psalm collection (compare Psalms 42–83 with Psalms 1–41 and especially Psalm 53 with Psalm 14). It may be due to the more universal outlook of the chapter with its reference to support from the Phoenicians and victory over the Philistines. Palmer Robertson suggests this with regard to the Elohim psalms.[46]

The minor differences between the two accounts with regard to David emphasise that though victory is due to God's help, David is God's instrument against the enemy. In his confession, instead of 'before me' (2 Sam. 5:20), David states that it is 'by my hand' that God had broken through his enemies (v. 11).

The contrast between Saul and David is striking in the passage. Whereas Saul 'asked' a medium in the face of the Philistine threat and did not enquire of God (1 Chron. 10:13), David 'asked' God (vv. 10 and 14). While Saul's head and armour were presented by the Philistines as trophies to their god (1 Chron. 10:9-10), David collects the images of their gods as spoil to be burnt (14:12). David 'did as God commanded' and proved faithful in burning the carved images by fire, unlike Saul who acted 'unfaithfully' in that he did not keep the word of Yahweh (1 Chron. 10:13). David's success against the Philistines thus begins to reverse the situation that existed at the time of Saul's death. It is like a return from an exilic position (see 1 Chron. 10:13-14).

It is possible the Chronicler had in mind Isaiah 28:21, especially as the text reads 'from Gibeon' (v. 16) rather than 'from Geba' (2 Sam. 5:25). In his oracle pronouncing his 'strange' work of judgment against Jerusalem, the prophet Isaiah recalls the occasion when God punished their enemies, breaking through upon the Philistines at Mount Perazim and also striking down the Canaanites in the 'valley of Gibeon' (see Josh. 10:11). Gibeon is only a few miles to the west of Geba and the Philistines were driven much further west to Gezer, so that the Chronicler is still informing us correctly of the enemy retreat. From his 'strange' or 'alien' work of fighting

46. O. Palmer Robertson, *The Flow of the Psalms: Discovering their Structure and Theology* (Phillipsburg: P&R, 2015).

against his own people, the Chronicler is encouraging the post-exilic community to appreciate that God's more familiar way, as Israel's history revealed, is to act decisively on behalf of his faithful people against enemy attack.

4. David's international fame (14:17)

14:17. Then David's name went out through all the lands, and Yahweh put the fear of him on all the nations.

The international outlook that is first hinted at in verse 1 is emphasised in this final comment, which finds no parallel in Samuel and reinforces what is stated in verse 2. It is similar to the Chronicler's later summary statements (see 2 Chron. 17:10; 20:29; etc.). Here it is made clear that the living God who has given victory to David over Israel's great enemy is none other than Yahweh, Israel's covenant-keeping God. Not only did David perceive that Yahweh had established him as king in Israel (v. 2) but the surrounding nations as well as the 'lands' of Israel (1 Chron. 13:2) were made aware of this fact and that he was a force to be reckoned with and someone who demanded respect. The phrase 'the fear of him' may be purposefully ambiguous, referring both to the fear of Yahweh and the fear of David.[47] When the Davidic covenant is introduced, it is emphasised that it is Yahweh who has made David's name great in the eyes of the world (see 1 Chron. 17:8).

Application

The Chronicler uses past experiences of God's help recorded in the Bible to encourage the post-exilic community to trust God. This, coupled with David's international renown, inspired God's people to look expectantly for the fulfilment of God's promises to David. David was a type of the Messiah who would be victorious over the evil one Himself, as Genesis 3:15 pronounces. Jesus is God's instrument of deliverance with whom God was well-pleased. He has 'broken through' to end the ultimate exile by Himself experiencing divine desertion (Mark 15:34). Because of this, God has highly exalted Him

---

47. See Klein, *1 Chronicles*, p. 343.

and given Him the name 'above every name' (Phil. 2:9; see Pss. 2:8-9; 72:17 and 89:27; Eph. 1:19-23).

The Philistines, like Edom and Babylon, become a type of all opposition to God and His people. David's example encourages believers now to resist the devil and to see him flee as the Philistines fled from David and his men. As God gave the sign of the heavenly army's movement in the tree tops, may similar signs of the Holy Spirit's activity be seen today, so that where the enemy has come in like a flood, God's people might see the dark powers of evil being pushed back and the work of God triumph.

The successful transfer of the ark (15:1–16:43)

The Chronicler makes clear that the worship of God is of fundamental importance to David and to the religious life of Israel. Concerning this second attempt to bring the ark to Jerusalem, much more detail is given by the Chronicler compared with the parallel text in 2 Samuel 6:12-19. The passage explains why the first attempt proved unsuccessful and indicates the right procedure for the ark's removal as set out in the Mosaic law. Great emphasis is placed on the role of the Levitical families in the ark's relocation, as well as their ongoing ministry in the sanctuaries at Jerusalem and Gibeon. The transfer of the ark followed by the psalm of thanksgiving takes centre stage (15:25-16:36), with David's arrangements concerning the priests and Levites surrounding the event (15:2-24; 16:37-42) and the entire section framed with references to the houses of David (15:1; 16:43).

> 15:1. He made houses for himself in the city of David; and he prepared a place for the ark of God, and pitched a tent for it. 2. Then David said that no one except the Levites should carry the ark of God, because Yahweh had chosen them to carry the ark of Yahweh and to serve him for ever. 3. And David assembled all Israel to Jerusalem to bring up the ark of Yahweh to its place, which he had prepared for it.

These introductory verses that announce the right procedure for carrying the ark find no parallel in the Samuel text. They especially fill out the brief reference to those 'bearing the ark' in 2 Samuel 6:13.

David's name does not appear as the subject of the first sentence (v. 1). The Chronicler assumes the reader will understand that it is the same David, whose fame and fear Yahweh had given him before the nations (1 Chron. 14:17). In continuing with his own house building projects (v. 1; see 1 Chron. 14:1), David had not forgotten his commitment to God concerning the ark. A site was cleared and a tent pitched in preparation for the ark's arrival in Jerusalem (see 2 Sam. 6:17). This special 'tent' is not to be confused with the tent of meeting that was to remain at Gibeon (1 Chron. 16:39).

Rather than in a cart pulled by oxen as on the previous occasion (1 Chron. 13:7, 9), similar to the example set by the pagan Philistines (see 1 Sam. 6), David ordered that the ark was to be carried by the Levites. This is what the Mosaic law directed and the Chronicler's language suggests that he had Numbers 4:15, Deuteronomy 10:8 and 18:5 in mind. As a united nation assembled to anoint David king and to make Jerusalem the capital (1 Chron. 11:1, 5), so representatives of 'all Israel' assembled together in Jerusalem to see the symbol of God's presence settled among them (v. 3; 1 Chron. 13:5).

15:4. Then David gathered the sons of Aaron and the Levites. 5. Of the sons of Kohath: Uriel the chief and 120 of his brothers. 6. Of the sons of Merari: Asaiah the chief and 220 of his brothers. 7. Of the sons of Gershom: Joel the chief and 130 of his brothers. 8. Of the sons of Elizaphan: Shemaiah the chief and 200 of his brothers. 9. Of the sons of Hebron: Eliel the chief and 80 of his brothers. 10. Of the sons of Uzziel: Amminadab the chief and 112 of his brothers.

15:11. And David called for Zadok and Abiathar the priests, and for the Levites: for Uriel, Asaiah, Joel, Shemaiah, Eliel and Amminadab. 12. And he said to them, 'You are the heads of the Levite fathers; sanctify yourselves, you and your brothers and bring up the ark of Yahweh, the God of Israel, to where I have prepared for it. 13. Because with reference to the first time when you were not *there*, Yahweh our God broke out against us, because we did not seek him according to the rule.' 14. So the priests and the Levites sanctified themselves to bring up the ark of Yahweh, the God of Israel. 15. Then the sons of the Levites carried the ark of God upon their shoulders with staves on them as Moses commanded, according to the word of Yahweh.

15:16. And David said to the chiefs of the Levites to appoint their brothers the singers, proclaiming on musical instruments:

harps, lyres and cymbals-to raise a joyful sound. 17. So the
Levites appointed Heman the son of Joel, and of his brothers,
Asaph the son of Berechiah; and of the sons of Merari their
brothers, Ethan, the son of Kushaiah 18. and with them their
brothers of the second *order*: Zechariah, Ben and Jaaziel and
Shemiramoth, Jehiel, Unni, Eliab, and Benaiah, and Maaseiah,
and Mattithiah, and Eliphelehu, and Mikneiah, and Obed-edom
and Jeiel the gatekeepers. 19. The musicians Heman, Asaph and
Ethan were to play on bronze cymbals, 20. and Zechariah and
Aziel and Shemiramoth and Jehiel and Unni and Eliab and
Maaseiah and Benaiah on harps according to Alamoth; 21. and
Mattithiah and Eliphelehu and Mikneiah and Obed-edom and
Jeiel and Azaziah to lead with lyres according to Sheminith. 22.
And Chenaniah *was* chief of the Levites in lifting: he directed in
lifting because he was skilled. 23. And Berechiah and Elkanah
were gatekeepers for the ark. 24. And Shebaniah and Joshaphat
and Nethanel and Amasai and Zechariah and Benaiah and
Eliezer the priests blew the trumpets before the ark of God.
Also Obed Edom and Jehiah were gatekeepers for the ark.

The occasion provided David with the opportunity of
gathering the priests ('the sons of Aaron', v. 4) as well as
the rest of the tribe of Levi. The priests were the ones who
blew the trumpets (v. 24) and offered the sacrifices (15:26 and
16:39-40). Though the term 'Levites' can denote the whole tribe
of Levi including the priests, it is used more often of those
from Levi's tribe who were not priests. These are the ones the
Chronicler particularly brings to our attention. Six groups
of Levites are listed, with details of each group following
the same pattern. The usual order for naming the first three
original sons of Levi is changed from Gershom (or Gershon,
see 1 Chron. 6:1,16), Kohath and Merari (Exod. 6:16-25;
1 Chron. 6:1) to Kohath, Merari and Gershom (vv. 5-7). Three
additional families are named but they also belong to the
Kohathites (vv. 8-10); they are Elizaphan, who is Uzziel's son
(Exod. 6:22; Num. 3:30; 2 Chron. 29:13), Hebron and Uzziel,
both of whom are Kohath's sons (1 Chron. 6:18; 23:19-20). The
six chiefs over their family groups include Uriel, Asaiah,
Joel, Shemaiah, Eliel and Amminadab and when the various
numerical figures from each group are added together they
total eight hundred and sixty-two, with five hundred and
twelve of them belonging to the Kohathites. By providing

such a large number of Kohathites, David was making sure this time round that the Mosaic law was followed correctly by providing enough men from this family to protect the ark and the holy vessels without touching them (Num. 3:27-32; 4:15).

Having introduced the six specially appointed Levites (vv. 4-10) whom David assembled, the text continues with David summoning and addressing the priests, the Levitical leaders and the six named chiefs. Zadok and Abiathar (v. 11) were the two high priests during David's kingship, the former serving at Gibeon (1 Chron. 16:39). According to the Mosaic law, the priests alone were allowed to handle the sacred ark (Num. 4:5-6,15), so their participation was as essential as those Levites appointed to carry it. They were all urged to 'sanctify' themselves (v. 12). All the sons of Levi were, of course, already separated by God for this work (Num. 3:5-6; Deut. 10:8), but for this special activity these priests and Levites were now called to 'make themselves holy'. Though the details are not described, their sanctification would probably have included bathing, the washing of their clothes and abstaining from sexual intercourse (see Exod. 19:10, 14-15; 40:12). Verse 14 declares that they carried out the requirements to the letter, with almost identical wording to verse 12 employed to emphasise the point. The ark had special significance and needed to be treated with proper respect. It was 'the ark of Yahweh, the God of Israel' (vv. 12,14; see 'the ark of God' in v. 15).

They are also reminded that it was their initial failure to transport the ark correctly that aroused Yahweh's anger (v. 13).[48] The use of the verb 'broke out' recalls the incident (1 Chron. 13:11), but instead of Uzzah's name being mentioned, David accepts that Uzzah's punishment was what they all deserved. Using the first person plural pronouns 'us' and 'our', David accepts guilt and does not seek to justify himself. Though, unlike Saul, they did seek Yahweh and the ark (1 Chron. 13:3), they 'did not seek' correctly. The phrase 'according to the rule' is the first of a number of

---

48. 'Because you did not' is an elliptical clause needing a predicate. Suggestions vary from 'carry it', to 'there'. The Hebrew form *lᵉmabbāri'šōnāh* is difficult. It is possibly made up of *lāmāh* ('why') plus *bāri'šōnāh* ('formerly', 'at first') or more simply an accumulation of prepositions *lᵉ*, *min* and *bᵉ* plus *ri'šōnāh* ('former', 'first') with the idea of 'with reference to the first time'.

occurrences where it is used for precise Levitical procedure (see 1 Chron. 23:31; 24:19; 2 Chron. 4:7, 20; 8:14; etc.). The proper way for carrying the ark is spelled out in verse 15 (see Num. 7:9). Again, it is emphasised that on this occasion the Kohathite Levites were obedient and did 'according to the word of Yahweh' as the Mosaic law commanded. The ark had 'poles' that were placed into rings on the ark ready for carriage and they were never to be taken out of the rings (see Exod. 25:13-15). The term 'staves', the Chronicler's word for 'poles', is also used for a yoke (Isa. 58:6).

The Chronicler concludes his account of the preparations for the ark's journey with David's employment of the Levitical musicians to express the joyfulness of the occasion (see 1 Chron. 12:40[41]). It was the 'chiefs of the Levites' (see vv. 4-11) who were given the task of appointing the three leading musicians and their assistants (v. 16).[49] The three musical instruments commonly used by the Levites are named. This time no 'tambourine' is mentioned (see 1 Chron. 13:8) and 'trumpets' are omitted because they were the responsibility of the priests. These singers 'proclaimed'.[50] Again, the Levite chiefs are obedient and appoint three leading musicians: Heman, Asaph and Ethan, representing each of the three main Levitical families (see vv. 5-7; 1 Chron. 6:31-48), although only Ethan's ancestor, Merari, is given (v. 17). Ethan is probably to be identified with Jeduthun (see 1 Chron. 16:41 and the Psalm headings to 39, 62 and 77). 'Kushaiah', his father, is an alternate form of 'Kishi' (see 1 Chron. 6:44).

The 'second' list is composed of Levite 'brothers' or relatives appointed to assist and fourteen are named (v. 18).[51] Jaaziel is written 'Aziel' in verse 20 and 'Jeiel' in 1 Chronicles

---

49. In this context, *mᵉšōrᵉrîm* 'singers' (Polel participle plural of *šîr*) could be translated more generally as 'musicians' according to Braun, *1 Chronicles*, p. 184, and likewise the noun *šîr* 'song' as 'musical'.

50. *mašmîʿîm* (Hiphil participle plural), literally 'causing to hear', could, in this context, be a musical term 'playing' or 'sounding', but 'proclaim' is better if the translation 'singers' is used. It may then be associated with 'prophetic singing' (see 1 Chron. 25:1-2).

51. Ben is omitted in several Hebrew MSS and the LXX and does not appear in verse 20 or 16:5. It may be that Zechariah's father is missing from the text and that instead of a person's name '*ben*' means 'the son of', reading 'Zechariah the son of ———'.

16:5. These names are repeated in verses 20-21 but Ben is omitted, Jaaziel is spelled Aziel (see 1 Chron. 16:5 where it is spelled Jeiel) and Azaziah's name is added. Whether Obed-edom (v. 18) is the Gittite from whose house the ark was taken (v. 25; 13:13-14) is not certain. While all those listed could have been gatekeepers (see 1 Chron. 9:17-27), from the way the text is written it is probable, in view of verse 24, that only Obed-edom and Jehiah acted in this capacity.

The Levite musicians are named again (vv. 19-21), this time to indicate the instruments they played. Appropriately, as the leading musicians, Heman, Asaph and Ethan were given the task of sounding the loud bronze cymbals (v. 19), while the first eight of the other Levites played the harps (v. 20) and the remaining six 'lead' with lyres (v. 21), both quieter stringed instruments. There is no certainty over the meaning of 'according to Alamoth' (see Ps. 46:1) and 'according to Sheminith' (see Pss. 6:1 and 12:1), which may be a reference to the tunes to be played rather than to the pitch.

Chenaniah (vv. 22,27) is another leader but his exact expertise is not immediately obvious, for the term *maśśā'* ('lifting') can refer, on the one hand, to 'lifting' the voice in song or to giving a prophetic 'utterance', or on the other hand, it could signify 'lifting' in the sense of carrying if the ark were in mind (2 Chron. 35:3). When the term again appears in verse 27 with the added expression 'the singers', it is clear that Chenaniah was chief in the area of raising the voice in song. The name 'Chenaniah' or 'Conaniah' occurs several times in Chronicles for various individuals associated with the Levites (1 Chron. 26:29; 2 Chron. 31:12; 35:9).

The references to the 'gatekeepers for the ark' (vv. 18, 23, 24) indicate their importance in preserving the ark's sanctity. They are presented by the Chronicler in such a way that they surround the priests who alone could blow the silver trumpets before the ark (vv. 23-24; Num. 10:8). Two gatekeepers, Berechiah and Elkanah, led the procession presumably to open the tent. Obed-edom and Jehiah (another form of Jeiel) are probably the ones mentioned in verse 18, having the double function of participating in the music and presumably, as gatekeepers, of closing up the tent after the event. The term 'gatekeeper' is used elsewhere with reference to the tabernacle or temple rather than specifically the ark. Among the occasions for trumpet blasts were days of gladness (Num. 10:10).

Application

The importance of obeying the revealed word of God is one of the concerns of the Chronicler as he instructs the people of his day. It remained important for many of the Jews during the Intertestamental period. Obeying God's word revealed in Scripture is also emphasised by the apostles (2 Tim. 3:16-17). The people of the post-exilic period in their concern to build their houses needed to be reminded constantly not to forget the importance of putting the Lord first as we see from the messages of the prophets of that period (Haggai and Zechariah and Malachi). Though David built houses for himself he also prepared a place for the ark of God, so Christians, in all the busyness of life, must be careful not to forget the place of communion with God in the home as well as of communal worship with God's people. It is interesting that the law of Moses gives no instruction concerning singing and music. They certainly sang spontaneously at the time of the exodus from Egypt (Exod. 15), but David uses the Levites, especially those with musical gifts, to encourage the praising of God on this special occasion and the Chronicler emphasises this Levitical function as he writes for the situation in the post-exilic period. For the church in the age of the Spirit, God has set down in His Word certain principles of communal worship but David's example also indicates freedom is given to us to express our devotion in song and music appropriate to the various occasions that arise and to use the gifts that members possess. Paul encourages singing to help and admonish believers and Peter urges Christians to use whatever gifts they have received to serve one another that in everything God may be glorified through Jesus Christ (Eph. 5:19-21; Col. 3:16-17; 1 Pet. 4:10-11).

15:25. So David and the elders of Israel and the commanders of thousands went to bring up the ark of the covenant of Yahweh from the house of Obed-edom with joy. 26 And because God helped the Levites who bore the ark of the covenant of Yahweh, they sacrificed seven bulls and seven rams. 27. And David was clothed with a robe of fine linen, also all the Levites who were carrying the ark and the musicians, and Chenaniah the chief of the musical lifting; also on David was an ephod of linen. 28. So all Israel was bringing up the ark of the covenant of Yahweh with shouting and with the sound of the horn, and with trumpets and with cymbals, playing loudly with harps and lyres. 29. And it was as the ark of the covenant of Yahweh came to the city of David, that Michal the daughter of Saul, looked out of the window and saw David the king leaping and laughing and she despised him in her heart.

At this point, Chronicles again parallels the 2 Samuel 6 text but in wording that emphasises the writer's concerns. From the more general term 'ark of God' (vv. 15, 24) through to the more specific designation 'ark of Yahweh the God of Israel' (vv. 12, 14), the ark is now referred to four times as the 'ark of the covenant of Yahweh' (vv. 25, 26, 28, 29). The ark, symbol of Yahweh's invisible presence and covenant relationship with His people, was to be the very centre of Israel's covenantal life in David's capital city. It was called the ark of the covenant for it contained Yahweh's covenant tablets, the Ten Commandments (Deut. 10:1-5, 8; see also Josh. 8:33). Through the nation's representatives ('the elders and commanders of thousands', v. 25), 'all Israel' were involved (v. 28; see v. 3). It was probably the joyous occasion ('with joy', v. 25) described in Psalm 68.[52]

This second attempt had God's approval for He 'helped' the Levites who were now 'carrying' the ark themselves, as He had 'helped' the Transjordanian tribes against the Hagrites and David against Saul (1 Chron. 5:20; 12:18[19]). 'God has power to help or to cast down' (2 Chron. 25:8). Appropriate sacrifices were offered through the appointed means, the personal pronoun 'they' (v. 26) referring to the Levites who were priests. This was in addition to the ones offered by David (2 Sam. 6:13; 1 Chron. 16:2). While Samuel merely states that David was wearing a 'linen ephod', the Chronicler explains that both king and all the Levites were dressed in robes of 'fine linen' made of byssus silk (v. 27;

2 Chron. 5:12). David's 'linen ephod' was an additional item of clothing associated with the priests (1 Sam. 2:18; 22:18) and to be distinguished from the ephod worn by the high priest (Exod. 28:1-39; Lev. 8:7; 1 Sam. 2:28; 14:3). The priestly garments worn by David together with his close supervision of the sacrifices (see 16:1-2) suggest that the Chronicler sees David as exercising a priestly role. Only the ram's 'horn' is referred to in 2 Samuel 6:15 but the Chronicler includes all the instruments previously mentioned (v. 28; see vv. 19-21). Compared with 2 Samuel, only briefly does the account reveal the attitude of Michal, Saul's daughter, to her husband's behaviour. David's concern for the ark and his enthusiasm over its arrival in the city he had made his capital, is in marked contrast to Saul's lack of interest in it. Saul's daughter has not been mentioned previously by the Chronicler as David's wife, but this fleeting reference is enough to indicate that she represented the same spirit as her father.

Application

Michal chose to follow in her father's footsteps rather than to be one with her husband in seeking God and rejoicing in the symbol of His presence. Here was a message for the Chronicler's own day and important for our own age. Do we follow those who have little or no interest in worshipping God or do we earnestly seek to be in tune with God and wholeheartedly serve Him? As the ark spoke of God among His people, so we have God in Christ dwelling among His people by His Spirit (Matt. 18:20; 1 Cor. 14:25; Col. 1:27). How central is Christ in our lives and worship? David's enthusiastic expression of devotion was not contrived. Times of spiritual awakening in the church have often been accompanied by leaping and laughing for joy as people have been taken up with God and His grace toward them. But at the same time our communal worship should be done decently and in order (1 Cor. 14:40). The whole incident concerning the ark's removal speaks both of fear and joy. Similarly, in times of revival when 'great power' and 'great grace' are evident (Acts 4:33), it can produce 'great fear' as well as 'great joy' (Acts 5:11; 8:8). As God helped the Levites who faithfully carried out God's will, so Paul could testify before Agrippa that in all his evangelistic activities he had obtained divine assistance, for he had only proclaimed what the Word of God through Moses and the prophets had indicated (Acts 26:22-23).

> 16:1. So they brought the ark of God and placed it in the middle of the tent which David had pitched for it; and they presented burnt offerings and peace offerings before God. 2. And when David had finished offering the burnt offerings and the peace offerings, that he blessed the people in the name of Yahweh. 3. And he distributed to every person of Israel, both man and woman, to everyone a loaf of bread, a piece of meat and a raisin cake.

This paragraph follows closely the text of 2 Samuel 6:17-19. As the specially prepared tent or tabernacle was erected in the wilderness (Exod. 40:2, 21), so David provided a tent in which to place the ark. For the Chronicler, it completes the statement of 1 Chronicles 15:1. The two main kinds of sacrifice were offered by David and the people, both representing atonement but in addition, the peace offerings were associated with fellowship, with portions of the meat being distributed widely (Lev. 7:11-18). It is for this reason that the otherwise unknown Hebrew term 'ešpār is translated 'piece of meat'. As king, David acted as a father figure over his people and so he blessed them (Gen. 27:4; 48:15; Exod. 39:43) and showed kindness to every individual in Israel. In such a way, David cemented Israel's unity. The whole incident depicts David as in some respects a second Moses who not only exercised some priestly functions but pitched a tent for the ark and blessed the people (Exod. 33:7; Deut. 33:1). The king's priestly role on this special occasion provides a type of that priest-king figure prophesied by David (Ps. 110:1,4).

Application

The church is at its best and united when Jesus Christ, our anointed priest and king, is central to its life and work. While the ark points us to God's covenant love in Christ toward His people, David provides us with a type of our Saviour who pitched His tent among us, died an atoning death and through whom God has blessed us with all spiritual blessings (John 1:14; Eph. 1:3). Before Jesus ascended He blessed His disciples (Luke 24:50-51). If we belong to the Christ who has redeemed us to God then we are truly blessed.

> 16:4. Then he set some of the Levites as ministers before the ark of Yahweh to commemorate, to thank, and to praise Yahweh, the God of Israel. 5. Asaph the head and his second Zechariah, Jeiel and Shemiramoth and Jehiel and Mattithiah and Eliab, and Benaiah and Obed-edom and Jeiel, with instruments of harps and lyres, and Asaph sounding with cymbals, 6. and Benaiah and Jahaziel the priests *blew* with trumpets regularly before the ark of the covenant of God. 7. On that day then David first appointed for thanksgiving to Yahweh by the hand of Asaph and his brothers.

At this point the Chronicler incorporates fresh material not found in 2 Samuel 6. He first introduces those Levites who were set apart to praise Yahweh (vv. 4-7), before presenting an example of the type of psalm that was sung on this special occasion (vv. 8-36a) and closing with the people's response (v. 36b). The phrase 'Yahweh the God of Israel' provides an *inclusio* (vv. 1 and 36).

David introduces a major innovation as part of the Jerusalem worship. While the main altar and tent still remained at this stage in Gibeon, the king appointed a group of Levites, that included priests, to have this distinct function of ministering in song 'before the ark' that was at rest in his capital city. They were commissioned to 'commemorate' as well as to express thanksgiving and praise. The last two terms speak for themselves and there are examples in the Psalter of praise and thanksgiving psalms that these Levites could have used as occasion demanded (see, for example, Psalms 29 and 30). There is uncertainty over how the first verb 'to commemorate' (literally 'to bring or cause to remember') is to be understood in this context. When used with God's name it has the sense of 'to invoke' (Exod. 20:24) but where David employs the word in his psalms and in the headings to Psalms 38 and 70, it suggests bringing his plight to God's remembrance and hence it is often associated with lament psalms. All three verbs are present in the following psalm (see vv. 8-12). Rather than seeing the terms as separate activities we should perhaps understand them as a way of expressing the comprehensive nature of this aspect of the communal

worship by the Levites.[53] Paul uses a similar build-up of terms
to emphasise the importance of prayer (Phil. 4:6). It is akin to
the eight synonyms for God's law in Psalm 119.

The Levitical group chosen from the list in the previous
chapter (15:16-24), consisted of ten members headed by
Asaph who played the cymbals (v. 5; see 15:19). Zechariah
was second in command and he with eight others played the
harps and lyres. The first named 'Jeiel' is probably another
way of pronouncing Aziel or Jaaziel (see 15:18, 20). Two priests
charged with blowing the trumpets (v. 6) were among this
select group to be in regular attendance before the ark.
When naming the priests in 1 Chronicles 15:24, Benaiah's
name appears immediately before Eliezer's and this might
suggest that this otherwise unknown priest Jahaziel (v. 6)
is another name for Eliezer, or, for some reason, replaced
Eliezer. Trumpet blowing by the priests was in the Mosaic
legislation (Num. 10:2, 8-10) and its function here was to aid
the communal worship (Ps. 98:6).

Asaph's prominent position as chief musician in Jerusalem
is highlighted along with the importance of David's position
in regulating the ongoing worship at the tent where the
ark rested (v. 7; see v. 37). It is later recorded that Asaph
'prophesied' under the direction of the king (1 Chron. 25:2).
Psalms 50 and 73–83 belong to the Asaph collection. The
psalm that follows is not said to have been composed for this
occasion. Rather, it is an example of the kind of thanksgiving
song of praise sung by the Levitical singers.[54]

16:8. O give thanks to Yahweh, call on his name; make known
his deeds among the peoples. 9. Sing to him, make music to him,
meditate on all his wonders. 10. Boast in his holy name; let the
heart of those who seek Yahweh rejoice. 11. Seek Yahweh and
his strength; seek his face regularly. 12. Remember his wonders
which he has done, his signs and the judgments of his mouth.
13. O seed of Israel, his servant, O sons of Jacob, his chosen ones.
14. He is Yahweh our God, his judgments are in all the earth.
15. Remember for ever his covenant, the word he commanded
for a thousand generations, 16. which he made with Abraham,

53. Selman, *1 Chronicles*, p. 167.

54. For the use of the same psalm or parts of a psalm in new contexts, see
Eveson, *Psalms* Vol. 1, p. 258.

and his oath to Isaac, 17. and established it for Jacob as a statute, for Israel as an everlasting covenant, 18. saying, 'To you I will give the land of Canaan, the portion of your inheritance.' 19. When you were few in number, like a little and sojourners in it, 20. and wandering about from nation to nation, and from a kingdom to another people, 21. he did not permit anyone to oppress them; and rebuked kings on their account, 22. 'Do not touch my anointed ones and do my prophets no harm.'

16:23. Sing to Yahweh, all the earth; bear good news of his salvation from day to day. 24. Declare his glory among the nations, his wonders among all the peoples. 25. For Yahweh is great and greatly to be praised, and he is to be feared above all gods. 26. For all the gods of the peoples are idols, but Yahweh made the heavens. 27. Splendour and majesty are before him; strength and joy are in his place. 28. Ascribe to Yahweh, O families of the peoples, give to Yahweh glory and strength. 29. Ascribe to Yahweh the glory of his name, lift up an offering and come before him. Worship Yahweh in holy adornment. 30. Tremble before him, all the earth; yes, the world is established, it shall not totter. 31. Let the heavens rejoice and let the earth be glad and let them say among the nations, 'Yahweh reigns!' 32. Let the sea roar and its fulness, let the field exult, and everything in it. 33. Then the trees of the forest shall give a ringing cry before Yahweh, for he comes to judge the earth. 34. Give thanks to Yahweh for he is good, for his steadfast love is for ever. 35. And say, 'Save us, O God of our salvation, and gather us and deliver us from the nations, to give thanks to your holy name, to boast in praising you. 36. Blessed be Yahweh, the God of Israel, from everlasting even to everlasting!' Then all the people said, 'Amen!' and praised Yahweh.

The Chronicler brings together a selection of praise and thanksgiving psalms that are found in the biblical Psalter, none of which have any heading indicating authorship. They could very well have come from the time when David brought the ark to Jerusalem and to have belonged to the Asaph collection. There are examples in the Psalter itself where passages from different psalms are combined to form a new psalm (compare Psalm 40:13-17 and Psalm 70; Psalm 108 and Psalms 57:7-11 and 60:5-12). The three psalms that make up this new composition all appear in Book Four of the Psalter (Psalms 90–106), psalms that were particularly appropriate to the Babylonian exilic situation. They are: Psalms 105:1-15

(vv. 8-22); 96:1-13 (vv. 23-33); 106:1 (v. 34); 106:47-48 (vv. 35-36). The overall use of this fresh model psalm would have been an encouragement to the post-exilic community to appreciate the continuity of worship from the days of David to their own times and to renew their faith in Yahweh and His promises.

Though seemingly derived from the three canonical psalms, this psalm must be viewed as a composition in its own right with the differences purposeful and thus needing no emendations. It begins with a call to thanksgiving and praise (vv. 8-13) and, typical of praise psalms, reasons for praise are given. God's people are urged to praise Yahweh on account of His promises (vv. 14-18) and the protection He gave the patriarchs (vv. 19-22). This is followed by a second call to sing praise and proclaim Yahweh's salvation but this time addressed to all the earth (vv. 23-24), for unlike the gods of the nations which are nonentities, Yahweh is real and active (vv. 25-27). A further call is given to the various people groups and families to worship this stunning God who reigns over the whole world and governs fairly (vv. 28-30). The whole cosmos, in fact, is called to make its contribution in expressing joyful praise to Israel's God (vv. 31-33). A final call to give thanks to Yahweh on account of His goodness and faithful love leads into an appeal for deliverance from the nations that God's people might continue to give thanks and praise God's holy name (vv. 34-35). The psalm closes with a doxology followed by the people's affirmation (v. 36).

The opening appeal to give thanks to Yahweh (v. 8) is matched by a similar call toward the close (v. 34) and sets the tone and theme for the whole psalm. To 'call' on Yahweh's name has more to do with proclaiming to all the nations who Israel's God is, than using His name as the basis of prayer, and the following imperative ('make known') confirms this. Yahweh's reputation and deeds are to be publicised before the people groups of the world. Again they are urged to sing, make music and meditate on His marvellous saving actions (v. 9; see vv. 12, 23, 24). God's people are called to boast in Yahweh's holy name (v. 10; see v. 35 and 1 Chron. 13:6). The worshippers who are exhorted to rejoice (see also v. 31) are ones who truly seek God. The terms used in verses 10 and 11 for 'seek' are especially important to the Chronicler for they express devotion to God and a desire to do His will rather than to look elsewhere (see 1 Chron. 10:13-14; 13:3; 15:13). Seeking God's 'strength' is closely associated with seeking His 'presence' and in this context may very well be a way of referring to the ark (see Pss. 78:61; 132:8).

As with most praise psalms, reasons accompany the call to praise. The people are to remember God's marvellous activity of old at the time of the exodus (v. 12; see v. 9). God's 'wonders' would refer particularly to the 'plagues' of Egypt (Exod. 7:3; Ps. 78:43) and the 'judgments of his mouth' to His decisions to punish Pharaoh (Exod. 6:6; 7:4; 12:12). God also pronounced such judgments against Israel (Jer. 1:16). These judicial decisions apply to 'all the earth' (v. 14b). Though Yahweh is Israel's God, He is no local god and this is why all people groups need to hear about Him (see vv. 1 and 14a). Whereas Psalm 105:6 reads 'seed of Abraham', our text has 'Israel' which then parallels 'Jacob' in the second line (v. 13). It further confirms the Chronicler's preference for 'Israel' as the way of referring to God's chosen people (see 1 Chron. 1:34; 2:1). There is another call for people to remember (v. 15)[55] but this time it is God's covenant with Abraham (v. 16; see Gen. 12:1-3, 7; 15:18; 17:1-14) and renewed with Isaac and Jacob (vv. 16-17; see Gen. 26:3-4; 28:13-14; 35:10-12). This covenant is unconditional and perpetual and attention is drawn particularly to the promise concerning Canaan (v. 18). It is their inherited 'portion' or 'allotment'. Again, for the encouragement of his people, the Chronicler applies the words of Psalm 105:12 to his own day by changing 'when they were' to 'when you were' (v. 19). It also indicates the solidarity of his generation with their ancestors. Like the patriarchs, Israel had been in exile as 'sojourners' and few in number and yet God had protected them (see Gen. 12:3a). In mind would be Abraham's time in Egypt and Jacob's move to Haran and later to Egypt, as well as the difficulties some of them had in producing children. It is Abraham who is particularly in mind (vv. 21-22; see Gen. 12:17; 14; 20:1-3), although the Philistine king also instructed his people not to touch Isaac

55. See verse 12. A plural imperative replaces the singular indicative where Yahweh is the subject as in Psalm 105:8.

and his wife (Gen. 26:11,29). Only here and in Psalm 105:15 are the terms 'anointed one' and 'prophet' found in parallel lines. While Abraham alone is called 'prophet' in Genesis 20:7, it is applied here, with the term 'anointed', to all the patriarchs. David was aware that even king Saul, his enemy, was the Lord's anointed and for that reason David would not kill him (1 Sam. 24:6; 26:9,11, etc.). The psalm by implication is applying it to Israel generally, which is why they existed after the exile even while still under foreign rule and 'slaves' (Ezra 9:8-9).

In verses 23-33, there is a universal summons to praise Yahweh. Many themes from the previous section reappear but now 'all the earth' is called to join in singing praise to Yahweh so that all nations and people groups might learn of Yahweh (vv. 23-24). Even the cosmos is encouraged to take part (vv. 31-33). The repeated calls 'to sing' praise to Yahweh as well as to sing 'a new song' found in Psalm 96:1-2 are dropped, leaving the content of what is to be announced and declared more prominent. The joyful news of God's salvation, the display of His stunning importance and His wonderful works ('wonders', vv. 23-24) are the points made. All the sons of Adam (see 1 Chron. 1:1) need to know that Yahweh is not like the gods of the other nations. They are nonentities but Yahweh is the creator God and to be praised and held in awe (vv. 25-26). In place of 'strength and beauty' the text reads 'strength and joy' and this couplet along with 'splendour and majesty' (v. 27) are like close aides associated with God. Joy is encouraged by the Chronicler on a number of occasions and here it is closely associated with the presence of the invisible God. Instead of 'sanctuary' our text reads 'place' and this is appropriate for the context as there was no sanctuary as such only a specially prepared place where the ark rested in a tent (1 Chron. 15:1, 3, 12). Psalm 96:6 takes for granted the presence of the temple. The same reason applies to 'come before him' which replaces 'come into his courts' (v. 27; see Ps. 96:8). What glory and strength God gives people is to be returned to Him in praise (v. 28). All nations are urged to give to Yahweh the honour due to Him. As lesser rulers brought tribute to the supreme overlord, so all the families of the earth are to show their allegiance, worshipping or doing obeisance before the majestic splendour of holiness with which Yahweh is arrayed.

Trembling in awe of His presence is the only right response from 'all the earth' (v. 30a), as the creator God and sovereign Lord has firmly established the inhabited world (v. 30b). Thus heaven and earth, sea and field can together be glad and declare that 'Yahweh reigns' (vv. 31-32; see Psalm 96 where the declaration 'Yahweh reigns' is placed after 'Tremble … all the earth' and before 'the world is established'). All are to rejoice on account of Yahweh's coming to judge the earth (Chronicles omits Psalm 96:10b and 13b).

In the final verses (vv. 34-36), there is a renewed call to give thanks (see v. 8) and the familiar refrain heard at different periods of Israel's history presents the reason (2 Chron. 5:13; 7:3; 20:21; Pss. 106:1; 107:1; 118:1, 29). Despite Israel's unfaithfulness, the good Yahweh (see Ps. 100:5; 2 Chron. 30:18) has shown kindness to His people and His enduring love never gives up on them. With slight but significant differences, the text of Chronicles having begun with the words of Psalm 106:1 ends with the closing two verses of that same psalm, where prayer is followed by praise instead of vice versa and thus providing a mirror image of the opening. In view of Yahweh's commitment toward Israel, Chronicles adds 'and say' to embolden the people to make the following passionate prayer. 'God of our salvation' replaces 'Yahweh our God' and along with the addition of 'deliver' strengthens the plea for God to 'save' (v. 35; see v. 23). Gathering and rescuing the people 'from the nations' could have applied to any period in Israel's history, including David's time, but the words would have been particularly appropriate during the exilic period and even after the return when God's people still thought of themselves in bondage to the Persians (Ezra 9:8-9). The appeal is made not for selfish ends but in order to express thanksgiving to God's holy name (v. 35; see v. 10) and in praising Him to 'boast' concerning Him. The psalm concludes with worship using the same doxology that brings Books One and Four of the Psalter to a close (Pss. 41:13; 106:48; see also 2 Chron. 2:12[11]; 6:4). When God is the object, the word 'blessed' suggests bowing the knee in submissive devotion (v. 36a). The Chronicler then adapts the final words of Psalm 106:48b, 'And let all the people say Amen! Praise Yah' ('Hallelujah) to the situation he is describing, where the people endorsed the song of thanksgiving by the Levites and 'praised Yahweh' (v. 36b).

Application

Like the calls in the Psalter, Chronicles uses this Davidic psalm to encourage the post-exilic community to praise Yahweh and to look to Him and the promises He has made. The presence of Yahweh in Jerusalem under the symbol of the ark is the setting for the psalm's message for the Chronicler's people not to give up hope concerning the coming of Yahweh (see Mal. 3:1-5). The knowledge that they were specially set apart to bear witness as anointed prophets, would have uplifted the spirits of the Jews after the exile. They are urged to make known Yahweh's wonderful deeds to the people groups of the earth so that they might fear Him.

Christians are prophets and priests teaching and exhorting each other as they sing God's praises and seeking to proclaim to all the world the good news of God's salvation. All need to be convinced that there is no God but Yahweh, the God and Father of our Lord Jesus Christ (1 Cor. 8:4-6). This God, who in Christ came to save His people from their sins, is coming to judge the earth (Acts 17:30-31). In this ministry, God's people are 'immortal' till their work on earth is done. The promised inheritance to all who belong to Abraham's seed through Christ finds its fulfilment in the new creation. Canaan symbolised that future new earth that God's people are to inherit (Matt. 5:5; Rom. 4:13-18; Heb. 6:12; 11:13-16; Rev. 21:1-7). In all our activities, we are urged to 'give thanks for everything to God the Father in the name of our Lord Jesus Christ (Eph. 5:20) and to add our Amens and Hallelujahs (2 Cor. 1:20; Rev. 19:1-6; 22:21). This particular psalm gives biblical warrant for producing fresh compositions for new situations using existing psalms or material found in our New Testaments.

> 16:37. So he left there, before the ark of the covenant of Yahweh, Asaph and his brothers to minister before the ark regularly as each day required. 38. And Obed-edom and sixty-eight of their brothers – and Obed-edom *was* the son of Jeduthun – and Hosah *were* gatekeepers. 39. And he left Zadok the priest and

his brothers the priests before the tabernacle of Yahweh in the high place at Gibeon, 40. to offer burnt offerings to Yahweh on the altar of burnt offering regularly morning and evening, according to everything written in the law of Yahweh which he commanded Israel. 41. And with them *were* Heman and Jeduthun and the rest of the chosen who were designated by name to thank Yahweh for his steadfast love is for ever. 42. And with them Heman and Jeduthun *had* trumpets and cymbals to play loudly and instruments for the song of God; and the sons of Jeduthun *were* for the gate. 43. Then all the people went, each to his house, and David turned to bless his house.

The narrative returns to where it left off at verse 7. David entrusted Asaph and his fellow Levitical singers to carry out their regular daily duties before the ark (see v. 5). Verse 38 concerns the Jerusalem gatekeepers. The two chief gatekeepers were Obed-edom who was a Kohathite of the Korah family (1 Chron. 26:1-4), the son of a different Jeduthun from the one who was a Merarite (1 Chron. 6:44), and Hosah who was a Merarite (see 1 Chron. 26:10-19; Num. 4:29-33). Obed-edom had this dual function both as a musician and gatekeeper (see 1 Chron. 15:24). Sixty-two of the gatekeepers belonged to Obed-edom's family, while the other six belonged to Hosah (see 1 Chron. 26:8,10-11), making sixty-eight in all.

Interestingly, although not directly relevant to the narrative, the Chronicler refers to the tabernacle and altar of burnt-offering at Gibeon. This city lay about five miles (eight kilometres) northwest of Jerusalem and is identified with modern El-Jib. It became a Levitical city in territory belonging to Benjamin (Josh. 18:25; 21:17). After the destruction of the Shiloh sanctuary by the Philistines (1 Sam. 4; Jer. 7:12), we know that the priests moved to Nob (1 Sam. 21). Following their slaughter (1 Sam. 22:6-23), Gibeon eventually became the site of the Mosaic tabernacle and bronze altar (1 Chron. 21:29). While most 'high places' were associated with Canaanite worship and led Israel into apostasy, 'the high place at Gibeon' (v. 39) was an exception as it was used for the worship of Yahweh (see Josh. 9:27). David appointed Zadok (1 Chron. 6:8) 'the priest' (the normal pre-exilic way of referring to the high priest), along with his fellow priests to serve at the altar, offering the daily burnt offerings at the set times specified in the Mosaic law (verse 40; 1 Chron. 6:49; see Exod. 29:38-42; Num. 28:1-8). Unlike 1 Chronicles 15:11, no mention is made in this context of Abiathar, possibly on account of his later involvement in the accession plot and the disgrace that followed (see 1 Kings 1–2).

In addition to the priests, David assigned two leaders from the musicians to serve at Gibeon, Heman a Kohathite and Jeduthun a Merarite (v. 41; 1 Chron. 6:33[18], 44[29]) along with other named Levites who had not been assigned to Jerusalem (see 1 Chron. 15:17-22). Like Asaph, their duties were to give thanks to Yahweh with the same kind of instruments used for accompaniment (vv. 41-42; see vv. 4-7). The refrain, 'for his steadfast love is for ever,' is a succinct and characteristic example of the content of both the hymns sung and the response of the worshippers (see v. 34; Ps. 136:1-26; etc.). Gatekeepers were also employed at Gibeon on account of the tabernacle being there and some of the sons of Jeduthun acted in this capacity as well as being singers (v. 42b; see 15:23-24).

To bring the whole narrative of the ark's transfer to Jerusalem to a conclusion, the Chronicler closes with words paralleled in 2 Samuel 6:19b-20a. The first part in both accounts rounds off the whole narrative, but whereas in Samuel the second part introduces the Michal episode (2 Sam. 6:20-23; see 1 Chron. 15:29), in Chronicles it acts as a very suitable introduction to what follows.

Each Israelite went back to his house, which, in this context, was a sign of peace and wellbeing. Having already blessed his people (16:2), David turned to bless his own house. The use of the word 'house' not only frames this section (see 15:1) but it prepares us for the term's frequent use in the following chapter (17:1, 4-6, 10, 12, 14, etc.).

Application

The Chronicler indicates, for the benefit of his people, the legitimate nature of the Gibeonite sanctuary and the unity that existed despite there being two sites, with the Levitical families carrying out similar duties in both places. At the same time, he stresses how the sacrifices were carried out precisely as ordained by the Mosaic law. The continuity of worship that was revealed under David served to encourage the Chronicler's first readers to remain faithful to Yahweh and to look to the day when the sacrifices would be obsolete with the coming of the antitype. Though the post-exilic people did not have the ark of the covenant, the Chronicler's reminder of its importance would have increased their longing for the presence of God's glory among them. Paul could speak of beholding the glory of God as a result of the coming of Jesus the Messiah and the Spirit of God (2 Cor. 3:7-18; 4:5-6; see also John 1:14)

Concerning the temple and dynasty (17:1-27)

Unlike the Samuel text, the immediately preceding words concerning David's house provide an appropriate introduction to this chapter which concerns David's desire to build a temple, the oracle of Nathan the prophet and David's prayer. However, Chronicles does now follow the parallel passage in 2 Samuel 7 quite closely but with some interesting differences that reveal the Chronicler's theology. Viewed in the light of the whole work, it is clear that this chapter has great significance in presenting the reigns of David and Solomon as jointly exhibiting something of God's rule on earth. The importance of the chapter for the Chronicler is seen in the repeated references to its contents in subsequent passages (1 Chron. 22:6-10; 28:2-10; 2 Chron. 6:15-17; 7:17-18). Though the word 'covenant' is not used, other biblical texts relating to these promises made by God to David do use the term (see 2 Sam. 23:5; Pss. 89:3, 28; 132:12; Isa. 55:3). The allusions to the patriarchal blessings would also suggest an extension of the Abrahamic covenant. It is with the play on the word 'house', found fourteen times in the chapter, that the narrative moves smoothly from David's own palace ('house') and his desire to build a temple ('house') for Yahweh, to Yahweh's promise to build David a lasting dynasty ('house') and to recognise a future temple ('house') built by David's son. The chapter divides as follows: David's plan (vv. 1-2); Nathan's oracle (vv. 3-15); and David's prayer response (vv. 16-27) which expresses amazement and praise (vv. 16-22) and acceptance that God would do what He had promised (vv. 23-27).

17:1. Now it was when David dwelt in his house that David
said to Nathan the prophet, 'Here I am dwelling in a house of
cedar, but the ark of the covenant of Yahweh is under curtains.'
2. Then Nathan said to David, 'Do all that is in your heart for
God is with you.'

David now resides in a very grand home ('house') but the ark
of the covenant that speaks of God's presence is lodged in a
simple nomadic tent ('curtains', v. 1; see 1 Chron. 14:1; 15:1).
The Chronicler makes no mention of David's rest from the
surrounding enemies (2 Sam. 7:1b) for he has yet to give further
details of enemy defeats in the following three chapters.
David's concern is to remedy the embarrassing disparity
between his own splendid home and the covering 'under'
which 'the ark of the covenant of Yahweh' (1 Chron. 15:25) had
been placed. David shared his good idea, not with the people
as previously (1 Chron. 13:1-3), but with a prophet. This is the
first mention of Nathan by the Chronicler and he is portrayed
as a trusted adviser to the king whose initial positive response
did not dampen the king's initiative. There was every reason
to encourage the king's pious thoughts, for Yahweh was with
him and had clearly established him as king (1 Chron. 11:9;
14:2), and Yahweh Himself actually accepted the correctness
of Nathan's assessment (see v. 8 below).

17:3. But it happened in that night that the word of God came
to Nathan, saying, 4. 'Go and say to David my servant, Thus
says Yahweh, you shall not build the house for me to dwell in.
5. For I have not dwelt in a house from the day that I brought
up Israel until this day but have been from tent to tent and
from dwelling *to dwelling.* 6. Wherever I have moved about in all
Israel, did I speak a word with one of the judges of Israel whom
I commanded to shepherd my people, saying, Why have you not
built for me a house of cedar? 7. And now thus shall you say to
my servant David, Thus says Yahweh of hosts, I took you from
the pasture, from following the sheep, to be prince over my
people Israel, 8. and I have been with you wherever you have
gone and have cut off all your enemies before you; and I will
make for you a name like the name of the great ones who are in
the earth. 9. And I will assign a place for my people Israel and
will plant them that they may dwell in their place and be shaken
no more nor shall sons of wickedness continue to wear them
out as before, 10. that is from the days that I commanded judges

over my people Israel; and I will subdue all your enemies. And I declare to you that Yahweh will build a house for you. 11. And it shall be when your days have been filled up for going with your fathers that I will raise up your seed after you that shall be from your sons, and I will establish his kingdom. 12. He will build for me a house, and I will establish his throne for ever. 13. I will be a father to him and he shall be a son to me; and I will not remove my steadfast love from him as I removed it from him who was before you. 14. And I will station him in my house and my kingdom for ever, and his throne will be established for ever.' 15. According to all these words and according to all this vision, thus did Nathan speak to David.

In a vision that same night (vv. 3, 15), God first made clear to Nathan that David would not build a temple (vv. 4-6) but on the positive side God stated that He would build him a dynasty (vv. 7-14). Both parts of the reply begin with the messenger formula: 'Thus says Yahweh (of hosts)' (vv. 4, 7). The king is addressed by God as 'my servant'. Altogether, this title occurs twelve times in the chapter. It denotes a privileged and responsible position and is restricted to God's true prophets and special individuals such as Abraham, Job, Moses, Isaiah, Zerubbabel and the Suffering Servant (Gen. 26:24; Num. 12:7-8; Josh. 1:1-2; 2 Kings 17:13; Job 1:8; 2:3; Ps. 105:6, 42; Isa. 20:3; 42:1; 52:13; Hag. 2:23).

The emphatic 'you' (v. 4) suggests that although David was not to build a temple, the idea itself was not wrong. God made clear that He had not demanded it in the past and had managed perfectly without one from the time of the exodus when it moved throughout Israel's wilderness wanderings and even in Canaan from Shiloh to Nob and now Gibeon. To support the nomadic, pastoral nature of the period, the judges are described as those who shepherded the people (v. 6). The mobile 'tent' is also referred to as the 'dwelling' (*miškān*, v. 5), the term found frequently in Exodus especially in connection with the presence of the 'Shekinah' glory. A larger more permanent structure does seem to have existed alongside the tabernacle by Eli's time at Shiloh and referred to as Yahweh's 'temple' which was later destroyed by the Philistines. The sanctuary itself, however, was still a tent (1 Sam. 1:9; 2:22; Jer. 7:12,14) and certainly not 'a house of cedar' (v. 6).

The positive message is introduced in a similar way (v. 7; see v. 4), with God's fuller title 'Yahweh of hosts' used to emphasise His power and authority. Here the emphatic 'I' contrasts with the 'you' of verse 4, indicating that it was Yahweh Himself who had chosen David, the humble shepherd boy, to become 'prince' or 'leader' over God's people (see 1 Chron. 11:2; Ps. 78:70-72) and who had been with him and given him victory over his enemies (v. 8). Saul and his allies would have been particularly in mind but perhaps the Philistines too. Just as the symbol of Yahweh's presence had moved about so He had been with all David's movements (vv. 6, 8). The promises made to David had implications for all God's people and called to mind the Abrahamic and Sinai covenants. David's name will be great (v. 8b; see Gen. 12:2), enemies will be subdued, Israel will be planted in the land, undisturbed and no longer worn out by wicked people (vv. 9-10; see Gen. 12:3; 13:14-17; 15:18-21; Exod. 15:17; Deut. 11:24-25). It is significant that in place of the 2 Samuel 7:11 text which reads 'rest', Chronicles has 'subdued'. The full rest did not come until Solomon's reign (see 1 Kings 5:4[18]).

In his important aside concerning David's subjects (vv. 9-10), where English texts translate with plural personal pronouns ('plant them that they … wear them out'), God describes 'my people Israel' using singular personal pronouns ('plant him that he … wear him out') to agree with the collective noun 'people' and perhaps with a reminder that Israel as a people was viewed as God's 'son' (vv. 9-10; see Exod. 4:22-23). It is also at this point that the oracle reaches a climax with the promise that, instead of a 'house' that David will build for Yahweh, Yahweh is going to build a 'house' for David. This 'house' will not be of stone and wood but a dynasty: a succession of heirs after David's death (vv. 10b-11). The royal 'seed' theme, so prominent in the patriarchal narratives, is echoed here (see Gen. 17:6, 16). The focus is on a successor to David from among his own sons and on establishing his kingdom. Interestingly, David's death is euphemistically described as 'to walk with' his ancestors (v. 11) rather than 'to lie' with them (see 2 Sam. 7:12). No mention is made of disciplining the 'seed' (see 2 Sam. 7:14b) for it is David's 'greater son' that is in mind and the temple He will build, rather than the whole

line of Davidic kings. Thus the oracle relates to the unnamed
'seed' who will build Yahweh's house and Yahweh in turn will
establish his throne for ever. David's son, Solomon, will be
presented as a type of this future ruler, His everlasting throne
and the 'house' He will build (v. 12). The temple building is
like 'circumcision in the case of the Abrahamic covenant'. It is
an 'act of human obedience by which God's covenant promise
is accepted and confirmed'.[56] God is committed to both David
and his son. Though the emphasis here is on establishing for
ever the throne of his son (vv. 12,14), the promise is made to
David, and it is later referred to as God's covenant with David
(2 Chron. 13:5; etc.).

The filial father-son relationship (v. 13) that Israel as a
people was promised at the exodus (Exod. 4:22) is applied
to Israel's king who represents God's people (see Pss. 2:7 and
89:27). It is the closest of bonds where Yahweh's steadfast
love is unconditional and He will not remove it in contrast
to what happened to Saul. Unlike the Samuel text, David's
predecessor is not actually named by the Chronicler and the
emphasis falls on Yahweh's direct involvement ('I will not
remove my steadfast love ...'), whereas the Samuel text reads
'my steadfast love will not depart ...' (2 Sam. 7:15).

The Chronicler's theological emphasis surfaces particularly
in verse 14 where in contrast to 2 Samuel 7:16, 'your house
and your kingdom ... your throne ...', Chronicles reads, 'in my
house and in my kingdom ... his throne ...'. David's 'throne'
and that of his son are to be seen not as two separate thrones
but one entity. In association with this insight and in so far as
Solomon was a type of this future seed, the David–Solomon
rule is to be viewed as manifesting God's kingdom on earth.
David's house is Yahweh's house where the ambiguity in
the term 'house' is purposeful, standing both for dynasty
and temple (see v. 12). Likewise, David's kingdom is also
Yahweh's kingdom. Later, it will be stated that Solomon 'sat
on the throne of Yahweh' (1 Chron. 29:23). Therefore, it is
Yahweh who has stationed David's seed on the throne and it
is Yahweh's rule through His appointed representative that
is being established. It was Yahweh who had turned 'the

56. Selman, *1 Chronicles*, p. 179.

kingdom' to David in the first place after the removal of Saul (1 Chron. 10:14). Three times the expression 'for ever' appears in the oracle, each time in connection with the Davidic rule (vv. 12, 14), and in David's prayer response it is found a further five times (vv. 22-24, 27).

Application

Nathan's initial response to David's well-meaning concern should remind church leaders of the importance of encouraging members who have constructive, well-meaning practical ideas. Nevertheless, they do still need to make sure that they do not run counter to God's revealed word.

The Chronicler, under divine inspiration, rightly interpreted Nathan's oracle to encourage his people to look to the true 'son' and 'seed' of David. To be reminded that the Davidic king's rule was an expression of God's rule kept alive the messianic hope expressed in the prophetic writings. Yahweh still reigned supreme and had already brought the people back to Jerusalem and they could be assured that the promises made to David would be fulfilled come what may. It is with the coming of Jesus the Messiah that all the Davidic promises find their ultimate fulfilment (Rom. 1:3-4). The eternal Son of the Father is also the messianic son of God. In His human nature God tabernacles among us and as a result of His atoning death, whereby the temple made with hands became obsolete, His resurrected body is now 'the tent of meeting between humanity and God'.[57]

With the Davidic covenant (see Ps. 89:3) and its promises, a new stage is reached in the fulfilment of the Abrahamic and Sinai covenants.[58] David's name is among the great ones and the people are now planted in the land. The Song of Moses at the Red Sea draws to a close by celebrating Yahweh's everlasting kingship and is immediately preceded by a glimpse into the future when the people would be 'planted' on Yahweh's own mountain where He would make and establish the sanctuary in which He would abide (Exod. 15:7-18; see

---

57. L. Michael Morales, *Who Shall Ascend the Mountain of the Lord? A biblical theology of the book of Leviticus* (Nottingham: Apollos, 2015), p. 263.

58. Selman, *1 Chronicles*, p. 179.

Zech. 6:12-13). These kingdom and temple references prepare for the time when both John the Baptist and Jesus proclaimed that the kingdom of God had drawn near in the person of Jesus the Messiah (Matt. 3:1; 4:17; Luke 17:20-21). Christians can be assured of the consummation when the kingdom of this world becomes the kingdom of our Lord and of His Christ and when representatives of the nations are seen in Zion where God and the Lamb are the city's temple (Rev. 21:22-24). Today the worldwide family of God already witnesses to the fulness that is yet to be.

> 17:16. And king David came and sat before Yahweh, and he said, 'Who am I, Yahweh God, and what is my house that you have brought me as far as this? 17. And this was a small thing in your eyes, God, and you have spoken concerning your servant's house for a distant time and regarded me as the upward turning of humanity, Yahweh God. 18. What more can David add to you for the honour of your servant and you know your servant. 19. O Yahweh, for the sake of your servant and according to your heart, you have done all this greatness, to make known all the great deeds. 20. Yahweh, there is no one like you and there is no God beside you, according to all we have heard with our ears. 21. Who is like your people Israel, one nation on the earth, whom God went to redeem for himself a people, to make for yourself a name for greatness and awesomeness, to drive out nations before your people whom you redeemed from Egypt. 22. And you made your people Israel to be your people for ever, and you, Yahweh, became their God.'

At this point, David is referred to as 'king' (v. 16; see v. 7) and having heard God's breath-taking words, he found a place to sit down 'before Yahweh', presumably in the tent he had erected for the ark, and there humbly poured out his expressions of astonishment at God's word to him (vv. 16-22) and his heartfelt desires that arose from hearing the plans that had been revealed to him (vv. 23-27). Sitting was not the usual posture for prayer (see Gen. 18:22; Num. 16:22; 1 Kings 8:54), but Elijah addressed God while sitting under a tree (1 Kings 19:4). They possibly sat because they were overwhelmed. Certainly, David's response to the oracle is one of bewilderment and excitement shown by the number of invocations ('God', 'Yahweh'), repetitions and rhetorical questions. At the same time, David remains respectful throughout the prayer, using the reverential title 'your servant' (vv. 17, 18-19, 23-27). All the main points of God's message to him are repeated back to God in the prayer and this reveals David's faith in God and His ability to keep His word. Overall, David's prayer response expresses his own insignificance in the light of God's magnanimity, his amazement at God's mighty acts in Israel's history and his hearty acceptance of God's promises by appealing to God to fulfil them. A similar prayer by David is found later (1 Chron. 29:10-19).

David begins by expressing his unworthiness 'Who am I ...?' (v. 16; see Exod. 3:11; Judg. 6:15). By adding 'what is my house ...?', David recognises that he and his family background do not merit the kind of status promised by God. It also indicates that he and his 'house' are one, a significant matter in the chapter and especially in his prayer (vv. 17, 23-25, 27). Various ideas have been proposed concerning the last phrase of verse 17. The text literally reads 'and you see me as the turning (tôr) of the man (hā'ādām) upwards'. In the parallel text (2 Sam. 7:19) it reads literally: 'this is the law/instruction (tôrāh) of the man' (hā'ādām). Both texts present a contrast between the 'small thing' that God has already done for David and what lies ahead for his descendants, 'for a distant time.' In addition, both passages suggest that God's promises to David have long-term significance for humanity. With David, an important turning point for the better in the history of humankind had been reached, a history that began with Adam ('ādām, 1 Chron. 1:1). It is interesting that the Chronicler reminds his readers of Genesis 2:4–3:24 by his use of 'Yahweh God' rather than 'Lord Yahweh' (vv. 16-17; see 2 Sam. 7:18-19). David views God's plans for himself and his descendants as benefiting not only Israel but the whole Adamic race. Here was to be the way whereby the royal victorious 'seed' would bring blessing to all nations (Gen. 3:15; 12:3; 49:8-12). No wonder he was so lost for words (v. 18)! There is no more he could add for the honour bestowed upon him. Like Abraham and the nation Israel, Yahweh 'knows' him (Gen. 18:19; Amos 3:2) in the sense of having chosen him to be in this special intimate relationship.

In place of 'for the sake of your word', Chronicles reads 'for the sake of your servant' (v. 19; see 2 Sam. 7:21), thus highlighting the promises God had already made concerning David (see 1 Chron. 14:2). David therefore acknowledges God's faithfulness to him in revealing His purposes. Added to this and in the light of David's own heart's desires (v. 2), David confesses that God has acted in accordance with his own heart's desire in this momentous disclosure concerning the future. All this leads David to praise God's uniqueness and the resulting uniqueness of Israel's status (vv. 20-22).

Yahweh's uniqueness means 'there is no one like' God and this was displayed and celebrated at the exodus (Exod. 15:11; see Ps. 86:8; Jer. 10:7). It also means that 'there is no God beside' Yahweh (Deut. 4:35; 32:39; 1 Sam. 2:2; Isa. 45:14, 21-22; Jer. 10:10). Israel is unique because this incomparable, only true God acted to redeem them to Himself, so that they might become His people 'for ever' and Yahweh might become their God. This relationship and commitment of Yahweh to Israel lies at the heart of the covenant bond. It echoes the well-known covenant formula, 'I will be your God and you shall be my people' (Lev. 26:12; Jer. 7:23; 11:4; Ezek. 36:28; 2 Cor. 6:16).

David here acknowledges that Israel is to be as enduring as the dynasty (v. 22; see vv. 12, 14). While the redemption from Egypt is mentioned by name (v. 21b), entrance into the promised land is only implied when David speaks of God driving out nations before them. In the process of accomplishing all these great acts of power, Yahweh's own reputation was enhanced in the eyes of the surrounding nations. Interestingly, no mention is made of driving out the gods of the nations as in the Samuel text (see 2 Sam. 7:23). For the Chronicler, this may have seemed unnecessary in view of the previous strong monotheistic statement. There is truth in the comment: 'what does not exist cannot be driven out'.[59]

17:23. 'So now, Yahweh, the word that you have spoken concerning your servant and concerning his house, let it be made firm for ever and do as you have spoken. 24. And let your name be made firm and be magnified for ever, saying, Yahweh of hosts, the God of Israel, is God for Israel, and the house of

---

59. Klein, *1 Chronicles*, p. 384.

David your servant will be established before you. 25. For you, my God, have revealed [literally 'you have uncovered the ear of …'] to your servant to build for him a house. Therefore your servant dared to pray before you. 26. And now, Yahweh, you are God, and you have spoken concerning your servant this good thing. 27. And now you have been pleased to bless the house of your servant to be for ever before you, for you, Yahweh, have blessed and it is blessed for ever.'

The opening words of verse 23 mark the change from affirmation and praise to prayer and satisfaction. David's prayer reveals his faith in the divine word, as he asks God to carry out what He has just promised. As God made a name for Himself at the time of the exodus (v. 21), so David prays that it would continue and even become greater. He is concerned that the watching world would appreciate that the mighty 'Yahweh of hosts' (see 11:9), Israel's God, far from being against his people, is 'for Israel' and the Davidic dynasty is therefore secure. David's personal relationship with God ('my God', v. 25; Pss. 22:1; 86:2) and the remarkable message he had received by revelation, enabled him to be bold in prayer,[60] while still expressing humility of spirit ('your servant'). The repetition ('And now', vv. 26, 27) and recognition of who David is speaking to ('you are God', v. 26), might seem unnecessary, but it is the expression of passionate, heartfelt religious devotion (see Dan. 9:15-19). David closes his prayer response not by petitioning God for blessing (see 2 Sam. 7:29) but by recognising the blessing he had already received in the amazing promises concerning his dynasty (vv. 25-27). In doing so, David also stressed the eternal nature of the promises by twice repeating the 'for ever' (v. 27) that he heard emphasised in Nathan's oracle (vv. 12, 14; see Ps. 72:17-19).

Application

At a time when God's people were feeling despondent and His name was dishonoured, David's prayer response would have

60. In the parallel text of 2 Samuel 7:27, the Hebrew verb *māṣā'* ('to find') has 'his heart' as the object and this translates: 'he found his heart to pray' meaning 'he took courage to pray'. In the Chronicler's text, there is no object so that most translations assume the Samuel text. However, it may be that the verb *māṣā'* in this context has the meaning 'to dare', which Klein adopts; see his *1 Chronicles*, p. 373.

been of some encouragement to them to trust God and to pray for the realisation of His amazing promises. The prayer also reminds us that God's promises should always be accepted in a humble, believing manner and appreciated for what they are and not received in any casual way. God owes us nothing and therefore we should be very grateful for His gracious plans concerning His people. David's response calls to mind Mary's humble submission and acceptance of God's incredible message through the angel Gabriel (Luke 1:38). We are encouraged to pray God's promises regarding God's kingdom as David does here (Matt. 6:10). As it was God's reputation that was important for David and not his own honour, so it should be for us. We should pray that God would act for the sake of His honour especially when the unbelieving world around mockingly asks, 'Where is their God?'

The passage is also a reminder today that there is actually only one true God. Other gods are nonentities and the result of demonic activity (Deut. 32:31; 1 Cor. 8:5-6; 10:19-20).[61] This is the God who has acted in history and it is in Jesus the Messiah that all God's promises find their fulfilment. If we belong to David's greater Son, we are a blessed and privileged people for the God and Father of our Lord Jesus Christ is committed to all who trust the Saviour. He is 'God to us', for He wonderfully benefits His people.

David's enemies subdued (18:1–20:8)

The section falls into three main literary passages headed by the phrase 'Now it happened after this': David's conquests and just rule (18:1-17); Ammonites and Arameans defeated (19:1–20:3); and Philistines defeated (20:4-8). David's campaigns against the Philistines actually begin and end the whole section (18:1; 20:4-8).

Whereas David's victorious exploits are scattered throughout 2 Samuel 8–23, Chronicles brings them neatly together in these chapters not for triumphalist reasons, but to impress upon his readership that Yahweh fulfilled the promise made in Nathan's oracle, 'I will subdue all your enemies' (1 Chron. 17:10). David is

61. See Daniel Strange, *'For their Rock is not as our Rock'*, *An evangelical theology of religions* (Nottingham: Apollos, 2014).

shown to be one of the great world warriors who had brought stability and rest for His people (1 Chron. 17:8-9). In addition, these military achievements prepare for the statement that David had 'shed much blood' and had 'made great wars' and was therefore not the right person to build Yahweh's house (1 Chron. 22:8). On the positive side, the spoils from these wars are set aside by David to beautify the temple that his son was to build (vv. 8, 11).

David's conquests and just rule (18:1-17)

This parallels the account in 2 Samuel 8. The Chronicler's formula at the end of verse 6 and 13 marks off the first two main paragraphs (vv. 1-6 and 7-13), leaving the final paragraph to list David's administrative officers (vv. 14-17).

> 1. Now it happened after this that David smote the Philistines and subdued them and took Gath and its daughter villages from the hand of the Philistines. 2. And he defeated Moab, and the Moabites became servants of David, bringing tribute. 3. David also defeated Hadadezer, the king of Zobah toward Hamath, when he went to set up his monument on the Euphrates river. 4. And David captured from him one thousand chariots, seven thousand horsemen and twenty thousand foot soldiers, and David hamstrung all the chariot horses, but from them he left a hundred chariots. 5. When the Arameans of Damascus came to help Hadadezer, king of Zobah, David also killed twenty-two thousand men of the Arameans. 6. Then David put *garrisons* in Aram of Damascus and the Arameans became servants to David, bringing tribute. And Yahweh saved David wherever he went.

Israel's early enemy, the Philistines, were entrenched in the western coastal region (1 Chron. 1:12). They had succeeded in controlling a large part of Israel after Saul's death but David won some initial victories over them (1 Chron. 14:8-16). In the campaign mentioned in verse 1, their defeat resulted in them being 'subdued'. This verb appears again in 1 Chronicles 20:4 also in connection with the Philistines. By enveloping this whole section with David's subjugation of the Philistines together with the 'hand' references ('hand of the Philistines' in 18:1; 'hand of David ... hand of his servants' in 20:8), suggests that the Chronicler presents the Philistines as a type of all the enemies of God and His people (see 1 Chronicles 17:10 where the verb 'subdue' is employed).

To the east lay Moab. Ruth, David's great-grandmother, was a Moabite and it was to Moab that David sent his parents for safety (Ruth 4:18-22; 1 Sam. 22:3-4). Why there was a battle in the first place is not known but it resulted in the Moabites becoming subservient to David and paying tribute (v. 2). The execution of two thirds of the Moabite captives mentioned in 2 Samuel 8:2 is omitted.

More detail is recorded of war in the north against the Arameans (vv. 3-10). The narrative is divided into two. First, verses 3-6 report David's victory over Hadadezer of Zobah as the latter was probably setting up a monument after reclaiming lost territory (see 1 Chron. 19:16-19). The name 'Hadadezer' is made up of Hadad, the personal name of the Canaanite god, Baal, and the word for 'help'. Remembering that 'help' is one of the Chronicler's key terms, it is ironic that Baal could offer no help and neither could the neighbouring powerful Aramean state of Damascus (v. 5). Zobah was the main Aramean kingdom at the time and lay to the north of Damascus. Hamath lay on the river Orontes further north of Zobah, about a hundred and fifty miles (242 kilometres) from Damascus.[62] It was clearly a considerable area that Hadadezer ruled, so his defeat by David was a truly remarkable achievement. Hamath was viewed as the northern boundary of the promised land (Num. 13:21; 34:8), corresponding to the ancient boundaries of the Egyptian district of Canaan.[63] David captured thousands of horsemen and foot soldiers and hamstrung the chariot horses, leaving only a hundred for his own use (v. 4).[64] With the defeat and destruction of so many of the Aramaeans of Damascus, David

---

62. The word translated 'monument' is *yāḏ* ('hand', v. 3) but often has the metaphorical sense of 'power'. It can also stand for 'monument' as in 1 Samuel 15:12; 2 Samuel 18:18. There is ambiguity as to whether it was Hadadezer or David who did the setting up.

63. See note 1, p. 232, in Gordon J. Wenham, *Numbers*, Tyndale Old Testament Commentaries (Leicester: Inter-Varsity, 1981) for a comment on the accuracy of the Bible's description of the Egyptian district of Canaan in the second half of the 13th century B.C. by Aharoni, *Land of the Bible*, p. 69.

64. Chronicles probably carries the better text than the 'seven hundred' in 2 Samuel 8:4.

was able to place garrisons[65] in the region and the defeated citizens became subject to him and, like Moab, paid tribute (v. 6). These examples of David's victories over surrounding enemies continue to indicate that Yahweh was with David to 'save' or 'preserve' him (v. 6b; 1 Chron. 11:9; 14:2; 17:8).

> 7. And David took the shields of gold which were on the servants of Hadadezer and brought them to Jerusalem. 8. Also from Tibhath and from Cun, cities of Hadadezer, David took a very large amount of bronze, with which Solomon made the bronze sea and the pillars and the bronze utensils. 9. Now when Tou, the king of Hamath, heard that David had defeated all the army of Hadadezer king of Zobah, 10. he sent Hadoram his son to king David to ask him for peace and to congratulate him because he had fought against Hadadezer and defeated him, for Tou had often been a warring man with Hadadezer. And as for all kinds of utensils of gold and silver and bronze, 11. these also king David dedicated to Yahweh, with the silver and the gold he had carried from all the nations: from Edom and from Moab and from the sons of Ammon and from the Philistines and from Amalek. 12. And Abshai the son of Zeruiah smote eighteen thousand Edomites in the Valley of Salt. 13. Then he placed garrisons in Edom, and all the Edomites became servants to David. And Yahweh saved David wherever he went.

The second paragraph of the chapter begins with the seizure by David of the golden war implements used by Hadadezer's men, all of which he brought to Jerusalem (v. 7). Other important cities in the kingdom of Zobah, from where David took much spoil, included Cun and Tibhath. Tibhath is mentioned in the Amarna Letters and lies just south of the modern-day Syrian city of Homs. It is noted that the large amount of bronze taken by David would be used later by Solomon in building the temple (v. 8; see 2 Chron. 3:17–4:18). This middle paragraph of the chapter ends with a peace settlement with Hamath and the defeat of the Edomites (vv. 9-13). Tou (also known as Toi in 2 Sam. 8:9), king of Hamath, showed his satisfaction at David's victory over his longstanding enemy, Hadadezer, by sending a deputation to David headed by his son Hadoram ('Hadad is exalted'). The Chronicler gives his actual name whereas

---

65. The word is missing in the Masoretic Text. The Versions and 2 Samuel 8:6 read 'garrisons'.

in 2 Samuel 8:10 the substitute name, Joram ('Yahweh is exalted'), is found (compare also Mephibosheth for Meribaal in 2 Samuel 4:4 and 1 Chronicles 8:34).

The costly gifts they brought were dedicated to Yahweh along with all the other spoils of war from every compass direction (v. 11). Again, Solomon had these dedicated items brought into the temple (2 Chron. 5:1). Of the five nations listed, the Philistines and Moabites have been mentioned earlier in the chapter, victory over Edomites in the south east is about to be introduced while victory over the Ammonites in the north east is covered in the following chapter. No campaign against the Amalekites of the south is recorded by the Chronicler (see 1 Sam. 30). It was David's nephew Abshai (spelled Abishai in the Samuel text) who was responsible for the decisive victory over the Edomites in the Valley of Salt, an area probably situated near the Dead Sea (vv. 12-13). In the heading to Psalm 60 the number slain is put at twelve not eighteen thousand. This variation is probably due to two different stages in the campaign. Like Moab and Aram (vv. 2, 6), Edom also became subservient to David and this would have been of special encouragement to his first readers in their concerns over Edom (see Mal. 1). Again, the paragraph closes with a reminder that it was Yahweh who 'saved' David in the sense of protecting him and granting him victory over his enemies (v. 13b; see v. 6b).

> 14. So David ruled over all Israel, and executed justice and righteousness for all his people. 15. And Joab the son of Zeruiah was over the army, and Jehoshaphat the son of Ahiud was recorder. 16. And Zadok the son of Ahitub and Abimelech the son of Abiathar, were priests, and Shavsha was secretary. 17 And Benaiah the son of Jehoiada was over the Cherethites and the Pelethites, and the sons of David were heads by the king's side.

The final paragraph (vv. 14-17) lists the officers in his administration but not before acknowledging that David's rule over all Israel, with the borders of his empire now extending from the Euphrates in the north to the Nile in the south, was one that exhibited sound moral practice ('justice' or 'judgement') based on sound moral principles ('righteousness'). Psalm 72:2 prays that the king's son will display these characteristics, a psalm that finds its realisation in Jesus the Messiah (see also Isa. 11:3-5; 42:1-4; Jer. 22:15). The dual appointees for each position are arranged in such a way that the military officers, Joab and Benaiah, form the outer ring, followed by the court administrators, Jehoshaphat and Shavsha, with the priests, Zadok and Abimelech, placed at the centre.

Joab, Abshai's brother (v. 12), was in charge of the regular army. He gained his position following the capture of Jerusalem (1 Chron. 11:6). Benaiah, who replaced Joab when Solomon became king (1 Kings 2:34-35), was in charge of the mercenaries. The Cherethites probably came originally from Crete but had settled in the Negev (1 Sam. 30:14). As for the Pelethites, their identity is unknown, although it has been suggested they were people from Philistia. Jehoshaphat remained a trusted civil servant under Solomon (1 Kings 4:3), though what the exact office of recorder entailed is unknown. Some scholars suggest a similarity to the Egyptian practice of making reports to the king. Shavsha, called Seraiah in the parallel text of 2 Samuel 8:17, probably acted as personal secretary to the king. Zadok the priest, the son of Ahitub (1 Chron. 6:12), has been mentioned in 1 Chronicles 15:11 along with Abiathar (see 1 Sam. 22:20; 2 Sam. 20:25). 'Abimelech' is perhaps an alternate pronunciation of the Ahimelech of 2 Samuel 8:17. It is likely that Abiathar and Ahimelech, father and son, carried out the priestly duties (1 Chron. 24:3, 6).

David's sons are placed outside this close administrative circle and described as 'heads' or 'chiefs' working under the authority of the king. The phrase translated 'by the king's side' is literally 'to the hand of the king' so that the word 'hand' frames the whole chapter (see v. 1). In 2 Samuel 8:18, David's sons are called 'priests' but clearly not in the Levitical sense. They may have acted as royal chaplains carrying out the king's wishes. The king did involve himself in some activities associated with the priests (see 1 Chron. 15:27; 16:2-3, 43; 21:26).

Application

Chronicles is concerned to show that promises made to David were fulfilled. The kingdom of God was seen on earth under the rule of Yahweh's viceregent. David became a model of just and stable rule and although far from perfect, he did foreshadow the just and flawless rule of the Messiah. The ancient boundaries of Canaan over which David had authority typify the new earth which will be characterised by righteousness (2 Pet. 3:13). The routing of the enemies of God's people, typified particularly by the Philistines and Edomites, is a reminder that the forces of wickedness will all be destroyed by Him who is called 'the Word of God' (Rev. 19:11-21).

Ammonites and Arameans defeated (19:1–20:3)

This account is similar to 2 Samuel 10:1–11:1 and 12:26, 30-31. The Chronicler assumes knowledge of David's kindness to Mephibosheth, Saul's grandson and the son of his close friend Jonathan, as well as David's affair with Bathsheba and the murder of her husband Uriah, which are found only in 2 Samuel 11:2–12:25. All relationships between Saul's family and David are assumed by the Chronicler (see 15:29) and only what served his message is included. In Samuel, the wars against Ammon and Aram frame the personal incidents in the life of David but in Chronicles, where personal details are kept to a minimum, his battles against the surrounding nations are much more closely integrated.

This is the second major passage introduced by the formula, 'Now it happened after this' (see 18:1; 20:4). It covers the humiliation that David's messengers suffered at the hands of the new Ammonite king (vv. 1-5), the Ammonite–Aramean coalition (vv. 6-9), followed by Joab's initial victory over the confederates (vv. 10-15), David's subsequent victory over the Arameans (vv. 16-19) and finally, the total defeat of the Ammonites by David and Joab (20:1-3). The final victory is no endnote as it might seem from 2 Samuel, for in Chronicles the two major battles with 'the sons of Ammon' form a frame around this section (19:1-15; 20:1-3).

> 19:1. Now it happened after this that Nahash the king of the sons of Ammon died, and his son became king in his place. 2. Then David said, 'I will deal loyally with Hanun the son of Nahash, because his father dealt loyally with me.' So David sent messengers to comfort him concerning his father. And

David's servants came to the land of the sons of Ammon to Hanun to comfort him. 3. But the chiefs of the sons of Ammon said to Hanun, 'In your eyes is David honouring your father, in that he sent comforters to you? Have not his servants come to you to search and to overthrow and to spy out the land?' 4. So Hanun took David's servants and shaved them, and cut off their garments in the middle as far as their hips, and sent them away. 5. Then *some* went and told David about the men. And he sent to meet them, for the men were greatly humiliated. And the king said, 'Remain in Jericho until your beards grow, then you can return.'

Nahash the Ammonite was defeated by Saul when he besieged Jabesh-gilead (1 Sam. 11:1-11) and it is possible that in the subsequent troubles between Saul and David, Nahash had sided with David and had remained good friends. Now that the Ammonite king had died David was eager to pay his respects to the king's son Hanun and to continue the friendly relationship by sending a delegation to convey condolences over his father's death (see 1 Kings 5:1(15). The relationship is described using the word 'loyal' (*ḥeseḏ*, v. 2), often translated as 'kindness' or in other contexts 'steadfast love'. It is an appropriate term for treaty relationships. Those who directed the new king in his thinking ('in your eyes', v. 3) were as lacking in wisdom as the young counsellors who were to advise Solomon's son, Rehoboam (2 Chron. 10). They assumed that David's motives were not sincere and if this event took place after David's victories over the Philistines, the Ammonites might have been suspicious of his intentions. Hanun's humiliating treatment of the envoys in attacking their dignity as males and treating them like prisoners of war (see Isa. 20:4; 47:2-3) was clearly a provocative act that broke all diplomatic conventions. It was an insult to David and the Israelite nation. David's concern for his civil servants reveals the sort of kindness he had sought to offer the Ammonite ruler. He advised them to stay in the Jericho region as that was the first major stopping-place after crossing the Jordan from Ammon to re-enter Israel (v. 5).

19:6. When the sons of Ammon saw that they had made themselves odious to David, Hanun and the sons of Ammon sent one thousand talents of silver to hire for themselves chariots and horsemen from Aram-naharaim, from Aram-maacah and from Zobah. 7. So they hired for themselves thirty-two thousand chariots and the king of Maacah and his people, and they came and encamped before Medeba. And the sons of Ammon gathered together from their cities and came to battle. 8. When David heard, he sent Joab and the whole army of warriors. 9. And the sons of Ammon came out and drew up in battle array at the entrance of the city, and the kings who had come were by themselves in the field. 10. Now when Joab saw that the face of the battle was set against him in front and behind, he chose some of all the choice men of Israel and they arrayed themselves against Aram. 11. But the rest of the people he placed in the hand of Abshai his brother; and they arrayed themselves against the sons of Ammon. 12. And he said, 'If Aram is too strong for me, then you shall save me, but if the sons of Ammon are too strong for you, then I will save you. 13. Be strong and let us show ourselves courageous on behalf of our people and on behalf of the cities of our God, and Yahweh will do what is good in his sight.' 14. So Joab and the people who were with him drew near before Aram for the battle, and they fled before him. 15. When the sons of Ammon saw that Aram had fled, they also fled from before Abshai his brother and they entered the city but Joab came to Jerusalem.

When the Ammonites realised there would be repercussions following their belligerent action, they set about preparing for war by obtaining support from their powerful northern neighbours, the Arameans. The whole episode reveals Ammon as the aggressor, with no mention of any revengeful reaction on the part of David. The only ominous note is the comment that the Ammonites had made themselves 'stink' or odious to David (v. 6). A thousand talents of silver was an incredible sum to obtain the services of these Arameans with their chariots and cavalry. Aram-naharaim ('Aram of the two rivers' or 'Aram of Mesopotamia') is the area of the Tigris and Euphrates in northern Syria (see v. 16) from where Balaam came, the pagan soothsayer who was employed by Moab with the assistance of Ammon to curse Israel (Num. 22:5). Zobah (see 1 Chron. 18:3-8) is the country ruled by Hadadezer. Aram-maacah lies south of Damascus and east of the Sea of Galilee near the northern settlement of Dan. The 'thirty-two thousand' is probably short-hand for the horsemen and foot soldiers as well as the 'chariots', and is the sum of the twenty thousand from Zobah and the twelve thousand from Tob mentioned in the Samuel text. That text also adds an additional one thousand troops belonging to what the Chronicler refers to as 'the king of Maacah and his people' (v. 7; see 2 Sam. 10:6). Not stated in Samuel is the place 'Medeba' where they assembled, a city south of Ammon on the borders of Moab. This would suggest that Moab was at least sympathetic to the Ammonite cause.

David sent Joab with his whole army of valiant men against this vast array of opponents (v. 8). The Ammonites were defending the city, presumably Medeba or the Ammonite capital Rabbah, and the Arameans were in the open country (v. 9). Joab found himself caught between the two forces but used it to his own advantage by dividing his army and taking a select number of his best troops against the Arameans whom he clearly saw as the greatest threat. The rest of the army he placed under the command of his brother Abshai (see 1 Chron. 18:12-13) to fight the Ammonites. In this formation the two divisions were also in a position to give mutual support if necessary (vv. 10-12). Joab's brief but stirring address to his brother and their forces is particularly significant and similar expressions urging action and the promise of divine assistance are found in later situations (vv. 12-13; see 2 Chron. 19:11; 32:7-8). It echoes the exhortation to Joshua (Deut. 31:7, 23; Josh. 1:6-9; see 1 Chron. 11:10). Joab's words indicated the true nature of the battle. This was a war not only on behalf of Israel but for 'the cities of our God' (v. 13), a unique expression in the Old Testament and probably referring to the cities belonging to the Transjordanian tribes. Rather than a prayer-wish, as with some translations, Joab's final words are a statement that reveals his trust in God in which he assures the troops that Yahweh will do what seems best to Him.

No sooner had Joab and his men approached the Arameans for battle than the enemy fled and this led to the Ammonites fleeing before Abshai and his troops and retreating to the city. Three times, the verb 'fled' is found with reference to the panic-stricken enemy. By way of contrast, Joab peacefully made his way back home to Jerusalem (vv. 14-15). The threat of battle was enough to scatter the Arameans, suggesting an unseen divine element that involved no military action and that made redundant Joab's strategic planning.

> 19:16. When the Arameans saw that they had been thrashed by Israel, they sent messengers and brought out the Arameans who were beyond the river and Shophach, the commander of the army of Hadadezer, was before them. 17. And when David was told, he gathered all Israel and crossed the Jordan and came to them and drew up in formation against them. So David drew up in battle array against the Arameans and they fought with him. 18. And the Arameans fled before Israel, and David killed of the Arameans seven thousand charioteers and forty thousand foot soldiers, and he put to death Shophach, the commander of the army. 19. And when the servants of Hadadezer saw that they had been thrashed by Israel, they made peace with David and served him. So the Arameans were not willing to save the sons of Ammon any more.

The narrative continues to show that Israel was not the aggressor. Having seen their mercenaries defeated in the campaign alongside the Ammonites, the Arameans took it upon themselves to initiate a second attack on Israel. They summoned the services of yet more Aramean allies only this time from the other side of the Euphrates ('beyond the river', v. 16). It was Hadadezer's army (see 1 Chron. 18:3) under the command of Shophach (spelled 'Shobach' in 2 Samuel 10:16) who heeded the call. On this occasion, instead of sending Joab and the standing army, David mustered 'all Israel' and himself took command and moved quickly to meet the Arameans on the other side of the Jordan. Unlike 2 Samuel 10:16-17 which mentions an unknown place called Helam, Chronicles has no reference to the battle site (v. 17). As in the first campaign, the Aramean forces again 'fled', only this time David pursued them and it resulted in the Aramean coalition receiving heavy losses including Shophach their commander (v. 18). There is some uncertainty concerning the numbers killed, with 2 Samuel 10:18 giving the figure of seven hundred charioteers to the Chronicler's seven thousand. The Samuel text also mentions a further forty thousand horsemen in place of the forty thousand foot soldiers in Chronicles. Maybe both figures are correct with different counting procedures being adopted.

The 'servants of Hadadezer' were the defeated vassal kings who had formed the coalition and they were eager to make peace with Israel. But unlike the Samuel text, the Chronicler emphasises that it was with 'David' that peace was made and that they served 'him'. It is David not Hadadezer who was now their real overlord and it resulted in the Arameans being 'not willing' to 'save' the Ammonites again (v. 19).

> 20:1. And it happened at the time of the turning of the year, at the time when kings go out *to war*, that Joab led out the valiant army and ravaged the land of the sons of Ammon, and came and besieged Rabbah but David remained in Jerusalem. And Joab smote Rabbah and overthrew it. 2. Then David took the crown of their king from his head, and found it to weigh a talent of gold and in it there was a precious stone; and it was placed on David's head. He also brought out the spoil of the city, a very great amount. 3. And he brought out the people who were in it and sawed *it* with the saw, with sharp irons and with saws. And thus David did to all the cities of the sons of Ammon. Then David and all the people returned to Jerusalem.

The first three verses of chapter 20 provide a condensed version of 2 Samuel 11–12. It relates how the Ammonites were themselves thoroughly defeated and subjugated and thus it completes the account that began with the humiliation of David's envoys at the hands of the newly installed king of Ammon (19:1-5). The first verse includes material found in the parallel text in Samuel where David's adultery with Bathsheba is introduced (see 2 Sam. 11:1) but it did not serve the Chronicler's purpose to include that incident. Besides, providing the time reference concerning the end of the wet winter season which made travel easier and food more plentiful, the material fitted nicely into the Chronicler's pattern to mention that David again remained in Jerusalem while Joab was the one who led out the troops against Ammon as happened at the beginning of this section relating to David's relations with Ammon (see 19:8). Joab's army now ravaged the very 'land' that the Ammonites had originally wrongly suspected David's envoys of reconnoitring (19:3). The verb 'to ravage' or 'destroy', used here for the first time, is one that will become more and more significant in Chronicles (see 1 Chron. 21:12, 15; 2 Chron. 12:7, 12; 21:7; 24:23; 25:16; 26:16; 27:2; 34:11; 35:21; 36:19).

Rabbah, the capital of the Ammonites (modern Amman), was first attacked by Joab and then after the final assault in which David was involved (2 Sam. 12:26-29), the city was destroyed by Joab (v. 1). David was clearly in Ammon not Jerusalem when the city was taken and received the king of Ammon's weighty golden crown (v. 2). It would have been too heavy to wear but it was briefly placed on David's head as a sign that he was now their overlord. It was an example of the gold plundered from such nations as Ammon that was mentioned earlier (1 Chron. 18:11). Much booty was also taken from the city before it was ruined (v. 2). There is some question over David's treatment of the inhabitants of Ammon (v. 3). The implied object of the verb 'to saw' is probably the city itself not the people (2 Sam. 12:31 has a different verb). Using various sharp iron tools,[66] it must be presumed that David sawed the city in the sense of tearing apart the city's fortifications.[67] The same was done to the other Ammonite cities. The Samuel text implies that the people were put to forced labour rather than gruesome torture as was once thought. The implements are typical of those used by labourers rather than executioners. Like Joab, David and all the people came back safely to Jerusalem (19:15b; 20:3b).

Application

Like many a general since, Joab gave a stirring appeal before entering the conflict. However, its content indicates the spiritual nature of the battle and is one of a number of such inspiring speeches before facing an enemy that we find in Chronicles. The outcome clearly suggests that unseen spiritual forces were at work to give victory to David and his people. It reminds us of the initial war that God started in Eden and of Paul's words that we do not war against flesh and blood but against principalities and powers and spiritual wickedness in heavenly places (Eph. 6:11-12).

---

66. The word *meḡērah* ('a saw') is from a root *grr*, 'to drag,' with the plural form (*meḡērôṯ*). Most English translations, including the AV, read *maḡezērôṯ* as 'axes' or 'cutting instruments' with one Hebrew MS and 2 Samuel 12:31. The verb *gāzar* means 'to cut, separate'.

67. See Klein, *1 Chronicles*, p. 408.

Philistines defeated (20:4-8)

This final section relating to David's campaigns against neighbouring nations is again introduced with the words, 'Now it happened after this' (1 Chron. 18:1; 19:1). It returns to wars against the Philistines (see 18:1) and records three encounters that are paralleled in 2 Samuel 21:18-22.

> 20:4. Now it happened after this that a battle was set up in Gezer with the Philistines; then Sibbecai the Hushathite killed Sippai, one born of the Rephaim and they were subdued. 5. And there was again war with the Philistines, and Elhanan the son of Jair killed Lahmi the brother of Goliath the Gittite; the shaft of his spear was like a weaver's beam. 6. And again there was war in Gath, and there was a man of such stature that he had six digits on each hand and foot, twenty-four altogether, and he also was born to the Raphah. 7. And when he taunted Israel, Jonathan the son of Shimea, the brother of David, killed him. 8. These were born to the Raphah in Gath; and they fell by the hand of David and by the hand of his servants.

Gezer was about twenty-five miles (forty kilometres) west of Jerusalem, an Ephraimite city of refuge (1 Chron. 6:67[52]), near the Philistine border. Earlier, David had struck down the Philistine army as far as Gezer (1 Chron. 14:16). The killing of the otherwise unknown Sippai, a descendant of ('one born of') the Rephaim, by one of David's mighty men, Sibbecai the Hushathite (see 1 Chron. 4:4;11:29), led to the defeat of the Philistines in this particular encounter (v. 4). The Rephaim were among the pre-Israelite inhabitants of Canaan, some known as Avvites and likened to the Anakim. Early Philistine settlers from Crete, called Caphtorites, had driven most of these giants out of the coastal region and they came to occupy areas both east and west of the Jordan (Gen. 14:5; 15:20; Deut. 2:10-11, 20-23; 3:11,13; Josh. 11:22; 12:4; 17:15).[68]

A second incident highlighted in Israel's confrontations with the Philistines involved another army hero, Elhanan (1 Chron. 11:26), who killed Lahmi the brother of the infamous Goliath. It is possible that 'Goliath' is an old Ugaritic name

---

68. See further on 2 Samuel 21:17-22 in Ronald F. Youngblood, '1 and 2 Samuel,' in *Expositor's Bible Commentary*, vol. 3 (Grand Rapids: Zondervan, 1988), pp. 863, 1059.

for a giant-hero,[69] and this would account for the apparent contradiction of 1 Samuel 17 in 2 Samuel 21:19. Like his brother, he possessed a spear that could be compared to that of a weaver's beam (1 Sam. 17:7).

The giant in the case of the third encounter is unnamed (vv. 6-7). It was his arrogant taunts, similar no doubt to those of Goliath and Sennacherib (1 Sam. 17:10, 25, etc.; 2 Chron. 32:17), that brought about his death by Jonathan, the son of Shimea, one of David's brothers (1 Chron. 2:13). The concluding note (v. 8) is probably explaining that these unusually massive men were the last of a long line of Rephaim[70] in Gath who served with the Philistines. David is associated with the victory not because he was actually involved but because it was done by his men. The references to David and Gath as well as the word 'hand' are a reminder of how this whole section concerning David's wars began (see 18:1).

Under David, Israel could at last dwell in safety, free from attack by neighbouring states, particularly the Philistines and the Rephaim who served them. David had saved them from the enemy nations (1 Chron. 16:35; 18:11) and the resulting peace that followed their subjugation, fulfilled God's promises first made to Abraham (Gen. 15:18-21), then to David (1 Chron. 17:10). It completed the work begun by Joshua.

Application

The Philistines become an early type of all God's enemies and those of His people. It was an encouragement to the post-exilic community and likewise for God's people in every age not to become disheartened at the power of whatever 'giants' they face and the slow progress that is often made to subdue them, but to look with anticipation to the fulfilment of God's purposes. There was something devilish about the remnants of the Anakim which needed to be destroyed (Num. 13:33; see Gen. 6:4). The identical word 'Rephaim' is used of the inhabitants of Sheol and often translated 'the dead' or 'shadowy ones' (Ps. 88:10[11]; Prov. 2:18; Isa. 14:9; 26:14, 19)

---

69. See Tsumurua, *1 Samuel*, p. 440.

70. Literally, 'to the Raphah' is probably a collective singular, rather than a proper name.

as if to indicate that those mighty ones have become weak and powerless as the verb 'to sink down, droop' from the same root letters suggests. David's victories become symbolic of David's greater Son who has won the decisive battle at Calvary but we do not yet see all things put under Him. There is a gradual elimination of all enemies. He must reign till all His enemies are under His feet, the last enemy giant to be destroyed being death (1 Cor. 15:25-26). Furthermore, the God of peace will soon crush Satan under our feet (Rom. 16:20).

David's census and the temple site acquired (21:1–22:1)

The whole incident parallels the text of 2 Samuel 24 but with significant differences. Unlike the Samuel passage, the Chronicler emphasises how it led directly to the place where the future temple was to be built and to David's own preparations toward that end. The account describes the poll (vv. 1-6), the punishment (vv. 7-15), the propitiation (vv. 16-27) and the place (21:28–22:1).

The poll (21:1-6)

> 21:1. Now Satan stood up against Israel and incited David to count Israel. 2. So David said to Joab and to the chiefs of the people, 'Go, number Israel from Beer-sheba to Dan and bring *the result* to me so that I may know their number.' 3. But Joab said, 'May Yahweh add to his people like them a hundred times! My lord the king, are not all of them my lord's servants? Why does my lord seek this? Why should he be for a cause of guilt for Israel?' 4. However, the king's word prevailed over Joab. So Joab went out, and travelled about through all Israel and came to Jerusalem. 5. Then Joab gave to David the number of the sum of the people. All Israel were a thousand thousands and a hundred thousand men who drew the sword; and Judah four hundred and seventy thousand men who drew the sword. 6. But Levi and Benjamin he did not count among them because the word of the king repulsed Joab.

Unlike the Samuel text, there is no indication of God's anger being aroused against Israel or its possible reference back to the narrative in 2 Samuel 21:1-14. In Chronicles, it is Satan who is against Israel. Following the references to the sinister Rephaim in the previous chapter, it is not a total surprise to hear of this malevolent spiritual being attacking Israel. Furthermore, in Chronicles it is Satan who moved David to number the people rather than the bold statement that Yahweh incited David against his own people to number them. Nevertheless, in both accounts David is held responsible for failing the test and falling into the temptation (see v. 8). There are only three direct references to 'Satan' in the Old Testament. In Job 1–2 and Zechariah 3:1-2 the word appears with the definite article suggesting the translation 'the Adversary', but here without the article it is a proper name. Some have suggested a human adversary is in mind, but all the indications are that this is a spiritual figure named Satan. The verb 'stood up' calls to mind the position of Satan standing at the right hand of Joshua the high priest (Zech. 3:1). Satan 'stood' similar to an adversary or accuser in a court of law (Ps. 109:6, 29). Interestingly, the verb 'incited' is found in connection with Satan's activity in Job's case (Job 2:3).

There was nothing inherently sinful in holding a census and there is much numbering of people throughout Chronicles without any indication of sin (1 Chron. 11:11; 23:1-5; 2 Chron. 17:14-19; 25:5). A census was usually taken for military or taxation purposes (Num. 1:3, 45; Exod. 30:11-16). This census was probably for military reasons as suggested by the term 'the sum' or 'muster' (*mip̱qār*) and the phrase, 'who drew the sword' (v. 5). Why this particular census was sinful is not specifically stated, neither here nor in the Samuel text, yet even Joab, the commander-in-chief of the army, found this one obnoxious (v. 6; 1 Chron. 2:16; 18:15). The boundaries of Israel are given in reverse order to the usual sequence 'from Dan to Beersheba' that is found elsewhere in Scripture and the parallel text in 2 Samuel 24:2 (v. 2; see also 2 Chron. 30:5 and 1 Chron. 13:5).

Coming after the account of battles and victories over 'flesh and blood' enemies in the previous chapters, the Chronicler focuses on this supernatural foe who 'incited' or 'moved' David to sin. As a result, Satan brought about a spiritual defeat that led to the destruction of thousands in Israel. Joab's reply (v. 3; see 1 Chron. 27:23-24) suggests that David's motives were wrong. The king was calling for a census that served no purpose except, it would seem, to bolster the king's ego (see Prov. 14:28). Instead of continuing to rest in Yahweh's promises to make the nation as numerous as the stars in the heavens and the sand on the seashore (Gen. 15:5; 22:17) and to give victory over his enemies, he was trusting in his own strength of numbers. Chronicles emphasises David's interest in 'numbers' rather than the people themselves (compare v. 2 with 2 Sam. 24:2). There was no good reason to count them and Joab warned that the king's action would lead to divine retribution for the nation (v. 3; see Exod. 30:12.)[71] The term 'guilt' or 'punishment' (*'ašmāh*) becomes an important word later (see 2 Chron. 24:18; etc.).

With objections overruled, the Chronicler briefly describes how Joab did the king's bidding by travelling or 'walking about' (v. 4) the country until he came back to Jerusalem. Interestingly, unlike the Samuel text, the same verbal form 'walk about' or 'roaming around' (the *hithpael* of the verb 'to walk') is used of Satan's activity in the earth in Job 1:7 and 2:2. The results diverge slightly from the Samuel text as the numbers are calculated differently in Chronicles. It is probable that 'thousand thousands' and 'hundred thousand' are not to be taken literally as one million one hundred thousand swordsmen (v. 5). The word 'thousand' can mean a large military 'unit' of up to a thousand men even when there were often considerably less than a thousand in a unit. Of the 'thousands' from the whole united kingdom of Israel, four 'hundred' and seventy 'thousand' ('units') were from Judah. The Chronicler also gives information not found in the Samuel text, stating that the king's command was repugnant to Joab (v. 6). It resulted in the commander's decision not to number two tribes: Levi, the tribe set apart for sacred duties (Num. 1:49; 2:33) and Benjamin, probably because in their territory lay both Gibeon where the tabernacle was situated and Jerusalem, the city of David, where the ark of Yahweh rested (Josh. 18:21-28; 1 Chron. 16:39).

Application

Ultimately, God is the one who is sovereign and He wills to permit whatever happens. God was clearly angry with Israel

---

71. The atonement money in Exodus 30:11-16 uses the same root letters as the word for 'sum' or 'muster' (*mip̄qār*) in verse 5.

for some reason (2 Sam. 24:1) and it was He who permitted Satan to incite David to sin. However, God does not tempt people to sin; rather, He tests them. It is Satan's evil work to tempt them. Here we have the mystery of divine providence. David could have resisted the temptation and would have passed God's test but that did not happen. Yet, out of this evil, God brought good. In the same way, it was in God's good plan that Christ should be betrayed and killed but it was Judas, inspired by Satan, who betrayed Him and it was through wicked hands under the leadership of the prince of darkness that He was killed.

The punishment (21:7-17)

21:7. This thing was displeasing in the sight of God, and he struck Israel. 8. Then David said to God, 'I have sinned greatly that I have done this thing; but now, take away, please, the iniquity of your servant, for I have acted very foolishly.' 9. So Yahweh spoke to Gad, David's visionary, saying: 10. 'Go and speak to David, saying, "Thus says Yahweh: three I am offering you; choose for yourself one of them that I may do *it* to you."' 11. So Gad came to David and said to him, 'Thus says Yahweh: Choose for yourself, 12. either three years of famine, three months of being swept away before your adversaries while the sword of your enemies overtakes you, or three days of the sword of Yahweh, even a plague in the land, with the angel of Yahweh destroying in all the territory of Israel. And now consider what reply I should return to the one who sent me.' 13. Then David said to Gad, 'I am greatly distressed; please let me fall into the hand of Yahweh for his mercies are very great, but into the hand of humanity let me not fall.' 14. So Yahweh gave a plague in Israel and seventy thousand persons from Israel fell. 15. And God sent an angel to Jerusalem to destroy it but as *he was about to* destroy, Yahweh saw and relented over the evil and he said to the destroying angel, 'Enough now; let your hand drop!' And the angel of Yahweh was standing by the threshing floor of Ornan the Jebusite. 16. And David lifted his eyes and saw the angel of Yahweh standing between earth and heaven with his drawn sword in his hand stretched out over Jerusalem. Then David and the elders, covered in sackcloth, fell upon their faces. 17. And David said to God, 'Did not I say to number the people? And it was I who sinned and did enormous evil; but these sheep – what have they done? Yahweh my God, please let your hand be against me and against my father's house, but against your people no fatal blow.'

Not only did David's census disgust Joab, but it was displeasing to God (literally, 'there was evil in the eyes of God concerning the thing', v. 7). God's reaction echoes His reaction to David's adultery and murder (2 Sam. 11:27b). Though the Chronicler did not include that sin he clearly expected his readers to be aware of it. This census was equally sinful. It was Satan's main concern to attack 'Israel', the people of God (v. 1), but he did so through enticing David their king to engage in an action that provoked God's anger. This led to God's striking Israel (v. 7; see 2 Sam. 12:15). It was thus through David's sin that Israel was punished (see v. 3b). The statement that God 'struck Israel' (v. 7) is not a reference to some initial punishment prior to the plague that Yahweh sent to kill seventy thousand Israelites (v. 14), but 'is a summarising introduction to the following paragraph'.[72]

David acknowledged his sin, taking full responsibility for his action, and sought God's forgiveness (v. 8). This is the first reference to the verb 'to sin' in Chronicles and the only use of the term 'iniquity' (ʿāwôn) in the entire work. Though David was contrite, as Israel's king his sin was not a private matter but had consequences for the whole nation. In addition, Yahweh was already angry with Israel (2 Sam. 24:1) and used the consequences of the king's folly to discipline His people. In the case of David's previous sinful actions recorded in the Samuel text, the prophet Nathan had been used to confront David (2 Sam. 12), but on this occasion it was David's close associate, the prophet Gad, who was sent by God to speak to David (vv. 9-13). He is described as the king's 'visionary'. There are two words used in Hebrew that are usually translated in English as 'seer', ḥōzeh and rōʾeh. They are both participial forms of their respective verbs for 'to see', and ḥōzeh is the term found here and a number of times throughout Chronicles. It is translated 'visionary' for it bears that kind of meaning and distinguishes it from rōʾeh 'seer', the more common verb for 'to see'. Gad was a court prophet who had been with David when he was fleeing from Saul (1 Sam. 22:5; see 1 Chron. 29:29;

72. Williamson, *1 and 2 Chronicles*, p. 145, contrary to Johnson, *1 and 2 Chronicles*, Vol. 1, p. 230 and Klein, *1 Chronicles*, p. 422.

2 Chron. 29:25). He was directed to offer the king a choice of punishment and when he appeared before David he proclaimed God's word using the typical messenger formula, 'Thus says Yahweh' (vv. 9-11). The three forms of divine judgment put to the king constituted a well-known trio of calamities: sword, famine and plague (see Jer. 14:12; etc.). It was a clear sign of Yahweh's kindness that only one was to be chosen, for all three occurred together in God's final curse on the nation (Jer. 44:13; Ezek. 14:21). Famine is reckoned in years,[73] defeat by the sword in months, and plague in days (v. 12). The Chronicler makes it clearer than in the Samuel text that the third option involved the direct action of Yahweh by referring to the plague as 'the sword of Yahweh' and 'the angel of Yahweh destroying ...'. It thus makes more understandable David's reasoning that it would be better to fall into Yahweh's hand than into human hands (v. 13; see 2 Chron. 19:6 for a similar contrast between Yahweh and humans). It was a 'destroying' (mašḥît) angel that slew the first-born Egyptians (Exod. 12:13, 23) and passed over Israel's dwellings where the blood of the Passover lambs was daubed. The heavenly being with Yahweh's sword calls to mind the one whom Joshua saw (Josh. 5:13-15) and who confronted Balaam (Num. 22:31), as well as the cherubim with a flaming sword guarding the way to the tree of life (Gen. 3:24). David was placed in an impossible position and it caused him 'great distress' (v. 13). In one sense, the last option seemed the most terrible of the three punishments. His considered choice, however, indicated David's close relationship to Yahweh. He committed himself and his people to the very one who is a consuming fire (Deut. 4:24) and who will by no means clear the guilty, and yet he does so on the basis that Yahweh also shows very great compassion, compassion he had already experienced after his sin with Bathsheba (Ps. 51:1[2]).

The Chronicler briefly reports that the plague sent by Yahweh resulted in the death of seventy thousand people or seventy military units (v. 14) and that it now threatened Jerusalem, the very place where David and his administration lived. Stress is

---

73. While Chronicles has 'three years', 2 Samuel 24:13 in the MT reads 'seven years' but this is thought to be due to a copying error but both figures could be correct if, instead of being taken literally, they are symbolic of a complete period of time.

laid on the destruction that is to be carried out by God's angel
(v. 15). Yahweh, who at the time of the great Flood, 'saw', 'was
sorry' and punished human 'evil' (Gen. 6:5-6), on this occasion
also 'saw' and 'was sorry' concerning the 'evil' in the sense of
the 'disaster'. David's reasoning and trust was soundly based.
God did indeed show compassion and relented and stopped the
destroying angel at the threshing-floor of Ornan the Jebusite.
Yahweh's sword still remained in the angel's hand but for the
moment at least the plague progressed no further (see v. 27).
The name 'Ornan' is spelled 'Araunah' in the Samuel text.
He belonged to one of the many Canaanite groups that had
inhabited the land prior to Joshua's conquest. The Jebusites had
retaken Jerusalem and it was Joab at David's command who
finally captured it so that it became the capital city of David's
kingdom (1 Chron. 11:4-9; see Josh. 15:63; 18:16; Judg. 1:21).
Ornan had managed to retain his property in the city and was
busy threshing wheat (v. 20), an indication that the incident
happened at the height of summer. The site was at the northern
point of the city and a good location for a threshing-floor.

The immediate reaction of David and the Jerusalem elders
was to fall on their faces at the threatening sight of the angel
(v. 16; Josh. 5:13-14). As a sign of their penitent grief they
were clothed in sackcloth, a coarse material usually made
of goats' hair and normally worn next to the skin (Joel 1:8;
Esther 4:1; Neh. 9:1; 2 Kings 6:30). David's confession and plea
is heightened in Chronicles. Again, he takes full responsibility
for the census (v. 17; see v. 8) and prays that the punishment
might fall on him and his family. He describes his folly as
'evil' which is how Yahweh viewed it (v. 7). Interestingly, he
refers to his people as 'sheep' with the implication that he
was their shepherd (see Num. 27:17; Isa. 63:11; Jer. 50:6). In his
earnest appeal, David addresses God in a way that continues
to indicate his personal relationship with Him: 'Yahweh my
God' (see 1 Chron. 11:19; 17:25; see also 2 Chron. 6:19, 40).

Application

The Lord will judge His people (Heb. 10:31). Though there
is great mercy and forgiveness with God, there are often
consequences for sinful action that cannot be avoided in this

world. Personal folly can often lead to others being involved in our sin and its effects. The God we are called to love is also to be revered, respected and held in awe. Lewis catches the thought well in those lines spoken by Mr Beaver about Aslan: 'Who said anything about safe? Course he isn't safe. But he's good. He's the King, I tell you.'[74]

The Covid-19 pandemic has been a reminder of the many plagues that have struck the world over the past two thousand years and the reactions to them. All such tragic happenings were seen as warnings of the great final day of wrath. As C. S. Lewis said in *The Problem of Pain,* that pain is God's 'megaphone to rouse a deaf world'.[75] In such troubles and pandemics, some are brought to the end of themselves to give glory to God while others, like Pharaoh in the time of the plagues of Egypt, harden their hearts and refuse to repent (see Exod. 9:34-35; Rev. 11:13; 16:8-9, 11, 21).

The angel of Yahweh is very closely associated with Yahweh Himself and comes with all the authority of God. This special supernatural divine messenger prepares us for 'the angel of the covenant' who is one with Yahweh (Mal. 3:1-2) and is described by John as the Word who was with God and who was God and who assumed flesh as the man Jesus the Messiah (John 1:1-18).

The propitiation (21:18-27)

18. Then the angel of Yahweh commanded Gad to say to David that David should go up to erect an altar for Yahweh on the threshing-floor of Ornan the Jebusite. 19. So David went up at the word of Gad which he had spoken in the name of Yahweh. 20. And Ornan turned and saw the angel and his four sons with him hid themselves; now Ornan was threshing wheat. 21. And David came to Ornan and Ornan looked and saw David. And he went out from the threshing-floor and bowed down before David with face to the ground. 22. Then David said to Ornan, 'Give me the site of the threshing-floor so that I may build on it an altar to Yahweh. Give it to me at the full price, that the plague may be held back from the people.' 23. And Ornan said to David, 'Take it for yourself and may my lord, the king, do that which is good in his eyes. See, I have given the cattle for the burnt offering

---

74. C. S. Lewis, *The Lion, the Witch and the Wardrobe,* chapter 8.

75. C. S. Lewis, *The Problem of Pain* (London: The Centenary Press, 1940), p. 81.

and the threshing sledges for the wood and the wheat for the grain offering; I have given the whole.' 24. But king David said to Ornan, 'No, for I insist acquiring it at the full price for I shall not take what belongs to you for Yahweh, nor offer up burnt offerings without cost.' 25. So David gave Ornan six hundred shekels of gold by weight for the site. 26. And David built there an altar to Yahweh, and he offered up burnt offerings and peace offerings. And he called to Yahweh and he answered him with fire from heaven on the altar of burnt offering. 27. Then Yahweh commanded the angel and he returned his sword to its sheath.

The Chronicler's account is fuller than the parallel passage in 2 Samuel 24 and there are echoes of earlier events such as Abraham's purchase of the cave of Machpelah and Gideon's dealings with an angel while threshing wheat (Gen. 23; Judg. 6:11-24). It is made very clear that the erection of an altar at Ornan's threshing-floor is not another good idea of David's. This is God's initiative that comes to David first through the angel to Gad and then from Gad to the king (v. 18). David himself meekly follows Gad's instructions which came with divine authority (v. 19). It is emphasised that the place of sacrifice is on a site not only owned by a foreigner but one who was a descendant of one of the cursed pre-Israelite inhabitants. Three times he is referred to as 'Ornan the Jebusite' (vv. 15, 18, 28).

Ornan's threshing-floor now becomes the focus of attention. First, Ornan, who was threshing wheat, saw the angel of destruction and he and his four sons hid themselves. Then David approached Ornan and immediately he went from the threshing area and prostrated himself before the king out of respect and submission. The bargaining then began with Ornan ready to give not only the site but the gifts for sacrifice. These included the grain offering that normally accompanied the burnt offering (Exod. 29:38-41). Ornan was another individual like Rahab and Ruth, representatives from outside Israel, who desired to belong to God's people. David could not accept this kind gesture; he recognised that he was duty bound to pay the full price for the site and offer his own costly sacrifices. Fifty shekels of silver was paid for the threshing-floor where the altar was erected (2 Sam. 24:24), whereas the six hundred shekels of gold was probably the full cost of

purchasing the whole area on which the future temple was to
be built. Abraham paid four hundred shekels of silver for the
burial site (Gen. 23:15). Burnt offerings produced a pleasing
aroma to God which meant that His wrath was appeased
while peace offerings provided additional propitiatory
offerings (see 1 Chron. 16:1). They also expressed complete
devotion to God and renewed fellowship, while the meat of
the peace offerings provided a fellowship meal. David offered
these sacrifices for himself and his people. There are two
significant factors mentioned by the Chronicler that are not
found in the Samuel text. First, David called on the name of
Yahweh who answered by fire (see 1 Kings 18:24, 37-38). It was
a reminder of God's original approval of the sacrificial system
in Leviticus 9:24 and it was a preview of what happened after
Solomon's dedication of the temple when fire consumed the
sacrifices (2 Chron. 7:1). Here was a further example of an
answer to prayer (see 1 Chron. 4:10; 5:20). Secondly, it is made
clear that God's wrath no longer hung over them in the form of
the angel's destructive sword stretched out over the city. The
atoning sacrifices had been offered, prayers were heard and so
the threat of plague was averted (see 2 Sam. 24:25; Exod. 30:12).

Application

Unlike paganism, where people try their best to appease the
gods, it is God alone who initiates the means for propitiating
His wrath. The merciful God restrained His wrath and
provided a just and righteous means for removing it. This is
the gospel. It all pointed forward to the occasion at Calvary's
cross, where 'mercy met the anger of God's rod' and where 'a
penalty was paid and pardon bought'.[76]

The emphasis on Ornan, the Gentile Jebusite, and his
interest in providing the temple site where David's sacrifices
appeased God's wrath, is a reminder of Gentile participation in
our Lord's death on a Roman cross and the Roman centurion's
confession that Jesus was the Son of God (Mark 15). It was at
the cross that the wall dividing Jew and Gentile was broken
down so that people of all nationalities might find forgiveness

---

76. From the hymn *Great is the Gospel* by Vernon Higham.

and be brought together as the one people of God to share together at the Lord's Table.

The place (21:28–22:1)

> 21:28. At that time, when David saw that Yahweh had answered him at the threshing-floor of Ornan the Jebusite, that he sacrificed there. 29. But the tabernacle of Yahweh which Moses had made in the wilderness and the altar of burnt offering were at that time in the high place in Gibeon, 30. and David was not able to go before it to seek God, for he was terrified of the sword of the angel of Yahweh. 22:1. Then David said, 'This is the house of Yahweh God, and this is the altar for burnt offerings for Israel.'

The account is brought to a climax with the reference to Yahweh's future house and the altar of burnt offering, the very heart of the Chronicler's concern (1 Chron. 22:1). The previous verses indicate why David did not go to Gibeon to 'seek' God during this period of judgment (21:29-30). He was afraid of the destructive angel's sword (see v. 16). David may well have sacrificed at Gibeon later and certainly Solomon did so (2 Chron. 1:3-6). Seeking God in worship and for guidance is stressed by the Chronicler. It was when David saw that Yahweh had graciously answered his prayers, and accepted his sacrifices (vv. 27-28), that he was convinced that the threshing-floor site was no one-off place of sacrifice but the site where the future temple was to be built. With similar words to what Jacob uttered when Yahweh appeared to Him at Bethel, David confessed that this was the place of God's residence (22:1; see Gen. 28:17, 22).

The Chronicler includes a reference to 'the tabernacle of Yahweh and the altar of the burnt offering' that Moses made which were at 'the high place' in Gibeon (v. 29). This more than hints that the new site for a temple and burnt offering altar 'for Israel' (22:1) will be the beginnings of the true fulfilment of the Mosaic requirements that emphasised they were not to offer burnt offerings at every place they saw but only in 'the place where Yahweh your God chooses to make his name to dwell' (Deut. 12:5, 10-14). Chronicles has first shown how Yahweh appointed David as king, then how Jerusalem became the capital with the divine presence symbolised by the ark of the covenant housed in a tent, then how David's dynasty will be an enduring one, how David's son will build God's house and now how Yahweh chose the site for the future temple (2 Chron. 3:1). In Chronicles, most of the attention for the remainder of David's reign concerns this temple and the son who will build it.

Application

Until the Messiah came and fulfilled the whole Mosaic sacrificial system, the God-appointed place of worship was important for carrying out the rituals. But Jesus taught that as a result of His sacrificial work at Calvary's cross there is no need for a temple made with hands.

Just as there was both overlap and continuity between the old Mosaic tabernacle set up at Gibeon with its altar of burnt offering and the new temple in Jerusalem, so there was a certain overlap immediately after Jesus's death, resurrection, ascension and giving of the Spirit with the apostles still attending the temple as well as assembling together as local churches in people's homes.

David's preparations for the temple (22:2-19)

There are no parallels in either Samuel or Kings for the events covering the closing years of David's reign such as are found in these final chapters of 1 Chronicles. They continue the theme commenced in chapter 17 concerning the future temple and the one appointed to build it. In this chapter, the Chronicler highlights David's provisions for building (22:2-5), David's instructions to Solomon (22:6-16), and David's exhortation to the leaders (22:17-19).

David's provisions for building (22:2-5)

22:2. So David commanded to collect the resident aliens who were in the land of Israel; and he appointed stonecutters to dress hewn stones to build the house of God. 3. And David prepared iron in abundance for nails for the doors of the gates and for the beam joints, and bronze in abundance that could not be weighed, 4. and cedar wood that could not be counted for the Sidonians and the Tyrians brought cedar wood in abundance to David. 5. And David said, 'Solomon my son is young and inexperienced, and the house to be built for Yahweh must be exceedingly magnificent, famous and glorious for all the lands, therefore I will make preparations for it.' So David made abundant preparations before his death.

This paragraph emphasises the huge quantity of supplies that David acquired in preparation for the temple (vv. 3 and 5b). The materials collected included stone, iron, bronze and cedarwood. Iron was used for nails in making the wooden doors and for tie-bars for the wooden beams.[77] David had previously received help from Hiram king of Tyre with cedars, masons and carpenters to build his own house (1 Chron. 14:1). This time he received cedarwood from Sidon as well as Tyre. Interestingly, the people of Sidon and Tyre contributed wood when the Jews came to rebuild the temple after the exile (Ezra 3:7). For this grand project, David also gathered the resident aliens from all over the land to do the preparatory work. The 'resident alien' or 'sojourner' (*gēr*) included Gibeonites and Canaanites who continued to live 'in the land of Israel' (v. 2; see 2 Chron. 2:17) after the conquest. They were ranked with the fatherless and widow as being defenceless. Clearly, Ornan the Jebusite was in a much better state than most resident aliens. The Israelites themselves had been resident foreigners in Egypt and were to remember this in their treatment of such people (Deut. 10:19). The representatives of the nations 'from whom Israel took its origins', as the introduction to Chronicles makes clear, are found among God's people preparing for the new temple.[78]

David's instructions to Solomon (22:6-16)

22:6. Then he called for Solomon his son and commanded him to build a house for Yahweh the God of Israel. 7. And David said to Solomon, 'My son, I had it in my heart to build a house to the name of Yahweh my God, 8. but the word of Yahweh came to me saying, "Much blood you have shed and great wars you have waged; you shall not build a house for my name, for much blood you have shed on the earth before me. 9. Here is a son being born to you who will be a man of rest, and I will give rest to him from all his enemies on every side; for Solomon will be his name and peace and quiet I will give to Israel in his days. 10. He will build

---

77. The only other occurrence of 'beam joints' in the Hebrew Bible is in 2 Chronicles 34:11.

78. See Johnstone, *1 and 2 Chronicles*, Vol. 1, p. 238.

a house for my name, and he will be a son to me and I will be
a father to him and I will establish the throne of his kingdom
over Israel for ever." 11. Now my son, may Yahweh be with you
and may you be successful and build the house of Yahweh your
God as he has spoken concerning you. 12. Only may Yahweh
give you discretion and understanding and give you charge
over Israel, to keep the law of Yahweh your God. 13. Then you
will succeed if you observe to do the decrees and the rulings
that Yahweh commanded Moses concerning Israel. Be strong
and courageous. Do not fear or be dismayed. 14. Now see, with
great pains I have provided for the house of Yahweh a hundred
thousand gold talents, and silver, a thousand thousands talents,
and of bronze and of iron that could not be weighed, for there is
so much; and timber and stone I have provided and you should
add more to them. 15. And with you in abundance are workers:
stone-cutters and craftsmen of stone and wood and all skilled
in every kind of work. 16. Of the gold, of the silver and of the
bronze and of the iron it could not be counted. Arise and work,
and may Yahweh be with you!'

It did not serve the Chronicler's purpose to mention anything
about Absalom and Adonijah and their unsuccessful yet deeply
disturbing attempts to obtain the throne from their father.
Nevertheless, this chapter assumes knowledge of Solomon's
coronation and the co-regency during the final years of
David's reign. It is at this point that the Chronicler reveals that
Solomon is the one ordained to succeed his father, and David
addresses him in a way similar to the charges given to Joshua
(Deut. 31:7-8; Josh. 1:6-9). In fact, there are strong similarities
between David's commissioning ('commanded him,' v. 6)
of Solomon to build the temple and the commissioning of
Joshua to take over the leadership from Moses to bring Israel
into Canaan. Further resemblances include the fact that, like
Moses, David was disqualified from carrying out a God-given
task which became the responsibility of his successor. There
is even, as with Joshua, this private charge to Solomon before
a later public one in 1 Chronicles 28.[79]

The royal succession is wholly seen in terms of building
the temple in a period of rest and peace. David's charge to

---

79. The Chronicler uses the verb *yr'* ('to fear') rather than the less common
verb *'rṣ* ('to be in terror') used in Joshua 1:9.

Solomon is in two parts: verses 7-10 look back while verses 11-16 contain an exhortation based on the review, with the words 'Now my son' (v. 11) providing the link between the two parts. The charge begins by mentioning David's idea of building an earthly house for God[80] using the term 'name' to refer to Yahweh's presence in the temple (v. 7). In David's mind are the words of Moses' sermon to Israel in the plains of Moab which speaks of the time when God would give His people rest in Canaan from their enemies and choose the place for Yahweh's 'name' to dwell (Deut. 12:10-11; see 2 Chron. 2:1[1:18]). He also refers to Yahweh's message, presumably the one that came through the prophet Nathan (v. 8; see 1 Chron. 17).

Many scholars make heavy weather of David's disqualification from building the temple. In Nathan's prophecy, it was first made plain that God had not up to that point demanded a permanent house to live in on earth but that He would build David a dynastic house and that it would be David's son who would build Yahweh's house. It was therefore not because God was opposed in principle to a temple. What is now disclosed is the reason why David was not allowed to build the temple. It was because of his wars and shedding of blood (v. 8) which had been a mark of his reign from the beginning, and the previous chapters (1 Chron. 18–20) have given some indication of the wars he fought to bring about peace for the nation. David's son would be the beneficiary of these peaceful conditions that would provide the setting for building Yahweh's house (vv. 9-10; see 1 Chron. 17:8-10). There is no thought that David's disqualification was due to him being ritually unclean on account of his wars, for if that were the case, it is unlikely he would have been allowed to build an altar and sacrifice (1 Chron. 21:26). Neither is there any suggestion that it was David's sin in ordering the census resulting in so many lives lost, that excluded him from building the temple. The shedding of blood is emphasised, but it is in the context of David's 'great wars' and it is shown to have been done 'before' or 'in front of' Yahweh. These were

---

80. 'I had it in my heart' is literally, 'I, it was with my heart'; see also 1 Chronicles 28:2; 2 Chronicles 6:7; 24:4; 29:10.

wars that had God's approval in order for peaceful conditions
to exist during the reign of his son (v. 9).

In contrast to David, who is termed 'a man of wars'
(1 Chron. 28:3), his son and successor is described uniquely
as 'a man of rest' (v. 9). While Joshua is said to have given
'rest' (*mᵊnûḥāh*; Josh. 1:13; 23:1) from war enabling Israel to set
up the tabernacle at Shiloh, nothing was said about Yahweh
having specially chosen the exact place (see Deut. 12:5, 10-11).

Yahweh's word to David speaks of Solomon having rest
from all his enemies 'roundabout' (v. 9), which suggests that
his is a 'rest' much greater than that in Joshua's day and the
intermittent rest during the Judges' period (Judg. 3:11, 30; 8:28).
Yahweh had also indicated to David the exact spot for the
temple (1 Chron. 21) in David's capital city where the ark, the
symbol of Yahweh's presence, had already been transferred in
anticipation of the chosen site. It is at the point where peace
and quiet are mentioned that David reports that it was Yahweh
who gave his son and successor the name 'Solomon' (*šᵊlōmôh*,
v. 9), which is a word play on the term 'peace' (*šālôm* – a state
of wellbeing). This unique information by the Chronicler
continues to emphasise that lasting peace and tranquillity[81]
had finally arrived in Israel with the accession of Solomon
(see also 1 Kings 4:24[5:4]) and thus provided the opportune
time for the earthly home of Yahweh's presence to be built.

Verse 10 brings the first part of the charge to a climax.
David closely follows the wording in Nathan's prophecy
(1 Chron. 17:12-13) concerning Solomon's special relationship
to Yahweh and his appointment to build Yahweh's house
together with the dynastic promise. The significant addition
is that the throne of Solomon's kingdom is 'over Israel'.

On the basis of these important promises, David begins to
encourage his son by the prayer-wish that Yahweh would be
with him (see 1 Chron. 11:9; Deut. 31:8; Josh. 1:5, 9) and that he
would 'prosper' or 'succeed' (v. 11). The actual exhortation is
surrounded by this concern for Yahweh's presence (vv. 11, 16). As
for the verb 'to prosper', it becomes an important theme for the
Chronicler which he will use with regard to Solomon's reign as

---

81. The noun 'tranquillity' or 'quiet' (*šeqeṭ*) is only found here in the Old
Testament but the verb from the same root occurs in Joshua 11:23; 14:15 and
elsewhere including 1 Chronicles 4:40 and 2 Chronicles 14:1.

well as of other kings (1 Chron. 29:23; 2 Chron. 7:11; 14:4-7; 20:20). Solomon's main task was to build the temple and David refers now to God as 'Yahweh your God' (vv. 11, 12) instead of 'Yahweh my God' (v. 7). Having been given this charge or commission to be Israel's king, Solomon needed heavenly wisdom ('discretion and understanding,' v. 12) to put into effect the Mosaic law which included statutes ('decrees') and ordinances ('rulings' or 'judicial decisions').[82] Solomon would be successful ('prosper'; vv. 11, 13; see Josh. 1:8) and enjoy covenant blessing if he kept God's commandments. The condition of obedience to God's law does not nullify the covenant promises but God uses such obedience to bring them to fulfilment.

Following the prayer-wish coupled with caution, comes the exhortation using familiar language that also occurs on subsequent occasions (v. 13b; see Deut. 31:7, 23; Josh. 1:9; 10:25; 1 Chron. 28:20; 2 Chron. 32:7). David then informs Solomon of the personal effort ('pains' or 'afflictions'; see Psalm 132:1 where the verbal form from the same word family is found) that had already gone into providing material and labourers for the building work, before giving the final appeal to be up and doing (vv. 14-16). The huge quantity of gold and silver as well as the vast amount of bronze and iron that could not be weighed is highlighted. Some think that the Chronicler is using hyperbole. On the other hand, it was not unknown in the ancient world for such large hoards to be acquired through conquest and the previous chapters have indicated the wealth that David obtained through gifts, the spoils of war and tribute (1 Chron. 18:6-8, 10-11; 20:2). The timber and stone as well as the bronze and iron were mentioned earlier (vv. 3-4). For the Old Testament writers, in common with other examples from the Ancient Near East, intellectual ability and natural skills such as carving wood, cutting stone and working with metal were examples of being 'wise' (v. 15, 'skilful'). Such 'wise' workers, gifted by God, were employed in the construction of the tabernacle and its furniture and Solomon would employ such men for building the temple (Exod. 28:3; 36:1-8; 2 Chron. 2:6, 12-13).

82. Syntactically, verse 12 is difficult but the general sense is clear. There is no good warrant, as in the English Standard Version, for making the second clause temporal 'that *when* he gives you charge ... you may keep'.

David's exhortation to the leaders (22:17-19)

22:17. David also commanded all the officials of Israel to help Solomon his son. 18. 'Is not Yahweh your God with you, and has he not given you rest on every side? For he has given into my hand the inhabitants of the land, and the land is subdued before Yahweh and before his people. 19. Now, give your heart and your soul to seek Yahweh your God, and rise and build the sanctuary of Yahweh God in order to bring the ark of the covenant of Yahweh and the holy vessels of God to the house that is to be built for the name of Yahweh.'

This concluding exhortation to Israel's leaders is probably a separate occasion to the later reference in 1 Chronicles 28:1. The 'help' that David himself had experienced from Israel's leaders (1 Chron. 12:1, 17, 18, 21, 22) he now expects to be given to his son (v. 17). Again, as in David's address to Solomon, reasons for the exhortation are presented (v. 18) before the call to be up and doing (v. 19). David again speaks of Yahweh as Solomon's God (v. 18; see vv. 10-11) and echoes the words of verse 9 concerning the rest that God had given 'on every side'. This rest that Solomon enjoyed was one that David's wars had secured on account of Yahweh's presence with them. Among 'the inhabitants of the land' that have been subdued in David's time, special mention has been made of the Hittites and Philistines (1 Chron. 11:4-9; 14:8-17; 20:4-8). For the Chronicler, it is with David that the land of Canaan was finally conquered completely. Joshua's conquest is seen as anticipating this ultimate conquest by the use of phrases from the Pentateuch and Joshua such as: 'the inhabitants of the land' (Exod. 23:31), 'the land is subdued before Yahweh and before his people' (Num. 32:22, 29; Josh. 18:1) and 'rest on every side' (Deut. 12:10; Josh. 21:44).

Seeking Yahweh is one of the important themes in Chronicles (for *dāraš*, 'to seek,' see 1 Chron. 10:13-14; 13:3; 28:9). As David exhorted the leaders, he indicated how they were to seek God. It must be with 'heart and soul', that is, with the whole of one's being (v. 19). Such seeking is not so much a passive waiting on God for guidance but an active seeking to obey God's revealed will. In this case it meant building the temple which is here referred to as the 'sanctuary' or 'holy place' (*miqdaš*), another of the Chronicler's significant terms. While in the Former Prophets, which includes Joshua to 2 Kings, the noun appears only once (Josh. 24:26), it is found seven times in Chronicles (see 1 Chron. 28:10; 2 Chron. 20:8; etc.). Its sacredness was due to its being the house built for Yahweh's name, the name being His revealed character. That 'name' is associated with 'the ark of the covenant of Yahweh', which was the pledge and token of God's holy presence and which made the temple special. It was to be the permanent resting place for Yahweh's presence on earth. The holy vessels are the ones belonging to the tabernacle that was at Gibeon (1 Chron. 16:39) where the table, lampstand and altar of incense stood. Solomon brought them into the temple when it was built and they were taken to Babylon when Jerusalem was destroyed (2 Chron. 5:5; 36:18). Significantly, they were later returned to Jerusalem by decree of Cyrus (Ezra 1:7-11).

Application

The Chronicler emphasises how David is one with Solomon in being responsible for the building of the temple. David was eager to build Yahweh's house and though not allowed to actually see it built, he was involved in the planning stage, in the acquiring of the materials (see 1 Chron. 18:8; 22:2-5), and in obtaining the workers, as well as bringing the ark to Jerusalem and acquiring the temple site. For the original readership this would have taught them to view the David–Solomon era as one entity and to look with anticipation to all that the prophets proclaimed concerning a future where there would be peace, rest and stability under a Davidic ruler. Furthermore, they were encouraged to expect Yahweh to come to His temple, especially as the second temple contained no token of God's presence nor had there been any supernatural glory cloud filling the place. Yet, the post-exilic prophets had promised a glorious future for the temple and that Yahweh would come to His temple (Hag. 2:1-9; Mal. 3:1). Christians live in the period when Messiah Jesus, who is Yahweh God, the second person of the Holy Trinity, did come to His temple and, in fact, brought the former administration to an end. Out of the old has arisen a new temple established at the cost of Messiah's blood through His war with Satan, the ancient enemy. We still await the final consummation when peace and rest in the land will extend throughout the earth and God's presence will be among His people. For the present, Christians are encouraged to live obedient lives and proclaim the praises of the one who has called them out of darkness into His marvellous light (1 Pet. 2:4-10).

David's organisation of the temple and community workers (23:1–27:34)

This section, which again has no parallel elsewhere in the Bible, is in two parts, the greater part concerns David's involvement in the duties associated in some way with the temple (chs. 23–26), whereas the second more succinct part concerns the wider community (ch. 27). Interestingly, in the introduction, the lay officials are mentioned first before the priests and Levites (v. 2) but in the lists that follow they are dealt with last (27:1-34). The focus of attention is thus directed to the Levites, dealing first with the three Levitical families of Gershon, Kohath and Merari and their duties (23:6-32). The Aaronic Levites, who are introduced in 23:13, are dealt with in more detail in 24:1-19 and this is followed by listing the non-Aaronic Levites from the families of Kohath and Merari (24:20-31) before introducing the Levitical musicians (25:1-31), gatekeepers (26:1-19), treasurers (26:20-28) and other Levites who had responsibilities outside the temple (26:29-32). This comprehensive list of religious, military and civil leaders who supported David toward the close of his reign provides further evidence of the well-ordered transition from David's reign to that of his son and indicates that the move to a more centralised government was not unique to Solomon.

The Levitical divisions and duties (23:1-32)

23:1. Now when David grew old and full of days, he made his son Solomon king over Israel. 2. And he gathered together all the officials of Israel and the priests and the Levites. 3. Now the Levites from aged thirty years and upward were numbered and their number per head of the males was thirty-eight thousand. 4. Of these, twenty-four thousand acted as overseers over the work of Yahweh's house, and six thousand officers and judges, 5. And four thousand gatekeepers and four thousand giving praise to Yahweh with the instruments that I made for offering praise. 6. And David divided them into divisions.

The chapter begins with a general heading that applies to the rest of 1 Chronicles. It comes close to the statement in 1 Kings 1:1, 'Now king David was old, advanced in days' but with 'full of' in place of 'advanced'. A similar idiom is used of Abraham, Isaac and Job (Gen. 25:8; 35:29; Job 42:17; see also 1 Chron. 29:28; 2 Chron. 24:15). It did not serve the Chronicler's purpose to include the account of the intrigue surrounding the succession to the throne and of David's own frailty recorded in 1 Kings 1–2. However, what has already been assumed in 1 Chronicles 22 is now clearly stated that in his final years David made his son Solomon king. The heading introduces again the close connection between the succession and the preparations for the new temple, only this time the focus is not on building material but on personnel. It shows how David and Solomon were one in this great enterprise, the co-regency providentially providing the obvious setting.

Verse 2 provides the introduction to the lists of temple staff and state officials that occupy our attention until the end of chapter 27. David gathered Israel's secular leaders as well as the priests and other Levites, a gathering different from the one the king assembled in 1 Chronicles 28:1. The following lists indicate where the Chronicler's interests lay. It is the Levites who are given pride of place. The term 'Levite' is often used in a comprehensive sense for all the personnel connected with the temple. Attention was first drawn to their central place in the Chronicler's thinking in his introduction (1 Chron. 6:1-81).

A census was taken of the Levites (vv. 3-5). Unlike David's previous census, in which Joab did not include the Levites (1 Chron. 21) and which served no good purpose, this poll followed the divine pattern revealed to Moses with a view to Levitical service in the temple (see Num. 1:47-53; 3:14-39; 4:1-49). The period of service fluctuated according to circumstances and ability, ranging from twenty, twenty-five or thirty and up to fifty and beyond (see Num. 4:35-36, 39-40, 43-44, 47-48; 8:24-26; 2 Chron. 31:17; Ezra 3:8). In verses 24 and 27 the Levites were numbered from twenty years and above. No doubt younger men would have been employed for heavy work. In the time of Moses, the number of Levites in the thirty to fifty age bracket was eight thousand, five hundred and eighty (Num. 4:48), while by David's time, the total aged from thirty upward is put at thirty-eight thousand. It may be that the Chronicler was using 'thousand' in the sense of 'clan' or 'group'. Of this figure, twenty-four 'thousand' may refer to temple supervisors and administrators or even to the priests and their attendants as in chapter 24 (see 2 Chron. 34:12-13; Ezra 3:8-9), six thousand 'officers and judges' (1 Chron. 26:29), four thousand 'gate-keepers' (see 1 Chron. 26) and four thousand musicians (see 1 Chron. 25). It is calculated that the temple staff amounted to about one in thirty of the adult male population.[83] David's interjection 'which I made' (v. 5; see 1 Chron. 28:19 for a further example) indicates his involvement in making musical instruments (see also Amos 6:5; 2 Chron. 7:6; 29:26-27; Neh. 12:36).

The first half of verse 6 concludes the introductions with the mention that David organised the Levites into divisions, similar to the parcelling out of the land to the tribes by Joshua (Josh. 11:23;12:7). A new section begins at 6b.

> 23:6b. Concerning Levi's sons, Gershon, Kohath and Merari. 7. Of the Gershonites: Ladan and Shimei. 8. The sons of Ladan the chief: Jehiel and Zetham and Joel, three; 9. the sons of Shimei: Shelomith and Haziel and Haran, three; these were the heads of the fathers of Ladan. 10. And the sons of Shimei: Jahath, Zina and Jeush and Beriah. These were the sons of Shimei, four; 11. And Jahath was the chief and Zizah the second; but Jeush and Beriah did not have many sons so they became a father's house, one muster.
>
> 12. The sons of Kohath: Amram, Izhar, Hebron and Uzziel, four. The sons of Amram: Aaron and Moses. 13. And Aaron, he and his sons, were set apart for ever to sanctify the most holy things, to burn incense before Yahweh, to minister to him and to bless in his name for ever. 14. But Moses, the man of God, his sons were named among the tribe of Levi. 15. The sons of Moses: Gershom and Eliezer. 16. The sons of Gershom: Shubael the chief. 17. And the sons of Eliezer were Rehabiah the chief; and Eliezer had no other sons, but the sons of Rehabiah were exceedingly many. 18. The sons of Izhar: Shelomith the chief.

---

83. Johnstone, *1 and 2 Chronicles*, Vol. 1, p. 245.

19. The sons of Hezron: Jeriah the chief, Amariah the second, Jahaziah the third and Jekameam the fourth. 20. The sons of Uzziel: Micah the chief and Isshiah the second.

23.21. The sons of Merari: Mahli and Mushi. The sons of Mahli: Eliezer and Kish. 22. And Eliezer died and had no sons, but only daughters; and the sons of Kish their brothers married them. 23. The sons of Mushi: Mahli and Eder and Jeremoth, three.

From verse 6b to 23, a segmented genealogy of Levi's family takes the line down four generations, five in the case of Moses. Previous Levi genealogies are found in Exodus 6:16-25; Numbers 3:17-20; and 1 Chronicles 6:1-30[5:27-16:15]. After mentioning the three sons of Levi, Gershon (spelled Gershom in 1 Chronicles 6:16[6:1]), Kohath and Merari, it is the Gershonite line that is first covered (vv. 7-11). Two sons of Gershon are listed: Ladan and Shimei. Ladan is either an alternate name for Libni (Exod. 6:17; Num. 3:18; 1 Chron. 6:17[6:2]; see 1 Chron. 26:21) or a prominent later descendant. Three sons of Ladan follow in verse 8, while in verse 9 another Shimei appears, different from the one in verses 7 and 10, and a descendant of Ladan. All the ones named belonging to Ladan's descendants come to six family heads, the largest of the Levitical groups. The descendants of Gershon's second son, Shimei, did not fare so well. Though four of his sons are named, only the first two, Jahath the chief and Zina, also called Zizah (vv. 10-11) the second, had numerous offspring; the other two, Jeush and Beniah, did not produce many descendants with the result that the two family households were reckoned as one for roster purposes.

Kohath's descendants are dealt with next (vv. 12-20). After naming Kohath's four sons, Amram, Izhar, Hebron and Uzziel (v. 12; see Exod. 6:18), special attention is given to Amram on account of his sons Aaron and Moses. Aaron and his sons have a special status and therefore his descendants are not reckoned among the Levites for roster duty like the descendants of his brother Moses. Aaron's family, who are described as 'set apart for ever', are given special duties that involved, in the first place, sanctifying or consecrating the most holy things (see Exod. 30:29). The 'most holy' (literally 'holy of holies') items included the incense and incense altar that was in front of the veil and ark of the covenant and in fact the whole tabernacle and its furnishings (Exod. 30:10, 25-29, 36; Ezek. 45:3). While Leviticus 16:2-3 calls the inner sanctum where the ark was situated 'the holy place', the Letter to the Hebrews refers to it as 'the most holy' (Heb. 9:12). Devoted objects and offerings can also be described as 'most holy' (Lev. 2:3, 10; 27:28). Aaron and his descendants were also set apart to 'burn incense' in Yahweh's presence. The verb is literally 'to make smoke', which could include burning on the main bronze altar. In addition, their work involved ministering to God on behalf of the people and blessing the people on behalf of God (see Deut. 10:8; 21:5). Such ministering would have included offering the sacrifices and caring for the lampstand and showbread, etc. It seems to have been the regular climax to the public worship after the sacrifices had been offered for the priests to pronounce the blessing on the assembled gathering in Yahweh's name. This they did by raising their hands toward the people (see Lev. 9:22-23). An Aaronic blessing is recorded in Numbers 6:23-27. The 'for ever' (v. 13) perhaps picks up the phrase 'to this day' in Deuteronomy 10:8, but the double use of it suggests that the Chronicler encourages the post-exilic community to remember that there has been this continuity from the time when the priests were first set apart right through not only to David but to their own day.

Moses is described as 'the man of God' (v. 14; see Deut. 33:1; Josh. 14:6; Ps. 90:1). The expression, first applied to Moses the prophet *par excellence*, describes Yahweh's spokesmen and emphasises their status in the eyes of the people. Both Samuel and David are referred to in this way, but the phrase appears many times with reference to Elijah and Elisha (2 Chron. 8:14; Neh. 12:24,36; 1 Sam. 9:6-19; 1 Kings 17:18, 24; 2 Kings 1:10; 4:7, 9, 21; etc.). Though Moses was the one who initially set apart Aaron and his sons for their priestly tasks, his descendants were not given that role but counted with the rest of the Levites for administrative duties (v. 14).

Thus it is only Amram's line through Moses that is produced here. His sons, Gershom and Eliezer, are by Moses' wife Zipporah (Exod. 2:22; 18:2-4). A certain Jonathan and his descendants, who is described as the 'son' ('descendant') of

Gershom, Moses' son, served as priests among the Danites until the exile (Judg. 18:30). Of Gershom's sons only one is named, Shubael (also spelled Shebuel; see 1 Chron. 24:20; 26:24), who is described as 'chief'. Gershom's second son, Eliezer, had only one son, Rehabiah, also described as 'chief' but he fathered many sons as his name suggests (v. 17; the root letters of his name (r-h-b) form words suggesting 'wide' or 'large'; see Rehoboth in Genesis 26:22).

From verses 18 to 20, descendants of the other sons of Kohath are shown. Shelomoth, the only son of Izhar, is nevertheless called 'chief' (see vv. 16-17). Exodus 6:21 names other sons of Izhar including the rebel Korah (Num. 16:1). This suggests that in some cases the term 'chief' used with a lone son may witness to other unnamed sons. Hezron has four sons named while Uzziel has two (a further three are named in Exod. 6:22; see also 1 Chron. 24:23-25).

Merari's family is dealt with in verses 21-23. For his two sons, Mahli and Mushi, see further 1 Chronicles 6:19[4], 29[14] (see also Exod. 6:19; Num. 3:20, 33; Ezra 8:18; 1 Chron. 24:26-30). The note concerning Eleazer, the son of Mahli, is interesting. He had no sons but only daughters, so his brother Kish's sons married them[84] as was allowed under the Mosaic law of inheritance (see Numbers 27:1-11 for the precedent set in the case of Zelophehad's daughters). Despite this ruling, it is most unlikely that daughters would have served as an independent Levitical house. For roster purposes they would have come under the house of Kish. Thus there are four heads of family houses for Merari (Kish, Mahli, Eder and Jeremoth (Jerimoth in 1 Chron. 24:30), nine for Kohath (Shubael, Rehabiah, Shelomoth, Jeriah, Amariah, Jahaziel, Jehaneam, Micah and Isshiah) and nine for Gershon, making twenty-two in all.

23:24. These were the sons of Levi by the house of their fathers, the heads of the fathers according to their muster, counting names per head, each doing the work of the service of Yahweh's house from the age of twenty years and upward. 25. For David said, 'Yahweh the God of Israel has given rest to his people and he tabernacles in Jerusalem for ever, 26. and also for the Levites, there is no need to carry the tabernacle or any of

---

84. The verb *nāśā'*, 'to lift', 'take,' often means 'to marry' in the post-exilic books (see Ezra 9:2, 12; 10:44; Neh. 13:23; 2 Chron. 11:21; 13:21; 24:3).

its vessels for its service.' 27. For by the last words of David these were the number of the sons of Levi, from aged twenty years and upward. 28. For their standing *was to be* at the side of the sons of Aaron for the service of Yahweh's house, over the courts and over the chambers and over the cleansing of everything that is holy, and the work of the ministry of God's house, 29. and for the rows of bread, and for the flour of the grain offering and for the unleavened wafers, and for the pan cakes, and for what is mixed, and for all measures and sizes. 30. And to stand each morning to give thanks and to give praise to Yahweh, and likewise at evening. 31. And to offer all burnt offerings to Yahweh for the Sabbaths, for the New Moons and for the appointed festivals, by number according to the ruling concerning them, regularly before Yahweh. 32. And they shall observe the regulation of the tent of meeting and the regulation of the holy place and the regulation of the sons of Aaron their brothers for the service of Yahweh's house.

Verse 24, taking up the brief reference in verse 9, makes clear in this summary statement that the foregoing names comprised a list of the heads of Levitical families from which David drew for administrative work in Yahweh's house. Though for census purposes the age at which Levites began service was set at thirty (v. 3; see Num. 4:3, 43), practical considerations meant that they often began work at an earlier age, a precedent having been set by God in the wilderness (Num. 8:24). The added note about David's final words gives the age twenty ruling more weight (v. 27). With the new era of peace and stability, Yahweh now resided or 'tabernacled' (*šākan*, v. 25) in Jerusalem 'for ever'. No longer would the Levites need to carry the ark, and this would also mean that, unlike the situation during the wilderness period (Num. 10:17; Deut. 10:8), there would be no need for them to transport any portable residence with its accompanying furniture and utensils (v. 26; see 2 Chron. 35:3), the implication being that there will be a permanent temple building. The word 'tabernacle' (*miškān*, v. 26) is from the same word family as 'to reside' or 'to tabernacle' (*šākan*, v. 25).

The duties of the Levites who are not priests are set out in some detail in verses 28-32 (see 1 Chron. 9:28-32). Primarily, their position or duty was to assist the priests in Yahweh's house (vv. 28, 32; see Num. 3:6; 18:1-4). This must not be thought of as some diminution in their status but in the light of what is envisaged in the proposed temple there is necessarily a change in their duties. In Solomon's temple there were two courts, an outer court for the people and an inner court for the priests (1 Chron. 28:6, 12; Jer. 26:2; 2 Chron. 4:9). The 'chambers' were side rooms off the courts (v. 28; 1 Chron. 9:26, 33; 28:12; Jer. 35:2, 4; 36:10, 12). Their task of 'cleansing' what was 'holy' probably had to do with making sure that every gift from the people for the priests was not polluted in any way. The Levites were also involved in preparing the 'rows of bread' (1 Chron. 9:32; Lev. 24:6; also termed 'bread of the Presence' from the literal 'bread of the face,' see Exod. 25:30; 35:13). Besides preparing this 'showbread' as it is traditionally called in English, they were responsible for the fine flour and other ingredients to make the grain offering cakes (1 Chron. 9:31; Lev. 2; 6:21[14]; 7:12) and for the standards of measurement and weight (v. 29; Lev. 19:35-36). Those Levites particularly responsible for music (see v. 5) were to be in attendance at the morning and evening sacrifices to praise God (v. 30; see 1 Chron. 16:4). The Levites also had the task of assisting the priests who offered the required number of burnt sacrifices on the various holy days and festivals 'regularly' (1 Chron. 16:6, 37, 40) throughout the religious year (v. 31; Num. 28–29; see 2 Chron. 8:13-14; Ezra 3:4). Only the priests were allowed to present the offerings and to administer the blood of the sacrifices (Num. 18:3).

In what amounts to a summary statement in verse 32, the Chronicler uses the old terms 'tent of meeting' and 'holy place' when referring to the temple and its inner sanctuary. The instructions concerning the Levites' temple duties would have included guarding the sanctuary from all unclean or unauthorised persons (Num. 1:53; 18:22-23) as well as attending to the needs of the priests as they ministered in Yahweh's house.

Application

The Chronicler's presentation of the final years of David's reign purposefully emphasises the unity and peaceful conditions of this period that overlapped with the beginning of Solomon's reign and the preparations for the future temple, particularly its personnel. Though the post-exilic temple bore no comparison to the splendour of the temple that Solomon built, the Chronicler sought to indicate that there was a definite continuity with the past to give inspiration and support to his own generation. The attention given to the Levites indicates his concern to embolden those of Levitical descent to be forward in their service at the restored temple following the exile in Babylon and not to be apathetic in their devotion (see Malachi).

With the finished work of the Messiah and the end of the Jerusalem temple (John 4:20-26; Mark 15:38), there is no place for Levites or sacerdotal priests. Principles, however, can be obtained from this passage for the smooth running of church life and the support to be given by deacons and others so that preachers might not be negligent in prayer and the ministry of the word (Acts 6:1-7).

The priests and other Levites (24:1-31)

The first nineteen verses deal with the priestly divisions, picking up on the brief statement in 23:13, while the rest of the chapter is a further genealogy of non-priestly Levites.

Priestly divisions (24:1-19)

24:1. Now the divisions of the sons of Aaron. The sons of Aaron: Nadab and Abihu, Eleazar and Ithamar. 2. And Nadab and Abihu died before their father and they had no sons, so Eleazar and Ithamar became priests. 3. And David and Zadok of the sons of Eleazar and Ahimelech of the sons of Ithamar divided them according to their muster in their service. 4. Now the sons of Eleazar were found more numerous in male heads than the sons of Ithamar, so they were divided: of the sons of Eleazar, sixteen heads according to house of fathers, and of the sons of Ithamar, eight according to their fathers' house. 5. And they divided them by lot, the one as the other, for they were officials of the sanctuary and officials of God, from the sons of Eleazar and among the sons of Ithamar. 6. And Shemaiah, the son of Nethanel, the scribe, from the Levites, wrote them down before the king and the officials and Zadok the priest and Abimelech the son of Abiathar and the heads of the fathers of the priests and the Levites, one father's house drawn for Eleazar and one always drawn for Ithamar.

7. Now the first lot came out to Jehoiarib, the second to
Jedaiah, 8. the third to Harim, the fourth to Seorim, 9. the fifth to
Malchijah, the sixth to Mijamin, 10. the seventh to Hakkoz, the
eighth to Abijah, 11. the ninth to Jeshua, the tenth to Shecaniah,
12. the eleventh to Eliashib, the twelfth to Jakim, 13. the thirteenth
to Huppah, the fourteenth to Jeshebeab, 14. the fifteenth to
Bilgah, the sixteenth to Immer, 15. the seventeenth to Hezir, the
eighteenth to Happizzez, 16. the nineteenth to Pethahiah, the
twentieth to Jehezekel, 17. the twenty-first to Jachin, the twenty-
second to Gamul, 18. the twenty-third to Delaiah, the twenty-
fourth to Maaziah. 19. These were their muster for their service
for entry to the house of Yahweh according to the ruling given
them by the hand of Aaron their father, as Yahweh the God of
Israel had commanded him.

The first six verses provide an introduction to the mustering
of the twenty-four priestly classes or offices. All four sons
of Aaron are listed and there is a reminder of why there
were only two family groups. The sudden death of Nadab
and Abihu who had no sons (see Lev. 10:1-5; Num. 3:4) meant
that it was only from the remaining two sons, Eleazar and
Ithamar, that the priestly lines were formed. Both these sons
worked with their father under Moses' directions but Eleazar
was appointed chief over the Levites, having the oversight of
those who were responsible for the sanctuary (Lev. 10: 6-20;
Num. 3:32). Not so much is said of Ithamar, but he was given
overall responsibility for recording the quantities of precious
metals used in constructing the tabernacle and overseeing
the duties of the Gershonites and Merarites in the tabernacle
(Exod. 38:21; Num. 4:28, 33; 7:8). Among the returnees from
Babylon with Ezra was a descendant of Ithamar by the name
of Daniel (Ezra 8:2). In dividing or apportioning the priests
(see 1 Chron. 23:6) for their duties of service, David had the
help of Zadok, a descendant of Eleazar (1 Chron. 6:3-8; 50-53
[5:29-35; 6:35-38]), and Ahimelech, the son of Abiathar and
grandson of Ahimelech who was killed by Saul (1 Chron. 18:16;
1 Sam. 22:20; 2 Sam. 8:17). Zadok is usually paired not with
Ahimelech but Abiathar (1 Chron. 15:11; see 2 Sam. 15:35;
17:15; 1 Kings 4:4) but perhaps, through his involvement in
the conspiracy to make Adonijah king, he had already been
demoted before being expelled from office after David's death

(1 Kings 1-2). It is significant that it is Zadok who is called 'the priest', not Ahimelech (vv. 3, 6).

Those families descending from Eleazar are said to be more numerous than those descending from Ithamar (v. 4). Nevertheless, this did not mean the Eleazarites received preferential treatment. All alike were selected for duty by means of casting lots (v. 5) and in none of the resulting twenty-four orders is there any indication of their family ties. In addition, the members of both priestly lines were viewed as of equal status in their most sacred of tasks, referring to them literally as 'officials of holiness' or 'sanctuary officials' (Isa. 43:28) and as either 'officials of God' or 'most distinguished officials' (v. 5).[85] Casting lots was used by Joshua in dividing up the promised land among the twelve tribes and in allocating the Levitical cities (Josh. 19:51; 21:1-40; 1 Chron. 6:54[39]). Whether this was done in association with the Urim and Thummim is not revealed (see Josh. 7:14-18; 1 Sam. 10:19-21; 14:38-45) but it was a means of obtaining direct guidance from God. The practice is first mentioned in connection with the day of Atonement when lots were cast as to which of the two goats was to become the scapegoat (Lev. 16:8). Concerning the priestly arrangements, the results of the lot were recorded by an otherwise unknown scribe called Shemaiah, who also belonged among the Levites (v. 6; see 'Shavsha' in 1 Chron. 18:16), and everything took place in the presence of the king and the other leaders. Strict fairness and lack of prejudice was thus maintained in the division of priestly duties. As there were sixteen family heads among the Eleazarites to the eight belonging to Ithamarites it is possible that the last part of verse 6 means that one lot was taken from each of the two families in turn until they reached sixteen with the final eight assigned to Eleazar's family, or that two were drawn for the Eleazarites for every one of the Ithamarites.[86]

---

85. It is possible that the term for God (Elohim) expresses the superlative: 'outstanding officers' (see perhaps Psalm 68:16[17]); A. B. Davidson, *Hebrew Syntax*, §34 Rem.6; D. Winton Thomas, 'A Consideration of Some Unusual Ways of Expressing the Superlative in Hebrew,' *Vetus Testamentum* 3 (1953) 209-24.

86. The MT repeats the verb 'drawn' or 'taken' (wᵉ'āḥuz 'āḥuz). Some Hebrew MSS and the LXX read 'and one' (wᵉ'eḥāḏ). But the double use of the word 'taken'

Verses 7-18 describe the twenty-four family heads that 'came out' by lot (see Josh. 16:1). Many of the names appear in post-exilic lists and perhaps named after their family heads but that is not certain, as in the case of Jeshua in verse 11 (see Ezra 2:2; Hag. 1:1; Zech. 3:1) and Eliashib in verse 12 (Neh. 3:1, 20-21; 12:22-23; 13:28). Some of the names listed have no parallel in the Bible, such as Seorim, Huppah, Jeshebeah, Happizzez and Gamul. For 'Jehoiarib' and 'Jedaiah' (v. 7) see 1 Chronicles 9:10, Ezra 2:36-39 and Nehemiah 11:10. From Jehoiarib arose the priestly Maccabean family of Mattathias (1 Macc. 2:1). From Harim (v. 8) were those who returned from exile (Ezra 2:36-39; Neh. 7:39-42) and Malchijah and Mijamin (v. 9) appear in post-exilic lists (Neh. 10:3[4], 7[8]; 12:5, 14, 17). The family of Hakkoz (v. 10) had difficulties proving their priestly legitimacy after the exile (Ezra 2:61-63; Neh. 7:63-65), whereas from Abijah comes Zechariah, the father of John the Baptist (Neh. 10:7[8]; 12:4, 17; Luke 1:5). Descendants of a Delaiah (v. 18) are among those exiles who returned who could not prove their ethnicity (Ezra 2:59-60; Neh. 7:62).

Verse 19 is a reminder that David's activity in ordering the priestly service was in accordance with the ruling that God had given to Aaron. Yahweh did speak directly to Aaron on a few occasions (see Lev. 10:8; Num. 18:1) but usually God's word to Aaron was mediated through Moses (Lev. 6:1-2[8-9]). Unlike the description of the tasks given to the Levites (23:28-32), the work of priests is not detailed.

Application

Drawing lots continued into the post-exilic period (Neh. 10:34[35]; 11:1; see also Purim in Esther 3:7; 9:23-32) and was even used, along with prayer, in appointing Matthias to replace Judas Iscariot (Acts 1:26). With the coming of the Spirit at Pentecost there is no further mention of this method of obtaining direct divine guidance in the Bible, although it has been employed by some churches particularly in the

may be a Hebrew idiom to give either interpretation (Williamson, *1 and 2 Chronicles*, p. 164; Klein, *1 Chronicles*, p. 467).

East, as well as Christian groups like the Moravians in the eighteenth century. The outcome of casting lots was not seen as a matter of luck or devilish divination but as having God's approval, and by this means God's people trusted Him to make known His will (Prov. 16:33; 18:18). This practice gives no biblical justification for gambling or any encouragement to participate in modern-day lotteries.

These twenty-four priestly divisions, who were descendants of Aaron's remaining sons, and appointed to minister in the temple according to Aaronic rules, emphasised the continuity of the priestly ministry and its enduring significance. For the post-exilic people, the re-establishment of these divisions and orders for daily rotation duties in the second temple was an encouragement to faith. Josephus describes a similar twenty-four system prior to the fall of Jerusalem in A.D. 70. John the Baptist's father, Zechariah, belonged to one of these orders, the order of Abijah, and Luke mentions his roster week of duty in the temple and the added responsibility given him, through the casting of lots, of offering incense in the holy place, on the very day when the angel appeared to him (Luke 1:5-11).

Continuity with the past is not to be despised by Christians. As we partake together of the Lord's Supper on the Lord's Day, for instance, it is amazing to think that we follow an historical tradition that goes back two thousand years to our Lord Himself on the night in which He was betrayed. The same applies to other elements in our communal worship such as the reading of Scripture, the singing of hymns, preaching, baptism and prayer (Mark 14:22-26; Acts 2:41-42; 20:7; 1 Cor. 10:16-17; 11:23-26; Eph. 5:18-21; Heb. 10:23-25).

Non-priestly Levites (24:20-31)

24:20. Now for the rest of the sons of Levi. For the sons of Amram: Shubael; for the sons of Shubael: Jehdeiah. 21. For Rehabiah: for the sons of Rehabiah the head: Isshiah. 22. For the Izharites: Shelomoth. For the sons of Shelomoth: Jahath. 23. And my sons: Jeriah, Amariah the second, Jahaziel the third, Jekameam the fourth. 24. The sons of Uzziel: Micah. The sons of Micah: Shamir. 25. The brother of Micah: Isshiah. For the sons of Issiah: Zechariah. 26. The sons of Merari: Mahli and Mushi, the sons of Jaaziah, Beno. 27. The sons of Merari by Jaaziah:

Beno, Shoham, Zaccur and Ibri. 28. For Mahli: Eleazar, who had
no sons. 29. For Kish: the sons of Kish: Jerahmeel. 30. Also the
sons of Mushi: Mahli, Eder and Jerimoth. These were the sons
of the Levites according to the house of their fathers'. 31. These
also cast lots as well as their brothers the sons of Aaron, in the
presence of David the king, Zadok, Ahimelech and the heads of
the fathers' belonging to the priests and Levites, the head fathers
as well as his youngest brother.

The rest of chapter 24 is concerned with the non-priestly
Levites who assisted the priests in their sacerdotal work (see
23:4a). By placing the non-priestly Levites around the priestly
division, the Chronicler draws attention to the importance of
the Aaronic priesthood.

The Gershonites seem not to be included in this list of
families from the tribe of Levi, only those from Kohath and
Merari. It is understandable for the list to commence with the
Kohathites for it follows the pattern set in chapter 23 where
the list of Kohathites also follows the note about the priests
(23:13, 16-20). Without mentioning Kohath or the intervening
descendants of Amram such as Moses or his sons Gershom
and Eleazar (23:14-16a), the list begins with Shubael (spelled
Shebuel in 23:16b). With Jehdeiah, a descendant of Shubael,
the list introduces an extra generation (v. 20). The same is the
case with Isshiah, the descendant of Rehabiah (v. 21).[87] Again,
with the descendants of Izhar, an extra generation, Jahath,
follows the name Shelomoth (v. 22; Shelomith in 23:18). Is the
reading 'my sons' (v. 23) an indication of the family belonging
to the author of the list or even of the Chronicler himself?[88]
Comparing the names that follow with those in 23:12 it is clear
that the descendants of Hebron, the third son of Kohath, are in
mind. Concerning the sons of Uzziel (see 23:20), a descendant
of Micah, Shamir, is added to this list (v. 24). Isshiah (Jesshiah
in 23:20), is referred to as Micah's brother and his descendant
is also named: Zechariah (v. 25). Thus, apart from the Hebron
family, an extra generation appears. Adding together the

---

87. As in the case of Ladan (23:8), the term 'head' or 'chief' comes immediately
after Rehabiah, suggesting that it belongs to him rather than with the name that
follows.

88. Without the Masoretic pointing, it could be read: 'And the sons of'. In the
margin of two Hebrew MSS is the reading, 'And the sons of Hebron.'

names of the final generation member of each family group brings the total to nine: Jehdeiah, Isshiah, Jahath, Jeriah, Amariah, Jahaziel, Jekameam, Shamir and Zechariah.

Levi's son, Merari, is explicitly mentioned along with the grandsons, Mahli and Mushi (see 23:21a). The second half of verse 26 and the following verse 27 are difficult.[89] Translating 'Beno' as 'his son' in verses 26-27 could mean that Jaaziah is an otherwise unknown son of Merari or perhaps a family member who traced his ancestry to him. Verse 27 would then read, 'The sons of Merari by Jaaziah his son: Shoham, Zaccur and Ibri.' Eleazar's situation (v. 28) has been described in the previous chapter (23:22), while Eleazar's brother, Kish, has a further generation added: an otherwise unknown Jerahmeel (v. 29). Verse 30 which mentions the three sons of Mushi is a repeat of 23:23-24. It is possible to see in this list (vv. 20-30) twenty-four non-priestly Levitical divisions to correspond with the priestly divisions (vv. 7-18). Josephus understood it in this way.

The chapter closes (vv. 30b-31) by using phraseology that parallels the introduction to the priestly divisions (vv. 4-6). In order to guarantee impartiality lots were again drawn in the presence of the same witnesses that oversaw the earlier occasion although there is no mention of the lay 'officials' (see v. 6).

Application

Not only does this list indicate the central place of the priests in the temple but it emphasises the important supportive role of these Levite families in assisting the priests. By this means the Chronicler sought to encourage the temple staff in the post-exilic period to work together in the daily routine of worship for the good of the people and the honour of God. In the context of the local church's life and worship, this Word of God should inspire Christians to act unitedly in serving the Lord and supporting the leadership (Gal. 6:6-10; Col. 3:12-17).

By adding a new generation of family heads to the list already given in the previous chapter and even introducing a new family member, the Chronicler shows the importance of

---

89. Instead of a proper name, the word 'beno' ($b^e n\hat{o}$) could be translated 'his son' in verses 26 and 27 suggesting that Jaaziah is Merari's son who had three not four sons: Shoham, Zaccur and Ibri.

the next generation taking over the duties from their fathers and of new families being added to their numbers. No one is so indispensable that they cannot be replaced in God's work. The next generation of believers must be encouraged to take responsibility in the Lord's service and those Christians with no previous family connections with the church are as entitled to serve as those with long-standing family ties to the fellowship (Heb. 13:7, 17). There is also no room in the church of God for preferential treatment to be given to those with more influence or important family connections (Gal. 5:26; James 2:1-9).

The Levitical musicians (25:1-31)

This chapter is concerned with the temple singers, who were first mentioned when the ark was brought to Jerusalem (1 Chron. 15:16-28). In verses 1-7, the three musical families are introduced and this is followed by a list of the singers from these families in the order in which the lot fell (vv. 8-31).

> 25:1. Also David and the commanders of the host for service separated the sons of Asaph and Heman and Jeduthun, who were to prophesy with lyres, with harps and with cymbals and the number of the men who worked according to their service was: 2. of the sons of Asaph: Zaccur and Joseph and Nethaniah and Asharelah; the sons of Asaph *were* under the hand of Asaph who prophesied under the hands of the king. 3. Of Jeduthun, the sons of Jeduthun: Gedaliah and Zeri and Jeshaiah, Hashabiah and Mattithiah, six, under the hands of their father Jeduthun, who prophesied with the lyre to give thanks and praise to Yahweh. 4. Of Heman, the sons of Heman: Bukkiah, Mattaniah, Uzziel, Shebuel and Jerimoth, Hananiah, Hanani, Eliathah, Giddalti and Romamti-ezer, Joshbekashah, Mallothi, Hothir, Mahazioth. 5. All these were the sons of Heman, the king's visionary, by the words of God, to raise up a horn. And God gave Heman fourteen sons and three daughters. 6. All these were under the hands of their father in the song of the house of Yahweh, with cymbals, harps and lyres for the service of the house of God; under the hands of the king *were* Asaph and Jeduthun and Heman. 7. And their number with their brothers trained in the song of Yahweh, all who were skilled, was two hundred and eighty-eight.

This first section is composed of an introduction (v. 1) that ends with a phrase that is repeated in the conclusion (v. 7): 'And

the number of them … was', with the term 'number' having
the meaning 'list' as in 1 Chronicles 11:11. The intervening
verses introduce the three leading musical families: Asaph
(v. 2), Jeduthun (v. 3) and especially Heman (vv. 4-6). The 'host
for service' is another way of describing the large 'army' of
non-Aaronic Levites and their 'commanders' or 'officials' (see
1 Chron. 15:16). The term 'host' or 'army', which is normally
found in military contexts and in the description of God
as 'Yahweh of hosts', is used here, as in the Pentateuch, for
the sanctuary 'service' of the Levites (Num. 4:3-4, 23, 30, 35;
etc.). 'Levitical service is just as integral to Israel's military
advance as the carrying of weapons.'[90] The military idea
is not entirely absent here, as was true of the ark of the
covenant (Num. 10:35-36) and so-called 'holy war' situations
(2 Chron. 20:22), but now with 'rest' from fighting having been
obtained and the ark permanently residing in Jerusalem, the
temple worship is seen as a means of maintaining that rest.

David and the Levitical leaders 'separated' (v. 1) the musical
families to this ministry in the temple. It is the same word that
is used for the original setting-apart of the Levites for their
particular work on behalf of their people (see Num. 8:14; 16:9).
The involvement of David in the musical side of the future
temple worship is not surprising. He played the harp and was
called 'the sweet psalmist of Israel' (2 Sam. 23:1). Half of the
compositions in the Book of Psalms are attributed to David.

The musical families are described as 'prophesying'
(vv. 1-3) and Heman is called the king's 'visionary' (*hōzeh*, v. 5),
a term that was used for the prophet Gad (see 1 Chron. 21:9)
and later applied to both Asaph and Jeduthun (2 Chron. 29:30;
35:15). 'Visionary' or 'seer', like 'man of God', was another
and perhaps, at one time, more popular way of referring to a
prophet (*nābî'*; 1 Sam. 9:8-10). Judging by the Chronicler's usage,
Asaph, Heman and Jeduthun seem to have been considered
prophets in exactly the same way as Gad and Nathan (see
2 Chron. 29:25; 35:15). They had messages from God that were
authoritative for the people. Their psalm compositions were
divinely inspired in exactly the same way as the message

---

90. Philip J. Budd, *Numbers*, Word Biblical Commentary 5 (Waco: Word
Books, 1984), p. 48.

of Jahaziel, a descendant of Asaph, who delivered a divine oracle to an assembly of God's people (2 Chron. 20:14-17).

As for the verb 'to prophesy', while the biblical evidence leads to the conclusion that the primary meaning of the verb is 'to proclaim a message from God' (see Amos 2:12; 3:8; 7:12; Ezek. 21:9,28; etc.), it could sometimes mean some kind of ecstatic behaviour that was a sign of being endued with a supernatural spirit and where no authoritative divine word was necessarily mentioned. This seems to be the situation with the seventy elders (Num. 11:24-29). Similarly, on two occasions, when Saul met up with a group of prophets who were 'prophesying' he started 'prophesying' with them, as had messengers that he had sent earlier, but no words of what they said were ever recorded. Saul even stripped himself naked as he prophesied and lay before Samuel. Interestingly, on the first occasion, the prophets were 'prophesying' with musical instruments (1 Sam. 10:5-6, 10-11; 19:20-24). There is also the occasion when an 'evil' spirit came upon Saul and he 'prophesied' but again, there is no hint that he was proclaiming anything (1 Sam. 18:10). This suggests that 'prophesying' sometimes expressed itself in abnormal behaviour that did not usually result in proclaiming intelligible speech (see Jer. 29:26).

With the Levitical musicians, there is no sign of abnormal behaviour. In fact, they prophesied under the directions ('under the hands of') of the king (vv. 2, 6). Prophesying through singing divinely inspired psalms of praise and thanksgiving seems to be in mind here. Miriam is called a prophetess by her action of leading the women in the song of Moses to musical accompaniment (Exod. 15:20-21). There are examples in the canonical prophets of prophetic words addressed to God (see Jer. 10:6-10) and the Asaph psalms are part of Scripture (Pss. 50; 73-83). The two stringed instruments, the lyre and harp, and the cymbals (vv. 1, 3, 6) are the ones regularly used in the sanctuary worship (2 Chron. 29:25; Pss. 33:2; 57:8[9]). These references to musical instruments in the context of prophesying are unlike those occasions when music was used to calm nerves and settle the mind (1 Sam. 16:23; 2 Kings 3:15).

The three musical Levitical families descend from each of the three sons of Levi: Asaph from Gershon, Jeduthun

(also called Ethan) from Merari, and Heman from Kohath
(1 Chron. 6:31-48; 15:17-19). Although Asaph is mentioned first
and was initially responsible for music and ministry 'before
the ark' in Jerusalem (1 Chron. 16:5, 7, 37), he provided the
least number of musical sons. For Asaph, four sons are named
and for Jeduthun, six,[91] whereas Heman has fourteen sons
and he, significantly, like the Aaronic priests, is descended
from the Kohathites (1 Chron. 6:33). Heman was blessed not
only with many sons, he also had three daughters (v. 5). The
text suggests that he received a promise from God ('words of
God') concerning a large family that would result in his being
exalted to a primary position. The phrase 'raise up a horn'
(v. 5) has nothing to do with sounding the horn. It is used
metaphorically for being raised to a powerful, triumphant
position (see 1 Sam. 2:1, 10; Ps. 75:10).

The last half of the list of Heman's sons has some unusual
names like Romamti-ezer, Joshbekashah and Mallothi.
From these names, some scholars have made recognisable
phrases that have led them to speculate that it witnesses to
poetic fragments or to the first lines of psalms. Actually, it
is easier to reconstruct such a psalm from the more familiar
names, beginning with Hananiah, Hanani, ('Be gracious to
me, Yah, be gracious to me') followed by Eliathah ('you are
my God'), than the more obscure later ones which require
much ingenuity on the part of the academic. But as far as the
Chronicler is concerned these words were definitely proper
names and each one appeared separately when the lots were
cast (vv. 13-31). Michael Wilcock playfully suggests that
Heman named these sons after his favourite psalms![92]

The first part of verse 6 could refer to the sons of all
the musical families and their ability to play the various
instruments, but the use of the singular 'father' suggests
that Heman's sons are particularly in mind and follows the
pattern for the other two families (see vv. 2-3). While the
families were under the authority of their individual father,
the three family heads were under the authority of the king

91. Only five are named. One Hebrew MS and the LXX provides the sixth
name, Shimei, after Jeshaiah; see verse 17.

92. Wilcock, '1 and 2 Chronicles' in the New Bible Commentary, 21st Century
Edition (Leicester: Inter-Varsity Press, 1994), p. 400.

('under the hands of', v. 6b). Verse 7 is the conclusion to the
first part of the chapter and a summary of what is to follow.
The twenty-four sons (vv. 2, 3, 5) from the three musical
families become themselves twenty-four heads of musical
groups like the priests, all of them considered 'brothers' and
competent ('skilful') musicians. The 'song of Yahweh' (v. 7),
like 'the song of the house of Yahweh' (v. 6), is used in the
sense of 'music' for the Lord in His temple. As the following
list makes clear, the two hundred and eighty-eight singers
are made up of the twenty-four leaders with twelve family
members ('his sons and his brothers') to each group. This is
much smaller than the original four thousand Levites who
praised Yahweh (1 Chron. 23:5).

Application

The Chronicler directs the post-exilic community to see the
temple staff and their activities in the worship of God as a
kind of military service. Praise has an important part to play
in the context of Israel's victory over enemies (see Ps. 149;
2 Chron. 20). Prayer and praise continue to be important
elements in the spiritual warfare of God's people. The great
spiritual and moral battle has been won at Calvary and while
there is a rest that Christians now enjoy in Christ, there
are supernatural evil powers to wrestle against before the
ultimate rest. Revelation 19 shows praise to God went up
when all the enemies of God and His people had been for
ever removed.

The canonical psalms, many of them attributed to David,
Asaph and other Levites, are there because they were inspired
by God and accepted as God's prophetic and authoritative
words (see 2 Chron. 29:30). The singing of the divine
compositions was viewed as prophesying in the sense of
proclaiming the prophetic word in praise and thanksgiving to
God. At the same time, the words would have instructed and
encouraged the people who heard them. The wish of Moses
and the prophecy of Joel (Num. 11:29; Joel 2:28-29) came to
realisation on the day of Pentecost when all God's people were
filled with the Spirit and began to proclaim the wonderful
works of God (Acts 2:11, 16-21). Paul urges Christians to be

filled with the Spirit, teaching and admonishing each other with psalms, hymns and spiritual songs and singing and giving thanks to the Lord (Eph. 5:18-21; Col. 3:16-17). As our prayers are to be guided and based on God's word so should our singing, and how uplifting and moving it often is to hear the prayers of God's people, young and old, male and female, and to sing the words of men and women who have composed hymns and songs that express so eloquently the truths of the gospel and the feelings of believers, following the biblical and authoritative tradition of David and all the poets of Old and New Testament times. Matthew Henry suggests that the prophesying mentioned by Paul in 1 Corinthians 11:4 and 14:24 was 'singing the praises of God'.

> 25:8. And they cast lots, duty for duty, the small like the great, teacher with pupil. 9. And the first lot came out for Asaph to Joseph, Gedaliah the second, he and his brothers and his sons, twelve. 10. The third Zaccur, his sons and his brothers, twelve. 11. The fourth to Izri, his sons and his brothers, twelve. 12. The fifth Nethaniah, his sons and his brothers, twelve. 13. The sixth Bukiah, his sons and his brothers, twelve. 14. The seventh Jesharelah, his sons and his brothers, twelve. 15. The eighth Jeshaiah, his sons and his brothers, twelve. 16. The ninth Mattaniah, his sons and his brothers, twelve. 17. The tenth Shimei, his sons and his brothers, twelve. 18. The eleventh Azarel, his sons and his brothers, twelve. 19. The twelfth to Hashabiah, his sons and his brothers, twelve. 20. For thirteen Shubael, his sons and his brothers, twelve. 21. For fourteen Mattithiah, his sons and his brothers, twelve. 22. For fifteen, for Jeremoth, his sons and his brothers, twelve. 23. For sixteen, for Hananiah, his sons and his brothers, twelve. 24. For seventeen, for Joshbekashah, his sons and his brothers, twelve. 25. For eighteen, for Hanani, his sons and his brothers, twelve. 26. For nineteen, for Mallothi, his sons and his brothers, twelve. 27. For twenty, for Eliathah, his sons and his brothers, twelve. 28. For twenty-one, for Hothir, his sons and his brothers, twelve. 29. For twenty-two, for Giddalti, his sons and his brothers, twelve. 30. For twenty-three, for Mahazioth, his sons and his brothers, twelve. 31. For twenty-four, for Romamti-ezer, his sons and his brothers, twelve.

As with the priests (1 Chron. 24:5) so with the musicians; fairness is achieved for roster duty by means of the lot (v. 8).

No exceptions were made for age, status or experience (see also 26:12-13).[93] The sequence is interesting: first the Asaph and Jeduthun families alternate (vv. 9-12); then there is an overlap with Heman's family (vv. 13-15) followed by the families of Heman and Jeduthun alternating (vv. 16 -22), with the final names all from Heman's family (vv. 23-31). Setting out the list in such a repetitive and fulsome way indicates how important these musicians were for the Chronicler in the temple worship.

Surprisingly, the list opens (v. 9) not in the same stylized way that is to follow for the rest of the twenty-four divisions. The family head ('Asaph) only appears in this verse but, on the other hand, there is no reference to 'his sons and his brothers, twelve', which is simply taken as read. When the first lot was cast, it fell not to Zaccur, the eldest son of Asaph, but Joseph the second son (see v. 2). There are alternative spellings or pronunciations for Zeri and Asharelah (v. 3), namely, Jizri (v. 11) and Jesharelah (v. 14). The same is the case for Uzziel, Shebuel and Jerimoth (v. 4) who are now written as Azarel (v. 18), Shubael (v. 20) and Jeremoth (v. 22). One who was not mentioned in the initial list of six sons belonging to Jeduthun (v. 3) is now named as Shimei (v. 17).

Application

It is clear that the Chronicler was concerned to see the musicians playing their part in the second temple (see 1 Chron. 9:33). The law of Moses gave no instructions concerning music and singing in the sanctuary. In fact, the only singing heard at Sinai was when the people started worshipping the golden calf (Exod. 32:18). It was a development that arose with the ark being brought to rest in Jerusalem. While the priests were still needed to offer the prescribed sacrifices, and other important ministries that lay at the heart of Israel's worship required from among the non-Aaronic Levites, the musical families are given this new important role in temple worship. This innovation was introduced by David, himself

93. The word *mišmeret*, 'charge', 'watch' (1 Chron. 23:3) when used with *lᵉ'ummat*, 'alike' may be an abridged way of meaning 'charge for charge' or 'duty for duty' (see 1 Chron. 26:16).

an accomplished instrument maker, musician and composer of songs (Amos 6:5; 1 Sam. 16:14-23; 2 Sam. 22; 23:1). He is also described as a prophet and there are compositions of his that are part of the canon of Scripture (Mark 12:36; Luke 20:42-43; Acts 2:25-28; 4:25-26). While in the presence of the awesome God at Sinai there was no singing, when Israel arrived in Canaan and the presence of God associated with the ark was at rest in the Jerusalem temple, then singing and joyful worship was established.

Although church choirs are often linked with Christian worship, the biblical emphasis under the new dispensation of the Holy Spirit, since Messiah's death and resurrection, is on all God's people involved in singing to God and by so doing encouraging and exhorting one another. Congregational singing was re-introduced into public worship as a result of the Protestant Reformation. Such singing first appeared as a result of the redemption from Egypt when Moses and Miriam led the male and female congregations (Exod. 15). The redemption accomplished through Christ's work on the cross calls for songs in praise of Jesus who has redeemed people to God by His precious blood from every language and nation.

The Levitical gatekeepers, treasurers and other officials (26:1-32)
The chapter concerns the gatekeepers (vv. 1-19), the treasurers (vv. 20-28) and other Levitical workers (vv. 29-32).

> 26:1. Concerning the divisions of the gatekeepers. Of the Korahites: Meshelemiah the son of Kore, from the sons of Asaph. 2. And Meshelemiah had sons: Zedekiah the firstborn, Jediael the second, Zebadiah the third, Jathneil the fourth, 3. Elam the fifth, Jehohanan the sixth, Eliehoenai the seventh. 4. And Obed-edom had sons: Shemaiah the firstborn, Jehozabad the second, Joah the third, Sachar the fourth, Nethanel the fifth, 5. Ammiel the sixth, Issachar the seventh, Peullethai the eighth, for God had blessed him. 6. Also to his son Shemaiah were born sons, rulers in the house of their father, for they were valiant warriors. 7. The sons of Shemaiah: Othni and Rephael and Obed, Elzabad, his brothers were valiant ones, Elihu and Semachiah. 8. All these were some of the sons of Obed-edom; they and their sons and their brothers *were* men of valour with strength for the service. Sixty-two of Obed-edom. 9. And Meshelemiah had sons and brothers, valiant ones, eighteen. 10. And Hosah, from

the sons of Merari, had sons: Shimri the head, (because he was not the firstborn, yet his father made him head); 11. Hilkiah the second, Tebaliah the third, Zechariah the fourth. All the sons and brothers of Hosah *were* thirteen.

12. These divisions of the gatekeepers, corresponding to the male heads, duties like their brothers, to serve in the house of Yahweh. 13. And they cast lots, small and great alike, according to the house of their fathers, for each gate. 14. The lot for the east fell to Shelemiah, and *for* Zechariah his son, a prudent counsellor, they cast lots and the lot came out for the north. 15. For Obed-edom for the south, and for his sons, the storehouses. 16. For Shuppim and Hosah *the lot came out* for the west, with the gate of Shallecheth on the road that goes up – duty for duty. 17. On the east *were* six Levites, on the north four each day, on the south four each day, and two each at the stores.

18. At the Parbar to the west, four at the road, two at the Parbar. 19. These were the divisions of the gatekeepers for the sons of the Korahites and for the sons of Merari.

The names of the gatekeeper family heads are listed (vv. 1-11), followed by the account of how each group was allotted for their particular duties (vv. 12-19). Gatekeepers have been mentioned earlier (1 Chron. 9:17-32; 15:18,24; 16:38; 23:5; see also Ezra 2:42; Neh. 11:19; 12:25). Though there were priests who guarded the entrance into the holy precinct (2 Kings 12:9[10]), it was given to these non-priestly Levites to take responsibility for guarding the entrance into the temple courts. It was an office that could be traced back to Moses' time, and David and Samuel had been involved in appointing them in their day too (1 Chron. 9:19b-22). The work was assigned to the descendants of two of Levi's sons, Kohath (vv. 1-9) and Merari (vv. 10-11). It is from Kohath's son Izhar that the Korahites came and Meshelemiah or Shelemiah (v. 1; see v. 14) is the first-mentioned leader, a descendant of Kore and Asaph (a shortened form of Ebiasaph [1 Chron. 6:37-38; 9:19, 21]). Of his seven sons that are named, the first is Zedekiah, a shrewd counsellor (v. 14), who was considered as important as Phinehas when mentioning the post-exilic gatekeepers (see 1 Chron. 9:20-21). All Meshelemiah's relatives ('sons and brothers') amounted to eighteen 'valiant' men (v. 9; literally 'sons of valour'). The term 'valour' is often used in military contexts and suggests the gatekeepers were strong men, like bouncers, who could eject unclean people and animals from the temple courts (see also vv. 6, 7, 8, 30-32; 1 Chron. 9:13; 2 Chron. 23:4-7,19).

Without any introduction, Obed-edom and his family are inserted into the paragraph dealing with Meshelemiah (vv. 4-8). This suggests that this was the Obed-edom the Gittite mentioned earlier in whose house the ark of God remained three months and who was involved in bringing it to its final resting place in Jerusalem (1 Chron. 13:13-14). Like Meshelemiah, he was a Korahite (see 1 Chron. 15:18, 21, 24; 16:5, 38) and was among the original Levitical musicians and gatekeepers. An eighth son is listed (v. 5), one more than Meshelemiah's male offspring, indicating that he was blessed over and above others, seven being a perfect number. Was this how God blessed him for providing a home for the ark (1 Chron. 13:14)? Children were considered a blessing from God and the names of some of his sons suggest that they were seen as heavenly gifts and rewards, as proclaimed in Psalm 127:3-5. The personal names, Issachar and Sachar, speak of 'reward' while Jehozabad and Nethanel refer to divine gifting. Interestingly, Jehozabad's nephew was called Elzabad and Shemaiah's son Obed is named after his grandfather Obed-edom (v. 7). While all sixty-two of Obed-edom's valiant relatives were particularly strong for the work to which they were called, attention is drawn to Elihu and Semachiah (vv. 7-8).[94]

As for the descendants of Merari, four sons of Hosah are named (v. 10; see 1 Chron. 16:38). It was usual for the firstborn to be 'head' (see v. 2), but though Hosah's son Shimri was not the firstborn, he was made the 'first' (v. 10). Normally, the firstborn would be expected to have this special status but clearly it was not automatic. It was the father's prerogative to grant this primary position (see 2 Chron. 11:22). This little note by the Chronicler is a reminder of other situations where firstborn rights gave way to other considerations (Gen. 48:19; 49:3-4; 1 Chron. 5:1-3).

While the previous appointments by lot were to arrange periods of service, in the case of the gatekeepers, lots were cast

---

94. In verse 6, the MT reads 'the dominions of the house of their father' where 'dominions' may be a case of the abstract being used for the concrete, i.e., 'the rulers'.

to determine placements at the temple gates as well as times of duty in Yahweh's house. Again, the lot ensured fairness ('small and great alike', v. 13). Gatekeepers were positioned in four directions (see 1 Chron. 9:24). To the area facing east the lot fell to Shelemiah, an abbreviated form of Meshelemiah (vv. 1, 14). It was not through luck but by divine guidance that the most important gate, known in post-exilic times as 'the king's gate' (1 Chron. 9:18), went to the most important family. Entrance through this gate would have been the most direct way into the sanctuary. Shelemiah's firstborn son, Zedekiah (v. 14), who had already been appointed by David to keep the tabernacle door (1 Chron. 9:21), was placed at the north gate. Zedekiah is described as a 'prudent' or 'shrewd' counsellor, suggesting that he had a royal position advising the king like Ahithophel and Jonathan, David's uncle (1 Chron. 27:32-33; 2 Sam. 15:12). Obed-edom had responsibility for the south gate facing the royal palace and his family were given an extra assignment of being in charge of the storehouses, the anterooms perhaps where some of the people's offerings were collected (see Neh. 12:25) before being transferred to the inner courts (see 1 Chron. 23:28).[95]

Nothing is known of Shuppim but he, with Hosah, must have belonged to Merari's descendants and assigned to guard the west side and also responsible for the 'Shallecheth gate' (v. 16). The name of this otherwise unknown gate is related to the verb 'to throw out' and it is suggested it may have been the gate from which the temple refuse, such as the ashes from the altar, were removed (Lev. 6:10-11).[96] The importance of the east side is reflected in the number of Levites assigned to this position, six instead of four each for the other three sides. In addition, at the antechambers, there were Levites working in pairs (v. 17). At the Parbar or 'colonnade' as it probably means (v. 18; 2 Kings 23:11),[97] a further two of Merari's family kept guard, assuming this columned structure was also on the west side. There is little point in seeking to calculate the number of gatekeepers stationed at any one time as the number of antechambers

95. This is the suggestion of Johnstone, *1 and 2 Chronicles*, Vol. 1, p. 262.

96. *Ibid*, p. 262.

97. In the *Temple Scroll* found at Qumran, the word 'parbar' or 'parvar' is used of the temple porch with columns.

is not given. What the Chronicler emphasises is that all the gatekeepers were taken from just the two families belonging to the Korahites and the Merarites (v. 19).

Application

Some of the personal names re-appear in the list of post-exilic gatekeepers and the Chronicler encourages those gatekeepers of his own day to be diligent in their service and to appreciate that their position in the second temple had a long history going back to David's appointment prior to the original temple built by Solomon. Because of the polluted sacrifices being offered in Malachi's day, the prophet wished that someone would close the doors to prevent unworthy sacrifices being offered (Mal. 1:10).

Gates feature considerably in Ezekiel's prophecy. The north gate was being used for idolatrous worship while it was from the east gate that Ezekiel saw the glory of Yahweh moving away from the temple. In his vision of the ideal temple he witnessed God's glory returning through this east gate, which was the gate reserved for the prince (Ezek. 10:19; 11:1, 23; 40:11-44; 43:1-5; 44:1-3; 46:1). In Revelation, the holy city is also God's temple full of His glory and with twelve gates representing Israel and twelve angels at the gates (Rev. 21:12-13, 21-27). Without the washing of regeneration by the Holy Spirit and the cleansing blood of the Messiah, God's Son, the heavenly temple would be closed to sinful human beings. The old children's hymn is indelibly imbedded in my mind and heart since I learnt it in church as a child:

> *There is a city bright,*
> *Closed are its gates to sin;*
> *Nought that defileth,*
> *Nought that defileth*
> *Can ever enter in.*
>
> *Saviour, I come to Thee!*
> *O Lamb of God, I pray,*
> *Cleanse me and save me,*
> *Cleanse me and save me,*
> *Wash all my sins away.*[98]

---

98. Mary Ann Sanderson Deck (1813-1903).

26:20. And the Levites: Ahijah *was* over the treasuries of the house of God and of the treasuries of the holy things. 21. The sons of Ladan, the sons of the Gershonite belonging to Ladan, the heads of the fathers belonging to Ladan the Gershonite: Jehieli. 22. The sons of Jehieli: Zetham and Joel his brother over the treasuries of the house of Yahweh. 23. Of the Amramites, the Izharites, the Hebronites and the Uzzielites: 24. and Shebuel the son of Gershom, the son of Moses, was leader over the treasuries. 25. And his brothers by Eliezer: Rehabiah his son, and Jeshaiah his son, and Joram his son, and Zichri his son, and Shelomith his son. 26. This Shelomoth and his brothers *were* over all the treasuries of the dedicated things that David the king and the heads of the fathers, the commanders of the thousands and the hundreds and the commanders of the army had dedicated. 27. From the spoil of battles they dedicated for the maintenance of the house of Yahweh. 28. Also all that Samuel the seer and Saul the son of Kish and Abner the son of Ner and Joab the son of Zeruiah had dedicated. All dedicated things *were* in the hand of Shelomoth and his brothers. 29. Of the Izharites: Chenaniah and his sons were for outside work over Israel, for officers and judges. 30. Of the Hebronites: Hashabiah and his brothers, one thousand seven hundred valiant ones, had the oversight of Israel beyond the Jordan westward for all the work of Yahweh and for the service of the king. 31. Of the Hebronites: Jerijah the head of the Hebronites according to the genealogy of fathers. In the fortieth year of David's reign search was made and valiant warriors were found among them in Jazer of Gilead. 32. And his brothers were two thousand seven hundred valiant ones, heads of the fathers, and king David appointed them over the Reubenites, and the Gadites and the half tribe of the Manassites for all the things of God and the things of the king.

If 'Ahijah' is the correct reading then it must be supposed that he was the overall treasurer of the two types of treasuries (v. 20). Otherwise, if the emendation, 'their brothers', is accepted, then it is a reference to all the Levite officials that follow.[99] Those associated with the treasuries of the house of Yahweh are mentioned in verses 21-22 and those over treasuries of the holy or dedicated gifts in verses 23-28.

---

99. Some argue that a *mem* has accidentally been dropped at the end of the word *'aḥiyyāh* so that instead of a personal name, it should read with the LXX 'their brothers' (*'aḥiyyām*). But there is no obvious reason for the omission of the *mem* and the LXX is no guarantee of a correct reading.

Descendants of Levi's sons Gershon and Kohath are among the treasurers, but there is no reference to any from Merari. Ladan the Gershonite is emphasised perhaps because he was also known as Libni (Exod. 6:17; 1 Chron. 23:7). Jehieli the chief and his sons (see 1 Chron. 23:8; 29:8) were responsible not only for the valuable temple vessels but probably also for the supplies for the daily sacrifices and offerings (see 1 Chron. 9:28-29).

Verse 23 mentions the four sons of Levi's second son, Kohath, and this introduces the families mentioned in the rest of the chapter. Amram's non-priestly line, the descendants of Moses, appears in verses 24-26; Izhar's line is mentioned in verse 29 and Hebron's descendants in verses 30-32. No reference is made to any duties assigned to the Uzzielites. It is unclear whether Shebuel (v. 24; spelled Shubael in 23:16) was the chief officer over all the treasuries as in verse 20 or more probably supervising Shelomoth and his brothers who were over the treasuries concerning the dedicated items (v. 26). This Shelomoth or Shelomith (see 1 Chron. 23:9, 18; 24:22)[100] is to be distinguished from the son of Shimei, the Gershonite (23:9) and the son of Izhar (23:18; 24:22). Mentioning Shebuel's descent from Moses indicates the importance of this responsible position for a non-priestly Levite. Rehabiah was a descendant of Moses' second son Eleazar (v. 25; 1 Chron. 23:15, 17). The 'dedicated' items included the spoils of war that David had originally dedicated to Yahweh (v. 26; 1 Chron. 18:7-8, 11; 20:1-2; 22:14). Special mention is made of the military leaders who also willingly dedicated what they had won in battle, some of which were used for the future maintenance and repair of the temple (v. 27; see Num. 31:25-54). Even items of war that Samuel,[101] Saul and the military generals, Abner and Joab, had dedicated to Yahweh, David carefully kept to be deposited in the treasuries (v. 28). This little piece of information highlights again the Chronicler's concern to show that all Israel even before David's coronation, including opponents like Saul,

---

100. The *Kethibh* reading in verse 25 is Shelomoth whereas the *Qere* has Shelomith. In verse 26, no alternative is given to the *Shelomoth* reading.

101. For 'seer' (*rō'eh*), see 1 Chronicles 25:5 where *hōzeh* is found. These two synonymous Hebrew words are masculine singular active participles of verbs for 'to see'.

as well as friends, though unknowingly, contributed to the temple support.

The Izharites under the leadership of Chenaniah and his sons were responsible for duties outside the temple as 'officers and judges' (v. 29; see 1 Chron. 23:4b). It may be that this included not only caring for the outside appearance of the temple but collecting tithes, temple taxes, dealing with local disputes and interpreting the Mosaic law (Deut. 17:9; 33:10). There were Levites serving as officers and judges in the time of Jehoshaphat (2 Chron. 19:8-11). In post-exilic times, two Levites had oversight of business 'outside' the temple (Neh. 11:16; see also 10:37-39[38-40]).

It is not clear how the work of the Hebronites differed from that of the Izharites but certainly their duties took them outside of Jerusalem, some having oversight of Israel west of the Jordan (v. 30) and others working among the Transjordanian tribes who are described using traditional language: 'the Reubenites, the Gadites and the half tribe of Manasseh' (v. 32; 1 Chron. 5:18; 12:37; see Deut. 29:8; Josh. 1:12; etc.). It was in the final year of David's reign (v. 31) that a search was made of Hebronites in the Levitical city of Jazar to the northeast, in Gilead (1 Chron. 6:81[66]), that led to valiant men from this area having responsibility for the east bank. Jerijah, the head of the Hebronites (v. 31), is spelled Jeriah in 1 Chronicles 23:19 and 24:23. The work on both sides of the Jordan is described as 'the work of Yahweh and for the service of the king' (v. 30) and suggests, along with the concluding words about the things relating to God and the king (v. 32), that their responsibilities included state as well as religious duties.

Application

The Chronicler encourages the Levites of the post-exilic community to be forward in serving their generation as their ancestors had done in the period of the united monarchy. Under the new covenant, there is no physical temple but all believers have their responsibilities in the spiritual temple that God is building. There are practical details that need attention, including maintenance of church buildings, and weekly duties to attend to such as setting out the communion table, washing up and greeting people at the door. Deacons may well be in charge of mundane items but every church member has a part to play.

Paul was careful in dealing with the gifts he received for Christ's work and for meeting the needs of poor Christians, by making sure that others were involved in collecting the donations (1 Cor. 16:1-4; 2 Cor. 9:1-5). The final words of this chapter (v. 32) are echoed in Jesus' famous answer to a question concerning paying taxes to Caesar: 'Give to Caesar the things that are Caesar's and to God the things that are God's' (Mark 12:17). In whatever society Christians live, they are urged to fear God and honour those in authority (1 Pet. 2:13-17).

Organising the state officers (27:1-34)

This is the second and more concise part of the section that began with the organisation of the temple staff (23:3–26:32). The final verses of the first part have prepared for this chapter by focusing on Levites who had duties outside the temple and dealt with affairs that concerned the king as well as God (26:30, 32). But in this chapter, the focus is on leaders other than the Levites. The lay offices of state include the army commanders of the monthly divisions (vv. 1-15), the officers of Israel's tribes (vv. 16-24), overseers of the king's property (vv. 25-31) and David's advisers and colleagues (vv. 32-34). The number twelve seems significant for the first three state leadership positions and seven for the final list. Though the chapter seems to have little to do with the temple, all the officials mentioned are important in providing support for the temple project (see 1 Chron. 28:1-2).

27:1. And the sons of Israel, according to their number, the heads of the fathers and the commanders of thousands and hundreds and their officers who served the king concerning every matter of the divisions which came and went out month by month for all the months of the year; the division of each was twenty-four thousand. 2. Over the first division of the first month *was* Jashobeam the son of Zabdiel and with regard to his division *were* twenty-four thousand. 3. *He was* from the sons of Perez, the head of all the commanders of the hosts for the first month. 4. And over the division of the second month *was* Dodai the Ahohite, and his division also had Mikloth the leader and with regard to his division *were* twenty-four thousand. 5. The third army commander for the third month *was* Benaiah the son of Jehoiada the high priest and with regard to his division *were* twenty-four thousand. 6. This was Benaiah who was a warrior of the thirty and over the thirty, and his division had Ammizabad his son. 7. The fourth for the fourth month *was* Asahel the brother of Joab, and Zebadiah his son after him and with regard to his division *were* twenty-four thousand. 8. The fifth for the fifth month *was* the commander Shamhuth the Izrah and with regard to his division *were* twenty-four thousand. 9. The sixth for the sixth month *was* Ira the son of Ikkesh the Tekoite and with regard to his division *were* twenty-four thousand. 10. The seventh for the seventh month *was* Helez the Pelonite from the sons of Ephraim and with regard to his division *were* twenty-four thousand. 11. The eighth for the eighth month *was* Sibbecai the Hushathite of the Zerahites and with regard to his division *were* twenty-four thousand. 12. The ninth for the ninth month *was* Abiezer the Anathothite of the Benjaminites and with regard to his division *were* twenty-four thousand. 13. The tenth for the tenth month *was* Maharai the Netophathite of the Zerahites and with regard to his division *were* twenty-four thousand. 14. The eleventh for the eleventh month *was* Benaiah the Pirathonite from the sons of Ephraim and with regard to his division *were* twenty-four thousand. 15. The twelfth for the twelfth month *was* Heldai the Netophathite of Othniel and with regard to his division *were* twenty-four thousand.

The heading in verse 1 probably applies to verses 2-15 rather than to the whole chapter. Solomon arranged for governors to provide supplies for the royal court every month which the Chronicler does not include in his work (see 1 Kings 4:7-19). Instead, information is recorded that indicates that David anticipated Solomon's action with this monthly militia roster under the leadership of military heroes dedicated to the king's service. The terms 'thousands' and 'hundreds' are used for military units that did not necessarily consist of those precise numbers. Altogether, the twelve divisions of twenty-four 'thousand' to each division came to two hundred and eighty-eight 'thousand' or 'units'.

The commanders named can be compared to the first sixteen names in 1 Chronicles 11:10-47. Jeshobeam (v. 2; see

11:11 and 2 Sam. 23:8) was one of David's mighty men and a descendant of Perez of the tribe of Judah (1 Chron. 2:4). He was placed in charge of all the unit commanders. Leadership of the second group was in the hands of two leaders: Dodai who was related to Eleazar and a Benjaminite (v. 4; see 11:12; 8:4) and Mikloth, possibly also from the same tribe (see 8:32; 9:37).[102] Benaiah, the son of Jehoiada, was one of David's trusted generals (vv. 5-6; see 18:17; 2 Sam. 8:18; 23:22-23) who became Solomon's commander-in-chief after executing Joab (1 Kings 1–2). Jehoiada, his father, was an Aaronite priest and leader of a troop that came to David at Hebron (see 11:22-24; 12:27[28] and v. 34 below). It should be remembered that priests and other Levites were not exempt from military service.

Asahel, the brother of Joab and one of David's elite warriors, was killed by Abner in the civil war that raged in the north before David became king of all Israel (v. 7; 2 Sam. 2:18-23; 23:24). The memory of his bravery is not forgotten by David. Though his son Zebadiah was the person in charge of the division by this time, the division continued to be associated with his father. The name Shamhuth (v. 8) is either unknown elsewhere or a variation of Shammoth or Shammah (1 Chron. 11:27; 2 Sam. 23:11). If the latter, then he was a native of Harod/Haror, possibly a site near Jerusalem (2 Sam. 23:25).[103] Ira, who was over the eighth division, came from Tekoa in Judah, the same city as the prophet Amos and the home of a wise woman (v. 9; 11:28; Amos 1:1; 2 Sam. 14:2; 23:26). Helez, a representative from Ephraim (v. 10; 11:27) is called 'the Pelonite' which seems to be a variant of 'Paltite' (2 Sam. 23:26). As for Sibbecai who belonged to the Zarhite clan (Gen. 38:30; 46:12), he came from Hushah, a city southwest of Bethlehem (v. 11; see 4:4; 11:29; 20:4). In charge of the ninth division was Abiezer, who hailed from the well-known Benjaminite city of Anathoth (v. 12; see 6:60[45]; 11:28). Another member of the Zarhite clan was Maharai (v. 13; see v. 11; 11:30). He was from Netophah, a place near Bethlehem (Ezra 2:22; Neh. 7:26). The eleventh captain was another Benaiah, but this one, like

---

102. The difficult phrase 'and his division and Mikloth the leader' is omitted in the LXX.

103. The Hebrew lacks the gentilic 'ite' in Izrahite (verse 8). Many scholars also change the name to Zarhites as in verses 11 and 13.

Helez, was from Ephraim (v. 14; see v. 10; 11:31). He came
from the city of Pirathon, some six miles (9.5 kilometres)
west of Shechem (see Judg. 12:15; 2 Sam. 23:30). The twelfth
captain is Heldai (v. 15), possibly the same as the one spelled
elsewhere as Heled and Heleb (11:30; 2 Sam. 23:29). He also,
like Maharai, came from Netophah, but was a descendant of
Othniel (Josh. 15:17). In all, seven captains would appear to
come from Judah, two from Benjamin, one from Levi, and
two from Ephraim.

> 27:16. Now over the tribes of Israel for the Reubenites *was* leader
> Eliezer the son of Zichri; for the Simeonites, Shephatiah the
> son of Maacah. 17. For Levi, Hashabiah the son of Kemuel; for
> Aaron, Zadok. 18. For Judah, Elihu from the brothers of David;
> for Issachar, Omri the son of Michael. 19. For Zebulun, Ishmaiah
> the son of Obadiah; for Naphtali, Jeremoth the son of Azriel.
> 20. For the sons of Ephraim, Hoshea the son of Azaziah; for the
> half-tribe of Manasseh, Joel the son of Pedaiah. 21. For the half
> of Manasseh in Gilead, Iddo the son of Zechariah; for Benjamin,
> Jaasiel the son of Abner. 22. For Dan, Azarel the son of Jeroham.
> These were the officials of the tribes of Israel. 23. But David did
> not take their number of those aged twenty years and under,
> because Yahweh had promised to multiply Israel like the stars of
> the heavens. 24. Joab the son of Zeruiah began to count but did
> not finish; for this wrath came upon Israel and the number was
> not put in the account of the Chronicles of king David.

This paragraph lists the leaders or local rulers in charge of
some of the Israelite tribes. They do not appear to be the
tribal elders (1 Chron. 11:3) but special officers appointed by
David. If this is the case, then already before Solomon took
over, there was a move toward a more centralised system of
government. The list begins with Leah's six sons in the order
of their birth: Reuben, Simeon, Levi, Judah, Issachar and
Zebulun (vv. 16-19a,). In Levi's case, there are two officers, one
over the non-priestly Levites and Zadok who was appointed
leader over the Aaronites, even though at this time he was
not high priest (v. 17). The leader over Judah is called Elihu
and, like Zadok, his father's name is not given. While he could
be another son of Jesse (see 1 Sam. 16:6-9, 1 Chron. 2:13-15
and 2 Chron. 11:18), the phrase 'from the brothers of David'
could mean from among David's relatives or kinsmen (see

1 Chron. 12:2 where Saul's 'brothers' are his relatives). Gad and Asher, the sons of Leah's maid, Zilpah, are not included. The remaining six tribes are associated with Rachel, Jacob's favourite wife. They are arranged in a significant order: the two outer names, Naphtali and Dan are the sons of Rachel's maid, Bilhah (vv. 19b, 22); the four central names begin with the offspring of Rachel's first son Joseph, namely Ephraim and Manasseh (west and east), followed by her second son, Benjamin (vv. 20-21). The 'half of Manasseh in Gilead' refers to that area, east of the Jordan, occupied by half of the Manasseh tribe (Num. 32:39). Whether the name 'Abner' (v. 21b) refers to the well-known cousin of Saul who was commander of Saul's army is uncertain as none of the other patronyms are familiar. Given the way the list is structured would strongly suggest that the omission of Gad and Asher was deliberate. The list is unique not only because of the reference to the Aaronites as well as the Levites, but in dividing Joseph into three rather than two tribes. Thirteen names are recorded, but it is clear that the inclusion of the Aaronites is an anomaly, for nowhere else are they ever considered to be a separate tribe. Perhaps it may be considered a parenthesis to separate the priesthood from the rest of the Levites and to show that Zadok already had the approval of David. This interesting list suited the Chronicler's purpose in expressing the unity of Israel for it incorporates an equal number from each side of Jacob's family.

Verses 23 and 24 indicate why no numbers are given in this tribal list as was recorded for the military divisions and why the number was not recorded in the annals of King David. For this particular census, David followed the Mosaic law and did not number those 'aged twenty years and under' (see Num. 1:3; etc.; 1 Chron. 23:24,27). To seek to count everyone called into question God's promise to Abraham (Gen. 15:5; 22:17; 26:4). The exact number was to be known only to God. On the other hand, for practical purposes, the over-twenties were counted in order to have some idea of numbers. Whether the reference to Joab not finishing the census denotes the 1 Chronicles 21 incident or this additional one is uncertain. But the point is not to transfer guilt from David to Joab as many scholars assume, but 'to show that behind the striking gap in official records lay the sovereign action of God'.[104] The count was aborted and the records were incomplete on account of God's 'wrath' (*qeṣep̄*), a term almost exclusively used for the divine wrath breaking out on God's people (see Num. 1:53; 18:5; Josh. 22:20; 2 Chron. 19:2, 10; 24:18; 29:8; 32:25-26). This is the only reference in the Bible to the 'Chronicles' of David (see 1 Kings 11:41 for Solomon). Literally, the word 'Chronicles' reads 'the words of the days' and it is this phrase that forms the Hebrew title of the books of Chronicles.[105]

> 27:25. And over the king's treasuries *was* Azmaveth the son of Adiel; and over the treasures in the field, in the cities, in the villages and in the towers *was* Jonathan the son of Uzziah. 26. And over those doing the work of the field, tilling the ground *was* Ezri the son of Chelub. 27. And over the vineyards *was* Shimei the Ramathite; and over that which was in the vineyards for the wine stores *was* Zabdi the Shiphmite. 28. And over the olive and sycamore trees in the Shephelah *was* Baal-hanan the Gederite; and over the oil stores *was* Joash. 29. And over the herds that fed in Sharon *was* Shitrai the Sharonite; and over the herds in the valleys *was* Shaphat the son of Adlai. 30. And over the camels *was* Obil the Ishmaelite; and over the she-asses *was* Jehdeiah the Meronothite. 31. And over the flocks *was* Jaziz the Hagrite. All these were the officials of the property which belonged to king David.

The closing words of this paragraph indicate that this list contains the names of the royal administrative officials (v. 31b). There are twelve in number. Two of the officers supervised the treasuries. Most probably the first concerned those located in Jerusalem for the second officer is said to have been over those treasures outside the capital in the countryside ('the field,' v. 25), including the watchtowers at the border posts. The Hebrew word for 'treasuries' was used in the previous chapter (26:20). One of David's warriors was called Azmaveth (1 Chron. 11:33; 2 Sam. 23:31) and he may be the one mentioned in verse 25, but the other official, Jonathan, is otherwise unknown.

---

104. Selman, *1 Chronicles*, p. 246.

105. The word 'account' (*mispār*, v. 24) is literally 'number' and is the same word in Hebrew that appears just before it. It is often viewed as dittography which the LXX corrects to read 'in the book of'. But 'number' can mean an 'account' (see Judg. 7:15).

Next in order were five officials in charge of agricultural affairs: one responsible for preparing the ground, possibly for producing grain (v. 26). Concerning the production of wine, one official supervised the vineyard workers and another, the storage of the wine (v. 27). Such wine cellars have been found dating back to about two centuries after David.[106] Two officials were also needed for overseeing the production of olive oil and its storage, in addition to having responsibility for the sycamore fig which was proverbially abundant in the Shephelah or lowland coastal area of Palestine and became the staple diet of the poor (v. 28; see 2 Chron. 1:15; 9:27; Amos 7:14). Baal-hanan is called 'the Gederite' as he came from Geder or Gederah, both of which are places in the lowland area (see Josh. 12:13; 15:36).

Finally, five officials had the oversight of the royal estates where the animals grazed. Over the herds of cattle was an official from the Sharon area where they were kept (v. 29). Appropriately, in charge of the camels was an Ishmaelite, a term that was used of nomadic desert tribes in general (v. 30; see Gen. 16:12; 37:25, 28; Judg. 8:24; 1 Chron. 2:17), but there is no certainty about Meronoth, the place from where the supervisor of donkeys originated (see Neh. 3:7). The female donkeys are particularly mentioned as they would have needed special supervision for breeding purposes. Interestingly, it was a Hagrite, a descendant of Hagar the mother of Ishmael, who was over the flocks. The Hagrites, like the Ishmaelites, were desert tribes living east of the Jordan and they were conquered by the Reubenites in the days of Saul, resulting in an abundance of camels and flocks being taken as booty (1 Chron. 5:10, 19-22; Ps. 83:6[7]).

> 27:32. And Jonathan, David's uncle, *was* a counsellor; a man of understanding and a scribe. And Jehiel the son of Hachmoni *was* with the king's sons. 33. And Ahithophel *was* counsellor to the king, and Hushai the Archite *was* the king's friend. 34. And after Ahithophel *was* Jehoiada the son of Benaiah, and Abiathar. And the commander of the king's army *was* Joab.

This list of personal influential counsellors can be compared to and contrasted with the earlier list of government officials in 1 Chronicles 18:15-17. Three of these royal advisers are

---

106. See Klein, *1 Chronicles*, p. 510.

otherwise unknown and included an uncle or relative of David called Jonathan who is described as a discerning scribe (v. 32). Earlier, Shavsha was the scribe (18:16). Jehiel is likewise unknown and his responsibility for the king's sons is not specified but it may have included acting as guardian or tutor. Hachmoni was the father of Jashobeam, one of David's chief warriors (1 Chron. 11:11), which makes it possible that Jehiel was Jashobeam's brother. Ahithophel and Hushai are well-known from the Samuel account, especially during Absalom's rebellion (v. 33; 2 Sam. 15-17), with Hushai regarded as David's 'friend' or personal confidant and adviser (2 Sam. 15:37; see 1 Kings 4:5 for Zabud who was 'friend' to Solomon). The successor to Ahithophel is named as Jehoiada, indicating that this list originated toward the end of David's reign. Though this Jehoiada, the son of Benaiah has been identified with the priestly line (see v. 5 and 18:17) and named after his grandfather, this is unlikely and thus must be treated as otherwise unknown. Both Abiathar the priest and Joab the army commander (v. 34) had been closely associated with David even before he became king and they remained loyal during Absalom's revolt against his father (1 Sam. 22:20; 26:6; 2 Sam. 15:24; 18:2). Joab's more personal advisory role was evident in his blunt words to David over his excessive display of grief when Absalom was killed (2 Sam. 19:5-8). Both men lost favour on account of their support for Adonijah so that when Solomon came to the throne, Abiathar was replaced by Zadok and Joab was put to death (1 Kings 1:7; 2:5-6, 26-35).

Application

The David–Solomon era is seen in idealistic terms as a unified whole and a little foretaste or picture of the future kingdom of God on earth. Such a presentation encouraged the civil and religious leaders of the Chronicler's own day to support the work of building for the future and to look expectantly for the anointed Ruler and his well-ordered kingdom of peace and stability (see Isa. 9:6-7). The allusion to God's promise to Abraham concerning innumerable descendants (v. 23) is a reminder to today's church not to be too concerned about numbers. The Lord knows those who are His (2 Tim. 2:19a) and the symbolic number of 144,000 elect ones that John heard, turns out, when he looked, to be a great multitude that no one could count from every nation, people group and language (Rev. 7:4, 9). It is the church's business to carry on bearing witness to Jesus and, instead of calculating numbers, the call is for everyone who names the name of the Lord to abstain from iniquity (Rev. 12:17; 2 Tim. 2:19b).

The climax to David's reign (28:1–29:30)
The final actions and speeches of David are recorded in this section and most of the material is unique to this book and of great theological significance. The Chronicler returns to the subject of the temple (see ch. 22) and details are given of the gifts made for its construction. The section falls into two parts, the first covers David's speech to the leaders and his son Solomon (28:1-21) and the second recounts David's final words, Solomon's enthronement, and David's death with an assessment of his life (29:1-30).

In chapter 28 David addresses first the leaders of Israel (vv. 1-8), then Solomon (vv. 9-10) before producing the temple plans (vv. 11-19) and addressing Solomon once more (vv. 20-21).

David's address to the leaders of Israel (28:1-8)

28:1. Now David assembled to Jerusalem all the officials of Israel: the officials of the tribes and of the divisions who served the king, the commanders of thousands and commanders of hundreds, and the officials of all the property and livestock of the king, and of his sons, with the eunuchs and the valiant ones, and all the valiant warriors. 2. And David the king rose on his feet and said, 'Hear me, my brothers and my people: I had it in my heart to build a house of rest for the ark of the covenant of Yahweh and for the footstool of the feet of our God, and had made preparations to build. 3. But God said to me, "You shall not build a house for my name, because you are a man of wars and have shed blood." 4. But Yahweh the God of Israel chose me from all the house of my father to be king over Israel for ever, for he chose Judah to be ruler; and from the house of Judah, the house of my father, and among the sons of my father, he took pleasure in me to make me king over all Israel. 5. And from all my sons – for Yahweh has given me many sons – he has chosen my son Solomon to sit on the throne of the kingdom of Yahweh over Israel. 6. And he said to me, "Solomon your son, he will build my house and my courts, for I have chosen him to be my son, and I will be his Father. 7. And I will establish his kingdom for ever if he is resolute to observe my commandments and my judgments, as at this day." 8. And now, in the sight of all Israel, the assembly of Yahweh, and in the hearing of our God, keep and seek all the commandments of Yahweh your God, that you may possess the good land and leave it as an inheritance for your sons after you for ever.'

This is not the same gathering of leaders mentioned in 1 Chronicles 23:2 but more like the one referred to in 1 Chronicles 22:17-19, where the presence of priests and Levites is not mentioned. It is the most complete description of the composition of an assembly in the whole of Chronicles and consists of the kind of military and state leaders especially detailed in chapter 27:1-31. It is described in verse 8 as an 'assembly of Yahweh'. The king gathered this assembly of Israel to witness the transfer of power from David to Solomon and to indicate that the new king's chief concern would be the building of the temple. Rather than the king's sons (v. 1) being seen as joint owners of the property, the text can be taken to read that the king's sons were present in the assembly.[107] David began his speech with a familiar call to listen (see 2 Chron. 13:4) but used a unique form of address (v. 2) in which the king humbly considered himself one with his people ('my brothers'; Deut. 17:15; see 1 Chron. 29:14).

Building a permanent home for the ark had been David's settled conviction for some time (1 Chron. 17:1; 22:7) and much of his language is familiar from his previous speeches. But here, fresh elements are introduced. The temple is to be 'a house of rest' for the ark, which is described as God's 'footstool' (v. 2), all reminders of Psalm 132:7-8, as well as to Mosaic times when the ark led the people through the wilderness and searched out a 'resting -place' for them, and the call for Yahweh's presence to rest with them (Num. 10:35-36). Here, this unique expression 'house of rest' is used of the temple in Jerusalem where the symbol of God's presence on earth

---

107. The *lᵉ* can either be possessive and so equivalent to the previous *lᵉ* 'belonging to the king and to his sons' or be translated 'as well as his sons', continuing the list of those who assembled.

was to rest. The 'footstool' image is a reminder that the home of the full splendour of God's presence remains in heaven. In general, heaven is God's throne and earth is His footstool (Isa. 66:1), but Zion and especially the temple is seen as His footstool (Pss. 99:5; 132:7, 13-14; Lam. 2:1). The ark as God's footstool pinpoints His presence more specifically.

David indicates that he had made preparations to build a temple (v. 2b) but this did not mean he had begun to do so before Yahweh rejected his idea. It relates to what subsequently happened (see 1 Chron. 22). David mentions again the reason why he was not allowed to construct the temple (v. 3). His role as a 'man of wars' who had 'shed blood' disqualified him from the task, but the removal of enemies was a necessary work in establishing peace (Deut. 12:9-11), in order that the 'man of rest' might accomplish the task (see 22:6-10; 1 Kings 5:3).

The divine election of Solomon is seen by David as part of a pattern, whereby God first chose David to be Israel's king, which in turn was due to God's choice of the tribe of Judah (v. 4; 1 Chron. 5:2). When Jacob 'gathered together' his sons, he prophesied that 'the sceptre would not depart from Judah', and the Asaph psalm indicates that God had it in mind all along that the ruler of God's people would arise not from Joseph but from Judah, that Mount Zion would be the place of God's special presence on earth, and that David would shepherd God's people (Gen. 49:8-12; Ps. 78:67-72). The reference to God's being pleased to make David king, who was just one among many of his father's sons, recalls the incident where David's older brothers were rejected and Samuel was divinely instructed to anoint the youngest (1 Sam. 16:1-13).

It is against this selection process background that David emphasised Solomon's election to office (see vv. 5, 6, 10; 29:1). Of all the many sons of David (see 1 Chron. 3:1-9; 14:3-7), it was Solomon who was chosen to follow his father (1 Chron. 22:9). The point is well made that the divine choice was finalised not with David but with Solomon and this made father and son equals, 'each personally and individually elected, as opposed to all the subsequent kings of Judah, who reign by virtue of God's promise to David.'[108] While the Samuel–Kings text

---

108. Japhet, *I & II Chronicles*, p. 488.

gives us all the gory details surrounding the rivalry between David's sons and the succession to the throne that involved Amnon, Absalom and Adonijah (2 Sam. 13–18; 1 Kings 1), Chronicles emphasises God's sovereign plan in the election of Solomon to be king.

Along with the stress on kingship over 'all Israel' (v. 4) is the point, hinted at earlier but now made explicit, that the Davidic throne is 'the throne of the kingdom of Yahweh' (v. 5; see 17:14), It is a theme that the Chronicler draws attention to a number of times (see 1 Chron. 29:11, 23; 2 Chron. 9:8; 13:8). If the ark is God's footstool, the earthly throne of David in Jerusalem is Yahweh's throne. In contrast to verse 3, David explains that God informed him that Solomon would build Yahweh's house along with its courts. The courts are prominent (v. 6; see v. 12), for that is where the people would congregate at festival time. The psalmists longed for and delighted in the courts of Yahweh, for there they met with the living God (Pss. 65:4[3]; 84:2[3]). David adds that his son's election involved a most intimate relationship with God (v. 6; see 1 Chron. 17:13; 22:10). He rules as God's earthly representative and because this kingdom belongs to God, it is established for ever. But there are conditions attached. It is only as the Davidic king remains true to God's commandments that his rule will continue.

With verse 8 David applies God's word to the leaders.[109] His exhortation is introduced most solemnly by calling on 'all Israel' to recognise that they are all observers to this charge ('in the sight of all the assembly …'; see Deut. 31:7, 30) and that God Himself is also a witness to what is said ('in the hearing of our God'; see 1 Tim. 5:21; 6:13; 2 Tim. 4:1). Of the many occurrences of the word 'assembly' (*qāhāl*) in Chronicles, this is the only occasion where the phrase 'assembly of Yahweh' is used. Further references to the term 'assembly' (*qāhāl*) appear in the following chapter (29:1, 10, 20; see 1 Chron. 13:2, 4). It recalls the time when Israel gathered at Sinai (or Horeb) to meet with Yahweh, which Moses calls 'the day of the assembly' (Deut. 9:10; 10:4; 18:16).

---

109. Both verbs, 'keep' and 'seek', as well as the prepositions and verbs that follow, are in the plural, indicating that the address is to the leaders and not to Solomon, as Pratt believes. See Richard L. Pratt, *1 and 2 Chronicles*, A Mentor Commentary (Fearn, Ross-shire: Christian Focus Publications, 1998), p. 192.

Instead of urging his people to receive Solomon as their king, as might have been expected, David calls on them to observe Yahweh's law. Neither the monarchy nor all the arrangements concerning the temple are ends in themselves;[110] the main issue is the keeping of God's commandments (Deut. 5:10). To 'seek' them means being intent on finding out God's will for their lives in what He has revealed through Moses and the prophets. God had a gracious purpose in this exhortation, the same point emphasised by Moses and expressed using similar language. It involved the possession of 'the good land' and the passing of it on 'as an inheritance' to succeeding generations (see Deut. 1:8; 4:21-22; 6:18).

David's address to Solomon (28:9-10)

28:9. And you, my son Solomon, know the God of your father and serve him with a whole heart and with a willing soul; for Yahweh searches all hearts and understands all the intent of the thoughts. If you seek him, he will be found by you; but if you forsake him, he will cast you off for ever. 10. See now, for Yahweh has chosen you to build a house for the sanctuary; be strong, and act.

It is here that David turns to address Solomon publicly and echoes the earlier private counsel (22:13). The exhortation consists of a series of imperatives ('know ... serve ... see ... be strong and act'), punctuated with words of encouragement and warning. The verb 'know' means more than acknowledging God. It speaks of that intimate, personal experience 'which arises between two persons who are committed wholly to one another in a relationship that touches mind, emotion, and will'[111] (see Jer. 31:34; Hosea 13:5; 1 Chron. 17:18). It results in appropriate actions (Jer. 22:16; Hosea 6:6). This was the kind of intimacy that David experienced, the man 'after God's own heart' and hence the title 'God of David your father' (see 2 Chron. 21:12). David had known men who were of one mind and wholehearted in making him king at Hebron (12:38). Here David urged Solomon to serve God with a 'whole' or 'perfect'

---

110. See the observation in Johnstone *1 and 2 Chronicles*, volume 1 p. 277 note 1.

111. J. A. Thompson, *The Book of Jeremiah*, The New International Commentary on the Old Testament (Grand Rapids: Eerdmans, 1980), p. 581.

heart and it led him later to pray that his son would have such a heart (29:19). A 'willing soul' is a person who takes pleasure in doing God's will (see Isa. 66:2b-4).

At this point, David broke off his exhortation to inform Solomon of two important truths concerning God that are meant primarily for the future king's encouragement. First, Yahweh takes account of motives behind human actions (see 29:18), as Hezekiah appreciated when the Passover was not kept according to the strict procedure of the law (2 Chron. 30). Secondly, with the words of Deuteronomy 4:29 in mind, David showed how right motives could be maintained. Solomon was urged to 'seek' (*dāraš*) God and warned not to 'forsake' or 'abandon' (*'āzab*) Him (see 2 Chron. 15:2,4). Seeking God with one's heart is equivalent to being faithful to Yahweh, the very opposite of honouring God with the lips alone (Isa. 29:13). Saul displayed his infidelity in that he did not seek Yahweh (1 Chron. 10:14). Such seeking can include repentance when sin has been committed (2 Chron. 7:14; Jer. 29:13; Amos 5:4-6). It will result in the blessing of being found by God, which means knowing God's favour and presence (Isa. 55:6-7). To leave or abandon Yahweh is one of the Chronicler's great concerns and he refers to it many times (v. 20; 2 Chron. 7:19, 22; 12:1,5; 13:10, 11; etc.). The solemn warning of being 'cast off' or 'rejected' (*zānaḥ*) by Yahweh for ever was something about which the psalmist was deeply troubled (Pss. 43:2; 44:9[10], 23[24]; 60:1[3], 10[12]; 74:1; 77:7[8]; 88:14[15]). Lamentations 3:31 encourages those who seek God to understand that though Yahweh disciplines His people, He will not cast them off for ever.

David's exhortation to Solomon continued with the reminder that God had chosen him for a specific purpose (v. 10). This was his life's work as king: to build the temple which is described here as 'a house' and a 'sanctuary' or 'holy place' (see 1 Chron. 22:19; 2 Chron. 20:8; 26:18; 29:21; 30:8; 36:17). The address concluded by urging Solomon to be strong and act (see 1 Chron. 22:13; Josh. 1:6-7,9; Ezra 10:4).

Application

The emphasis is on Yahweh as both transcendent and immanent. The high and holy one who dwells in eternity does come to live among his people. He did not despise Solomon's temple as a picture of the future reality in Jesus and the church. For Isaiah, the Lord looked for and promised to dwell with humble, contrite hearts that trembled at God's word (Isa. 66:1-2; 57:15; see also Mal. 3:16-17).

Choosing David and his descendants to rule and the choice of Zion as the place of God's presence on earth belong together. At the time when the Chronicler was writing, the people had a temple in Jerusalem as a guarantee of the complete fulfilment of God's purposes in the appearance of a Davidic ruler who would reign in a Zion where God would be for ever present with His people (see Isa. 11:1, 9). While Zerubbabel and his family encouraged the possibility of the continuation of David's line (1 Chron. 3:19; Hag. 2:23), hope needed to be kept alive when there was so much to disappoint. These Old Testament passages relating to God's kingship through His anointed ruler prepare for the Gospels and their emphasis on the 'coming near' of God's kingdom in the ministry of Jesus, the chosen one who was obedient, beloved and well-pleasing to God.

The Old Testament assembly finds fulfilment in the Messiah. Jesus had this Old Testament background in mind concerning God's people as an 'assembly' when He informed Peter that on the rock of his confession concerning Jesus as the Messiah he would build the church. In addition, he described it in a way that put him as an equal with Yahweh, for instead of referring to Yahweh's assembly/church, he spoke of 'my assembly/church' (Matt. 16:18).

The temple plans (28:11-19)

> 28:11. Then David gave to his son Solomon the plan of the vestibule and its houses, and its treasuries, and its upper rooms and its inner chambers, and the house of the mercy seat, 12. even the plan of all that was on his mind: for the courts of the house of Yahweh and for all the surrounding chambers; for the treasuries of the house of God and for the treasuries for the dedicated things; 13. also for the divisions of the priests and the Levites and for all the work of the service of the house of Yahweh; and for all the vessels of service in the house of Yahweh. 14. For the gold by weight for the gold belonging to all the vessels of every kind of service; for all the silver vessels by weight, for all

silver vessels of every kind of service. 15. And for the weight of the golden lampstands and their lamps, gold by weight for each lampstand and its lamps; and for the silver lampstands by weight, for the lampstand and its lamp, according to the service of each lampstand; 16. and the gold *by* weight for the tables of the rows, for each table, and silver for the silver tables; 17. also pure gold the forks and the basins and the cups, and the golden bowls by weight for each bowl; and for the silver bowls by weight for each bowl; 18. and refined gold by weight for the altar of incense; and gold for the plan of the chariot, the cherubim that spread and covered the ark of the covenant of Yahweh. 19. Everything in writing from Yahweh's hand upon me, he taught, all the workings of the plan.

This paragraph is highly significant with its reference to the divinely revealed temple plan (v. 19), recalling the tabernacle design and all its furnishings shown to Moses on Mount Sinai by Yahweh (Exod. 25:9, 40). The same word for plan or pattern is used on both occasions (*taḇnît*), whereas different terms are employed for Ezekiel's eschatological temple blueprint (Ezek. 40:45-48; 41:5-14; 43:10). Despite some difficulties in translating verse 19, the text makes clear that the plan David gave Solomon was a document written under divine inspiration. It is for this reason some consider verse 12 should be seen as a further indication that the plan was divinely given, translating the literal text '… all that was in the spirit with him' to mean all that the Holy Spirit gave him.[112] Most older commentators as well as the LXX consider the literal phrase '… all that was in the spirit with him' to mean David's own spirit. There are other occasions in Chronicles where 'spirit' means the human spirit (see 2 Chron. 21:16; 36:22), but it is made very clear in Amasai's case that he spoke under the influence of the divine Spirit (1 Chron. 12:18[19]). What this paragraph does make plain is that the plans in David's mind (v. 12) were ones God had given him to understand and to place in writing (v. 19). He is a second Moses and the temple has the same validity as the Israelite tabernacle. As in the Exodus account, where the tabernacle arrangement and its

112. See Wilhelm Rudolph, *Die Chronikbücher*, Handbuch zum Alten Testament (Tübingen: Mohr, 1955), p. 186; Jacob M. Myers, *1 Chronicles*, Anchor Bible (New York: Doubleday, 1965) pp. 188, 190; Selman, *1 Chronicles*, p. 253.

furnishings are set out first and then its actual construction recorded later (Exod. 25–27, 36–40), so in Chronicles, the plan for the temple is described at this point with 2 Chronicles 3–4 detailing its construction.

Verse 11 describes the temple itself with its various rooms. 'Vestibule' or 'porch' ('ûlām) does often mean the area at the top of the stairs flanked by two pillars (see 2 Chron. 3:4), but it is probably used here for the whole temple (see 2 Chron. 29:7, 17), with 'houses' standing for its various rooms including the holy place, sometimes called the hall or nave of the temple (hêkal; 1 Kings 6:3). The most sacred room, known as the holy of holies (Exod. 26:33-34; 1 Kings 6:16) or simply 'holy place' in Leviticus 16:2-3 or 'inner sanctuary' (dᵉbîr; 1 Kings 6:19-20, wrongly translated as 'oracle' in the AV), is here described uniquely as 'the house of the atonement' or 'the room of the propitiation'. This is the only place outside the books of Moses where the term 'atonement place' or 'mercy seat' is found (see Exod. 25:17; Lev. 16; Num. 7:89) and it draws attention again to the link between the tabernacle and the temple. It was in this 'house' that the ark of the covenant, Yahweh's footstool, found rest (v. 2). In the tabernacle the 'mercy seat' was actually a covering of pure gold that was placed on top of the ark (Exod. 25:21).

Another unique phrase related to the ark of the covenant appears at the end of the paragraph: 'the plan of the chariot' (v. 18). Together with the word 'plan' and 'mercy seat' at the beginning (v. 11), it forms a frame around all that the divine blueprint contained concerning the temple buildings, clergy duties, furnishings and utensils (vv. 12-18). The golden cherubim, 'spread out' by their wings, were placed on the mercy seat and therefore covered the ark (Exod. 25:18-21; 1 Kings 6:23-28; 8:6-7; 1 Chron. 13:6; 2 Chron. 3:13; 5:8). They are likened to a 'chariot' and recall Ezekiel's vision of the glory of Yahweh where cherubim and wheels within wheels suggest some kind of chariot-like vehicle (Ezek. 1 and 10; see Ps. 18:10[11]; 2 Kings 2:11-12). Interestingly, the golden altar of incense is closely associated with the ark of the covenant as was the case in the tabernacle (v. 18a; Exod. 30:1-10; see Heb. 9:4). It was in this area that Yahweh met with the representatives of the people (Exod. 25:22; 30:6; 1 Chron. 6:49[34]; 2 Chron. 2:4).

The 'treasuries' (v. 11; see 26:20-28) were of two types: those 'of the house of God' and 'those of the dedicated' offerings (v. 12; see 1 Chron. 18:11) and housed in buildings adjacent to the sanctuary (1 Kings 6:5). Again the courts are mentioned (v. 12; see v. 6) and the arrangements for the temple services (v. 13a; see v. 6 and 1 Chron. 24:1; 26:1, 19). Attention is particularly drawn to the utensils used in the temple services and to the weight of the precious metals used in making them (vv. 13b-17). This list includes gold and silver lampstands and lamps (v. 15), golden tables for the rows of bread or 'the showbread', silver tables (v. 16) and golden forks, basins and cups as well as gold and silver bowls (v. 17). The tabernacle account likewise draws attention to the various vessels to be used by the priests (Exod. 25:29; 37:16).

Application

The one element, the ark of the covenant, missing in the second temple is the very item that is given particular prominence in this passage (vv. 2, 11, 18) as it has in previous chapters (13; 15:1-3, 12, 14-15, 23-29; 16:1, 4, 6, 37; 22:19). What the ark, mercy seat and cherubim symbolised, namely, the glory of Yahweh present among His people, is the missing element for the post-exilic community, but their prophets encouraged the people to look forward to the reality (Hag. 2:7; Mal. 3:1). With the coming of Jesus, the apostles looked at the glory of God in the face of Jesus (John 1:1-18).

Attention is drawn particularly to the temple vessels because these were items taken to Babylon at the time of the exile and which were all returned when the Jews were allowed back to Jerusalem and constructed the temple (2 Chron. 36:7, 10, 18; Ezra 1:7-11). They provided continuity with the past and encouraged the people to look to the full realisation of God's promises concerning the temple and the land. Through the two thousand years of Christian history, the Church of Jesus Christ continues and Christians are encouraged by the constants of the preaching of God's authoritative word, the observance of Christian baptism and the Lord's Supper, and the fellowship and love of God's people.

David addresses Solomon (28:20-21)

> 28:20. And David said to his son Solomon, 'Be strong and of good courage and act; do not fear or be dismayed, for Yahweh God, my God, is with you. He will not fail you or forsake you until all the work for the service of the house of Yahweh is completed. 21. And here are the divisions of the priests and the Levites for all the service of the house of God; and with you in all the work will be every skilled volunteer for every kind of service; also the officials and all the people will be entirely at your command.'

David encouraged Solomon using the same familiar language that has been used previously and even earlier in the present chapter (v. 10; 1 Chron. 22:13; see Josh. 1:6, 9; 8:1). The recognition that Yahweh is with Solomon and the promise that David's God will not abandon him before the construction of the temple is complete is the very best assurance that could be given. These words of exhortation which were spoken in the presence of the officials and commanders were a reminder to them that the leadership was now passing to Solomon and that he had the full approval of both God and David. It invites parallels with the transfer of leadership from Moses to Joshua (Deut. 31:6, 8; Josh. 1:5). Both Moses and David were great leaders of their people who were not allowed to see all they had hoped to accomplish but nevertheless they took important initial steps that would be completed by their successors.

The 'divisions of the priests and Levites' (v. 21) that were also in the plan (see v. 13a) are given to Solomon for the ongoing worship that would take place in the temple. As there were skilled workers and other willing helpers who were involved in the work of constructing the tabernacle (Exod. 25:2; 28:3; 31:6; 35:5, 30-35; 36:1-8), so skilled volunteers (literally 'willing in the wisdom', v. 21) are put at the disposal of Solomon and he is assured of the support of the leaders and all the people.

Application

In this short paragraph, the Chronicler wished to encourage the post exilic community to be committed to the temple and its services. The passage serves to prick the consciences of God's people today in their commitment to their local church and to see the work of living stones being added to the spiritual house of God. Willing, committed workers using whatever skills God gives His people are to be used in the service of God for the building of His church (Rom. 12:4-8; 1 Pet. 4:8-11).

The theme of God being with His people is taken up by Isaiah and applied to the messianic ruler Himself: Immanuel 'God with us' (Isa. 7:14). We pray with Phillips Brooks, 'O come to us, abide with us, Our Lord Immanuel.'[113]

Israel's gifts for the temple (29:1-9)

29:1. Then David the king said to the whole assembly, 'Solomon my son, whom alone God has chosen, is young and inexperienced and the work is great, for the palace is not for humans but for Yahweh God. 2. And according to all my strength I have provided for the house of my God, the gold for the gold *things* and the silver for the silver and the bronze for the bronze, the iron for the iron and the wood for wood *things*, onyx stones and inlaid ones, glistening stones and variegated, and all kinds of precious stones and stones of alabaster in abundance. 3. In addition, because I have taken pleasure in the house of my God the special treasure of gold and silver that I have given to the house of my God over and above all that I have provided for the holy house: 4. three thousand talents of gold from the gold of Ophir, and seven thousand talents of refined silver for overlaying the walls of the houses; 5. of gold for the gold *things* and silver for the silver and for all the work by the hand of the craftsmen. Who then will offer himself willing to consecrate himself today to Yahweh?' 6. Then the officials of the fathers and the officials of the tribes of Israel and the commanders of the thousands and the hundreds and including the officials of the king's work offered themselves willingly. 7. And they gave for the service of the house of God five thousand talents and ten thousand darics of gold, and ten thousand talents of silver and eighteen thousand talents of bronze, and one hundred thousand talents of iron. 8. And those with whom *precious* stones were found, gave them to the treasury of the house of Yahweh, under the hand of Jehiel the Gershonite. 9. Then the people rejoiced on account of offering themselves willingly, for with a whole heart they offered willingly to Yahweh; and David the king also rejoiced with great rejoicing.

113. The carol 'O little town of Bethlehem'.

David had given generously toward the temple and now he invited the representatives of the people to follow his example (vv. 1-5) and they responded most willingly (vv. 6-9).

The passage highlights the enormity of the task. Though Solomon is the one chosen by God to succeed David and given the responsibility of building the temple (28:5-6), he was relatively young and inexperienced (1 Chron. 22:5). According to Josephus, he was still in his teens. The addition of the word 'alone' in connection with God's choice of Solomon is a reminder of Adonijah's attempt to succeed David as king (1 Kings 1–2). By using the unusual term 'palace' for the temple, a term that also has the meaning of 'citadel' or 'fortress (*bîrāh*, v. 1; see also v. 19), David indicated that this was to be a sturdy, massive construction resembling the kind of fortress palace or citadel that is mentioned often in the Persian period (Neh. 1:1; 2:8; 7:2; Esther 3:15; Dan. 8:2; etc.). This was no royal residence for humans; it was for Yahweh God, the God of creation and David's God (see Gen. 2:4–3:24 where the divine epithet 'Yahweh God' is first used; see 28:20).

David had already mentioned the great trouble he had taken to prepare the materials for building the temple (1 Chron. 22:14; 28:2) and now the details of what he had contributed are mentioned (vv. 2-5a). David lists the materials offered, commencing with the most valuable metals from gold down to the less valuable iron and then the wood (see 1 Chron. 22:3,14). The precious stones are next mentioned but there is uncertainty concerning the meaning of some, especially the glistening variegated stones and the 'stones of alabaster'. The word *pûḵ* ('glistening') is used of black make-up for the eyes (2 Kings 9:30) and hard cement (Isa. 54:11), while the word for 'variegated' is used mainly of colourful cloth and in one case of the variety of colour in an eagle's feathers (Exod. 26:36; Ezek. 17:3). So it is possible that the verse begins with gems and precious stones and ends with colourful linen.

Besides this material belonging to the kingdom, David also donated from his own personal collection, from his 'special treasure' (v. 3, *sᵉgullāh*; see Eccles. 2:8), a term often used to describe the people of God (see Exod. 19:5; Deut. 14:2; Mal. 3:17; also Titus 2:14; 1 Pet. 2:9). God had taken pleasure in David

(1 Chron. 28:4) and now David takes pleasure in the house of his God by providing an abundance of material from his private property for the temple which is called 'the holy house' (see 2 Chron. 36:17). It is not anachronistic to refer to the gold from Ophir (v. 4; see 1 Chron. 1:23). David clearly received this high-quality gold before Solomon's trading arrangement with that foreign country (2 Chron. 8:18). The quantities are immense especially when the three thousand talents of gold are compared with the twenty-nine talents of gold used for the tabernacle (Exod. 38:24). By way of comparison, the queen of Sheba brought Solomon a hundred and twenty talents of gold (2 Chron. 9:9,13; 1 Kings 10:10, 14). There was no thought of coating the walls of the various temple 'houses' or rooms with a finishing slither of plaster (Ezek. 13:10). They were to be overlaid with gold!

Having shown by example his willingness to offer sacrificially to the work of building the temple, David called for a willingness on the part of Israel's leadership to give generously. The phrase 'to consecrate' (v. 5) translates the Hebrew idiom 'to fill the hand'. It is a technical expression mainly used for commissioning someone to the priestly office (Exod. 28:41; 29:29, 35; etc. and 2 Chron. 13:9; 29:31). By giving willingly to the work of the temple, Israel, as a kingdom of priests (Exod. 19:6), would express their own dedication to the service of God and His temple.

All the leaders and commanders (see 1 Chron. 27:25-31; 28:1) are referred to, using the same term 'officials' or 'chiefs' (śārîm) in each case. Verse 6 is the only occasion in Chronicles where the word 'official' is found with 'fathers' (it appears once in Ezra 8:29). All the other references are to 'heads of the fathers' (1 Chron. 8:6, 10; etc.). The word 'household' or 'family line' is implied; only occasionally is the full form given ('heads of the house of the fathers' as in 1 Chronicles 7:40; 24:4). The leaders followed the king's example with their very generous freewill offerings that included, like David's gifts, gold, silver, bronze, iron and precious stones (vv. 6-8).

These stones were given to Jehiel (see 1 Chron. 23:7-8; 26:21-22) who had charge of the treasury of Yahweh's house (v. 8). The amounts are overwhelming and the round numbers in thousands may well be a means of emphasising through hyperbole that the people's contributions far exceeded those of the king. The ten thousand golden darics, on the other hand, is understood to be a much more reasonable amount (v. 7). It is believed that 'darics' only came into use under king Darius I and named after the Persian ruler (Ezra 6:1; 8:27). If this is the case, it suggests that the Chronicler updated the original currency in the same way that the Authorised (King James) Version updated the same word to 'drams' for its day.

Expressions of joy and gladness are noted by the Chronicler at significant moments in the life of the nation, including David's coronation and the bringing of the ark to Jerusalem (1 Chron. 12:40[41]; 15:25; 16:10,31) and on numerous other occasions later (see 2 Chron. 6:41; 7:10; 15:15; etc.). Both David and the people rejoiced at the way they had all been able to give so generously and willingly to Yahweh. It was a wholehearted giving. A 'whole' or 'perfect' heart is another of the Chronicler's favourite expressions to convey his concern for wholehearted devotion to God. The men who made David king did so wholeheartedly and David urged Solomon, praying that he would serve God with a 'whole' or 'perfect' heart (1 Chron. 12:38[39]; 28:9; 29:19).

Application

Leaders are to show by example their eagerness in serving God. Old Testament worship at its best was no cold, legalistic religion. The Chronicler inspires his own people by these examples to wholehearted, sincere devotion in place of the careless, often half-hearted attitude that was too often evident. Malachi had to stir up such people who showed by their poor-quality offerings how little they thought of God.

Paul spends time speaking of giving and informs us that the Lord loves a cheerful giver: willing giving not by constraint. Jesus taught not to give in order to be seen for personal advantage and that it is more blessed to give than to receive (Matt. 6:1-4; Acts 20:35). While David was an example to Israel in free-will offerings, Paul presents us with the example of Christ (2 Cor. 8–9). How generous are we as Christians in giving to the Lord's work for the extension of His kingdom both locally and worldwide?

David's final prayer (29:10-20)

29:10. So David blessed Yahweh in the sight of all the assembly and David said, 'Blessed are you Yahweh God of Israel, our father, for ever and ever. 11. To you, Yahweh, is the greatness and the power and the beauty and the eminence and the majesty, indeed, everything in the heavens and the earth; to you, Yahweh, is the kingdom, and you are exalted as head over all. 12. Both riches and honour come from you and you reign over all and in your hand are strength and power, and it is in your hand to make great and to give strength to all. 13. And now, our God, we give thanks to you and praise your splendid name. 14. But who am I and who are my people that we should be able to offer willingly like this? For from you *come* all things and from your hand we have given you. 15. For we are resident aliens before you and temporary visitors like all our fathers. Our days on the earth are like a shadow, and there is no hope. 16. Yahweh our God, all this abundance that we have provided to build you a house for your holy name is from your hand and is all your own. 17. And I know, my God, that you test the heart and take pleasure in uprightness. In the uprightness of my heart I have willingly offered all these *things*, and now with joy I have seen your people, who are present here, to offer willingly to you. 18. Yahweh, God of Abraham, Isaac and Israel, our fathers, keep this for ever, the inclination of the thoughts of the heart of your people and establish their heart toward you; 19. and give to Solomon my son a perfect heart to keep your commandments, your declarations and your statutes and to do *them* all and to build the palace for which I have made preparation.'

20. Then David said to all the assembly, 'Bless now Yahweh your God.' So all the assembly blessed Yahweh the God of their fathers, and they bowed and prostrated themselves to Yahweh and to the king.

David's powerful public prayer of thanksgiving consists of an introduction (v. 10a) that leads to worship with declarations of God's greatness and sovereignty (vv. 10b-12), continues with humble thanksgiving (vv. 13-16) and closes with petition for his people and for Solomon (vv. 17-19).

The introduction indicates the kind of prayer it is. Only a few people are said to 'bless Yahweh' (Gen. 24:48; Deut. 8:10; Josh. 22:33; 2 Chron. 20:26; 31:8). Such benedictions are not of the same order as God blessing people, in the sense of graciously giving them what they need. Blessing God, as the Hebrew verb implies (*bāraḵ*), means bowing the knee to Him, reverently giving to Him the worship that He is owed. David therefore begins by paying homage to Yahweh (v. 10b), but unusually he does so directly in the second person: 'Blessed are you' (see the only other occurrence in Ps. 119:12). Normally, Yahweh is blessed indirectly using the third person: 'Blessed be Yahweh' (see 1 Chron. 16:36; Ps. 28:6; etc.). Yahweh is the God of Jacob their 'father' or 'ancestor', here referred to as 'Israel' which is typical in Chronicles (1:34; see v. 18 below). It is unlikely that 'father' is referring to God (see v. 20). This God is to be honoured for ever (see 1 Chron. 16:36).

The reason for such worship is that 'greatness' (1 Chron. 17:19), 'power' or 'might' (Ps. 106:2, 8), 'beauty' or 'splendour' (see v. 13; Ps. 96:8), 'eminence' (1 Sam. 15:29) and 'majesty' (1 Chron. 16:27) belong to Yahweh (v. 11). Indeed, the God of Israel is the creator of the entire universe and therefore owns it (see Ps. 115:15). It is in the context of God's choice of Solomon as the next king that David is prompted to acknowledge that sovereignty belongs to Yahweh, something the Chronicler stresses throughout his work (either using *mamlāḵāh* as here or using *malkûṭ* as in 1 Chron. 28:5). The Davidic kings ruled as God's representatives: they sat on God's throne in Jerusalem (see v. 23) and the Davidic kingdom was to be an expression of God's rule (see 2 Chron. 13:8). But David emphasises that it is God who is supreme over all (v. 11c; see also v. 12a). The riches and honour, such as David and later his son enjoyed (see v. 28; 2 Chron. 1:1,12), derive from God for He has the power to give freely (v. 12).

In verse 13, David includes thanksgiving in his praise to God's 'splendid' name (see v. 11; Isa. 63:14) and, as his focus shifts to the specific context of the freewill offerings for building the temple, he expresses his humble amazement and unworthiness that he and his people had the power or ability to give so willingly (see 1 Chron. 17:16; 2 Chron. 2:6). Again, David is aware that boasting is totally out of place for they are all utterly dependent on God and they have only given a portion of what God has given them (v. 14). This truth is emphasised by the confession (v. 15) that, like the patriarchs, they have no permanent home in this present world but are like foreigners, resident in Canaan ('resident aliens'), or like 'temporary visitors' or 'sojourners'. They are like Abraham who had no land of his own and the nation itself was to remember the impermanent nature of their position even when they received Canaan as a gift, especially when it came to their treatment of aliens (Gen. 23:4; Lev. 19:33-34; 25:23; Ps. 39:12[13]). Furthermore, human life itself is as fleeting as a shadow (Pss. 102:11[12]; 144:4; Eccles. 6:12; 8:13). Any effort on the part of humans to become immortal is hopeless. And so David repeats the point (v. 16) that they owe it to the God who in fact owns everything, even 'the abundance' of what they were able to give toward building the temple for God's 'holy name' (1 Chron. 16:35). They are merely stewards of the provisions God had given them.

In verse 17, David introduces his petition by acknowledging that both he and the people have had worthy motives. He is aware that God is the one who tests people's intentions (28:9; see Jer. 12:3) and is pleased with 'uprightness', and he confesses that he has had a right attitude in the gifts he has offered (see Ps. 17:3). What is more, David indicates the joyful way the people had responded (v. 17; see vv. 6-9). The petition begins by appealing to the God of the patriarchs (v. 18; see v. 10), the covenant-keeping God. His prayer is first for the people, that their present commitment would not be a one-off expression of devotion but an ongoing inner attitude (see 1 Chron. 28:9). David is aware that only God can bring about such piety for by nature the human heart is deceitful and evil (Gen. 6:5; Jer. 17:9-10). His one prayer for Solomon is that God would also deal with his inner self, giving him that perfect heart to keep the Mosaic law (God's commandments, declarations and statutes) and to carry out the building project. Again, the special term 'citadel' or 'fortress palace' is employed for the temple (v. 19; see v. 1), which thus frames this powerful prayer relating to the people's willing contributions towards the temple.

In verse 20, David urges the assembled gathering to 'bless' Yahweh their God. Blessing God means submissive worship and the people showed this not only by what they said but by prostrating themselves before Yahweh (see v. 10). What was spoken is not actually mentioned but it would have been something like David's own expressions praising God's character and actions (see vv. 10-12; Pss. 41:13; 72:18-19; etc.). What is unique is that the people not only bowed down and prostrated themselves before God but also before the king. One or other of the two verbs are employed elsewhere to show homage to humans, for example, Ornan prostrated himself before David (1 Chron. 21:21). But here, both verbs are found in a context where king and God are coupled together. This does not mean that David was considered a god and given the same honour as Yahweh; nevertheless, the king was closely associated with Yahweh for the king's throne was Yahweh's throne (see v. 23; 1 Chron. 28:5).

Application

There are parallels between what is expressed in poetic language by David in praise to Yahweh and the contents of a number of the Psalms (see Pss. 71; 96:6; 106:2, 8; 115:15; 124:8; etc.). The Chronicler presents David's prayer as an encouragement to his community to use such psalms in praise to God and at the same time to become more committed to God and His kingdom interests.[114] What is said of Yahweh is the kind of language applied to Jesus, the slain Lamb (Rev. 5:12). The doxology at the end of the Lord's Prayer echoes these words of David (Matt. 6:13b of the traditional text). Like David, Paul teaches that we have no right to boast over the things we possess. He criticises the Corinthians: 'What did you have that you did not receive? If then you received it, why do you boast as if you did not receive it?' (1 Cor. 4:7).

The fleeting nature of life in this world is emphasised by James; and Hebrews speaks of Christians, like the patriarchs, as having no permanent home here (Heb. 11:13-16; 13:14; James 4:14 see 1 Pet. 1:1; 2:11). Any human endeavour to escape death is a hopeless task. Only Jesus has gained the victory over death, by Himself passing through it, and He assures His followers of their own bodily resurrection to life in the new creation.

While David was not to be worshipped as God, this occasion does point us to great David's greater Son (see Ps. 45:6; Heb. 1:8-9). We can honour Him as God for He is one

---

114. See Braun, *1 Chronicles*, pp. 283-285.

with the Father and the Spirit in the Holy Trinity. Jesus sits on God's throne and we give the same worship to the Lamb as to God (Rev. 3:21; 5:13-14), while, at the same time, we are warned not to fall down in worship before men or angels (Rev. 19:10; 22:8-9).

It is true that Christians are called to worship and serve God in the whole of life, every day of the year. However, this does not rule out worship that involves personal and communal humble adoration, prayer, song and hearing and receiving God's word. As the creatures in heaven bow in such worship, so believers in this world are to bow heart and mind, yes, and body too with bowed head and bended knee (1 Cor. 14:25).

Solomon anointed king (29:21-25)

> 29:21. And the following day, they sacrificed sacrifices to Yahweh and offered burnt offerings to Yahweh, a thousand bulls, a thousand rams, a thousand lambs, with their libations and sacrifices in abundance for all Israel. 22. So they ate and drank before Yahweh on that day with great joy, and they made Solomon the son of David king the second time, and they anointed *him* to be prince for Yahweh and Zadok to be priest. 23. And Solomon sat on the throne of Yahweh as king instead of David his father; and he prospered and all Israel obeyed him. 24. And all the officials and the valiant ones and also all the sons of king David pledged allegiance to king Solomon. 25. And Yahweh made Solomon exceedingly great in the sight of all Israel and he gave him royal majesty that had not been on any king before him in Israel.

The enthronement of Solomon is made to emerge seamlessly from the events of the previous day when David ended his prayer and encouraged the assembly to worship the Lord (vv. 18-20). It was in the context of worship that Solomon was confirmed as king (vv. 21-22). David's son had, of course, already been anointed king by Zadok at Gihon in a rather rushed and tense atmosphere that is not recorded by the Chronicler (1 Kings 1). On this more grand and peaceful occasion, in the presence of all the leaders of Israel, Solomon is recognised as king a 'second time' (v. 22).[115] In David's case,

---

115. See Selman, *1 Chronicles*, pp. 261-2 in support of the MT.

he was anointed three times (1 Sam. 16:13; 2 Sam. 2:4; 5:3). Such occasions demanded a large number of animals to be sacrificed, but the three thousand animals slaughtered is a relatively small sum in comparison with the one hundred and forty-two thousand animals sacrificed at the dedication of the temple (2 Chron. 7:4-5). The 'burnt offerings' were all consumed by fire as propitiatory sacrifices and were expressive of the people's wholehearted devotion to God (Lev. 1; 6:8-13), while the other 'sacrifices' were the peace or fellowship offerings (see 1 Chron. 16:1-3), which meant that portions of meat could be eaten by the people as they communed together joyfully (Lev. 3; 7:11-21). Little is known of the 'drink offerings' but they accompanied the burnt offerings (Exod. 29:40-41; Num. 28:7-10). At David's own coronation there was much eating and drinking, as also happened when the ark rested in Jerusalem (1 Chron. 12:39-40; 16:1-3) and at Adonijah's abortive coronation (1 Kings 1:25). The feasting with great joy was all part of their worship of God for it was done 'before Yahweh' (v. 22).

Solomon was anointed as Yahweh's 'prince' or 'leader' (*nāgîd*, v. 22), a term sometimes used to refer to a king-designate or crown prince (see 1 Chron. 5:2; 11:2; 17:7; 1 Sam. 9:16; 10:1). He was not king in his own right but ruled as regent. Yahweh is the true king. Interestingly, Zadok is introduced as priest. Abiathar had disqualified himself on account of his involvement in the plot to make Adonijah king and Zadok took his place (1 Kings 1:7; 2:26-27, 35). He has been mentioned a number of times as a priest or leader (1 Chron. 6:53[38]; 12:28; 15:11; 16:39; 18:16; 24:3, 6, 31; 27:17), but here he is being recognised by popular approval as sole priest or as high priest at the dawn of this new era. Though it is not actually stated, it is possible that the verb 'anointed' does duty for Zadok as well as Solomon. Priests were specially anointed and often referred to as the anointed priest (see Exod. 40:12-15; Lev. 4:3; 8:1-12).

In his concluding remarks concerning the coronation of Solomon, the Chronicler indicates again that the throne on which Solomon sat was Yahweh's throne, not merely David's throne, as it states in 1 Kings 2:12 (see 1 Chron. 17:14; 28:5). Solomon was also blessed by God in that he prospered.

'Prosperity' or 'success' is another of the Chronicler's themes expressing God's blessing on those who were faithful to Him (1 Chron. 22:11, 13; 2 Chron. 20:20; 26:5; 32:30). Such prosperity included not only riches and fame but stability of government, evidenced by the fact that the people were obedient to him, and all Israel's leaders, military men and David's sons submitted themselves to him (vv. 23-24). The phrase 'pledged allegiance' translates the Hebrew idiom 'put a hand under' (v. 24), which may well have arisen from an ancient oath-taking ceremony similar to the one undertaken by Abraham's servant and later by Joseph (Gen. 24:1-3; 47:29).

The Chronicler assumes his readers know that Solomon's kingdom was only established after the expulsions and executions recorded in 1 Kings 1–2. Unusually, the achievements of Solomon's reign are mentioned even before David's death is announced (v. 25). The God whom David had acknowledged as the one who had the power to 'make great' (v. 12) had made Solomon 'exceedingly great'. In fact, it was Benaiah's wish that Yahweh would make Solomon's throne greater than David's (1 Kings 1:37, 47). Interestingly, Yahweh had previously made Joshua great in the sight of all Israel (Josh. 3:7; 4:14). Solomon is depicted as a second Joshua with David as a new Moses. The kind of 'majesty' or 'splendour' (sometimes translated 'honour' or 'glory') that is God's (1 Chron. 16:27; Ps. 8:1[2]) and that is applied to the ark (Ps. 78:61) and the messianic Branch (Zech. 6:13) is uniquely bestowed on Solomon (see Pss. 21:5[6]; 45:4[5]). Not even David, whose kingdom was highly 'exalted' ('made great'; 1 Chron. 14:2), had such royal majestic splendour. The adverb 'exceedingly' (v. 25) is another of the Chronicler's favourite words (1 Chron. 14:2; 22:5; 23:17; 29:3; 2 Chron. 1:1; 16:12; 17:12; 20:19).

Application

Solomon's rule is idealised and seen as the culmination of David's rule. The Chronicler's method indicates the unity of David and Solomon's reigns. This preview of the kingdom of God on earth is brought to the attention of God's people in the post-exilic period to create that longing for it to come in all its glory, not only to exist in a small part of the Middle East but to embrace the whole world. Jesus instructed His followers to pray for the coming of God's kingdom. That kingdom is associated with the Messiah, Jesus, and the psalms point us to Him, as do the Song of Solomon and the prophetic writings.

David's death and summary of his life (29:26-30)

> 29:26. And David the son of Jesse reigned over all Israel. 27. And the days he reigned over Israel were forty years. In Hebron he reigned seven years and in Jerusalem he reigned thirty-three *years*. 28. And he died in good old age, full of days, riches and honour, and Solomon his son reigned in his place. 29. Now the acts of David, the first and the last, there they are written in the words of Samuel the seer and in the words of Nathan the prophet, and in the words of Gad the visionary, 30. with all his reign, his power and the events which came on him and on Israel and on all the kingdoms of the lands.

David's reign is first summarised and his successor named (vv. 26-28) and the paragraph closes by citing other sources for David's life (vv. 29-30). It sets a pattern for similar summary statements in the case of almost all the kings that follow.

The Chronicler presents a much fuller summary of David's reign than the one in 1 Kings 2:10-12. It begins with the reminder of David's humble origins: 'the son of Jesse' (v. 26; see Ps. 72:20). At the same time, the phrase is used as an *inclusio* to the whole section concerning David's reign (see 1 Chron. 10:14). It is emphasised that David ruled over 'all Israel' (see 1 Chron. 11:1-3; 28:4-5) for forty years. Even his reign in Hebron is considered to have been over all Israel. The imprecise seven-year rule in Hebron follows 1 Kings 2:11 (see 1 Chron. 3:4; 2 Sam. 5:5 for the exact period). Though David's physical strength was diminished, as the account in 1 Kings 1:1-4 suggests, this did not mean that he was immobile and helpless, as he was healthy and active enough to be involved in all the events that led to Solomon's enthronement. Any lingering doubts readers may have are corrected by the Chronicler as he uses traditional language to indicate that David died well, like some of the patriarchs (v. 28; 1 Chron. 23:1; Gen. 15:15; 25:8; 35:29; Job 42:17). Even by Moses' time, seventy was considered a reasonable life span (Ps. 90:10). His riches and wealth were gifts of Yahweh and evidences of His favour (v. 12; 2 Chron. 1:11-12).

In addition to the canonical books of Samuel and Kings with which the Chronicler assumes readers are familiar, other sources are noted. These would have given further information concerning David's deeds and the events that befell him and the nation, as well as details concerning those foreign kingdoms that came under his control (vv. 29-30; see 1 Chron. 18-20).

The three prophets named were personally involved at different stages in David's life: Samuel at the beginning (1 Chron. 11:3); Nathan in David's desire to build the temple (1 Chron. 17); and Gad in the choice of the temple site (1 Chron. 21:9-13,18-19). It is very possible that their personal accounts relating to David's rule were used by both the prophetic authors of Samuel–Kings and the Chronicler. It is interesting that each prophet is given a different title, perhaps one that was particularly associated with them: 'seer' (rō'eh), 'prophet' (nāḇî') and 'visionary' (ḥōzeh, usually translated 'seer', as the word is synonymous with rō'eh).

The unique closing phrase, 'all the kingdoms of the lands' (kol-mamlᵊḵōṯ hā'ᵃrāṣôṯ), is a reminder of how Chronicles begins by setting the roots of Israel among the founders of the kingdoms of this world. Now, a representative number of those kingdoms has been brought under the influence of the Davidic ruler (see 1 Chron. 16:28-29). Interestingly, at the end of the Chronicler's work, it is Cyrus the Persian ruler who confesses that Yahweh has given to him 'all the kingdoms of the land/earth' (kol-mamlᵊḵôṯ hā'āreṣ, 2 Chron. 36:23).

Application

While Luke mentions his procedure and sources at the beginning of his presentation of Jesus' life and ministry (Luke 1:1-4), the Chronicler informs us of his sources at the close of his treatment of David. His work is based on historical material. Though these ancient texts are lost to us, we can be sure that all that is necessary for our spiritual wellbeing has been preserved in the authoritative, God-breathed canonical Scriptures of Samuel–Kings and Chronicles.

In Psalm 2:8 Yahweh says to His anointed, 'Ask of me and I will give you the nations as your inheritance.' The judgment on Edom by Obadiah which ends with the words 'and the kingdom will belong to Yahweh' (v. 21) is underlined by Chronicles' account of David and would have been an encouragement to disenchanted Jews of the post-exilic era (Mal. 1:1-14). Jesus was tempted to receive the kingdoms of the world if He would only fall down and worship the devil, but He resisted and instead received them by His victory on the cross over the ruler of this world (Matt. 4:8-10; John 12:20-33). The good news is now preached to all nations (Matt. 24:14; 28:18-20; Luke 24:46-47), and the final book of the Bible looks expectantly to the time when the kingdom of this world will become the kingdom of God and of His Messiah (Rev. 11:15).

Group Study Questions

Part One: Israel's Roots
(1 Chronicles 1:1–9:34)

1. Why is the Bible so interested in all the nations of the world?

2. What nations stand out in the lists and why do you think they do so?

3. What is significant about the tribes of Levi, Benjamin and Judah?

4. Is there such a thing as a pure race?

5. In what way does Zerubbabel typify Jesus?

6. How does Jabez remind us of Jesus?

7. What encouragements to pray are found in the whole of this first part?

8. What are the encouragements for the Christian in studying history?

9. Consider the theme of curse and exile in Chronicles.

10. Communal worship is no substitute for daily godly living – discuss.

11. In what way does Samuel resemble Jesus?

12. What was 'the ark of the covenant'? Why was it important and why do you think it was no longer needed after the exile?

13. What did Jesus mean by saying that 'salvation is of the Jews'?

14. Why was the nation Israel only an alien in Canaan?

15. Should churches invest heavily in preparing men to be gospel preachers and pastors?

16. Show how God does not despise northern regions.

17. Indicate the important place of women in the Bible.

18. In what ways does the Chronicler stress the unity of Israel and how can it be applied to the church?

19. Draw out the significance of the prophetess Anna in Luke 2:36-38 from the text of Chronicles.

20. From your reading of 1 Chronicles 1-9, what are the Chronicler's main points that he is to develop in the remainder of his work?

21. Show the importance of good biblical tradition.

Part Two: The David-Solomon Kingdom
(I Chronicles 9:35–2 Chronicles 9:28)

1. Indicate why a person's bodily remains should be treated with dignity.

2. How is the description of Israel's defeat under Saul a preview of the events surrounding Israel's Babylonian exile?

3. Consider how the Chronicler's presentation of David would have encouraged the post-exilic community.

4. What early evidences of the Holy Spirit's power do we find in 1 Chronicles?

5. 'God's time is always the right time' – Have you found this to be true in your own experience?

6. Why are God's people on earth in a war situation? When and how will it end?

7. How does 1 Chronicles 13 help us understand Hebrews 12:28-29?

8. Consider how expressions of joy in worship can co-exist with respect for God.

9. What did the ark of God signify?

10. What does the Old Testament tabernacle typify?

11. How was the kingdom of God seen on earth in Old Testament times and how does it prepare for the preaching of John the Baptist and Jesus?

12. Why was David's census wrong and why is the Chronicler's account different from the parallel passage in Samuel?

13. Indicate the differences between pagan and biblical sacrifices.

14. Do the instructions given to the Levites have anything to say about the running of our churches today?

15. Is there any place for Christians to engage in 'casting lots'?

16. Consider the place of music in the life of the church and the individual believer.

17. Do you agree that we cannot properly understand what the New Testament means by church without considering the Old Testament background?

18. What are the benefits – and dangers – of tradition?

19. Under the new covenant, are there obligatory as well as free-will offerings?

20. Does worshipping God in the whole of life every day mean there is no place for special communal worship on the Lord's Day?

21. Why does the Chronicler idealise and stress the united rule of David and Solomon?

22. Consider the continuity and discontinuity between Solomon's temple and the post-exilic temple. How does the reality far surpass those shadowy pictures and types?

23. What do we mean by God's transcendence and immanence? In what ways can both be true of God?

Bibliography

Commentaries

Ackroyd, P. R. *I & II Chronicles, Ezra, Nehemiah* Torch Bible Commentaries (London: SCM, 1973).

Braun, R. L. *1 Chronicles* Word Bible Commentary 14 (Waco: Word Books, 1986).

Bolen, T. *The Date of the Davidic Covenant* (JETS 65, 2022).

Dillard, R. B. *2 Chronicles* Word Bible Commentary 15 (Waco: Word, 1987).

Japhet, S. *I & II Chronicles* The Old Testament Library (London: SCM, 1993).

Johnstone, W. *1 and 2 Chronicles*, vol. 1: *1 Chronicles 1–2 Chronicles 9: Israel's Place Among the Nations*; vol. 2: *2 Chronicles 10–36: Guilt and Atonement* JSOT Suppl. Series 160 (Sheffield: Sheffield Academic Press, 1993).

Knoppers, G. N. *1 Chronicles 1–9 A New Translation with Introduction and Commentary* Anchor Bible 12A (New York: Doubleday, 2004).

1 Chronicles 10–29 A New Translation with Introduction and Commentary Anchor Bible 12B (New York: Doubleday, 2004).

Merrill, E. H. *Kingdom of Priests* (Grand Rapids: Baker, 1987).

Murphy, J. G. *The Books of Chronicles* Hand-Books for Bible Classes (Edinburgh: T & T Clark, undated).

Myers, Jacob M. *I Chronicles: Introduction, Translation and Notes* Anchor Bible 12 (New York: Doubleday, 1965).

II Chronicles: Translation and Notes Anchor Bible 13 (New York: Doubleday, 1965).

Payne, J. Barton. '1, 2 Chronicles' pp. 301-562 in *The Expositor's Bible Commentary* editor F. E. Gaebelein vol. 4 (Grand Rapids: Zondervan Publishing House, 1988).

Pratt, Richard L. *1 and 2 Chronicles*, A Mentor Commentary (Fearn, Ross-shire: Christian Focus Publications, 1998).

Rudoph, W. *Chronikbücher* Handbuch zum Alten Testament (Tübingen: Mohr, 1955).

Selman, M. J. *1 and 2 Chronicles*, 2 vols. Tyndale Old Testament Commentaries (Leicester: Inter-Varsity Press, 1994).

Wilcock, M. *The Message of Chronicles*, The Bible Speaks Today (Leicester: Inter-Varsity Press, 1987).

'1 and 2 Chronicles' in 21st Century edition of *The New Bible Commentary* eds. Carson, France, Motyer, Wenham (Leicester: Inter-Varsity Press, 1994), pp. 388-419.

Willi, T. *Die Chronik als Auslegung* (Göttingen: Vandenhoeck & Ruprecht, 1972).

Williamson, H. G. M. *1 and 2 Chronicles*, The New Century Bible Commentary (London: Marshall Morgan & Scott, 1982).

Supplementary works

Ackroyd, Peter R. 'The Chronicler as Exegete,' *JSOT* 2 (1977), pp. 2-32.

The Chronicler in his Age, JSOT Sppl. Series 101 (Sheffield: Sheffield Academic Press, 1991).

'The Temple Vessels: A Continuity Theme', *Supplements to Vetus Testamentum* 23 (1972), pp. 166-181, and reprinted in *Studies in the Religious Tradition of the Old Testament* (London: SCM Press, 1987) chapter 4.

Braun, R. L. 'Solomonic Apologetic in Chronicles', *JBL* 92, 1973, pp. 503-16.

'Solomon, the Chosen Temple Builder: The Significance of 1 Chronicles 22, 28, 29 for the Theology of Chronicles', *JBL* 95, 1976, pp. 581-90.

'A Reconsideration of the Chronicler's Attitude toward the North', *JBL* 96, 1977, pp. 59-62.

Butler, T. C. 'A Forgotten Passage from a Forgotten Era (1 Chr xvi. 8-36), VT 28 (1878) pp. 142-50.

Dillard, R. B. 'Reward and Punishment in Chronicles: the Theology of Immediate Retribution' *WTJ* 46 (1984), pp. 164-72.

Evans, Paul. 'Divine Intermediaries in 1 Chronicles 21– An Overlooked Aspect of the Chronicler's Theology,' *Biblica* 85.4 (2004), pp. 545-58.

Eveson, P. H. 'Prayer Forms in the Writings of the Chronicler,' unpublished M.Th. dissertation (University of London, 1979).

Graham, M. P., McKenzie, S. L. and Knoppers, G. N. (eds.), *The Chronicler as Theologian. Essays in Honour of Ralph W. Klein*, JSOT (London: T & T Clark, 2003).

McKenzie S. L. and Suppl. Series 371 (London: T & T Clark International, 2003).

Japhet, S. 'The Supposed Common Authorship of Chronicles and Ezra–Nehemiah Investigated Anew,' *VT* 18, 1968, pp. 332-372.

The Ideology of the Book of Chronicles and Its Place in Biblical Thought (Frankfurt am Main: Peter Lang, 1997 revised edition).

Johnson, M. D. *The Purpose of the Biblical Genealogies: With Special Reference to the Setting of the Genealogies of Jesus.* 2nd edition (Cambridge: Cambridge University Press, 1988).

Kelly, Brian E. *Retribution and Eschatology in Chronicles* JSOT Suppl. Series 211 (Sheffield: Sheffield Academic Press, 1996).

Mason, Rex. *Preaching the Tradition. Homily and hermeneutics after the exile* (Cambridge: Cambridge University Press, 1990).

Meyers, J. M. 'The Kerygma of the Chronicler,' *Interpretation* 20 (1966), pp. 257-73.

Murray, D. F. 'Retribution and Revival: Theological Theory, Religious Praxis, and the Future in Chronicles,' *JSOT* 88 (2000), pp. 77-99.

Plöger, O. 'Reden und Gebete im deuteronomistischen und chronistischen Geschichtswerk' in *Festschrift für Günther Dehn* ed. W. Schneemelcher (Neukirchen: Kreis Moers, 1957) pp. 35-49.

Theokratie und Eschatologie 1959 translated by S. Rudman as *Theology and Eschatology* (Oxford: Blackwell, 1968).

von Rad, G. 'The Levitical Sermon in I and II Chronicles' in *The Problem of the Hexateuch and other Essays* (Edinburgh: 1966), pp. 267-80.

Riley, William. *King and Cultus in Chronicles. Worship and the Reinterpretation of History* JSOT Suppl. Series 160 (Sheffield: Sheffield Academic Press, 1993).

Wenham, J. 'Large Numbers in the Old Testament,' *Tyndale Bulletin* 18 (1967), pp. 19-53.

Williamson, H. G. M. 'The Accession of Solomon,' *VT* 26 (1976), pp. 351-61.

Israel in the Books of Chronicles (Cambridge: Cambridge University Press, 1977).

'Eschatology in Chronicles' *Tyndale Bulletin* 28 (1977), pp. 115-154.

Zvi, Ehud Ben. *History, Literature and Theology in the Book of Chronicles* (London: Equinox Publishing, 2006).

Subject Index

M

N

T

tabernacle

Scripture Index

The Focus on the Bible Commentary Series
Old Testament

Genesis: The Beginning of God's Plan of Salvation - Richard P. Belcher
ISBN 978-1-84550-963-7
Exodus: God's Kingdom of Priests - Allan Harman
ISBN 978-1-52710-025-1
Deuteronomy: The Commands of a Covenant God - Allan Harman
ISBN 978-1-84550-268-3
Joshua: No Falling Words - Dale Ralph Davis
ISBN 978-1-84550-137-2
Judges: Such a Great Salvation - Dale Ralph Davis
ISBN 978-1-84550-138-9
Ruth & Esther: There is a Redeemer and Sudden Reversals - David Strain
ISBN 978-1-52710-234-7
1 Samuel: Looking on the Heart - Dale Ralph Davis
ISBN 978-1-85792-516-6
2 Samuel: Out of Every Adversity - Dale Ralph Davis
ISBN 978-1-84550-270-6
1 Kings: The Wisdom and the Folly - Dale Ralph Davis
ISBN 978-1-84550-251-5
2 Kings: The Power and the Glory - Dale Ralph Davis
ISBN 978-1-84550-096-2
1 Chronicles: Adam to David - Philip H. Eveson
ISBN 978-1-85792-935-5
2 Chronicles: Solomon to Cyrus - Philip H. Eveson
ISBN 978-1-85792-936-2
Job: The Mystery of Suffering and God's Sovereignty - Richard P. Belcher, Jr.
ISBN 978-1-52710-002-2
Psalms 1-89: The Lord Saves - Eric Lane
ISBN 978-1-84550-180-8
Psalms 90-150: The Lord Reigns - Eric Lane
ISBN 978-1-84550-202-7
Proverbs: Everyday Wisdom for Everyone - Eric Lane
ISBN 978-1-84550-267-6
Ecclesiastes: The Philippians of the Old Testament - William D. Barrick
ISBN 978-1-84550-776-3

Song of Songs: A Biblical, Theological, Allegorical, Christological Interpretation - James M. Hamilton Jr
ISBN 978-1-78191-560-8
Isaiah: A Covenant to be Kept for the Sake of the Church - Allan Harman
ISBN 978-1-84550-053-5
Jeremiah & Lamentations: The Death of a Dream and What Came After - Michael Wilcock
ISBN 978-1-78191-148-8
Daniel: A Tale of Two Cities - Robert Fyall
ISBN 978-1-84550-194-5
Hosea: The Passion of God - Tim Chester
ISBN 978-1-78191-368-0
Joel & Obadiah: Disaster and Deliverance - Iwan Rhys Jones
ISBN 978-1-78191-602-5
Amos: An Ordinary Man with and Extraordinary Message - T. J. Betts
ISBN 978-1-84550-727-5
Jonah, Michah, Nahum, Nahum & Zephaniah - John L. Mackay
ISBN 978-1-85792-392-6
Haggai, Zechariah & Malachi: God's Restored People - John L. Mackay
ISBN 978-1-85792-067-3

*Song of Songs: A Biblical-Theological, Allegorical, Christological
Interpretation* – James M. Hamilton Jr.
ISBN 978-1-78191-396-3

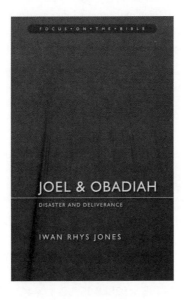

Joel and Obadiah: Disaster and Deliverance
– Iwan Rhys Jones
ISBN 978-1-78191-602-5

The Focus on the Bible Commentary Series

New Testament

Matthew: A Call for Unity and Responsibility in the Church - John D. Hannah
ISBN 978-1-78191-146-4

Luke 1–13: The Year of the Lord's Favor - Dale Ralph Davis
ISBN 978-1-5271-0638-3

Luke 14–24: On the Road to Jerusalem - Dale Ralph Davis
ISBN 978-1-5271-0642-0

John: Jesus Christ is God - William F. Cook
ISBN 978-1-78191-717-6

Acts: Witnesses to Him - Bruce Milne
ISBN 978-1-84550-507-3

Romans: The Revelation of God's Righteousness - Paul Barnett
ISBN 978-1-84550-269-0

1 Corinthians: Holiness and Hope of a Rescued People - Paul Barnett
ISBN 978-1-85792-598-2

2 Corinthians: The Glories & Responsibilities of Christian Service - Geoffrey Grogan
ISBN 978-1-84550-252-2

Galatians: God's Proclamation of Liberty - Joseph A. Pipa Jr
ISBN 978-1-84550-558-5

Ephesians: Encouragement and Joy in Christ - Paul Gardner
ISBN 978-1-84550-264-5

Philippians: Rejoicing and Thanksgiving - David Chapman
ISBN 978-1-84550-687-2

Colossians & Philemon: So Walk in Him - John Woodhouse
ISBN 978-1-84550-632-2

1 & 2 Thessalonians: Triumphs and Trials of a Consecrated Church - Richard Mayhue
ISBN 978-1-85792-452-7

James: Wisdom for the Community - Christopher Morgan and B. Dale Ellenburg
ISBN 978-1-84550-335-2

1 & 2 Peter & Jude: Christians Living in an Age of Suffering - Paul Gardner
ISBN 978-1-85792-338-4

1, 2 & 3 John: Redemption's Certainty - John D. Hannah
ISBN 978-1-78191-771-8

Revelation: The Compassion and Protection of Christ - Paul Gardner
ISBN 978-1-85792-329-2

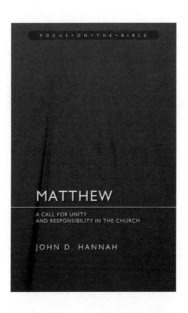

Matthew: A Call for Unity and Responsibility in the Church –
John D. Hannah
ISBN 978-1-78191-146-4

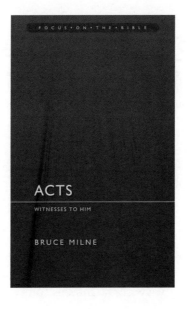

Acts: Witnesses to Him – Bruce Milne
ISBN 978-1-84550-507-3

Christian Focus Publications

Our mission statement –

STAYING FAITHFUL
In dependence upon God we seek to impact the world through literature faithful to His infallible Word, the Bible. Our aim is to ensure that the Lord Jesus Christ is presented as the only hope to obtain forgiveness of sin, live a useful life and look forward to heaven with Him.

Our Books are published in four imprints:

CHRISTIAN FOCUS

popular works including biographies, commentaries, basic doctrine and Christian living.

CHRISTIAN HERITAGE

books representing some of the best material from the rich heritage of the church.

MENTOR

books written at a level suitable for Bible College and seminary students, pastors, and other serious readers. The imprint includes commentaries, doctrinal studies, examination of current issues and church history.

CF4•K

children's books for quality Bible teaching and for all age groups: Sunday school curriculum, puzzle and activity books; personal and family devotional titles, biographies and inspirational stories – because you are never too young to know Jesus!

Christian Focus Publications Ltd,
Geanies House, Fearn, Ross-shire,
IV20 1TW, Scotland, United Kingdom.
www.christianfocus.com